BUSINESS FORECASTING WITH ACCOMPANYING EXCEL-BASED FORECASTX™ SOFTWARE

BUSINESS FORECASTING WITH ACCOMPANYING EXCEL-BASED FORECASTX™ SOFTWARE

J. Holton Wilson
Central Michigan University

Barry Keating
University of Notre Dame

John Galt Solutions, Inc.

Boston   Burr Ridge, IL   Dubuque, IA   Madison, WI   New York   San Francisco   St. Louis
Bangkok   Bogotá   Caracas   Kuala Lumpur   Lisbon   London   Madrid   Mexico City
Milan   Montreal   New Delhi   Santiago   Seoul   Singapore   Sydney   Taipei   Toronto

McGraw-Hill Higher Education

A Division of The **McGraw-Hill** *Companies*

BUSINESS FORECASTING WITH ACCOMPANYING EXCEL-BASED FORECASTX™ SOFTWARE
Published by McGraw-Hill, an imprint of The McGraw-Hill Companies, Inc. 1221
Avenue of the Americas, New York, NY, 10020. Copyright © 2002, by The McGraw-Hill
Companies, Inc. All rights reserved. No part of this publication may be reproduced or
distributed in any form or by any means, or stored in a database or retrieval system,
without the prior written consent of The McGraw-Hill Companies, Inc., including,
but not limited to, in any network or other electronic storage or transmission, or
broadcast for distance learning.
Some ancillaries, including electronic and print components, may not be available to customers
outside the United States.

This book is printed on acid-free paper.

domestic   2 3 4 5 6 7 8 9 0 DOC/DOC 0 9 8 7 6 5 4 3
international   2 3 4 5 6 7 8 9 0 DOC/DOC 0 9 8 7 6 5 4 3

ISBN   0-07-231266-1

Senior sponsoring editor: *Scott Isenberg*
Editorial assistant: *Lee Stone*
Senior marketing manager: *Zina Craft*
Senior project manager: *Jean Hamilton*
Production supervisor: *Rose Hepburn*
Media producer: *Greg Bates*
Designer: *Damian Moshak*
Associate supplement producer: *Vicki Laird*
Cover design: *Damian Moshak*
Cover illustration: *Tom White*
Typeface: *10/12 Times Roman*
Compositor: *Interactive Composition Corporation*
Printer: *R. R. Donnelley & Sons Company*

Library of Congress Cataloging-in-Publication Data

Wilson, J. Holton, 1942–
    Business forecasting with accompanying Excel-based ForecastX™ software / J. Holton
Wilson and Barry Keating.—4th ed.
        p.   cm.
    "The major change to the fourth edition of the text is the integration of the user-friendly
and powerful Excel-based forecasting software"—Preface.
    Includes index.
    ISBN 0-07-231266-1
    1. Business forecasting.   I. Keating, Barry, 1945–   II. Title.

HD30.27 .W56   2001
658.4'0355'02855369—dc21   2001042730

INTERNATIONAL EDITION ISBN 0-07-112136-6
Copyright © 2002. Exclusive rights by The McGraw-Hill Companies, Inc., for manufacture and export.
This book cannot be re-exported from the country to which it is sold by McGraw-Hill.
The International Edition is not available in North America.

www.mhhe.com

To Eva, Ronnie, and Clara
To Robert Vincent Keating

The fourth edition of *Business Forecasting with Accompanying Excel-Based Fore-castX™ Software* builds on the success of the first three editions. While a number of significant changes have been made in this fourth edition, it remains a book about fore-casting methods for managers, for forecasting practitioners, and for students who will one day be business professionals who have a need to understand practical issues related to forecasting. Our emphasis is on authentic learning of the forecasting methods that practicing forecasters have found most useful. *Business Forecasting with Accompany-ing Excel-Based ForecastX™ Software* is written for students and others who want to know how it's really done.

The major change to the fourth edition of the text is the integration of user-friendly and powerful Excel-based forecasting software. The software, ForecastX™, has been made available through an agreement with John Galt Solutions, Inc. Every method dis-cussed in the text can be implemented with this software. We have tested the software thoroughly in class environments. Students find the software easy to use, even without a manual or other written instructions. However, we have provided a brief introduction to the use of ForecastX™ at the end of each relevant chapter. While we are confident that faculty and students will enjoy using this widely adopted, commercially successful software, the text can be used without reliance on this particular package.

All data files are provided on the CD in Excel format so that they can be easily used with almost any forecasting or statistical software. As with previous editions, nearly all data in the text are real, such as domestic car sales and private housing starts. In addition, we have continued the use of an ongoing case involving forecasting sales of The Gap at the end of chapters to provide a linkage from chapter to chapter. Links to many excellent sources of data are included on the CD and are referenced in the text. These are especially useful for student projects and for additional exercises instructors may wish to develop.

Also included on the instructor's CD are answers to text problems, test preparation software, banks of test questions for each chapter, and PowerPoint templates for each figure and table in the text, which can be used to master overheads or in electronic pre-sentations using a run-time version of PowerPoint (also included on the CD).

Comments from the field by forecasting practitioners provide quick insights into issues and problems faced daily by individuals who are actively engaged in the fore-casting process. These provide a very practical perspective from the "real world" to help students appreciate the relevance of the concepts presented in the text.

Today, most business planning routinely begins with a sales forecast. Whether you are an accountant, a marketer, a human resources manager, or a financial analyst, you will have to forecast something sooner or later. This book is designed to lead you through the most helpful techniques to use in any forecasting effort. The examples we offer are, for the most part, based on actual historical data much like the data you may encounter in your own forecasts. The techniques themselves are explained as procedures that you may replicate with your own data.

The authors would like to thank the students at the University of Notre Dame and Central Michigan University for their help in working with materials included in this book during development. Their comments were invaluable in preparing clear expositions and meaningful examples for this fourth edition. The final product owes a great debt to the inspiration and comments of our colleagues, especially Professor Thomas Bundt of the Oregon Graduate Institute, Portland. In addition, we would like to thank the staff at John Galt Solutions, Inc., especially Kai Trepte and Annemarie Omrod, for their advice and counsel regarding the ForecastX™ software, and Dan A. Kiely of Wyeth-Ayerst Global Pharmaceuticals for his assistance in providing an excellent application of event forecasting.

Adopters of the first three editions who have criticized, challenged, encouraged, and complimented our efforts deserve our thanks. The authors are particularly grateful to the following faculty who used earlier editions of the text and have provided comments that have helped to further improve this fourth edition.

Paul Altieri, Central Connecticut State University

Margaret M. Capen, East Carolina University

Ali Dogramaci, Rutgers, the State University of New Jersey

Robert Fetter, Yale University

Benito Flores, Texas A & M University

Kenneth Gaver, Montana State University

Rakesh Gupta, Adelphi University

Joseph Kelley, California State University, Sacramento

Thomas Kelly, BMW of Canada

Krishna Kool, University of Rio Grande

John Mathews, University of Wisconsin, Madison

Elam McElroy, Marquette University

Thomas Needham, US Bancorp

Gerald Platt, San Francisco State University

Melissa Ramenofsky, University of Southern Alabama

Helmut Schneider, Louisiana State University

Stanley Schultz, Cleveland State University

Nancy Serafino, United Telephone

Donald N. Stengel, California State University, Fresno

Kwei Tang, Louisiana State University

Dick Withycomb, University of Montana

In addition, the following reviewers have provided insights that have helped to make this edition better than it would have been without their thoughtful comments:

Thomas P. Chen, St. John's University

Ronald L. Coccari, Cleveland State University

Lewis Coopersmith, Rider University

Farzad Farsio, Montana State University

Joseph McCarthy, Bryant College

Rob Roy McGregor, University of North Carolina, Charlotte

John C. Nash, University of Ottawa

We are especially grateful to have worked with the following publishing professionals on our McGraw-Hill/Irwin book team:

Brent Gordon, Publisher

Scott Isenberg, Supporting Editor

Lee Stone, Developmental Editor

Zina Craft, Marketing Manager

Jean Hamilton, Project Manager

Vicki Laird, Supplements Coordinator

Greg Bates, New Media Producer

We hope that all of the above, as well as all new faculty, students, and business professionals who use the text, will be pleased with the fourth edition.

J. Holton Wilson
Holt.Wilson@cmich.edu
Barry Keating
Barry.P.Keating.1@nd.edu

BRIEF CONTENTS

C O N T E N T S

3   Moving Averages and Exponential Smoothing   99

4   Introduction to Forecasting with Regression Methods   139

8   Combining Forecast Results   341

9   Forecast Implementation   377

Index   405

1 INTRODUCTION TO BUSINESS FORECASTING

If you can get the
forecast right, you
have the potential
to get everything
else in the supply
chain right.

I believe that forecasting or demand management may have the potential to add more value to a business than any single activity within the supply chain. I say this because if you can get the forecast right, you have the potential to get everything else in the supply chain right. But if you can't get the forecast right, then everything else you do essentially will be reactive, as opposed to proactive planning. Al Enns, Director of Supply Chain Strategies, Motts North America, Stamford, Connecticut.[1]

Introduction

If you are reading this text as part of the course requirements for a college degree consider yourself fortunate. Many college graduates, even those with degrees in business or economics, do not ever study forecasting, except as a sidelight in a course that has other primary objectives. And yet, we know that forecasting is an essential element of most business decisions.

The need for personnel with forecasting expertise is growing.[2] For example, Levi Strauss only started its forecast department in 1995 and now has a full time forecasting staff of thirty. Many people filling these positions have had little formal training in forecasting and are paying thousands of dollars to attend educational programs. In a survey conducted by the Institute of Business Forecasting it was found that there were substantial increases in the staffing of forecasters in full-time positions within American companies.

---

[1]Sidney Hill, Jr., "A Whole New Outlook," *Manufacturing Systems* 16, no. 9, September 1998, pp. 70–80.

[2]Chaman L. Jain, "Explosion in the Forecasting Function in Corporate America," *Journal of Business Forecasting*, Summer 1999, p. 2.

1

Quantitative Forecasting Has Become Widely Accepted

We might think of forecasting as a set of tools that helps decision makers make the best possible judgments about future events. In today's rapidly changing business world such judgments can mean the difference between success and failure. It is no longer reasonable to rely solely on intuition, or one's "feel for the situation," in projecting future sales, inventory needs, personnel requirements, and other important economic or business variables. Quantitative methods have been shown to be helpful in making better predictions about the future course of events,[3] and a number of sophisticated computer software packages have been developed to make these methods accessible to nearly everyone. There is a danger, however, in using canned forecasting software unless you are familiar with the concepts upon which the programs are based.

This text and its accompanying computer software have been carefully designed to provide you with an understanding of the conceptual basis for many modern quantitative forecasting models, along with programs that have been written specifically for the purpose of allowing you to put these methods to use. You will find both the text and the software to be extremely user-friendly. After studying the text and using the software to replicate the examples we present, you will be able to forecast economic and business variables with greater accuracy than you might now expect. But a word of warning is appropriate. Do not become so enamored with quantitative methods and computer results that you fail to *think* carefully about the series you wish to forecast. Personal judgments based on practical experience and/or thorough research should always play an important role in the preparation of any forecast.

> Personal judgments based on practical experience and/or thorough research should always play an important role in the preparation of any forecast.

Forecasting in Business Today

Business decisions almost always depend on some forecast about the course of events. Virtually every functional area of business makes use of some type of forecast. For example:

1. Accountants rely on forecasts of costs and revenues in tax planning.
2. The personnel department depends on forecasts as it plans recruitment of new employees and other changes in the workforce.
3. Financial experts must forecast cash flows to maintain solvency.
4. Production managers rely on forecasts to determine raw-material needs and the desired inventory of finished products.
5. Marketing managers use a sales forecast to establish promotional budgets.

> The sales forecast is often the root forecast from which others, such as employment requirements, are derived.

The sales forecast is often the root forecast from which others, such as employment requirements, are derived. As early as the mid-1980s a study of large American-operated firms showed that roughly 94 percent made use of a sales forecast.[4] The ways

---

[3]J. Holton Wilson and Deborah Allison-Koerber, "Combining Subjective and Objective Forecasts Improves Results," *Journal of Business Forecasting* 11, no. 3 (Fall 1992), pp. 12–16.
[4]Ibid., pp. 12–16.

in which forecasts are prepared and the manner in which results are used vary considerably among firms.

As a way of illustrating the application of forecasting in the corporate world we will summarize aspects of the forecasting function in eight examples. In these examples you may see some terms with which you are not fully familiar at this time. However, you probably have a general understanding of them, and when you have completed the text you will understand them all quite well.

Bell Atlantic

At Bell Atlantic, the forecasting process begins with the collection of historical data on a monthly basis.[5] These data are saved both for service classifications and geographic regions. The Demand Forecasting Group at Bell Atlantic developed a data warehouse so that the data can be shared and integrated across the entire corporation. In preparing forecasts, subjective forecasting methods are used along with time-series methods, and regression modeling based on economic, demographic, and other exogenous variables. The forecasts are continually monitored and compared with actual results monthly and annually to ensure that Bell Atlantic meets customer needs.

Columbia Gas

Columbia Gas of Ohio (Columbia) is a large natural gas utility that delivers over 300 billions of cubic feet (BCF) of natural gas annually.[6] Columbia develops two kinds of forecasts, which they refer to as the *Design Day Forecast* and the *Daily Operational Forecast.* The former is used to determine gas supply, transportation capacity, storage capacity, and related measures. This forecast is used primarily for supply and capacity planning. Over a seven-year period the average mean absolute percentage error in their Design Day Forecast was 0.4 percent.

The Daily Operational Forecast is used primarily to ensure that supplies are in balance with demand over five-day spans. As would be expected, the average errors for these shorter term forecasts have been higher at about 3 percent. The forecasts are based to a large degree on regression models (see Chapters 4 and 5) in which demand is a function of such variables as current-day temperatures, previous-day temperatures, wind speed, and day of the week.

Segix Italia

Segix Italia is a pharmaceutical company in Italy that produces products that are sold domestically and are exported to countries in Europe, such as Belgium, Holland, Germany, and England, as well as to African, South American, Asian, and Middle

---

[5]Sharon Harris, "Forecasting with Demand Forecasting Group Database at Bell Atlantic," *Journal of Business Forecasting,* Winter 1995–96, p. 23.

[6]H. Alan Catron, "Daily Demand Forecasting at Columbia Gas," *Journal of Business Forecasting* 19, no. 2 (Summer 2000), pp. 10–15.

Eastern countries.[7] The forecasting function at Segix is housed within the marketing group, and forecasts are reviewed by the marketing director and the sales director, both of whom may make subjective adjustments to the forecasts based on market forces not reflected in the original forecasts. The forecasts are prepared monthly for seven main prescription drug products. The monthly forecasts are then aggregated to arrive at annual forecasts. These forecasts are used to develop targets for sales representatives.

Pharmaceuticals in Singapore

In this example we look at some survey results related to forecasting by pharmaceutical firms in Singapore.[8] The survey included many well-known firms, such as Glaxo Wellcome, Bayer, Pfizer, Bristol-Myers Squibb, and others. Respondent forecasters were from across business areas such as management, marketing, finance, and operations. The primary uses of forecasts were found to be: allocation of corporate resources for human resources planning, and for promotions, strategic planning, and setting sales quotas. Both quantitative methods and personal judgments were found to be important in the development of forecasts.

Fiat Auto

Top management at Fiat considers the forecasting function as an essential aspect of their decision-making process.[9] Midway through the 1990s Fiat was selling over 2 million vehicles annually and employed some 81,000 people in Italy and about another 38,000 overseas. All functional areas in the company make use of the forecasts that are prepared primarily in the Planning, Finance, and Control Department and in the Product Strategy Department. Macroeconomic data such as gross domestic product, the interest rate, the rate of inflation, and raw-material prices are important inputs in Fiat's forecasting process. At Fiat forecasts are first prepared for total sales of vehicles, engines, and gears, and then broken down to specific stock-keeping units (SKUs). Sales are measured by orders rather than shipments because their system is customer driven.

Douglas Aircraft

In discussing how forecasts are prepared at Douglas Aircraft, Adrian LeRoy and Adam Pilarski relate how two alternative forecasts are reconciled within the company.[10] Since the number of passenger-miles flown is an important determinant of airplane sales, they prepare two passenger-miles forecasts: a top-down forecast and a bottom-up forecast.

---

[7]Anna Maria Rosati, "Forecasting at Segix Italia: A Pharmaceutical Company," *Journal of Business Forecasting,* Fall 1996, pp. 7–9.

[8]Louis Choo, "Forecasting Practices in the Pharmaceutical Industry in Singapore," *Journal of Business Forecasting* 19, no. 2 (Summer 2000), pp. 18–20.

[9]Anna Maria Rosati, "Forecasting at Fiat Auto," *Journal of Business Forecasting,* Spring 1996, pp. 28–29.

[10]Adrian D. LeRoy and Adam Pilarski, "The Way to Improve Accuracy—Douglas Aircraft's Experience," *Journal of Business Forecasting* 4, no. 2 (Summer 1985), pp. 10–12.

The former starts with an econometric forecast of the entire market for each of 32 regions of the world. These regional forecasts are then broken down for individual airlines that serve each market. Another forecast begins with a separate econometric model for each of the top 50 airlines in the world (which includes about 85 percent of the market) for each market. Less sophisticated forecasts for another 110 airlines are added to arrive at a bottom-up forecast for each market. The total of 160 airlines accounts for about 98 percent of the market. The econometric models are augmented with commonsense judgments about the industry in arriving at final forecasts for the two approaches, which are then reconciled.

Trans World Airlines

Paul Biederman, director of economic analysis and forecasting at TWA, has the responsibility for revenue forecasting for the entire company.[11] TWA's financial plan for each year is driven by his revenue forecasts, which are done twice each year. A first forecast for the following year is prepared in the November of the previous year. This forecast is then recalibrated in May of the forecast year. Thus, for the 1998 year a forecast is prepared in November 1997 and that forecast is updated in May 1998. Ultimately the revenue forecasts are combined with expense estimates that come from the office of the controller. In addition to these short-term forecasts, TWA prepares long-term forecasts for equipment planning.

Rather than forecasting each market separately and adding them together to get the total company forecast, TWA uses a top-down and industry-share approach. They start by forecasting total industry passenger traffic and then they estimate TWA's share of the total. The reason for the top-down approach is related to data availability issues. Total industry data are available for each month within a week after the end of the month. On the other hand, it takes about nine months to get market-by-market data from the U.S. Department of Transportation. TWA uses a combination of regression and trend models in developing annual forecasts, which are then converted to a monthly basis according to seasonal relationships.

Brake Parts, Inc.

Brake Parts, Inc. (BPI) is a manufacturer of replacement brake parts for both foreign and domestic cars and light trucks.[12] They have nine manufacturing plants and seven distribution centers in the United States and Canada. Overall, BPI has roughly 250,000 stock-keeping units at various distribution locations (SKULs) to forecast. The development and implementation of a multiple forecasting system (MFS) has saved BPI over $6 million per month, resulting from sales not being lost due to stockouts. The MFS used at BPI uses up to 19 time-series forecasting techniques, such as a variety of

[11]Paul S. Biederman, "The Role of Forecasting at Trans World Airlines," *Journal of Business Forecasting,* Fall 1993, pp. 3–4.

[12]John T. Mentzer and Jon Schroeter, "Multiple Forecasting System at Brake Parts, Inc.," *Journal of Business Forecasting,* Fall 1993, pp. 5–9.

exponential smoothing methods, and causal regression models in tandem. Forecasts are first developed with a time-series method and then the errors, or residuals, are forecast using regression. The two forecasts are then added together and provided to management in a form that allows management to make subjective adjustments to the forecasts.

Forecasts are evaluated using three measures: percent error (PE), mean absolute percent error (MAPE), and year-to-date mean absolute percent error (YTD MAPE). The first two of these are common error measures but the third is somewhat unique. The YTD MAPE is used to give management a feeling for how each forecast is performing in the most current time frame. The PE and MAPE contain errors that have occurred at any time in the historical period and thus may not reflect how well the method is working currently.

These examples illustrate the role forecasting plays in eight representative firms. Similar scenarios exist in thousands of other businesses throughout the world and, as you will see in the following section, in various nonbusiness activities as well.

Forecasting in the Public and Not-for-Profit Sectors

The need to make decisions based on judgments about the future course of events extends beyond the profit-oriented sector of the economy. Hospitals, libraries, blood banks, police and fire departments, urban transit authorities, credit unions, and a myriad of federal, state, and local governmental units rely on forecasts of one kind or another. Social service agencies such as the Red Cross and the Easter Seal Society must also base their yearly plans on forecasts of needed services and expected revenues.

Brooke Saladin, working with the research and planning division of the police department in a city of about 650,000 people, has been effective in forecasting the demand for police patrol services.[13] This demand is measured by using a call-for-service work-load level in units of hours per 24-hour period. After a thorough statistical analysis, five factors were identified as influential determinants of the call-for-service work load (W):

POP	a population factor
ARR	an arrest factor
AFF	an affluence factor
VAC	a vacancy factor
DEN	a density factor

The following multiple-regression model was developed on the basis of a sample of 40 cruiser districts in the city:

$$W = 5.66 + 1.84\text{POP} + 1.70\text{ARR} - 0.93\text{AFF} + 0.61\text{VAC} + 0.13\text{DEN}$$

Using the remaining 23 cruiser districts to test this model, Saladin found that "the absolute error in forecasting workload ranged from 0.07827 to 1.49764, with an average

---

[13]Brooke A. Saladin, "A Police Story with Business Implications and Applications," *Journal of Business Forecasting* 1, no. 6 (Winter 1982–83), pp. 3–5.

of 0.74618."[14] This type of model is useful in planning the needs for both personnel and equipment.

In Texas, the Legislative Budget Board (LBB) is required to forecast the growth rate for Texas personal income, which then governs the limit for state appropriations. The state comptroller's office also needs forecasts of such variables as the annual growth rates of electricity sales, total nonagricultural employment, and total tax revenues. Richard Ashley and John Guerard have used techniques like those to be discussed in this text to forecast these variables and have found that the application of time-series analysis yields better one-year-ahead forecasts than naive constant-growth-rate models.[15]

Dr. Jon David Vasche, senior economist for the California Legislative Analysis Office (LAO), is involved with economic and financial forecasting for the state. He has noted that these forecasts are essential, since the state's budget of over $70 billion must be prepared long before actual economic conditions are known.[16] The key features of the LAO's forecasting approach are:

1. *Forecasts of national economic variables.* The Wharton econometric model is used with the adaptations that reflect the LAO's own assumptions about such policy variables as monetary growth and national fiscal policies.
2. *California economic submodel.* This model forecasts variables such as trends in state population, personal income, employment, and housing activity.
3. *State revenue submodels.* These models are used to forecast the variables that affect the state's revenue. These include such items as taxable personal income, taxable sales, corporate profits, vehicle registrations, and cash available for investment.
4. *Cash-flow models.* These models are used to forecast the flow of revenues over time.

In developing and using forecasting models, "the LAO has attempted to strike a balance between comprehensiveness and sophistication on the one hand, and flexibility and usability on the other."[17] LAO's success is determined by how accurately it forecasts the state's revenues. In the three most recent years reported, the "average absolute value of the actual error was only about 1.6 percent."[18] Errors of 5 percent or more have occurred when unanticipated movements in national economic activity have affected the state's economy.

---

[14]Ibid., p. 5.

[15]Richard Ashley and John Guerard, "Applications of Time-Series Analysis to Texas Financial Forecasting," *Interfaces* 13, no. 4 (August 1983), pp. 46–55.

[16]Jon David Vasche, "Forecasting Process as Used by California Legislative Analyst's Office," *Journal of Business Forecasting* 6, no. 2 (Summer 1987), pp. 9–13; and "State Demographic Forecasting for Business and Policy Applications," *Journal of Business Forecasting*, Summer 2000, pp. 23–30.

[17]Jon David Vasche, "Forecasting Process as Used by California Legislative Analyst's Office," *Journal of Business Forecasting* 6, no. 2 (Summer 1987), pp. 9, 12.

[18]Ibid., p. 12.

A multiple-regression forecasting model has been developed to help forecast a hospital's nursing staff requirements.[19] This model forecasts the number of patients that need to be served and the nature of care required (e.g., pediatric or orthopedic) for each month, day of the week, and time of day. Such models have become very valuable for directors of nursing personnel in determining work schedules.

In a study of a hospital that holds over 300 beds, we have found that the forecasting methods discussed in this text are effective in forecasting monthly billable procedures (BILLPROC) for the hospital's laboratories.[20] The primary purpose of producing monthly forecasts is to help laboratory managers make more accurate staffing decisions in the laboratory. Also, an accurate forecast can help in controlling inventory costs and in providing timely customer service. This can streamline operations and lead to more satisfied customers.

For preparing short-term forecasts of billable procedures, two models are used: a linear-regression model and Winters' exponential-smoothing model. The linear-regression model is based on inpatient admissions, a time index, and 11 monthly dummy variables to account for seasonality. The second model is a Winters' exponential smoothing that incorporates a multiplicative seasonal adjustment and a trend component.

The root-mean-squared error (RMSE) is used to evaluate the accuracy of forecast models at the hospital. The first annual forecast, by month, of billable procedures for the laboratory prepared with these quantitative methods provided good results. The linear-regression model provided the most accurate forecast, with an RMSE of 1654.44. This was about 3.9 percent of the mean number of procedures per month during that year. The Winters' model had a higher RMSE of 2416.91 (about 5.7 percent of the mean number of procedures per month). For the entire fiscal year in total, the forecast of the annual number of laboratory procedures resulted in an error of only 0.7 percent.

Forecasting and Supply Chain Management

In recent years there has been increased attention to supply chain management issues. In a competitive environment businesses are forced to operate with maximum efficiency and with a vigilant eye toward maintaining firm cost controls, while continuing to meet consumer expectations in a profitable manner. To be successful, businesses must manage relationships along the supply chain more fully than ever before.[21]

We can think of the supply chain as encompassing all of the various flows between suppliers, producers, distributors (wholesalers, retailers, etc.), and consumers. Throughout this chain each participant, prior to the final consumer, must manage supplies, inventories, production, and shipping in one form or another. For example, a manufacturer that makes cellular phones needs a number of different components to assemble

---

[19]F. Theodore Helmer, Edward B. Opperman, and James D. Suver, "Forecasting Nursing Staffing Requirements by Intensity-of-Care Level," *Interfaces* (June 1980), pp. 50–55.

[20]J. Holton Wilson and Steven J. Schuiling, "Forecasting Hospital Laboratory Procedures," *Journal of Medical Systems,* December 1992, pp. 269–79.

[21]See, for example, David Simchi-Levi, Philip Kaminsky, and Edith Simchi-Levi, *Designing and Managing the Supply Chain,* (New York: Irwin/McGraw-Hill), 2000.

the final product and ultimately ship it to a local supplier of cellular phone services or some other retailer. One such component might be the leather carrying case. The manufacturer of the carrying case may have suppliers of leather, clear plastic for portions of the case, fasteners, dyes perhaps, and possibly other components. Each one of these suppliers has its own suppliers back one more step in the supply chain. With all of these businesses trying to reduce inventory costs (for raw materials, goods in process, and finished products), reliability and cooperation across the supply chain become essential.

Forecasting has come to play an important role in managing supply chain relationships. If the supplier of leather phone cases is to be a good supply chain partner it must have a reasonably accurate forecast of the needs of the cellular phone company. The cellular phone company, in turn, needs a good forecast of sales to be able to provide the leather case company with good information. It is probably obvious that if the cellular phone company is aware of a significant change in sales for a future period, that information needs to be communicated to the leather case company in a timely manner.

To help make the entire supply chain function more smoothly, many companies have started to use collaborative forecasting systems in which information about the forecast is shared throughout the relevant portions of the supply chain. Often, in fact, suppliers have at least some input into the forecast of a business further along the supply chain in such collaborative forecasting systems.[22] Having good forecasts at every stage is essential for efficient functioning of the supply chain.

At the beginning of the text, at the very start of page one, you read the following quote from Al Enns, Director of Supply Chain Strategies, at Motts North America:

> I believe that forecasting or demand management may have the potential to add more value to a business than any single activity within the supply chain. I say this because *if you can get the forecast right, you have the potential to get everything else in the supply chain right.* But if you can't get the forecast right, then everything else you do essentially will be reactive, as opposed to proactive planning.[23]

This is just one example of the importance business professionals are giving to the role of forecasting.

There is another issue that is partially related to where a business operates along the supply chain that is important to think about when it comes to forecasting. As one gets closer to the consumer end of the supply chain the number of items to forecast tends to increase. For example, consider a manufacturer that produces a single product that is ultimately sold through discount stores. Along the way it may pass through several intermediaries. That manufacturer only needs to forecast sales of that one product (and, of course, the potentially many components that go into the product). But, assume that Wal-Mart is one of the stores that sells the product to consumers throughout the United States. Just think of the tens of thousands of stock-keeping units (SKUs) that Wal-Mart

To help make the entire supply chain function more smoothly, many companies have started to use collaborative forecasting systems in which information about the forecast is shared throughout the relevant portions of the supply chain.

---

[22]Many forecasting software packages facilitate collaborative forecasting by making the process Web-based so that multiple participants can potentially have access to, and in some cases input into, the forecast process.

[23]Sidney Hill, Jr., "A Whole New Outlook." *Manufacturing Systems* 16, no. 9, September 1998, pp. 70–80. (Emphasis added.)

sells and must forecast. Clearly the methods that the manufacturer considers in preparing a forecast can be much more labor intensive than the methods that Wal-Mart can consider. Wal-Mart will be limited to applying forecasting methods that can be easily automated and can be quickly applied. This is something you will want to think about as you study the various forecast methods discussed in this text.

Computer Use and Quantitative Forecasting

In today's business environment computers are readily available to nearly everyone. There was a time when only very large business enterprises had the resources to spend on computer systems, and within those businesses access to the computer's power was limited. Today things are quite different. The cost of large-scale computer systems has dropped significantly, and microcomputers have made computer technology available to virtually any business professional interested in utilizing it. As early as 1966 a study reported that 68 percent of the companies surveyed used computers in preparing forecasts.[24] In 1986 a survey of economists found that over 93 percent used a computer in developing forecasts.[25] A similar study of marketing professionals found that about 87 percent were using computers in forecasting. Just over 30 percent of the marketing professionals surveyed who use a computer in developing forecasts relied solely on a microcomputer.[26] It is clear that microcomputers are currently the primary computational tool for the preparation of forecasts.

The widespread availability of computers has contributed to the use of quantitative forecasting techniques, many of which would not be practical to carry out by hand. Most of the methods described in this text fall into the realm of quantitative forecasting techniques that are reasonable to use only when appropriate computer software is available. A number of software packages, at costs that range from about $100 to many thousands of dollars, are currently marketed for use in developing forecasts. You will find that the software that accompanies this text will enable you to apply the most commonly used quantitative forecasting techniques to data of your choosing.

The use of microcomputers or PCs (personal computers) in forecasting has been made possible by rapid technological changes that have made these desktop (or laptop) computers very fast and capable of storing and processing large amounts of data. User-friendly software makes it easy for people to become proficient in using forecasting programs in a short period of time. Dr. Vasche has said in this regard that "reliance on such PC systems has given state economists added flexibility in their forecasting work. By minimizing use of mainframe computers, it has also reduced the state's costs of preparing forecasts."[27] The same is true in most business situations as well. The dominance of PC forecasting software is clear at the annual meetings of the major

---

[24]Spyros Makridakis, Steven C. Wheelwright, and Victor E. McGee, *Forecasting: Methods and Applications,* 2nd ed. (New York: John Wiley & Sons, 1983), p. 782.

[25]Barry Keating and J. Holton Wilson, "Forecasting: Practices and Teachings," *Journal of Business Forecasting* 6, no. 3 (Winter 1987–88), p. 12.

[26]J. Holton Wilson and Hugh G. Daubek, "Marketing Managers Evaluate Forecasting Methods," *Journal of Business Forecasting* 8, no. 1 (Spring 1989), p. 20.

[27]Vasche, "Forecasting Process," p. 12.

forecasting associations. At these meetings various vendors of PC-based forecasting software packages display and demonstrate their products.

The importance of quantitative methods in forecasting has been stressed by Charles W. Chase, Jr., who was formerly director of forecasting at Johnson & Johnson Consumer Products, Inc., and now works in a similar capacity for Wyeth-Ayerst Global Pharmaceuticals. He says, "Forecasting is a blend of science and art. Like most things in business, the rule of 80/20 applies to forecasting. By and large, forecasts are driven 80 percent mathematically and 20 percent judgmentally."[28]

Subjective Forecasting Methods

Quantitative techniques using the power of the computer have come to dominate the forecasting landscape. However, there is a rich history of forecasting based on subjective and judgmental methods, some of which remain useful even today. These methods are probably most appropriately used when the forecaster is faced with a severe shortage of historical data and/or when quantitative expertise is not available. In some situations a judgmental method may even be preferred to a quantitative one. Very long-range forecasting is an example of such a situation. The computer-based models that are the focal point of this text have less applicability to such things as forecasting the type of home entertainment that will be available 40 years from now than do those methods based on expert judgments. In this section several subjective or judgmental forecasting methods are reviewed.

Sales-Force Composites

The sales force can be a rich source of information about future trends and changes in buyer behavior. These people have daily contact with buyers and are the closest contact most firms have with their customers. If the information available from the sales force is organized and collected in an objective manner, considerable insight into future sales volumes can be obtained.

Members of the sales force are asked to estimate sales for each product they handle. These estimates are usually based on each individual's subjective "feel" for the level of sales that would be reasonable in the forecast period. Often a range of forecasts will be requested, including a most optimistic, a most pessimistic, and a most likely forecast. Typically these individual projections are aggregated by the sales manager for a given product line and/or geographic area. Ultimately the person responsible for the firm's total sales forecast combines the product-line and/or geographic forecasts to arrive at projections that become the basis for a given planning horizon.

While this process takes advantage of information from sources very close to actual buyers, a major problem with the resulting forecast may arise if members of the sales force tend to underestimate sales for their product lines and/or territories.[29] This

---

[28]Charles W. Chase, Jr., "Forecasting Consumer Products," *Journal of Business Forecasting* 10, no. 1 (Spring 1991), p. 2.

[29]Robin T. Peterson, "Sales Force Composite Forecasting—An Exploratory Analysis," *Journal of Business Forecasting* 8, no. 1 (Spring 1989), pp. 23–27.

behavior is particularly likely when the salespeople are assigned quotas on the basis of their forecasts and when bonuses are based on performance relative to those quotas. Such a downward bias can be very harmful to the firm. Scheduled production runs are shorter than they should be, raw-material inventories are too small, labor requirements are underestimated, and in the end customer ill will is generated by product shortages. The sales manager with ultimate forecasting responsibility can offset this downward bias, but only by making judgments that could, in turn, incorporate other bias into the forecast. Robin Peterson has developed a way of improving sales-force composite forecasts by using a prescribed set of learned routines as a guide for salespeople as they develop their forecasts.[30]

These sets of learned routines are referred to as *scripts,* which can serve as a guide in developing an essentially subjective forecast. An example of a hypothetical script adapted from Peterson's work follows:

> Review data on gross domestic product
> Review forecasts of gross domestic product
> Review industry sales data for the preceding year
> Review company sales data for the preceding year
> Review company sales forecasts for the previous years
> Survey key accounts concerning their purchasing plans
> Review last year's sales data in the salesperson's territory
> Review the employment situation in the salesperson's territory
> Do a simple trend projection of sales in the salesperson's territory
> Examine competitors' actions in the salesperson's territory
> Gather internal data about the company's promotional plans
> Gather internal data about the company's product introduction plans
> Gather internal data about the company's customer service plans
> Gather internal data about the company's credit-granting plans
> Check to see if there are planned changes in the company's pricing structure
> Evaluate the pricing practices of competitors
> Track the company's sales promotions
> Track the competitors' sales promotions

A script such as this can be developed, based on interviews with successful salespeople concerning procedures they have used in preparing their forecasts.

Surveys of Customers and the General Population

In some situations it may be practical to survey customers for advanced information about their buying intentions. This practice presumes that buyers plan their purchases and follow through with their plans. Such an assumption is probably more realistic for

---

[30]Robin T. Peterson, "Improving Sales Force Composite: Forecasting by Using Scripts," *Journal of Business Forecasting,* Fall 1993, pp. 10–14.

industrial sales than for sales to households and individuals. It is also more realistic for big-ticket items such as cars or personal computers than for convenience goods like toothpaste or tennis balls.

Survey data concerning how people feel about the economy are sometimes used by forecasters to help predict certain buying behaviors. One of the commonly used measures of how people feel about the economy comes from a monthly survey conducted by the University of Michigan Survey Research Center (SRC). The SRC produces an Index of Consumer Sentiment (ICS) based on a survey of 500 individuals, 40 percent of whom are respondents who participated in the survey six months earlier and the remaining 60 percent are new respondents selected on a random basis. This index has its base period in 1966, when the index was 100. High values of the ICS indicate more positive feelings about the economy than do lower values. Thus, if the ICS goes up, one might expect that people are more likely to make certain types of purchases.

Jury of Executive Opinion

The judgments of experts in any area are a valuable resource. Based on years of experience, such judgments can be useful in the forecasting process. Using the method known as the *jury of executive opinion,* a forecast is developed by combining the subjective opinions of the managers and executives who are most likely to have the best insights about the firm's business. To provide a breadth of opinions, it is useful to select these people from different functional areas. For example, personnel from finance, marketing, and production might be included.

The person responsible for making the forecast may collect opinions in individual interviews or in a meeting where the participants have an opportunity to discuss various points of view. The latter has some obvious advantages such as stimulating deeper insights, but it has some important disadvantages as well. For example, if one or more strong personalities dominate the group, their opinions will become disproportionately important in the final consensus that is reached.

The Delphi Method

The Delphi method is similar to the jury of executive opinion in taking advantage of the wisdom and insight of people who have considerable expertise about the area to be forecast. It has the additional advantage, however, of anonymity among the participants. The experts, perhaps five to seven in number, never meet to discuss their views; none of them even knows who else is on the panel.

The Delphi method can be summarized by the following six steps:

1. Participating panel members are selected.
2. Questionnaires asking for opinions about the variables to be forecast are distributed to panel members.
3. Results from panel members are collected, tabulated, and summarized.
4. Summary results are distributed to the panel members for their review and consideration.

5. Panel members revise their individual estimates, taking account of the information received from the other, unknown panel members.

6. Steps 3 through 5 are repeated until no significant changes result.

Through this process there is usually movement toward centrality, but there is no pressure on panel members to alter their original projections. Members who have strong reason to believe that their original response is correct, no matter how widely it differs from others, may freely stay with it. Thus, in the end there may not be a consensus.

The Delphi method may be superior to the jury of executive opinion, since strong personalities or peer pressures have no influence on the outcome. The processes of sending out questionnaires, getting them back, tabulating, and summarizing can be speeded up by using advanced computer capabilities, including networking and e-mail.[31]

Some Advantages and Disadvantages of Subjective Methods

Subjective (i.e., qualitative or judgmental) forecasting methods are sometimes considered desirable because they do not require any particular mathematical background of the individuals involved. As future business professionals, like yourself, become better trained in quantitative forms of analysis, this advantage will become less important. Historically, another advantage of subjective methods has been their wide acceptance by users. However, our experience suggests that users are increasingly concerned with how the forecast was developed, and with most subjective methods it is difficult to be specific in this regard. The underlying models are, by definition, subjective. This subjectivity is nonetheless the most important advantage of this class of methods. There are often forces at work that cannot be captured by quantitative methods. They can, however, be sensed by experienced business professionals and can make an important contribution to improved forecasts. Wilson and Allison-Koerber have shown this dramatically in the context of forecasting sales for a large piece of food-service equipment produced by the Delfield Company.[32] Quantitative methods reduced errors to about 60 percent of those that resulted from the subjective method that had been in use. When the less accurate subjective method was combined with the quantitative methods, errors were further reduced to about 40 percent of the level when the subjective method was used alone. It is clear from this result, and others, that there is often important information content in subjective methods.

The disadvantages of subjective methods were nicely summarized by Charles W. Chase, Jr., when he was with Johnson & Johnson Consumer Products, Inc. He stated that "the disadvantages of qualitative methods are: (1) they are almost always biased; (2) they are not consistently accurate over time; (3) it takes years of experience for someone to learn how to convert intuitive judgment into good forecasts."[33]

---

[31]See, for example, Bernard S. Husbands, "Electronic Mail System Enhances Delphi Method," *Journal of Business Forecasting* 1, no. 4 (Summer 1982), pp. 24–27.

[32]Wilson and Allison-Koerber, "Combining Subjective and Objective Forecasts," p. 15.

[33]Charles W. Chase, Jr., "Forecasting Consumer Products," p. 4.

New-Product Forecasting

Quantitative forecasting methods, which are the primary focus of this text, are not usually well suited for predicting sales of new products, because they rely on a historical data series to establish model parameters. Often judgmental methods are better suited to forecasting new-product sales because there are many uncertainties and few known relationships. One way to deal with the lack of known information in the forecasting of new products is to incorporate a modified version of the Delphi method. This was done by Ken Goldfisher while he worked in the Information Services Division of the Nabisco Foods Group. Goldfisher has also found some relatively simple quantitative methods, such as moving averages, to be helpful in developing new-product forecasts at Nabisco.[34]

Various market research activities can be helpful in new-product forecasting. Surveys of potential customers can provide useful preliminary information about the propensity of buyers to adopt a new product. Test-market results and results from the distribution of free samples can also provide estimates of initial sales. On the basis of predictions about the number of initial innovators who will buy a product, an S-shaped market-penetration curve can be used to forecast diffusion of the new product throughout the market.

Terry Anderson has described a process for new-product forecasting at Howmedica that is based on various judgmental factors.[35] It begins with an estimate of the total number of customers, based on a consensus within the marketing and sales groups. A customer usage rate is derived based on experience with past new introductions. Inventory requirements are also included in making projections.

Whitlark, Geurts, and Swenson have used customer purchase intention surveys as a tool to help prepare forecasts of new products.[36] They describe a three-step process that starts with the identification of a demographic profile of the target market, then the probability of purchase is estimated from survey data, and finally a forecast is developed by combining this probability with information on the size of the target market. A sample of consumers from the target market are asked to respond to an intent-to-purchase scale such as: definitely will buy; probably will buy; might or might not buy; probably will not buy; and definitely will not buy. Probabilities are then assigned to each of the intention-to-buy categories, using empirical evidence from a longitudinal study of members of the target market covering a length of time comparable to the length of time for the proposed forecast horizon. An example of these probabilities for a three- and a six-month time horizon is shown in Table 1–1. Note that the probabilities of purchase increase as the time horizon increases.

Applying this method to two products produced good results. For the first product the three-month forecast purchase rate was 2.9 percent compared with an actual

---

[34]Ken Goldfisher, "Modified Delphi: A Concept for New Product Forecasting," *Journal of Business Forecasting* 11, no. 4 (Winter 1992–93), pp. 10–11; and Ken Goldfisher and Colleen Chan, "New Product Reactive Forecasting," *Journal of Business Forecasting* 13, no. 4 (Winter 1994–95), pp. 7–9.

[35]Anderson, "Demand Forecasting at Howmedica," pp. 2–3.

[36]David B. Whitlark, Michael D. Geurts, and Michael J. Swenson, "New Product Forecasting with a Purchase Intention Survey," *Journal of Business Forecasting* 10, no. 3 (Fall 1993), pp. 18–21.

TABLE 1–1   **Probabilities Assigned
to Purchase-Intention Categories**

Intention-to-Purchase Category	Three-Month Time Horizon	Six-Month Time Horizon
Definitely will buy	64%	75%
Probably will buy	23%	53%
Might or might not buy	5%	21%
Probably will not buy	2%	9%
Definitely will not buy	1%	4%

Adapted from Whitlark et al., p. 20.

purchase rate of 2.4 percent. In the six-month time horizon the forecast and actual rates were 15.6 percent and 11.1 percent, respectively. Similar results were found for a second product. In the three-month horizon the forecast and actual percents were 2.5 percent versus 1.9 percent, while in the six-month forecast horizon the forecast was 16.7 percent and the actual was 16.3 percent.

Two Simple Naive Models

The simplest of all forecasting methods is to assume that the next period will be identical to the present. You may have used this method today in deciding what clothes to wear. If you had not heard a professional weather forecast, your decision about today's weather might be based on the weather you observed yesterday. If yesterday was clear and the temperature was 70°F, you might assume today to be the same. If yesterday was snowy and cold, you might expect a similar wintry day today. In fact, without evidence to suggest otherwise, such a weather forecast is quite reasonable. Forecasts based solely on the most recent observation of the variable of interest are often referred to as "naive forecasts."

   In this section we will use such a method, and a variation on it, to forecast the quarterly U.S. average annual unemployment rate using data for 1990Q1 through 1999Q4. These data are given in Table 1–2 and are shown graphically in Figure 1–1. In both forms of presentation you can see that the unemployment rate (UR) varied considerably throughout this period, from a low of 4.1 percent in 1999Q4 to a high of 7.6 percent in 1992Q2 and 1992Q3. The fluctuations in most economic and business series (variables) are usually best seen after converting the data into graphic form, as in Figure 1–1. You should develop the habit of observing data in graphic form when forecasting.

   The simplest naive forecasting model, in which the forecast value is equal to the previous observed value, can be described in algebraic form as follows:

$$F_t = A_{t-1}$$

(c1t2)   **TABLE 1–2**   **U.S. Average Quarterly Unemployment Rate**

Year	Quarter	Unemployment Rate	Year	Quarter	Unemployment Rate	
1990	1	5.3%	1995	2	5.7%	
1990	2	5.3%	1995	3	5.7%	
1990	3	5.7%	1995	4	5.6%	
1990	4	6.1%	1996	1	5.5%	
1991	1	6.6%	1996	2	5.5%	
1991	2	6.8%	1996	3	5.3%	
1991	3	6.9%	1996	4	5.3%	
1991	4	7.1%	1997	1	5.3%	
1992	1	7.4%	1997	2	5.0%	
1992	2	7.6%	1997	3	4.9%	
1992	3	7.6%	1997	4	4.7%	
1992	4	7.4%	1998	1	4.7%	
1993	1	7.1%	1998	2	4.4%	
1993	2	7.1%	1998	3	4.5%	
1993	3	6.8%	1998	4	4.4%	
1993	4	6.6%	1999	1	4.3%	
1994	1	6.6%	1999	2	4.3%	
1994	2	6.2%	1999	3	4.2%	
1994	3	6.0%	1999	4	4.1%	
1994	4	5.6%	2000	1	4.0%	←Holdout period
1995	1	5.5%				

FIGURE 1–1

U.S. Average Quarterly Unemployment Rate (same as c1t2)

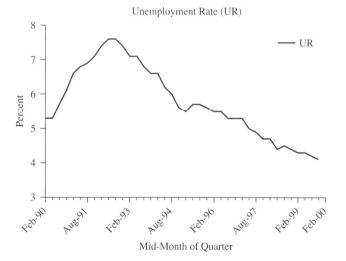

The U.S. average unemployment rate (UR) from 1990Q1 (Feb-90) through 1999Q4 (Nov-99) shows a low of 4.1% in 1999Q4 and a high of 7.6% in 1992Q2 and 1992Q3. A plot such as this is helpful to a forecaster to see the nature of the data to be forecast.

where F_t represents the forecast value for time period t and A_{t-1} represents the observed value one period earlier $(t-1)$. In terms of the unemployment-rate data we wish to forecast, the model may be written as:

$$URF_t = UR_{t-1}$$

where URF_t is the unemployment-rate naive forecast number 1 at time period t and UR_{t-1} is the observed unemployment rate one period earlier $(t-1)$. We call this *naive forecast one* because we will very shortly look at another naive forecast.

This first naive forecast was done using Excel. The results are shown in Table 1–3 along with measures of how well the model did. These measures will be discussed shortly.

TABLE 1–3   **U.S. Unemployment Rate (UR) and a Naive Forecast (URF)**   (c1t3)

Mid-Month of Quarter	Unemployment Rate (UR)	Unemployment Rate Naive Forecast (URF)	Error = Actual (UR) Minus Forecast (URF)	Squared Error	Historic Period Error Measures
Feb-1990	5.3%				
May-1990	5.3%	5.3%	0.0%	0.00%	Mean error (ME) = −0.031%
Aug-1990	5.7%	5.3%	0.4%	0.16%	
Nov-1990	6.1%	5.7%	0.4%	0.16%	
Feb-1991	6.6%	6.1%	0.5%	0.25%	Mean absolute error (MAE) = 0.200%
May-1991	6.8%	6.6%	0.2%	0.04%	
Aug-1991	6.9%	6.8%	0.1%	0.01%	
Nov-1991	7.1%	6.9%	0.2%	0.04%	Mean percent error (MPE) = −0.72%
Feb-1992	7.4%	7.1%	0.3%	0.09%	
May-1992	7.6%	7.4%	0.2%	0.04%	
Aug-1992	7.6%	7.6%	0.0%	0.00%	Mean absolute percent error (MAPE) = 2.82%
Nov-1992	7.4%	7.6%	−0.2%	0.04%	
Feb-1993	7.1%	7.4%	−0.3%	0.09%	
May-1993	7.1%	7.1%	0.0%	0.00%	Mean-squared error (MSE) = 0.046%
Aug-1993	6.8%	7.1%	−0.3%	0.09%	
Nov-1993	6.6%	6.8%	−0.2%	0.04%	
Feb-1994	6.6%	6.6%	0.0%	0.00%	Root-mean-squared error (RMSE) = 0.215%
May-1994	6.2%	6.6%	−0.4%	0.16%	
Aug-1994	6.0%	6.2%	−0.2%	0.04%	
Nov-1994	5.6%	6.0%	−0.4%	0.16%	
Feb-1995	5.5%	5.6%	−0.1%	0.01%	
May-1995	5.7%	5.5%	0.2%	0.04%	
Aug-1995	5.7%	5.7%	0.0%	0.00%	
Nov-1995	5.6%	5.7%	−0.1%	0.01%	
Feb-1996	5.5%	5.6%	−0.1%	0.01%	
May-1996	5.5%	5.5%	0.0%	0.00%	
Aug-1996	5.3%	5.5%	−0.2%	0.04%	
Nov-1996	5.3%	5.3%	0.0%	0.00%	
Feb-1997	5.3%	5.3%	0.0%	0.00%	
May-1997	5.0%	5.3%	−0.3%	0.09%	
Aug-1997	4.9%	5.0%	−0.1%	0.01%	
Nov-1997	4.7%	4.9%	−0.2%	0.04%	
Feb-1998	4.7%	4.7%	0.0%	0.00%	

(continued)

TABLE 1–3 *(Continued)*

Mid-Month of Quarter	Unemployment Rate (UR)	Unemployment Rate Naive Forecast (URF)	Error = Actual (UR) Minus Forecast (URF)	Squared Error	Historic Period Error Measures
May-1998	4.4%	4.7%	−0.3%	0.09%	
Aug-1998	4.5%	4.4%	0.1%	0.01%	
Nov-1998	4.4%	4.5%	−0.1%	0.01%	
Feb-1999	4.3%	4.4%	−0.1%	0.01%	
May-1999	4.3%	4.3%	0.0%	0.00%	
Aug-1999	4.2%	4.3%	−0.1%	0.01%	
Nov-1999	4.1%	4.2%	−0.1%	0.01%	
Feb-2000	4.0%	4.1%	−0.1%	0.01%	← Holdout period

This table shows the simple naive forecast for the unemployment rate where $URF_t = UR_{t-1}$.

FIGURE 1–2

U.S. Average Unemployment Rate and a Naive Forecast (data same as c1t3)

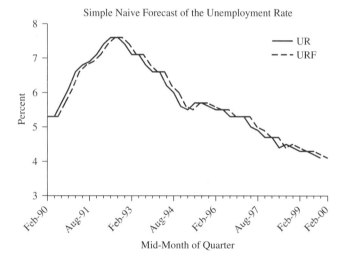

The U.S. average unemployment rate (UR) from 1990Q1 (Feb-90) through 1999Q4 (Nov-99) and a naive forecast (URF).

Note that each forecast value simply replicates the actual value for the preceding year. These results are presented in graphic form in Figure 1–2, which clearly shows the one-period shift between the two series. The forecast for every quarter is exactly the same as the actual value for the quarter before.

One might argue that in addition to considering just the most recent observation, it would make sense to consider the direction from which we arrived at the latest

TABLE 1–4   U.S. Unemployment Rate (UR) and a Modified Naive Forecast (URF2)

Mid-Month of Quarter	Unemployment Rate (UR)	Unemployment Rate Modified Naive Forecast (URF2)	Error = Actual (UR) Minus Forecast (URF2)	Squared Error	Historic Period Error Measures
Feb-1990	5.3%				
May-1990	5.3%			0.00%	Mean error (ME) = −0.017%
Aug-1990	5.7%	5.30%	0.40%	0.16%	
Nov-1990	6.1%	5.90%	0.20%	0.04%	
Feb-1991	6.6%	6.30%	0.30%	0.09%	Mean absolute error (MAE) = 0.050%
May-1991	6.8%	6.85%	−0.05%	0.00%	
Aug-1991	6.9%	6.90%	0.00%	0.00%	
Nov-1991	7.1%	6.95%	0.15%	0.02%	Mean percent error (MPE) = −0.36%
Feb-1992	7.4%	7.20%	0.20%	0.04%	
May-1992	7.6%	7.55%	0.05%	0.00%	
Aug-1992	7.6%	7.70%	−0.10%	0.01%	Mean absolute percent error (MAPE) = 2.56%
Nov-1992	7.4%	7.60%	−0.20%	0.04%	
Feb-1993	7.1%	7.30%	−0.20%	0.04%	
May-1993	7.1%	6.95%	0.15%	0.02%	Mean-squared error (MSE) = 0.033%
Aug-1993	6.8%	7.10%	−0.30%	0.09%	
Nov-1993	6.6%	6.65%	−0.05%	0.00%	
Feb-1994	6.6%	6.50%	0.10%	0.01%	Root-mean-squared error (RMSE) = 0.182%
May-1994	6.2%	6.60%	−0.40%	0.16%	
Aug-1994	6.0%	6.00%	0.00%	0.00%	
Nov-1994	5.6%	5.90%	−0.30%	0.09%	
Feb-1995	5.5%	5.40%	0.10%	0.01%	
May-1995	5.7%	5.45%	0.25%	0.06%	
Aug-1995	5.7%	5.80%	−0.10%	0.01%	
Nov-1995	5.6%	5.70%	−0.10%	0.01%	
Feb-1996	5.5%	5.55%	−0.05%	0.00%	
May-1996	5.5%	5.45%	0.05%	0.00%	
Aug-1996	5.3%	5.50%	−0.20%	0.04%	
Nov-1996	5.3%	5.20%	0.10%	0.01%	
Feb-1997	5.3%	5.30%	0.00%	0.00%	
May-1997	5.0%	5.30%	−0.30%	0.09%	
Aug-1997	4.9%	4.85%	0.05%	0.00%	
Nov-1997	4.7%	4.85%	−0.15%	0.02%	
Feb-1998	4.7%	4.60%	0.10%	0.01%	
May-1998	4.4%	4.70%	−0.30%	0.09%	
Aug-1998	4.5%	4.25%	0.25%	0.06%	
Nov-1998	4.4%	4.55%	−0.15%	0.02%	
Feb-1999	4.3%	4.35%	−0.05%	0.00%	
May-1999	4.3%	4.25%	0.05%	0.00%	
Aug-1999	4.2%	4.30%	−0.10%	0.01%	
Nov-1999	4.1%	4.15%	−0.05%	0.00%	
Feb-2000	4.0%	4.05%	−0.05%		← Holdout period

observation. If the series dropped to the latest point, perhaps it is reasonable to assume some further drop. Alternatively, if we have just observed an increase, it may make sense to factor into our forecast some further increase. Such adjustments can be made in a second naive forecasting model, which includes some proportion of the most recently observed rate of change in the series. In general algebraic terms the model becomes

$$F_t = A_{t-1} + P(A_{t-1} - A_{t-2})$$

where F_t is the forecast for period t, A_{t-1} is the actual observation at period $t - 1$, A_{t-2} is the observed value at period $t - 2$, and P is the proportion of the change between periods $t - 2$ and $t - 1$ that we choose to include in the forecast.

Applying this second naive model to the unemployment-rate data, we have

$$URF2_t = UR_{t-1} + P(UR_{t-1} - UR_{t-2})$$

where $URF2_t$ represents the unemployment-rate modified naive forecast for time period t; UR_{t-1} and UR_{t-2} are the observed unemployment rates one and two periods earlier, respectively; and P is the fraction of the most recent change in the unemployment rate that is now included in our forecast. This is illustrated with $P = 0.5$ in Table 1–4.

Let us look closely at the highlighted value in Table 1–4 to help you see the exact calculations that are involved in developing this forecast. To get the forecast for 1992Q1 (Feb-1992, denoted as F92 in the subscript), we take the observed value for 1991Q4 (Nov-1991) and adjust it by including some information from the most recent trend. (For illustrative purposes we have used one-half of that recent change, but one could try other values to see whether improved forecasts are possible.) Thus, the highlighted value (i.e., the forecast for Feb-1992, $URF2_{F92}$) is:

$$URF2_{F92} = UR_{N91} + 0.5(UR_{N91} - UR_{A91})$$
$$= 7.1 + 0.5(7.1 - 6.9)$$
$$= 7.1 + 0.5(.2)$$
$$= 7.1 + .1$$
$$= 7.2$$

All forecast values have been rounded to two decimal places. The values for this second naive forecast of the unemployment rate are shown in graphic form in Figure 1–3, along with the actual unemployment rate for each quarter.

Evaluating Forecasts

You have now looked at two alternative forecasts of the yearly unemployment rate in the United States. Which forecast is best depends on the particular year or years you look at. For example, the first model (URF) did a better job of forecasting the unemployment rate for Aug-1992 (1992Q3), whereas the second model (URF2) did a better job for

FIGURE 1–3

*Unemployment
Rate and Modified
Naive Forecast
(c1t4–c1f3)*

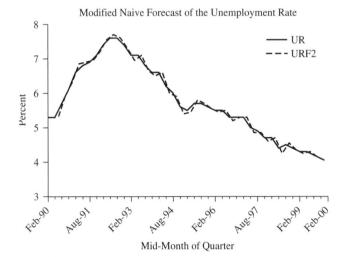

This figure shows the actual unemployment rate (solid line = UR)
and the modified naive model's forecast value (dashed line = URF2).
The forecast values were calculated by the following naive model:
$URF2_t = UR_{t-1} + 0.5(UR_{t-1} - UR_{t-2})$.

Nov-1999 (1999Q4). Results for these two periods are summarized as follows (the
better forecast in each period is in boldface):

Quarter	*UR*	*URF*	*URF2*
		Forecasts	
Aug-1992	7.6%	**7.6%**	7.7%
Nov-1999	4.1%	4.2%	**4.15%**

It is rare to find
one model that is
always best for
any given set of
business or
economic data.

In retrospect it is easy to say which forecast was better for any one period. However, it is rare to find one model that is always best for any given set of business or
economic data. But we need some way to evaluate the accuracy of forecasting models
over a number of periods so that we can identify the model that generally works the best.
Among a number of possible criteria that could be used, seven common ones are the
mean error (ME), the mean absolute error (MAE), the mean percentage error (MPE), the
mean absolute percentage error (MAPE), the mean-squared error (MSE), the root-
mean-squared error (RMSE), and Theil's U.

To illustrate how each of these is calculated, let

A_t = Actual value in period t

F_t = Forecast value in period t

n = Number of periods used in the calculation

1. The mean error is calculated as:

$$\text{ME} = \frac{\Sigma(A_t - F_t)}{n}$$

2. The mean absolute error is then calculated as:

$$\text{MAE} = \frac{\Sigma|A_t - F_t|}{n}$$

3. The mean percentage error is calculated as:

$$\text{MPE} = \frac{\Sigma[(A_t - F_t)/A_t]}{n}$$

4. The mean absolute percentage error is calculated as:

$$\text{MAPE} = \frac{\Sigma|(A_t - F_t)/A_t|}{n}$$

5. The mean-squared error is calculated as:

$$\text{MSE} = \frac{\Sigma(A_t - F_t)^2}{n}$$

6. The root-mean-squared error is:

$$\text{RMSE} = \sqrt{\frac{\Sigma(A_t - F_t)^2}{n}}$$

7. Theil's U can be calculated in several ways, two of which are shown here.

$$U = \sqrt{\Sigma(A_t - F_t)^2} \div \sqrt{\Sigma(A_t - A_{t-1})^2}$$

$$U = \text{RMSE (model)} \div \text{RMSE (no-change model)}$$

The no-change model used in calculating Theil's U is the basic naive forecast model described above, in which $F_t = A_{t-1}$.

For criteria one through six, lower values are preferred to higher ones. For Theil's U a value of zero means that the model forecast perfectly (no error in the numerator). If $U < 1$, the model forecasts better than the consecutive-period no-change naive model; if $U = 1$, the model does only as well as the consecutive-period no-change naive model; and if $U > 1$, the model does not forecast as well as the consecutive-period no-change naive model.

The values for these measures, for both forecasts of the unemployment rate (URF and URF2), are shown in Table 1–5. From these results we see that in this case all seven of the measures indicate that URF2 is the more accurate forecast. Thus, in this example we have consistent evidence that URF2 is better than URF. Usually you can expect mixed results.

Mean error (ME) and mean percentage error (MPE) are not often used as measures of forecast accuracy because large positive errors ($A_t > F_t$) can be offset by large negative errors ($A_t < F_t$). In fact, a very bad model could have an ME or MPE of zero.

TABLE 1–5   **Seven Measures of Forecast Accuracy for Two Alternative Unemployment Rate Forecasts**

Error Measure	Forecast 1 URF	Forecast 2 URF2
ME	−.031	−.017
MAE	.200	.050
MPE	−.72%	−.36%
MAPE	2.82%	2.56%
MSE	.046	.033
RMSE	.215	.182
Theil's U	1.000	.847
Number of times best	0	7

ME and MPE are, however, very useful as measures of forecast bias. A negative ME or MPE suggests that, overall, the forecasting model overstates the forecast, while a positive ME or MPE indicates forecasts that are generally too low.

The other measures (MAE, MAPE, MSE, RMSE, and Theil's U) are best used to compare alternative forecasting models for a given series. Because of different units used for various series, only MAPE and Theil's U should be interpreted across series. For example, a sales series may be in thousands of units, while the prime interest rate is a percentage. Thus, MAE, MSE, and RMSE would be lower for models used to forecast the prime rate than for those used to forecast sales.[37]

Throughout this text we will focus on root-mean-squared error (RMSE) to evaluate the relative accuracy of various forecasting methods. The RMSE is easy for most people to interpret because of its similarity to the basic statistical concept of a standard deviation, and it is one of the most commonly used measures of forecast accuracy.

All quantitative forecasting models are developed on the basis of historical data. When measures of accuracy, such as RMSE, are applied to the historical period, they are often considered measures of how well various models fit the data (i.e., how well they work "in sample"). To determine how accurate the models are in actual forecasts ("out of sample"), a holdout period is often used for evaluation. It may be that the best model "in sample" may not hold up as the best "out of sample."[38] Terry Anderson, of Howmedica, has said, "We often test models for their accuracy by preparing expost forecasts (forecasts for which actuals are known). This helps us in selecting an appropriate model."[39] In most examples throughout the text we will evaluate forecast methods using a holdout period.

---

[37]Brian P. Mathews and Adamantios Diamantopoulos, "Towards a Taxonomy of Forecast Error Measures," *Journal of Forecasting,* August 1994, pp. 409–16.

[38]Pamela A. Texter and Peg Young, "How Accurate Is a Model That Fits Best the Historical Data?" *Journal of Business Forecasting* 8, no. 4 (Winter 1989–90), pp. 13–16; and Spyros Makridakis, "Accuracy Measures: Theoretical and Practical Concerns," *International Journal of Forecasting*, December 1993, pp. 527–29.

[39]Anderson, "Demand Forecasting at Howmedica," p. 4.

Using Multiple Forecasts

When forecasting sales or some other business or economic variable, it is usually a good idea to consider more than one model. We know it is unlikely that one model will always provide the most accurate forecast for any series. Thus, it makes sense to "hedge one's bets," in a sense, by using two or more forecasts. This may involve making a "most optimistic," a "most pessimistic," and a "most likely" forecast. In our example of forecasting the unemployment rate, using the two naive models described in previous sections, we could take the lowest forecast value in each year as the most optimistic, the highest as the most pessimistic, and the average value as the *most likely*. The latter can be calculated as the mean of the two other forecast values in each year. That is:

$$\text{Most likely forecast} = \frac{\text{URF} + \text{URF2}}{2}$$

In making a final forecast, we again stress the importance of using well-reasoned judgments based on expertise regarding the series under consideration.

This is the simplest way to combine forecasts.

The purpose of a number of studies has been to identify the best way to combine forecasts to improve overall accuracy.[40] After we have covered a wider array of forecasting models, we will come back to this issue of combining different forecasts (see Chapter 8). For now, we just want to call attention to the desirability of using more than one method in developing any forecast. In making a final forecast, we again stress the importance of using well-reasoned judgments based on expertise regarding the series under consideration.

Sources of Data

The quantity and type of data needed in developing forecasts can vary a great deal from one situation to another. Some forecasting techniques require only the data series that is to be forecast. These methods include the naive methods discussed in previous sections as well as more sophisticated time-series techniques such as time-series decomposition, exponential smoothing, and ARIMA models, which will be discussed in subsequent chapters of this text. On the other hand, multiple-regression methods require a data series for each variable included in the forecasting model. This may mean that a large number of data series must be maintained to support the forecasting process.

The most obvious sources of data are the internal records of the organization itself. Such data include unit product sales histories, employment and production records, total revenue, shipments, orders received, inventory records, and so forth. However, it is surprising how often an organization fails to keep historical data in a form that facilitates the development of forecasting models. Often, monthly and/or quarterly data are discarded after three or four years. Thus, models that depend on such data may be difficult to develop. Another problem with using internal data is getting the cooperation necessary to make them available both in a form that is useful and in a timely manner. As better information systems are developed and made available through computer technology, internal data will become even more important and useful in the preparation of forecasts.

---

[40]For example, see Wilson and Allison-Koerber, "Combining Subjective and Objective Forecasts."

For many types of forecasts the necessary data come from outside the firm. Various trade associations are a valuable source of such data, which are usually available to members at a nominal cost and sometimes to nonmembers for a fee. But the richest sources of external data are various governmental and syndicated services.

You will find a wealth of data available on the Internet.[41] Using various search engines you can uncover sources for most macroeconomic series that are of interest to forecasters. The specific uniform resource locators (URLs, i.e., Web addresses) may change over time, but when you find that one of your favorites has disappeared it is likely that a new search will find it in another location on the Web.

Forecasting Domestic Car Sales

In each chapter of the text where new forecasting techniques are developed, we will apply at least one of the new methods to preparing a forecast of domestic car sales (DCS). As you will see, there is a fair amount of variability in how well different methods work for this very important economic series. The data we will be using are shown graphically in Figure 1–4 and in tabular form in Table 1–6. As you see from the table, we have quarterly domestic car sales figures from 1980Q1 through 1999Q2. The data represent domestic car sales in thousands of units and have not been seasonally adjusted. After this chapter we will discuss only each new forecast of DCS and will not repeat the original data. We will, however, keep a running summary of the root-mean-squared errors for the various models used.

In this chapter we apply a modified naive model to forecast domestic car sales. The model is:

$$DCSF_t = DCS_{t-4}$$

where $DCSF_t$ is the forecast of domestic car sales for time t and DCS_{t-4} is the actual domestic car sales four quarters earlier. As seen in Table 1–6, the level of domestic car sales for 1999Q2 (DCS_{Jun-99}) was 1,951.00. Thus our forecast for 2000Q2 (DCS_{Jun-00}) is 1,951.00.

FIGURE 1–4

Domestic Car Sales in Thousands of Units (c1t6–c1f4)

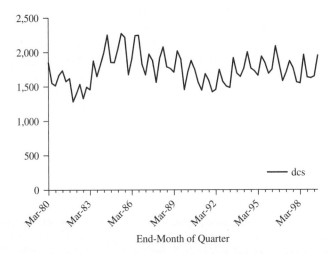

(c1t6–c1f4) TABLE 1–6 **Domestic Car Sales**

End Month of Quarter	Domestic Car Sales (thousands of units)	End Month of Quarter	Domestic Car Sales (thousands of units)	
Mar-1980	1,849.90	Jun-1990	1,878.20	
Jun-1980	1,550.80	Sep-1990	1,752.10	
Sep-1980	1,515.30	Dec-1990	1,560.40	
Dec-1980	1,665.40	Mar-1991	1,445.10	
Mar-1981	1,733.00	Jun-1991	1,683.90	
Jun-1981	1,576.00	Sep-1991	1,586.60	
Sep-1981	1,618.50	Dec-1991	1,421.30	
Dec-1981	1,281.30	Mar-1992	1,455.40	
Mar-1982	1,401.40	Jun-1992	1,746.10	
Jun-1982	1,535.30	Sep-1992	1,571.70	
Sep-1982	1,327.90	Dec-1992	1,503.40	
Dec-1982	1,493.60	Mar-1993	1,483.50	
Mar-1983	1,456.90	Jun-1993	1,917.90	
Jun-1983	1,875.80	Sep-1993	1,690.30	
Sep-1983	1,646.20	Dec-1993	1,642.30	
Dec-1983	1,814.10	Mar-1994	1,762.30	
Mar-1984	1,994.60	Jun-1994	2,001.50	
Jun-1984	2,251.80	Sep-1994	1,766.60	
Sep-1984	1,854.30	Dec-1994	1,724.80	
Dec-1984	1,851.00	Mar-1995	1,658.20	
Mar-1985	2,042.20	Jun-1995	1,938.40	
Jun-1985	2,272.60	Sep-1995	1,845.30	
Sep-1985	2,217.70	Dec-1995	1,686.90	
Dec-1985	1,672.20	Mar-1996	1,749.40	
Mar-1986	1,898.70	Jun-1996	2,087.70	
Jun-1986	2,242.20	Sep-1996	1,837.10	
Sep-1986	2,246.90	Dec-1996	1,579.50	
Dec-1986	1,827.20	Mar-1997	1,704.10	
Mar-1987	1,669.30	Jun-1997	1,870.60	
Jun-1987	1,972.80	Sep-1997	1,769.70	
Sep-1987	1,878.20	Dec-1997	1,561.80	
Dec-1987	1,560.60	Mar-1998	1,547.30	
Mar-1988	1,914.00	Jun-1998	1,961.60	
Jun-1988	2,076.00	Sep-1998	1,633.10	
Sep-1988	1,787.10	Dec-1998	1,621.90	
Dec-1988	1,762.30	Mar-1999	1,646.30	
Mar-1989	1,707.40	Jun-1999	1,951.00	
Jun-1989	2,018.60	Sep-1999	1,821.60	
Sep-1989	1,898.50	Dec-1999	1,562.80	← Holdout period
Dec-1989	1,453.60	Mar-2000	1,746.50	
Mar-1990	1,706.20	Jun-2000	1,914.40	

Table 1–7 and Figure 1–5 show how this naive model has fared over the historical period. The root-mean-squared error for this modified naive model for the period from 1981Q1 through 1999Q2 is 187.129. For the four quarters from 1999Q3 through 2000Q2 the RMSE is 112.255.

TABLE 1–7   **Domestic Car Sales (DCS) and a Modified Naive Forecast of Domestic Car Sales (DCSF)**   (c1t7–c1f5)

End-Month of Quarter	Domestic Car Sales (DCS) *(thousands of units)*	Domestic Car Sales: Naive Forecasting Model Using a Four Quarter Lag (DCSF)	Error	Suqared Error	
Mar-1980	1,849.90				
Jun-1980	1,550.80				
Sep-1980	1,515.30				
Dec-1980	1,665.40				
Mar-1981	1,733.00	1,849.90	−116.90	13,665.61	
Jun-1981	1,576.00	1,550.80	25.20	635.04	
Sep-1981	1,618.50	1,515.30	103.20	10,650.24	
Dec-1981	1,281.30	1,665.40	−384.10	147,532.81	
Mar-1982	1,401.40	1,733.00	−331.60	109,958.56	
Jun-1982	1,535.30	1,576.00	−40.70	1,656.49	
Sep-1982	1,327.90	1,618.50	−290.60	84,448.36	
Dec-1982	1,493.60	1,281.30	212.30	45,071.29	
⋮	⋮	⋮	⋮	⋮	
Mar-1997	1,704.10	1,749.40	−45.30	2,052.09	
Jun-1997	1,870.60	2,087.70	−217.10	47,132.41	
Sep-1997	1,769.70	1,837.10	−67.40	4,542.76	
Dec-1997	1,561.80	1,579.50	−17.70	313.29	
Mar-1998	1,547.30	1,704.10	−156.80	24,586.24	Historical
Jun-1998	1,961.60	1,870.60	91.00	8,281.00	period
Sep-1998	1,633.10	1,769.70	−136.60	18,659.56	RMSE =
Dec-1998	1,621.90	1,561.80	60.10	3,612.01	187.129
Mar-1999	1,646.30	1,547.30	99.00	9,801.00	
Jun-1999	1,951.00	1,961.60	−10.60	112.36	
Sep-1999	1,821.60	1,633.10	188.50	35,532.25	Holdout
Dec-1999	1,562.80	1,621.90	−59.10	3,492.81	period ← Holdout period
Mar-2000	1,746.50	1,646.30	100.20	10,040.04	RMSE =
Jun-2000	1,914.40	1,951.00	−36.60	1,339.56	112.555

Overview of the Text

Business Forecasting has been organized in such a way that by working consecutively through the text you will gradually develop a rather sophisticated forecasting capability. In this first chapter you have been given an introduction to business forecasting that has included three naive models.

The second chapter provides a discussion of data exploration through visualization, an overview of model-selection criteria, and a review of some statistical concepts that will be helpful as you learn about additional forecasting methods.

Chapter 3 presents moving-average and exponential smoothing techniques. These methods are widely used, quite simple from a computational standpoint, and often very

FIGURE 1–5

*Domestic Car Sales
(DCS) and a
Modified Naive
Forecast of
Domestic Car Sales
(DCSF) in
Thousands of Units
(c1t7–c1f5)*

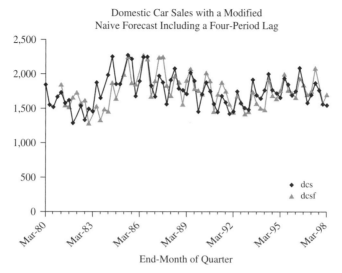

Domestic Car Sales with a Modified
Naive Forecast Including a Four-Period Lag

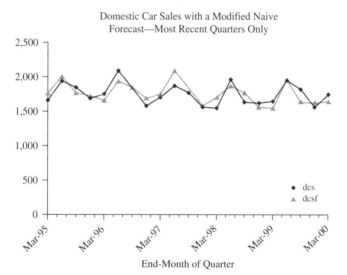

Domestic Car Sales with a Modified Naive
Forecast—Most Recent Quarters Only

*The upper panel shows the entire time frame. The lower panel
focuses on the most recent years. The actual values (DCS) are
represented by the dark line and the forecast values (DCSF) are
shown by the lighter line.*

accurate. Chapter 4 provides an explanation of simple linear-regression analysis and
its applications to business forecasting. Both simple trend models and simple two-
variable causal models are presented. In Chapter 5 the simple regression model is
expanded to include more than one independent variable. Multiple-regression models
are applied to specific forecasting problems, and a method for accounting for
seasonality is presented.

Classical time-series decomposition, discussed in Chapter 6, provides accurate forecasts for many series. In addition, it can be used to develop seasonal indexes that help identify the degree of seasonality in the data. These indexes can also be used to deseasonalize the data series. ARIMA forecasting models are presented in Chapter 7.

Chapter 8 contains a discussion of alternative methods for combining individual forecasts to take advantage of information contained in different methods to improve forecast accuracy. Chapter 9 focuses on how to select appropriate forecasting methods for a particular situation and on how to establish an effective forecasting process. The role of judgments based on experience with the series to be forecast is stressed once more.

At the end of each chapter you will find suggested readings that will provide additional insight into the topics covered. In addition, a set of exercises in each chapter will help you to validate your understanding of the material. Many of these exercises will also help you to become proficient in the use of the ForecastX™ software.

Comments from the Field

N. Carroll Mohn
Manager of field services, European Community Group, in the Corporate Marketing Research Department of The Coca-Cola Company.[*]

Why Try to Forecast?

Forecasts are critical inputs to a wide range of business decision-making processes. From letters, teaching forecasting, managing the function, and consulting work, I know that many people are striving to get a practitioner's grasp of the subject—some feeling for the applied state of the art and its science.

As forecasters, at one time or another, we have to ask ourselves why we should try to forecast in the first place. First, the power of forces such as economics, competition, markets, social concerns, and the ecological environment to affect the individual firm is severe and continues growing. Secondly, forecast assessment is a major input in management's evaluation of different strategies at business decision-making levels. Thirdly, the inference of *no* forecasting is that the future either contains "no significant change" or there is ample time to react "after the fact."

Forecasting is far too important to the organization not to have appropriate management and resource backing. Each firm must develop its own *explicit* forecast system so that alternative courses of action can be identified.

We can see the future coming if we know what to look for because many things often progress in an astonishingly orderly manner over time. This consistent progress provides a basis for forecasting. At the same time, many things respond to needs, opportunities, and support resources. If these driving forces can be identified, we believe future progress can be forecast.

---

[*]Adapted from an address given at the Fourth Annual Conference of the International Association of Business Forecasters, Philadelphia, September 1989.

INTEGRATIVE CASE
FORECASTING SALES OF THE GAP

Part 1: Background of The Gap and Its Sales

Throughout the text we will be using The Gap sales in an integrative case at the end of each chapter. In these cases, concepts from the chapter will be applied to this sales series. In this chapter we will apply concepts as well as provide an overview of the company.

The Gap: An Introduction

Few retailers have accomplished what The Gap has. The Gap has managed to successfully market its retail stores and the apparel they carry. In 1992, The Gap was the number two clothing brand in America, and in 1994 they placed in the top 25 of the 50 most recognizable brands in the United States. There are only two private-brand retailers that achieved this coveted brand image for their stores' products: Victoria's Secret and The Gap. While many other retailers, such as The Limited, lost strong brand images, The Gap continued to redefine its strategy and managed to maintain market dominance. By the end of 1995, The Gap operated over 1,500 stores in its four domestic divisions, which include The Gap, GapKids, Banana Republic, and the Old Navy Clothing Co. The Gap's fifth division, its International Division, operated 164 stores by the end of 1995 in countries such as Canada, the United Kingdom, France, Germany, and Japan.

The first Gap store was opened in 1969 by founder Donald Fisher, who decided to open a store after he had a problem exchanging a pair of Levi's jeans that were an inch too short. He felt that there was a need for a store that would sell jeans in a full array of sizes. He opened his first store in San Francisco, which advertised that it had "four tons" of Levi's. The store was an instant success and The Gap stores were on their way to national prominence. Levi's were the mainstay of The Gap's business, and due to Levi Strauss & Co.'s fixed pricing, Fisher maintained a 50 percent margin on the sales of these jeans. This changed in 1976, however, when the Federal Trade Commission prohibited manufacturers from dictating the price that retailers could charge for their products. There was suddenly massive discounting on Levi's products, which drastically cut The Gap's margins. Fisher recognized the need to expand his product offerings to include higher-margin items, and therefore began to offer private-label apparel.

In 1983, Fisher recruited Millard Drexler as president, with his objective being to revamp The Gap. Drexler did this by liquidating their existing inventories and focusing on simpler, more classic styles that offered the consumer "good style, good quality, good value." The Gap started to design its own clothes to fit into this vision. The Gap already had formed strong relationships with manufacturers from their earlier entry into the private-label business. This enabled them to monitor manufacturing closely, which kept costs low and quality high. The Gap's strategy didn't end with high-quality products. Drexler paid equally close attention to visual presence of the stores. He replaced the old pipe racks and cement floors with hardwood floors and attractive tables and shelves with merchandise neatly folded, which made it easier for the customers to shop. As new merchandise came in, store managers were given detailed plannograms, which told them precisely where the items would go. With this control, Drexler ensured that each Gap store would have the same look, and would therefore present the same image to the customer.

The Gap capitalized on these same concepts as they entered the kids' clothing market. The idea originated after Drexler was disappointed with the lack of selection he found while shopping for his own child. Drexler organized a meeting with his employees who had children to discuss their thoughts about the children's clothing market. Their mutual frustration with the selection of children's clothing triggered the idea for GapKids. Drexler and his team believed that they could use the same merchandising principles that made The Gap a success and apply them to the children's clothing market. GapKids was launched in 1986, and was a success in its first year of operation with sales of $2 million.

Drexler's retailing prowess also became evident when he turned around the poor performance of the Banana Republic division. In 1983, The Gap bought Banana Republic, which featured the then-popular safari-style clothing. This trend toward khakis had been brought on by the popularity of movies such as *Raiders of the Lost Ark* and *Romancing the Stone.* By 1987, Banana Republic's sales had reached $191 million. Then the safari craze ended, and this once popular division lost roughly $10 million in the two years that followed. Banana Republic was repositioned as a more upscale Gap, with fancier decor as well as more updated fashions that offered a balance between sophistication and comfort. By 1992, the chain was once again profitable, with about $300 million in sales.

Although these other Gap divisions had grown and prospered, the traditional Gap stores began to falter in the early 1990s. Coupled with the effects of a retailing recession, their strong emphasis on basic styles had made them a target of competition. The market became flooded with "Gap-like" basics. Other retailers were also mimicking their presentation strategy, and started folding large-volume commodity items such as jeans, T-shirts, and fleece, some selling them at substantially lower prices. Drexler and his team recognized that several major changes were taking place in the retailing environment, and they needed to identify ways to respond to this competition if they were to continue to grow.

One way The Gap responded to increasing competition was to revise its merchandise mix. Customers were shifting away from the basics toward more fashion items, in gender-specific styles. To respond to this trend, The Gap took advantage of aggressive changes already underway in their inventory management programs, which gave them faster replenishment times. This enabled The Gap to reduce its inventories in basics by as much as 40 percent, giving them more room for hot-selling, high-profit items. In addition to shifting to more fashion, The Gap also fine-tuned its product mix so that merchandise would be more consistent between stores.

Another way that The Gap has responded to increased competition and changing retailing trends was by entering into strip malls. This move has been facilitated in part by the reduction of available spaces in large malls. As fewer spaces became available, retailers wishing to expand have had to explore other possible options. Many strip centers have been upgraded in response to this trend, and retailers found that they could offer their customers easier access to stores and more convenient parking than they could in their traditional mall locations. With carefully placed geographic locations, retailers also discovered that they could often do the same volume that they could in the large malls. Additionally, strip-center rents are substantially lower than those of their mall counterparts. Their common charges are sometimes a mere 25 percent of what they would be in a typical large mall.

As other retailers and discounters found success by knocking off The Gap's classic styles and their presentation standards, The Gap responded by entering the "discount" market itself in 1993, with the transformation of 48 of its lowest-performance stores into "Gap Warehouse" stores. By doing so, The Gap capitalized on the new surge of price-conscious consumers. Gap Warehouse stores offer Gap-type styles at prices about 30 percent lower than The Gap apparel.

Their success with this discount concept led to the launch of the Old Navy Clothing Co. in April 1994, which targeted consumers in households with incomes between $20,000 and $50,000, who make about one-half of the nation's $150 billion apparel purchases each year. Old Navy stores carry a different assortment of apparel than traditional Gap stores. They differentiate themselves from The Gap stores by offering alternative versions of basic items, with different fabric blends that enable them to charge lower retail prices. In fact, 80 percent of their assortment retailed at $22 or less. There are other ways in which The Gap differentiates its Old Navy stores from their traditional Gap stores, however. To help keep costs down, they also scaled down the decor of these stores, with serviceable concrete floors and shopping carts instead of the hardwood floors found in The Gap. They are venturing away from The Gap's traditional means of advertising for these new stores and are offering more short-term promotions. Old Navy stores are further positioning themselves as one-stop-shopping stores by offering clothing for the whole family in one location.

With its current mix of stores, The Gap has successfully carved out a position for itself in every retail clothing category. Table 1–8 shows the distribution of store types late in 2000. Although there have been some hurdles along the way, The Gap has proven that it has the ability to respond to changes in the retail environment and has, therefore, managed to stay in the race. This is evidenced by the increased quarterly sales shown in Table 1–9 and the graphic in Figure 1–6.

TABLE 1–8 The Gap Store Count in Late 2000

Store Type	Number
The Gap Domestic	2,002
The Gap International	503
Banana Republic	389
Old Navy	648
Total	3,542

Source: http://gapinc.com/about/store_count.htm

TABLE 1–9 The Gap Sales and a Modified Naive Forecast (c1t9–c1f6gap)

Date	The Gap Sales ($000) (Gap)	The Gap Sales: Naive Forecasting Model Using a Four Quarter Lag (GapF)	Error (Gap − GapF)	Squared Error
Mar-1985	105,715.00			
Jun-1985	120,136.00			
Sep-1985	181,669.00			
Dec-1985	239,813.00			
Mar-1986	159,980.00	105,715.00	54,265.00	2,944,690,225.00
Jun-1986	164,760.00	120,136.00	44,624.00	1,991,301,376.00
Sep-1986	224,800.00	181,669.00	43,131.00	1,860,283,161.00
Dec-1986	298,469.00	239,813.00	58,656.00	3,440,526,336.00
Mar-1987	211,060.00	159,980.00	51,080.00	2,609,166,400.00
Jun-1987	217,753.00	164,760.00	52,993.00	2,808,258,049.00
Sep-1987	273,616.00	224,800.00	48,816.00	2,383,001,856.00
Dec-1987	359,592.00	298,469.00	61,123.00	3,736,021,129.00
Mar-1988	241,348.00	211,060.00	30,288.00	917,362,944.00
Jun-1988	264,328.00	217,753.00	46,575.00	2,169,230,625.00
Sep-1988	322,752.00	273,616.00	49,136.00	2,414,346,496.00

(continued)

TABLE 1–9   (*Continued*)

Date	The Gap Sales ($000) (Gap)	The Gap Sales: Naive Forecasting Model Using a Four Quarter Lag (GapF)	Error (Gap − GapF)	Squared Error	
Dec-1988	423,669.00	359,592.00	64,077.00	4,105,861,929.00	
Mar-1989	309,925.00	241,348.00	68,577.00	4,702,804,929.00	
Jun-1989	325,939.00	264,328.00	61,611.00	3,795,915,321.00	
Sep-1989	405,601.00	322,752.00	82,849.00	6,863,956,801.00	
Dec-1989	545,131.00	423,669.00	121,462.00	14,753,017,444.00	
Mar-1990	402,368.00	309,925.00	92,443.00	8,545,708,249.00	
Jun-1990	404,996.00	325,939.00	79,057.00	6,250,009,249.00	
Sep-1990	501,690.00	405,601.00	96,089.00	9,233,095,921.00	
Dec-1990	624,726.00	545,131.00	79,595.00	6,335,364,025.00	
Mar-1991	490,300.00	402,368.00	87,932.00	7,732,036,624.00	
Jun-1991	523,056.00	404,996.00	118,060.00	13,938,163,600.00	
Sep-1991	702,052.00	501,690.00	200,362.00	40,144,931,044.00	
Dec-1991	803,485.00	624,726.00	178,759.00	31,954,780,081.00	
Mar-1992	588,864.00	490,300.00	98,564.00	9,714,862,096.00	
Jun-1992	614,114.00	523,056.00	91,058.00	8,291,559,364.00	
Sep-1992	827,222.00	702,052.00	125,170.00	15,667,528,900.00	
Dec-1992	930,209.00	803,485.00	126,724.00	16,058,972,176.00	
Mar-1993	643,580.00	588,864.00	54,716.00	2,993,840,656.00	
Jun-1993	693,192.00	614,114.00	79,078.00	6,253,330,084.00	
Sep-1993	898,677.00	827,222.00	71,455.00	5,105,817,025.00	
Dec-1993	1,060,230.00	930,209.00	130,021.00	16,905,460,441.00	
Mar-1994	751,670.00	643,580.00	108,090.00	11,683,448,100.00	
Jun-1994	773,131.00	693,192.00	79,939.00	6,390,243,721.00	
Sep-1994	988,346.00	898,677.00	89,669.00	8,040,529,561.00	
Dec-1994	1,209,790.00	1,060,230.00	149,560.00	22,368,193,600.00	
Mar-1995	848,688.00	751,670.00	97,018.00	9,412,492,324.00	
Jun-1995	868,514.00	773,131.00	95,383.00	9,097,916,689.00	
Sep-1995	1,155,930.00	988,346.00	167,584.00	28,084,397,056.00	
Dec-1995	1,522,120.00	1,209,790.00	312,330.00	97,550,028,900.00	
Mar-1996	1,113,150.00	848,688.00	264,462.00	69,940,149,444.00	
Jun-1996	1,120,340.00	868,514.00	251,826.00	63,416,334,276.00	
Sep-1996	1,383,000.00	1,155,930.00	227,070.00	51,560,784,900.00	
Dec-1996	1,667,900.00	1,522,120.00	145,780.00	21,251,808,400.00	
Mar-1997	1,231,186.00	1,113,150.00	118,036.00	13,932,497,296.00	Historical
Jun-1997	1,345,221.00	1,120,340.00	224,881.00	50,571,464,161.00	period
Sep-1997	1,765,939.00	1,383,000.00	382,939.00	146,642,277,721.00	RMSE =
Dec-1997	2,165,479.00	1,667,900.00	497,579.00	247,584,861,241.00	233,091.90
Mar-1998	1,719,712.00	1,231,186.00	488,526.00	238,657,652,676.00	
Jun-1998	1,904,970.00	1,345,221.00	559,749.00	313,318,943,001.00	
Sep-1998	2,399,900.00	1,765,939.00	633,961.00	401,906,549,521.00	
Dec-1998	3,029,900.00	2,165,479.00	864,421.00	747,223,665,241.00	
Mar-1999	2,277,700.00	1,719,712.00	557,988.00	311,350,608,144.00	Holdout
Jun-1999	2,453,300.00	1,904,970.00	548,330.00	300,665,788,900.00	period
Sep-1999	3,045,386.00	2,399,900.00	645,486.00	416,652,176,196.00	RMSE =
Dec-1999	3,858,939.00	3,029,900.00	829,039.00	687,305,663,521.00	654,976.00

FIGURE 1–6

The Gap Sales and a Naive Forecast with a Four Quarter Lag (c1t9–c1f6gap)

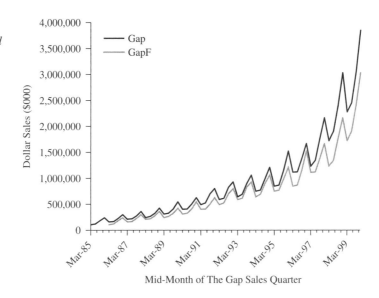

Case Questions

1. Based on the tabular and the graphic presentations of The Gap sales data, what do you think explains the seasonal pattern in their sales data?

2. Using a modified naive forecasting method, such as the one used for domestic car sales in this chapter, make a forecast of The Gap sales for the four quarters of 1999

using data only through 1998. Based on inspection of the graph of The Gap sales, what is your expectation in terms of forecast accuracy?

3. Calculate the RMSE for your forecast of the four quarters of 1999, given that the actual sales were as shown in Table 1–9 (see the shaded holdout period).

Solutions to Case Questions

1. The seasonal pattern is one in which sales typically have a small increase from the first to the second quarter, followed by a considerable increase in the third quarter and yet another large increase in the fourth quarter. The third quarter increase is related to back-to-school buying, while the increase in the fourth quarter is caused by the Christmas shopping season.

2. The model would be: GAPF = GAPSALES(-4). GAPF represents the forecast values, while GAPSALES(-4) is the actual value four periods earlier. An inspection of The Gap sales series would lead one to expect that a naive forecasting model with a lag of four periods would pick up the seasonality fairly well but would not account for the upward trend in The Gap sales. This can be seen in the graph of actual and pre-

dicted values in Figure 1–6. The actual values are consistently above the forecast values.

3. The actual and predicted values for 1999Q1 through 1999Q4 are shown below. The RMSE for these four quarters is: RMSE = 654,976.0. This is about a 23 percent error, based on the average quarterly sales for the year (2,908,831.25).

	GAPSALES	*GAPF*
1999Q1	2,277,700	1,719,712
1999Q2	2,453,300	1,904,970
1999Q3	3,045,386	2,399,900
1999Q4	3,858,939	3,029,900

The RMSE for the 1986Q1 through 1998Q4 historic period was 233,091.9. One reason the RMSE was so much lower in the historic period is that the level of sales over that period was also much lower. Also, the increasing trend in the sales series means that simply using a four-quarter lag to forecast will result in consistently larger errors over time.

Case References

Arlen, Jeffrey. "Gap Knocks Off Gap." *Discount Store News* (Sept. 6, 1993), p. A8.

——. "It's a Trend." *Discount Store News* (Sept. 6, 1993), p. A5.

Cuneo, Alice. "Gap Floats Lower-Price Old Navy Stores." *Advertising Age* (July 25, 1994), p. 36.

Edelson, Sharon. "Strip Centers: The Chain Reaction." *WWD* (Aug. 9, 1995), p. 9.

http://gapinc.com

Mitchell, Russell. "A Bit of a Rut at The Gap." *Business Week* (Nov. 30, 1992), p. 100.

——. "The Gap: Can the Nation's Hottest Retailer Stay on Top?" *Business Week* (March 9, 1992), p. 58.

——. "The Gap Dolls Itself Up." *Business Week* (March 21, 1994), p. 46.

——. "A Humbler Neighborhood for The Gap." *Business Week* (Aug. 16, 1993), p. 29.

Popiel, Leslie A. "Old Navy Store Is Gap's Answer to the Penny-Pinching Shopper." *Christian Science Monitor* (Oct. 28, 1994), p. 8.

Street, Pamela. "Old Navy Fills Off-Price Gap for The Gap." *Daily News Record* (March 31, 1994), p. 3.

The Gap, Inc. 1999 Annual Report.

Wilson, Marianne. "The Magic of Brand Identity." *Chain Store Age Executive* (Feb. 1994), p. 66.

ABOUT FORECASTX™: THE SOFTWARE ON THE CD WITH YOUR *BUSINESS FORECASTING WITH ACCOMPANYING EXCEL-BASED FORECASTX™ SOFTWARE* TEXT

The ForecastX™ Wizard is part of the ForecastX™ Product Family. It is an easy-to-use tool that will assist you in defining and improving your forecasting process.

This tutorial for ForecastX™ Wizard Version 3.8 will show you how easy it is to create accurate forecasts with ForecastX™. The examples that follow are designed to explain some of the ways that the ForecastX™ Wizard enables you to take advantage of the power and accuracy of ForecastX™.

The ForecastX™ Wizard utilizes the ForecastX™ Engine to assist in decision making through one-step forecasting. INSEAD University's M3 competition rated ForecastX™ one of the most accurate forecasting tools in the world among all forecasting products. This level of accuracy usually comes with significant complexity requiring extensive understanding of statistical methods, rewriting the format of your particular data series, and/or having to import your data into someone else's forecasting tool. ForecastX™ enables all levels of users—novices, intermediates, and expert statisticians—to become expert forecasters. Many well-known organizations use ForecastX™ because of its accuracy, sophistication, and ease of use. Some examples are shown in Table 1–10.

john gAlt
The Forecast Xperts

TABLE 1–10   Some Representative Users of ForecastX™

Automotive	Healthcare
BMW Mexico	Abbott Laboratories
Kawasaki Motors	Wyeth-Lederle
Consumer Products	**Manufacturing**
Reckitt Benckiser	Callaway Golf
Sunbeam Corporation	El Dupont
The Hoover Company	Essilor of America
	John Deere & Co.
	Pentax
Energy	
BP Amoco	**Retail**
Commonwealth Edison	Levis Mexico
Florida Power & Light	Petro Shopping Centers
	Sears Rocbuck & Co.
Financial	Yankee Candle Co.
Capital One	
Visa International	**Telecommunications**
Wells Fargo	AT&T Wireless
	Motorola
	Verizon Wireless
Food Services	
Chef America	**Technology**
Dean Foods	3Com
Keebler Company	Agilent Technology
Oberto Sausage	America Online
Piccadilly Cafeteria, Inc.	Lexmark International
Government	**Universities**
Air Force Logistics Agency	Drexel University
California Department of Health	Illinois Institute of Technology
U.S. Navy	University of Notre Dame

ForecastX™ Wizard Benefits

- Spend valuable time defining your forecasting process instead of formatting your data.
- Perform profitability analyses with your events and promotions.
- Plan successful new products.
- See where your promotion plan stacks up against best case–worst case scenarios.
- Work directly in Microsoft® Excel for increased efficiency and analytical power.

ForecastX™ Functionality

The ForecastX™ Wizard includes advanced functionality and enables organizations and individuals to further enhance their decision-making process. In addition to smoothing techniques, the functionality of ForecastX™ also encompasses easy-to-use forecasting through ProCast™, which provides expert selection to complex forecasting methods such as Box-Jenkins and regression modeling. This range of functionality makes ForecastX™ a solution that never stops growing with the end-user. For instance, nonstatisticians can use ForecastX™ to produce fast, accurate forecasts with a few clicks in an environment they are familiar with: Microsoft® Excel. At the same time, advanced mathematicians can use ForecastX™ to determine all the seasonal indices and smoothing parameters of their data sets. Some other features of ForecastX™ include:

- Multilevel forecasting
- Product life-cycle management
- Expert selection methodology that includes new product optimization
- Customize all forecasting parameters and settings
- Easy-to-use data cleansing to remove outliers and missing values, apply tracking signals, and adjustments
- Supports beginning and expert statisticians
- Interactive regression with linear and nonlinear models and simulation

ForecastX™ Features

The ForecastX™ Wizard is designed to make accurate forecasting as easy as possible. Users can either allow the Wizard to set forecasting parameters and measures, or define the parameters according to what they know about their data. Listed below are some features explained in the tutorial as well as others that are explained in the User's Guide.

- Unlimited batch forecasting
- No data preparation required
- An add-in that is fully integrated with Excel 97 (and later versions)
- Customized management and audit trail reports
- Advanced scenario management for what-if analyses
- Promotional modeling with best case–worst case simulations
- One-step forecasting with ProCast™ (Expert selection)

Table 1–11 provides a list of the technical and statistical methods included in ForecastX™.

TABLE 1–11   ForecastX™ Technical and Statistical Methods

john gAlt
The Forecast Xperts

Forecast Techniques
Adaptive exponential smoothing
Box-Jenkins (ARIMA modeling)
Brown's double exponential smoothing
Brown's triple exponential smoothing
Census II X-11 (additive and
   multiplicative)
Croston's intermittent method
Decomposition (additive and
   multiplicative)
Event/promotional modeling
Exponential smoothing
Gompertz curve
Holt's double exponential smoothing
Holt's Winters exponential smoothing
   (additive and multiplicative)
Linear regression
Logistic curve
Moving average
New product forecasting
Polynomial regression
Probit curve
ProCast
Simple regression
StepWise regression with dynamic
   lagging
Weighted moving average

Input/Output
Array level
Individual level

Replenishment Statistics
Safety-stock

Accuracy Statistics
Adjusted R-square
AIC

BIC
Confidence intervals
Durbin-Watson
Error
Ljung box
Mean absolute error
Mean absolute percent error
Mean error
Mean-squared error
Normality error
R square
Standard deviation of error
Sum of squared error
Theil's statistic
Tracking error

Random Functions
Beta
Binomial
Cauchy
Exponential
Exponential mix
Gamma
Geometric
Hyper geometric
Logarithmic
Negative binomial
Normal
Poisson
Student T
Triangular
Uniform
Uniform discrete
Von Mises
Weibull

Descriptive Statistics
Autocorrelation

Autocovariance
Box-Cox
Box-Pierce
Coefficient of determination
Coefficient of variance
Correlation coefficient
Covariance
Difference
Histogram
Kurtosis
Log
Max
Mean
Mean absolute deviation
Mean square deviation
Median
Min
Mode
Partial autocorrelation coefficient
Range
Root mean square
Skewness
Standard deviation
Sum of square deviation
Variance

Distributions
Chi-squared
Erlang B
Erlang C
Lognormal
Normal distribution
Poisson

Data Cleansing
Replace missing values
Replace outliers

Provided courtesy of John Galt Solutions, Inc.

System Requirements for Using ForecastX™

The following minimum requirements are necessary to use ForecastX™.

- A 486X-based machine.
- Microsoft® Windows® 95, 98, or NT.

- A minimum of 8MB of memory (32MB recommended).
- Microsoft® Office 97 (or later) is required to run the ForecastX™ Wizard.

Installing ForecastX™

Installing ForecastX™ is very straightforward. After starting the setup program, simply follow the Setup Wizard as described below.

- Insert the ForecastX™ CD into your CD drive.
- Within Windows® Explorer, select your CD drive.
- Double click **Setup.exe.**
- Follow the Setup Wizard. You will come to the **Call John Galt to Complete Installation** screen. Click **Yes.**
- The **John Galt Development, Inc.: Install Key** screen appears. Call (312) 701-9026 and give John Galt's representative the server code displayed to receive your 32-digit License Key.
- When you get the License Key, enter it in the box called **Key.**
- Click **Install Key.** There will be a brief pause.
- When you return to the **John Galt Development, Inc.: Install Key** screen, click **Exit.**
- You will be prompted to update HTML help. Click **Yes.**
- ForecastX™ is successfully installed.

GETTING STARTED: PROCAST™ JUMP STARTS YOUR FORECASTING PROCESS

ForecastX™ enables users to perform a literal one-step, accurate forecast, known as ProCast™. This function has two requirements: you need to have data to forecast, and you need to click the **ProCast** button on the ForecastX™ Wizard. The amount of data does not limit ProCast™ at all; you can run ProCast™ on a single data series or create an *unlimited batch forecast*. Once ProCast™ has been activated, ForecastX™ will determine the best forecasting technique for each data series in your particular data set. ProCast™ chooses from among the most complex forecasting techniques, including Croston's intermittent model, automatic Box-Jenkins ARIMA modeling, regression analysis, and many smoothing techniques. By literally clicking only once on the ForecastX™ Wizard, you can produce fast, accurate, and easy-to-read results.

In addition, the ForecastX™ Wizard can handle multiple descriptive labels.

The One-Step Forecast with ProCast™

Session 1: The One-Step ProCast™

- Open the **ForecastX_Samples.xls** spreadsheet that accompanies ForecastX™, and click the tab below labeled **ProCast.** The spreadsheet can also be opened by selecting the menu item **ForecastX Excel Wizard Demo** from the **ForecastX** menu located within the Windows® **Program Files** menu.
- When the spreadsheet opens, select a cell that contains data to be forecasted. On the right side of the Microsoft® Excel toolbar, click the **ForecastX™** icon to start the Wizard.

ForecastX™ uses several automatic features when it first captures your data.

The Intelligent Data Recognizer:

- Automatically detects that your data is arranged in rows.
- Determines the data range to be forecasted.
- Determines that your data has dates and that the dates are monthly.
- Determines that your data contains descriptive labels.

You are now ready to forecast your data.

1. Simply click the **ProCast** button to complete your forecast! (The button is in the lower right-hand corner of the ForecastX™ Wizard.)

ForecastX™ automatically produces a Standard Report that appears on a separate worksheet. The new worksheet lists what forecasting method ForecastX™ chooses for each data series. The fitted and forecasted values are listed below the actual values for each series.

When you scroll to the right on the spreadsheet, you will notice that ForecastX™ has listed the forecasted values in bold. To the right of the forecasted values, ForecastX™ has produced four accuracy statistics that help you determine how trustworthy the forecast is.

	AO	AP	AQ	AR	AS	AT	AU	AV
	Oct-00	Nov-00	Dec-00		Mean Absolute Percentage Error (MAPE)	R-Square	Mean	Standard Deviation
3	4,989.51	5,098.34	5,097.94		4.85%	69.34%	5,313.33	597.31
5	3,093.04	3,083.37	3,073.76		6.20%	76.15%	3,477.33	615.76
7	10,124.73	10,643.01	11,161.29		14.30%	58.89%	3,700.00	1,389.24

- **Mean Absolute Percentage Error** tells you the overall average of the error measurements ForecastX™ produced.
- **R-Square** value lets you know how well the fitted values compare to the actual values.
- **Mean** gives you the average value of each series.
- **Standard Deviation** tells you how far away each data point is from the average data point in the data set.

You have just produced an accurate, one-step forecast with ProCast™. Another example of ForecastX™ strength is how well ProCast™ can handle dirty data.

In the ForecastX™ Wizard, ProCast™ will also take new product growth curves into consideration. Go to the **Forecast Method** tab and configure ProCast™ for New Product growth curves.

Outlier Removal Using ProCast™

To improve the accuracy of your forecast, ForecastX™ can test whether outliers (e.g., missing data) exist.

Using the same spreadsheet, **ForecastX_Samples.xls,** and the worksheet **ProCast,** open the ForecastX™ Wizard.

1. With the Data Capture screen open, click the **Data Cleansing** button.
2. To replace bad data, check the **Yes** box under **Replace Outliers.**
3. Click **OK** to return to the **Data Capture** screen.
4. Click the **Reports** tab. This will bring up the **Report Options** screen. From the **Report Options** screen, uncheck **Standard,** and check the **Audit** box and click **Finish!**

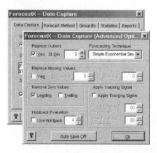

All the error measurements have significantly decreased, which means that you have given yourself a better and more reliable picture of the future.

Top-Down Allocation Using ProCast™

What if you need to forecast an entire product line or grouping of products? The **Group By** tab will perform top-down and bottom-up allocation.

Using the same spreadsheet, **ForecastX_Samples.xls,** and the worksheet **Batch Forecasting,** open the ForecastX™ Wizard.

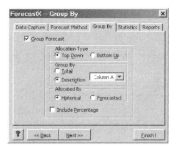

1. With the **Data Capture** screen open, click on the **Group By** tab.
2. Under **Group By,** check the **Group Forecast** box.
3. Under **Allocation Type,** mark the **Top Down** circle.
4. Under **Group By,** mark the **Description** circle. Make sure that **Column A** is showing in the pull-down box.
5. Under **Allocated By,** make sure the **Historical** circle is marked and click **Finish!**

Products that had intermittent demand forecast better by using this allocation and the overall forecast of the example has improved again.

Event and Promotional Modeling

If there is a special occasion or promotional event, ForecastX™ will take this into account while you develop your forecast.

By working with the marketing department, it is possible to identify major promotions that impact sales. By marking these impacts over time, ForecastX™ will be able to enhance the forecast based on the promotional plan.

Using the same spreadsheet, **ForecastX_Samples.xls,** and the worksheet **Event Modeling** tab, highlight **Month** and **Newspaper Sales** data (rows 1–40, columns A and B) and open the ForecastX™ Wizard.

1. With the **Data Capture** screen open, double-check **ForecastX™ Intelligent Data Recognizer,** making sure it has arranged your data by columns. (By the way, this is the hardest part of using ForecastX™.)
2. Click the **Reports** tab, and deselect **Standard** and check the **Append** box.

	Normal_NewEver	Arial		10		B	I	U						$ % ,			
	G34		=														

	A	B	C	D	E	F	G	H
1	Month	Newspaper Sales	Marketing Plan		Market Index		Description	
2	Oct-95	2,400	0		0		Business as usual	
3	Nov-95	2,260	0		1		Phone solicitation	
4	Dec-95	1,900	0		2		Three month free subscription offer	
5	Jan-96	1,794	0		3		Fifty percent off one year subscription	
6	Feb-96	2,300	0		4		Year end renewal drive	
7	Mar-96	2,870	0					
8	Apr-96	3,130	0					
9	May-96	2,980	0					
10	Jun-96	2,550	0					
11	Jul-96	3,620	1					
12	Aug-96	5,480	2					
13	Sep-96	5,360	3					
14	Oct-96	3,160	4					

3. Click **Finish** and you're done! ForecastX™ has appended the results to your current data set.

Using the same spreadsheet, **ForecastX_Samples.xls,** and the worksheet **Event Modeling** tab, highlight **Month** and **Newspaper Sales** data (rows 1–40, columns A and B) and open the ForecastX™ Wizard.

1. With the **Data Capture** screen open, click the **Forecast Method** tab. It will bring you to the **Method Selection** screen.
2. Under **Forecasting Techniques** use the pull-down bar to select **Event Model.**
3. Under **Event Flags** click inside the box. This will bring up the **Data Selection** screen.
4. Define the event flag data range and then click **Done.** This brings you back to the **Forecast Method** screen.
5. Click the **Report** tab to bring up the **Report Options** screen. Uncheck the **Standard** report, check **Audit** and click **Finish!**

	A	B	C	D	E	F	G
1	Month	Newspaper Sales	Marketing Plan		Market Index		Description
2	Oct-95	2,400	0		0		Business as usual
3	Nov-95	2,260	0		1		Phone solicitation
4	Dec-95	1,900	0		2		Three month free subscription offer
5	Jan-96	1,794	0		3		Fifty percent off one year subscription
6	Feb-96	2,300	0		4		Year end renewal drive
7	Mar-96	2,870	0				
8	Apr-96	3,130	0				
9	May-96	2,980	0				
10	Jun-96	2,550	0				
11	Jul-96	3,620	1				
12	Aug-96	5,480	2		Data Selection		✕
13	Sep-96	5,360	3				
14	Oct-96	3,160	4		[ForecastXTrainingSet.xls]Event Modeling'!$	_	Done
15	Nov-96	2,440	0				

The results from the **Audit Trail** graph provide you with additional statistical data. (By selecting the **More** tab on the **Statistics** screen, additional statistical choices may be added.) This report includes an event index, which represents each events lift factor over the base forecast.

Suggested Readings and Web Sites

Adams, F. Gerard. *The Business Forecasting Revolution.* New York: Oxford University Press, 1986.

Armstrong, J. Scott. "Forecasting for Environmental Decision Making." In *Tools to Aid Environmental Decision Making.* Eds. V. H. Dale and M. E. English. New York: Springer-Verlag, 1999, pp. 192–225.

Armstrong, J. Scott. *Principles of Forecasting: A Handbook for Researchers and Practitioners.* Norwell, MA: Kluwer Academic Publishers: The Netherlands, 2001.

Chase, Charles W., Jr. "Forecasting Consumer Products." *Journal of Business Forecasting* 10, no. 1 (Spring 1991), pp. 2–6.

Jain, C. L. "Forecasting at Colgate-Palmolive Company." *Journal of Business Forecasting* 11, no. 1 (Spring 1992), pp. 16–20.

Makridakis, Spyros. "Accuracy Measures: Theoretical and Practical Concerns." *International Journal of Forecasting,* December 1993, pp. 527–29.

Mathews, Brian P.; and Adamantios Diamantopulos. "Towards a Taxonomy of Forecast Error Measures." *Journal of Forecasting* (August 1994), pp. 409–16.

Meade, N. "Evidence for the Selection of Forecasting Methods." *Journal of Forecasting* 19, no. 6, 2000, pp. 515–35.

Mentzer, John T.; and Jon Schroeter. "Multiple Forecasting System at Brake Parts, Inc." *The Journal of Business Forecasting* 14, no. 3 (Fall 1993), pp. 5–9.

Moriarty, Mark M.; and Arthur J. Adams. "Management Judgment Forecasts, Composite Forecasting Models, and Conditional Efficiency." *Journal of Marketing Research* (August 1984), pp. 239–50.

Rosati, Anna Maria. "Forecasting at Segix, Italia: A Pharmaceutical Company." *Journal of Business Forecasting* 17, no. 3 (Fall 1996), pp. 7–9.

Van Vught, F. A. "Pitfalls of Forecasting: Fundamental Problems for the Methodology of Forecasting from the Philosophy of Science." *Futures* (April 1987), pp. 184–96.

Wilson, J. Holton; and Deborah Allison-Koerber. "Combining Subjective and Objective Forecasts Improves Results." *Journal of Business Forecasting* 11, no. 3 (Fall 1992), pp. 12–16.

Wilson, J. Holton; and Steven J. Schuiling. "Forecasting Hospital Laboratory Procedures." *Journal of Medical Systems* (December 1992), pp. 269–79.

http://www.economagic.com

http://forecasting.cwru.edu

http://wwwforecastingprinciples.com

http://www-marketing.wharton.upenn.edu/forecast/dictionary.pdf

Exercises

1. Write a paragraph in which you compare what you think are the advantages and disadvantages of subjective forecasting methods. How do you think the use of quantitative methods relates to these advantages and disadvantages?

2. Suppose that you work for a U.S. senator who is contemplating writing a bill that would put a national sales tax in place. Because the tax would be levied on the sales revenue of retail stores, the senator has asked you to prepare a forecast of retail store sales for year 8, based on data from year 1 through year 7. The data are:

(c1p2)

Year	Retail Store Sales
11	1,225
2	1,285
3	1,359
4	1,392
5	1,443
6	1,474
7	1,467

a. Use the first naive forecasting model presented in this chapter to prepare a forecast of retail store sales for each year from 2 through 8.

b. Prepare a time-series graph of the actual and forecast values of retail store sales for the entire period. (You will not have a forecast for year 1 or an actual value for year 8.)

c. Calculate the root-mean-squared error for your forecast series using the values for year 2 through year 7.

3. Use the second naive forecasting model presented in this chapter to answer parts (*a*) through (*c*) of Exercise 2. Use $P = 0.2$ in preparing the forecast. Which model do you think works the best? Explain why. (c1p3)

4. Suppose that you work for a major U.S. retail department store that has outlets nationwide. The store offers credit to customers in various forms, including store credit cards, and over the years has seen a substantial increase in credit purchases. The manager of credit sales is concerned about the degree to which consumers are using credit and has started to track the ratio of consumer installment credit to personal income. She calls this ratio the credit percent, or CP, and has asked that you forecast that series for year 8. The available data are:

(c1p4)	Year	CP
	1	12.96
	2	14.31
	3	15.34
	4	15.49
	5	15.70
	6	16.00
	7	15.62

a. Use the first naive model presented in this chapter to prepare forecasts of CP for years 2 through 8.

b. Plot the actual and forecast values of the series for the years 1 through 8. (You will not have an actual value for year 8 or a forecast value for year 1.)

c. Calculate the root-mean-squared error for your forecasts for years 2 through 7.

5. Go to the library and look up annual data for population in the United States from 1981 through the most recent year available. One good source for such data is the

Economic Report of the President, published each year by the U.S. Government Printing Office. This series is also available at a number of Internet sites, including http://www.economagic.com.

Plot the actual data along with the forecast you would get by using the first naive model discussed in this chapter. (c1p5)

6. Pick a corporation you are interested in and go to the library to find annual reports for that company. Look at five consecutive annual reports and find the firm's total revenue for each of those years. Plot the firm's actual revenue along with the forecast of revenue you would get by using the first naive model discussed in this chapter.

7. Go to the library and find the most recent edition of *U.S. Industrial Outlook,* published annually by the U.S. Department of Commerce. Write a paragraph in which you summarize the information given there for passenger cars.

8. CoastCo Insurance, Inc., is interested in developing a forecast of larceny thefts in the United States. It has found the following data:

(c1p8)	Year	Larceny Thefts*	Year	Larceny Thefts*
	1	4,151	10	7,194
	2	4,348	11	7,143
	3	5,263	12	6,713
	4	5,978	13	6,592
	5	6,271	14	6,926
	6	5,906	15	7,257
	7	5,983	16	7,500
	8	6,578	17	7,706
	9	7,137	18	7,872

*Data are in thousands.

Plot this series in a time-series plot and make a naive forecast for years 2 through 19. Calculate the RMSE and MAD for years 2 through 18. On the basis of these measures and what you see in the plot, what do you think of your forecast? Explain.

9. As the world's economy becomes increasingly interdependent, various exchange rates between currencies

have become important in making business decisions. For many U.S. businesses, the Japanese exchange rate (in yen per U.S. dollar) is an important decision variable. This exchange rate (EXRJ) is shown in the following table by month for a two-year period:

(c1p9)	Period	EXRJ	Period	EXRJ
	Year 1		Year 2	
	M1	127.36	M1	144.98
	M2	127.74	M2	145.69
	M3	130.55	M3	153.31
	M4	132.04	M4	158.46
	M5	137.86	M5	154.04
	M6	143.98	M6	153.70
	M7	140.42	M7	149.04
	M8	141.49	M8	147.46
	M9	145.07	M9	138.44
	M10	142.21	M10	129.59
	M11	143.53	M11	129.22
	M12	143.69	M12	133.89

Prepare a time-series plot of this series, and use the naive forecasting model to forecast EXRJ for each month from year 1 M2 (February) through year 3 M1 (January). Calculate the RMSE for the period from year 1 M2 through year 2 M12.

2 THE FORECAST PROCESS, DATA CONSIDERATIONS, AND MODEL SELECTION

Introduction

In this chapter we will outline a forecasting process that is a useful guide to the establishment of a successful forecasting system. It is important that forecasting be viewed as a process that contains certain key components. This process includes the selection of one or more forecasting techniques applicable to the data that need to be forecast. This, in turn, depends on the type of data that are available. In selecting a forecasting model, one should first evaluate the data for trend, seasonal, and cyclical components.

In evaluating a data series for its trend, seasonal, and cyclical components, it is useful to look at the data in graphic form. In this chapter we evaluate data for real gross domestic product (GDP), U.S. billings of the Leo Burnett advertising agency, private housing starts, domestic car sales, and The Gap sales to see which time-series components exist in each. This chapter also includes a review of statistics and an introduction to the use of autocorrelation coefficients, which can provide useful information about the underlying components in a time series.

The Forecast Process

The forecast process begins with recognizing the need to make decisions that depend on the future—and unknown—value(s) of some variable(s). It is important for managers who use forecasts in making decisions to have some familiarity with the methods used in developing the forecast. It is also important for the individuals involved in developing forecasts to have an understanding of the needs of those who make decisions based on the forecasts. Thus, good communication among all involved with forecasting is paramount.

There are a variety of ways in which one could outline the overall forecasting process. We have found the sequence shown below to be a useful paradigm.

1. Specify objectives
2. Determine what to forecast
3. Identify time dimensions
4. Data considerations
5. Model selection
6. Model evaluation
7. Forecast preparation
8. Forecast presentation
9. Tracking results

This flow of relationships in the forecasting process will be discussed in more detail in Chapter 9, after a base of understanding of quantitative forecasting methods has been established.

It may seem obvious that the forecasting process should begin with a clear statement of objectives that includes how the forecast will be used in a decision context. Objectives and applications of the forecast should be discussed between the individual(s) involved in preparing the forecast and those who will utilize the results. Good communication at this phase will help to ensure that the effort that goes into developing the forecast results in improved decision outcomes.

The second step of the process involves specifying explicitly what to forecast. For a traditional sales forecast, one must decide whether to forecast unit sales or dollar sales. Should the forecast be for total sales, or sales by product line, or sales by region? Should it include domestic sales, export sales, or both? A hospital may want to forecast patient load, which could be defined as admissions, discharges, patient-days, or acuity-days. In every forecasting situation, care must be taken to carefully determine exactly what variable(s) should be forecast.

Next, two different issues that relate to the time dimensions of the forecast need to be considered. One of these dimensions involves the length and periodicity of the forecast. Is the forecast needed on an annual, a quarterly, a monthly, a weekly, or a daily basis? In some situations an even shorter time period may be necessary, such as in forecasting electricity demand for a generating facility. The second time dimension to be considered is related to the urgency of the forecast. If there is little time available before the forecast is needed, the choice of methods that can be used will be limited. When forecasting is established as an ongoing process, there should be ample time to plan for the use of any forecasting technique.

The fourth element of the forecasting process involves a consideration of the quantity and the type of data that are available. Some data may be available internally, while other data may have to be obtained from external sources. Internal data are often the easiest to obtain, but not always. Sometimes data are not retained in a form that makes them useful for a particular forecast. It is surprising how frequently we find that data are kept only on an annual basis rather than for shorter periods such as quarterly or monthly. Similarly, we often run into situations where only dollar values are available rather than units. External data are available from a wide variety of sources, some of which were discussed in Chapter 1. Most external sources provide data in both printed and electronic form.

Model selection, the fifth phase of our forecasting process, depends on a number of criteria, including:

1. The pattern exhibited by the data
2. The quantity of historic data available
3. The length of the forecast horizon

Table 2–1 summarizes how these criteria relate to the quantitative forecasting methods that are included in this text. While all of these criteria are important, the first is the most important. We will discuss the evaluation of patterns in data and model selection in greater detail after completing our review of the forecasting process.

The sixth phase of the forecasting process involves testing the models on the specific series that we want to forecast. This is often done by evaluating how each model works in a retrospective sense. That is, we see how well the results fit the historic data that were used in developing the models. Measures such as the root-mean-squared error (RMSE) are typically used for this evaluation. We often make a distinction between *fit* and *accuracy* in evaluating a forecast model. *Fit* refers to how well the model works retrospectively. *Accuracy* relates to how well the model works in the forecast horizon (i.e., outside the period used to develop the model). When we have sufficient data, we often use a "holdout" period to evaluate forecast accuracy. For example, suppose that you

> *Fit* refers to how well the model works retrospectively. *Accuracy* relates to how well the model works in the forecast horizon.

TABLE 2–1 A Guide to Selecting an Appropriate Forecasting Method[1]

Forecasting Method	Data Pattern	Quantity of Historical Data (Number of Observations)	Forecast Horizon
Naive	Stationary	1 or 2	Very short
Moving averages	Stationary	Number equal to the periods in the moving average	Very short
Exponential smoothing			
Simple	Stationary	5 to 10	Short
Adaptive response	Stationary	10 to 15	Short
Holt's	Linear trend	10 to 15	Short to medium
Winters'	Trend and seasonality	At least 4 or 5 per season	Short to medium
Regression-based			
Trend	Linear and nonlinear trend with or without seasonality	Minimum of 10 with 4 or 5 per season if seasonality is included	Short to medium
Causal	Can handle nearly all data patterns	Minimum of 10 per independent variable	Short, medium, and long
Time-series decomposition	Can handle trend, seasonal, and cyclical patterns	Enough to see two peaks and troughs in the cycle	Short, medium, and long
ARIMA	Stationary or transformed to stationary	Minimum of 50	Short, medium, and long

[1]The methods presented in this table are the most commonly used techniques. There are many other methods available, most of which are included in the ForecastX™ software that accompanies this text.

have 10 years of historic quarterly sales data and want to make a two-year forecast. In developing and evaluating potential models, you might use just the first eight years of data to forecast the last two years of the historical series. RMSEs could then be calculated for the two holdout years to determine which model or models provide the most accurate forecasts. These models would then be respecified using all 10 years of historic data, and a forecast would be developed for the true forecast horizon. If the models selected in phase 6 did not yield an acceptable level of accuracy, you would return to step 5 and select an alternative model.

Phase 7, forecast preparation, is the natural result of having found models that you believe will produce acceptably accurate results. We recommend that more than one technique be used whenever possible. When two, or more, methods that have different information bases are used, their combination will frequently provide better forecasts than would either method alone. The process of combining forecasts is sufficiently important that Chapter 8 is devoted to this topic.

The eighth phase of the forecasting process involves the presentation of forecast results to those who rely on them to make decisions. Here, clear communication is critical. Sometimes technicians who develop forecasts become so enamored with the sophistication of their models that they focus on technical issues rather than on the substance of the forecast. In both written and oral presentations, the use of objective visual representations of the results is very important.[2]

Finally, the forecasting process should include continuous tracking of how well forecasts compare with the actual values observed during the forecast horizon. Over time, even the best of models are likely to deteriorate in terms of accuracy and need to be respecified, or replaced with an alternative method. Forecasters can learn from their mistakes. A careful review of forecast errors may be helpful in leading to a better understanding of what causes deviations between the actual and forecast series.

Trend, Seasonal, and Cyclical Data Patterns

The data that are used most often in forecasting are time series. For example, you might have sales data by month from January 1970 through December 2001, or you might have the number of visitors to a national park every year for a 30-year period, or you might have stock prices on a daily basis for several years. These would all be examples of time-series data.

Such time series can display a wide variety of patterns when plotted over time. Displaying data in a time-series plot is an important first step in identifying various component parts of the time series. A time series is likely to contain some, or all, of the following components:

Trend

Seasonal

Cyclical

Irregular

---

[2]An excellent discussion of how to present information in graphic form can be found in Edward R. Tufte, *The Visual Display of Quantitative Information* (Cheshire, Conn.: Graphics Press, 1983).

Let us first define and discuss each of these in general terms, and then we will look at several specific data series to see which components we can visualize through graphic analyses.

The *trend* in a time series is the long-term change in the level of the data. If, over an extended period of time, the series moves upward, we say that the data show a positive trend. If the level of the data diminishes over time, there is a negative trend. Data are considered *stationary* when there is neither a positive nor a negative trend (i.e., the series is essentially flat in the long term).

A *seasonal* pattern occurs in a time series when there is a regular variation in the level of the data that repeats itself at the same time each year. For example, ski lodges in Killington, Vermont, have very regular high occupancy rates during December, January, and February (as well as regular low occupancy rates in the spring of the year). Housing starts are always stronger in the spring and summer than during the fall and winter. Retail sales for many products tend to peak in November and December because of Christmas sales. Most university enrollments are higher in the fall than in the winter or spring and are typically the lowest in the summer. All of these patterns recur with reasonable regularity year after year. No doubt you can think of many other examples of time-series data for which you would expect similar seasonal patterns.

A *cyclical* pattern is represented by wavelike upward and downward movements of the data around the long-term trend. Cyclical fluctuations are of longer duration and are less regular than are seasonal fluctuations. The causes of cyclical fluctuations are less readily apparent as well. They are usually attributed to the ups and downs in the general level of business activity that are frequently referred to as *business cycles.*

The *irregular* component of a time series contains the fluctuations that are not part of the other three components. These are often called *random* fluctuations. As such, they are the most difficult to capture in a forecasting model.

To illustrate these components, let us analyze two specific sets of data. One of these is a quarterly macroeconomic series, real gross domestic product (GDP, in 1996 dollars), which many forecasters refer to as a *prime mover* because of its important influence on many other variables in the economy. The second series we will analyze is quarterly industry level data on private housing starts (PHS). Later in the chapter we will also evaluate domestic car sales for these time-series components. The integrative case at the end of this chapter also involves a similar evaluation of the sales of The Gap stores.

Figure 2–1 shows a times-series plot of real GDP on a quarterly basis starting with 1980Q1 and ending with 2000Q4. From a visual inspection of this graph, it is fairly easy to see that there has been a positive trend to GDP over the 21-year period shown. The long-term trend is shown by the straight line in Figure 2–1. (In later chapters, you will learn how to determine an equation for this long-term trend line.) In this graphic representation of the raw data along with the trend line, the wavelike cyclical movement of GDP above and below the long-term trend can also be discerned. Thus, GDP is nonstationary and has a cyclical component. Because GDP is nonstationary, some models would not be appropriate in forecasting GDP (see Table 2–1). Later in this chapter we will show one method that could be used to transform GDP to a stationary series.

FIGURE 2–1

Real Gross Domestic Product and Long-Term Trend (Billions of 1996 Dollars) (c2f1)

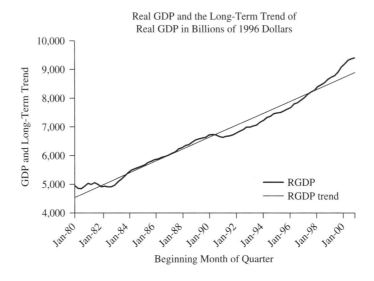

FIGURE 2–2

Quarterly Values of Private Housing Starts (PHS) in Thousands of Units (c2f2)

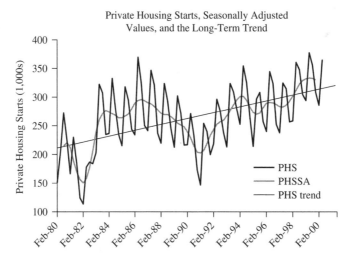

Private housing starts (PHS) are plotted in Figure 2–2 for the period from 1980 through 2000, on a quarterly basis. Probably the most striking feature of this visualization of the private housing starts data is the regular and sharp upward and downward movements that repeat year after year. This indicates a seasonal pattern, with housing starts reaching a peak in the spring of each year. Overall, there also appears to be some upward trend to the data and some cyclical movement as well.

The straight line in Figure 2–2 shows the long-term trend in the PHS series. The third line, which moves above and below the long-term trend but is smoother than the plot of PHS, is what the PHS series looks like after the seasonality has been removed.

FIGURE 2–3

U.S. Billings of the Leo Burnett Advertising Agency on an Annual Basis for 1950 through 1995 (c2f3)

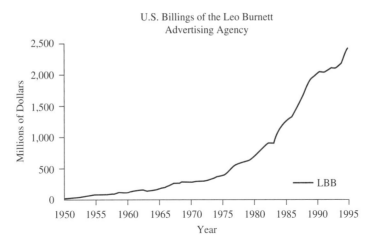

Such a series is said to be "deseasonalized," or "seasonally adjusted," and is represented by PHSSA (the "SA" at the end of the name is meant to indicate that the data have been seasonally adjusted). By comparing PHSSA with the trend, the cyclical nature of private housing starts becomes clearer. You will learn how to deseasonalize data in Chapter 6.

Now let us turn to a visual analysis of firm-specific data. Figure 2–3 shows U.S. billings of the Leo Burnett advertising agency (LBB), one of the largest firms in this industry. Data are shown on an annual basis from 1950 through 1995. Clearly, there is an upward trend in the data, and it is a trend that appears to be accelerating (i.e., becoming increasingly steep). You will learn to forecast such nonlinear trends later in this text. There does not appear to be a cyclical component to the series, and since these are annual data, there is no need to consider seasonality.

Data Patterns and Model Selection

The pattern that exists in the data is an important consideration in determining which forecasting techniques are appropriate.

As discussed earlier in this chapter, the pattern that exists in the data is an important consideration in determining which forecasting techniques are appropriate. On the basis only of the pattern of data, let us apply the information in Table 2–1 to determine which methods might be good candidates for forecasting each of the three specific series just discussed and plotted in Figures 2–1 through 2–3.

For GDP, which has a trend and a cycle but no seasonality, the following might be appropriate:

Holt's exponential smoothing

Linear regression trend

Causal regression

Time-series decomposition

Because of the cycle component, the last two may be better than the first two.

Private housing starts (PHS) have a trend, seasonality, and a cycle. Therefore, some likely candidate models for forecasting PHS would include:

Winters' exponential smoothing

Linear regression trend with seasonal adjustment

Causal regression

Time-series decomposition

Again, the existence of a cycle component would suggest that the latter two may be the best candidates.

For U.S. billings of Leo Burnett advertising (LBB), there is a nonlinear trend, with no seasonality and no cycle. Thus, the models most likely to be successful are:

Nonlinear regression trend

Causal regression

In subsequent chapters of the text, we will return to these series from time to time as examples. By the time you finish with the text you will be able to develop good forecasts for series that exhibit a wide variety of data patterns. After a review of some statistical concepts, we will return to an evaluation of data patterns that goes beyond the simple, yet powerful, visualization of data and that will be of additional help in selecting appropriate forecasting techniques.

A Statistical Review[3]

The approach that we will take in this discussion is more intuitive than theoretical. Our intent is to help you recall a small part of what is normally covered in an introductory statistics course. We begin by discussing descriptive statistics, with an emphasis on measures of central tendency and measures of dispersion. Next we review two important statistical distributions. These topics lead to statistical inference, which involves making statements about a population based on sample statistics. We then present an overview of hypothesis testing and finish with a discussion of correlation.

Descriptive Statistics

We often want to use numbers to describe one phenomenon or another. For example, we might want to communicate information concerning the sales of fast-food restaurants in a community. Or we might want to describe the typical consumption of soft drinks in U.S. households. Or we might want to convey to someone the rate at which sales have been increasing over time. All of these call for the use of descriptive statistics.

When we want to describe the general magnitude of some variable, we can use one or more of several *measures of central tendency*. The three most common measures of central tendency are the mean, median, and mode. To grasp each of these measures, let us consider the data in Table 2–2. These data represent 25 consecutive months of

---

[3]Students with a good statistical background may be able to skip this section.

(c2t2) **TABLE 2–2 Twenty-Five Consecutive Months of Total Sales**

Month	Sales	Month	Sales
1	3	14	4
2	4	15	7
3	5	16	3
4	1	17	4
5	5	18	2
6	3	19	5
7	6	20	7
8	2	21	4
9	7	22	5
10	8	23	2
11	1	24	6
12	13	25	4
13	4		

computer sales for a small office-products retailer. The *mode* is the response that occurs most frequently. If you count the number of times each value for sales is found in Table 2–2, you obtain the following results:

Sales	Number of Occurrences
1	2
2	3
3	3
4	6
5	4
6	2
7	3
8	1
13	1
Total	25

Since the largest number of occurrences is 6 (for sales of four computers), the mode is 4.

The *median* is the value that splits the responses into two equal parts when they are arrayed from smallest to largest. In this set of data, the median is 4. This is shown in the following diagram:

Responses Arrayed from Low to High

$$\underbrace{1\ 1\ 2\ 2\ 2\ 3\ 3\ 3\ 4\ 4\ 4\ 4}_{12\ \text{Values}}\quad \textcircled{4}\quad \underbrace{4\ 5\ 5\ 5\ 5\ 6\ 6\ 7\ 7\ 7\ 8\ 13}_{12\ \text{Values}}$$

↑
↓
Median

There are 12 numbers to the left of the circled 4, and 12 numbers to the right. When there are an even number of observations, the median is the midpoint of the two center values. For example, in the series 1, 4, 6, 10, the median is 5. Note that the median may be a number that is not actually in the data array.

The *mean* is the arithmetic average of all the numbers in the data set. To find the mean, add up all the values and divide by the number of observations. If the set of numbers is a population, rather than a sample, the mean is designated by the Greek mu (μ). It is calculated as:

$$\mu = \sum_{i=1}^{N} X_i / N$$

where the subscript i is used to identify each X value and

$$\sum_{i=1}^{N} X_i$$

means the sum of all the values of X_i, in which i ranges from 1 to N. X is simply a shorthand way of representing a variable. For the data in Table 2–2, $X_3 = 5$ and $X_{15} = 7$. N represents the total number of elements, or observations, in the population. In this case $N = 25$. Adding up all 25 values, we get:

$$\sum X = 115$$

Note that we have dropped the subscript here. This will often be done to simplify the notation. The population mean is then:

$$\mu = \sum X / N = 115/25 = 4.6$$

If the data represent a sample (i.e., a portion of the entire population), the mean is designated $\overline{X}$ and the number of elements in the sample is designated n. Thus, a sample mean is:

$$\overline{X} = \sum_{i=1}^{n} X_i / n$$

If the data in Table 2–2 represented a sample of months, the mean would be calculated as:

$$\overline{X} = \sum X / n = 115/25 = 4.6$$

All three of these measures of central tendency provide some feel for what we might think of as a "typical case." For example, knowing that the median and mode for sales are both 4 and the mean is 4.6 gives you an idea about what is a typical month's sales.

These sales data are plotted over time in Figure 2–4, along with the trend line. You see in this plot that sales fluctuate around a nearly flat trend. Thus, this sales series is stationary.

We have seen that for the data in Table 2–2, the mean is 4.6, and both the mode and the median are 4.0. Note that the mean is above both of the other measures of central tendency. This can result when there is one relatively large value (in this example, the 13). That large value pulls up the mean but has little or no effect on the median or

FIGURE 2–4

*Sales and Sales
Trend* (c2f4)

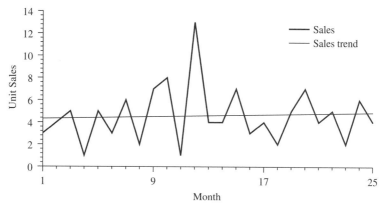

*For this sales series, the trend is almost perfectly flat, so that the data are
stationary. Note that the level of the trend line is fairly close to the sample
mean of 4.6.*

mode. Without that observation the median and mode for this example would still be 4,
but the mean would be 4.25 (4.25 = 102/24).

Let us now consider dispersion in data. A measure of dispersion tells us something
about how spread out (or dispersed) the data are. Such information helps us to gain a
clearer picture of the phenomenon being investigated than we get by looking just at a
measure of central tendency. Look, for example, at the following two data sets marked
A and *B:*

A:	18	19	20	21	22
B:	0	10	20	30	40

In both cases the mean and median are 20. (Since no value occurs more frequently than
the others, there is no mode.) However, the two data sets are really very different. Measures of dispersion can be helpful in conveying such a difference.

The simplest measure of dispersion is the *range,* which is the difference between
the smallest value and the greatest value. In Table 2 2 the smallest value is 1 (observations 4 and 11); the greatest is 13 (observation 12). Thus,

$$\text{Range} = \text{Greatest value} - \text{Smallest value}$$

$$= 13 - 1$$

$$= 12$$

For the two data sets *A* and *B* just given, the range for *A* is 4 and the range for *B* is 40.

Think for a moment about the different perception you get from the following two
statements:

"The data set *A* has a mean of 20 and a range of values equal to 4, from 18 to 22."

"The data set *B* has a mean of 20 and a range of values equal to 40, from 0 to 40."

You can see how much your perception is affected by knowing this measure of dispersion in addition to the mean.

Two other measures of dispersion, the variance and the standard deviation, are probably the ones that are most used. The standard deviation is a measure of the "average" spread of the data around the mean. Thus, it is based on the mean and tells us how spread out the data are from the mean. The variance is the square of the standard deviation.

The calculation of sample and population standard deviations and variances can be shown in the shorthand of mathematical expressions as follows (let X_i represent the ith observation):

	For a Sample	*For a Population*
Standard deviation	$S = \sqrt{\dfrac{\sum(X_i - \overline{X})^2}{n-1}}$	$\sigma = \sqrt{\dfrac{\sum(X_i - \mu)^2}{N}}$
Variance	$S^2 = \dfrac{\sum(X_i - \overline{X})^2}{n-1}$	$\sigma^2 = \dfrac{\sum(X_i - \mu)^2}{N}$

For the computer sales data in Table 2–2, the calculations of the standard deviation and variance are illustrated in Table 2–3. Note that the sum of the unsquared differences between each observation and the mean is equal to zero. This is always true. Squaring the differences gets around the problem of offsetting positive and negative differences. The standard deviation for the sales data is (assuming the data represent a sample) 2.582 units around a mean of 4.6. That is, the "average" spread around the mean is 2.582. The corresponding variance is 6.667 "units squared." You can see that the interpretation of the variance is a bit awkward. What is a "squared computer"? Because of this squaring of the units of measurement, the variance is less useful in communicating dispersion than is the standard deviation. In statistical analysis, however, the variance is frequently far more important and useful than the standard deviation. Thus, both are important to know and understand.

Look back at the two small data sets *A* and *B* referred to earlier. For both sets the mean was 20. Assuming that these are both samples, the standard deviations are:

$$\text{For } A: \quad S = 1.58$$
$$\text{For } B: \quad S = 15.8$$

You see that knowing both the mean and the standard deviation gives you a much better understanding of the data than you would have if you knew only the mean.

The Normal Distribution

Many statistical distributions are important for various applications. Two of them—the normal distribution and Student's t-distribution—are particularly useful for the applications in forecasting to be discussed in this text. In this section we will describe the normal distribution. We will consider the t-distribution in a later section.

The normal distribution for a continuous random variable is fully defined by just two characteristics: the mean and the variance (or standard deviation) of the variable. A graph of the normal distribution has a bell shape such as the three distributions shown (c2t3) **TABLE 2–3   Calculation of the Standard Deviation and Variance for the Computer Sales Data (Assuming a Sample)**

Observation Number	Computer Sales (X_i)	$(X_i - \bar{X})$	$(X_i - \bar{X})^2$
1	3	−1.6	2.56
2	4	−0.6	0.36
3	5	0.4	0.16
4	1	−3.6	12.96
5	5	0.4	0.16
6	3	−1.6	2.56
7	6	1.4	1.96
8	2	−2.6	6.76
9	7	2.4	5.76
10	8	3.4	11.56
11	1	−3.6	12.96
12	13	8.4	70.56
13	4	−0.6	0.36
14	4	−0.6	0.36
15	7	2.4	5.76
16	3	−1.6	2.56
17	4	−0.6	0.36
18	2	−2.6	6.76
19	5	0.4	0.16
20	7	2.4	5.76
21	4	−0.6	0.36
22	5	0.4	0.16
23	2	−2.6	6.76
24	6	−1.4	1.96
25	4	−0.6	0.36
Total	115	0.0	160.00

$$\text{Mean} = \bar{X} = \frac{\Sigma X_i}{n} = \frac{115}{25} = 4.6$$

$$\text{Variance} = S^2 = \frac{\Sigma (X_i - \bar{X})^2}{n - 1} = \frac{160}{25 - 1} = 6.667$$

$$\text{Standard deviation} = S = \sqrt{\frac{\Sigma (X_i - \bar{X})^2}{n - 1}} = \sqrt{\frac{160}{24}} = \sqrt{6.667} = 2.582$$

in Figure 2–5.[4] All such normal distributions are symmetrical around the mean. Thus, 50 percent of the distribution is above the mean and 50 percent is below the mean. It follows that the median must equal the mean when the distribution is normal.

---

[4]Technically, these are probability density functions, for which the area under the curve between any two points on the horizontal axis represents the probability of observing an occurrence between those two points. For a continuous random variable, the probability of any particular value occurring is considered zero, because there are an infinite number of possible values in any interval. Thus, we discuss only probabilities that values of the variable will lie between specified pairs of points.

FIGURE 2–5

*Three Normal
Distributions*

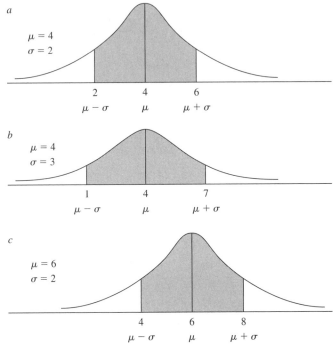

*The top and middle distributions have the same mean but different
standard deviations. The top and bottom distributions have the same
standard deviation but different means.*

In Figure 2–5, the top graph represents the normal curve for a variable with a population mean of 4 and a standard deviation of 2. The middle graph is for a variable with the same mean but a standard deviation of 3. The lower graph is for a normal distribution with a mean of 6 and a standard deviation of 2. While each is unique, the three graphs have similar shapes, and they have an important common feature: for each of these graphs the shaded area represents roughly 68 percent of the area under the curve.

This brings us to an important property of all normal curves. The area between one standard deviation above the mean and one standard deviation below the mean includes approximately 68 percent of the area under the curve. Thus, if we were to draw an element at random from a population with a normal distribution, there is a 68 percent chance that it would be in the interval $\mu \pm 1\sigma$. This 68 percent is represented by the shaded areas of the graphs in Figure 2–5.

If you remember that the normal distribution is symmetrical, you will realize that 34 percent must be in the shaded area to the left of the mean and 34 percent in the shaded area to the right of the mean. Since the total area to the right (or left) of the mean is 50 percent, the area in either tail of the distribution must be the remaining 16 percent (these are the unshaded regions in the graphs in Figure 2–5).

If one extends the range to plus or minus two standard deviations from the mean, roughly 95 percent of the area would be in that interval. And if you go out three standard deviations in both directions from the mean, about 99 percent of the area would be included. These concepts can be summarized as follows:

$\mu \pm 1\sigma$ includes about 68% of the area

$\mu \pm 2\sigma$ includes about 95% of the area

$\mu \pm 3\sigma$ includes about 99% of the area

These three rules of thumb are helpful to remember.

In Figure 2–5 you saw three similar yet different normal distributions. How many such distributions are there? There may be billions of them. Every variable or measurement you might consider could have a different normal distribution. And yet any statistics text you look in will have just one normal distribution. The reason for this is that every other normal distribution can be transformed easily into a *standard* normal distribution called the Z-distribution. The transformation is simple:

$$Z = \frac{X - \mu}{\sigma}$$

In this way any observed value (X) can be standardized to a corresponding Z-value. The Z-value measures the number of standard deviations by which X differs from the mean. If the calculated Z-value is positive, then X lies to the right of the mean (X is larger than μ). If the calculated Z-value is negative, then X lies to the left of the mean (X is smaller than μ).

The standard normal distribution is shown in the lower part of Figure 2–6. Note that it is centered on zero. A normal distribution for product sales (X) with a mean of 50 and a standard deviation of 10 is shown immediately above the standard normal distribution. For every value of X there is a corresponding value for Z, which can be found by using the transformation shown in the preceding equation. Let us calculate the Z-values that correspond to $X = 40$ and to $X = 65$:

$$Z = \frac{X - \mu}{\sigma}$$

For $X = 40$, $\qquad Z = \dfrac{40 - 50}{10} = -1$

For $X = 65$, $\qquad Z = \dfrac{65 - 50}{10} = 1.5$

Through this process every normal variable can be transformed to the standard normal variable Z.

Although this standardization is a simple process, it is very powerful and opens the door to answers for many questions. For example, suppose we want to know what percent of sales would be between the mean of 50 and 65. Since the sales variable can so easily be transformed into the standard normal variable, Z, we can answer such a

FIGURE 2–6

*Transformation
to the Standard
Normal
Distribution*

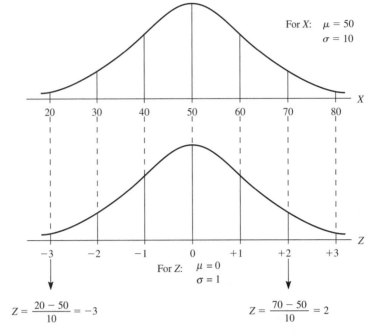

For X: $\mu = 50$
         $\sigma = 10$

For Z: $\mu = 0$
         $\sigma = 1$

$$Z = \frac{20 - 50}{10} = -3 \qquad\qquad Z = \frac{70 - 50}{10} = 2$$

The normal distribution for the sales variable, represented by X, is shown above the standard
normal distribution. Any level of sales can be transformed to the standard normal variable, Z,
as follows:

$$Z = \frac{X - \mu}{\sigma}$$

Two representative calculations are shown.

question with the help of the standard normal table shown as Table 2–4. The Z-value that
corresponds to sales of 65 ($X = 65$) is:

$$Z = \frac{65 - 50}{10} = 1.5$$

Looking for $Z = 1.5$ in Table 2–4, we find that the area under the normal curve between
the midpoint (the mean for sales, or $Z = 0$) and $Z = 1.5$ is 0.4332. Thus, 43.32 percent
of sales would be in the interval between 50 and 65.

Let us look at one more example. What percent of sales would be greater than 30?
The shaded area of the following normal curve is the area of interest:

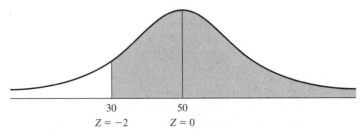

TABLE 2–4   **The Standard Normal Distribution**[*]

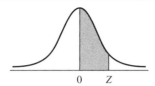

Z	.00	.01	.02	.03	.04	.05	.06	.07	.08	.09
0.0	.0000	.0040	.0080	.0120	.0160	.0199	.0239	.0279	.0319	.0359
0.1	.0398	.0438	.0478	.0517	.0557	.0596	.0636	.0675	.0714	.0753
0.2	.0793	.0832	.0871	.0910	.0948	.0987	.1026	.1064	.1103	.1141
0.3	.1179	.1217	.1255	.1293	.1331	.1368	.1406	.1443	.1480	.1517
0.4	.1554	.1591	.1628	.1664	.1700	.1736	.1772	.1808	.1844	.1879
0.5	.1915	.1950	.1985	.2109	.2054	.2088	.2123	.2157	.2190	.2224
0.6	.2257	.2291	.2324	.2357	.2389	.2422	.2454	.2486	.2518	.2549
0.7	.2580	.2612	.2642	.2673	.2704	.2734	.2764	.2794	.2823	.2852
0.8	.2881	.2910	.2939	.2967	.2995	.3023	.2051	.3078	.3106	.3133
0.9	.3159	.3186	.3212	.3238	.3264	.3289	.3315	.3340	.3365	.3389
1.0	.3413	.3438	.3461	.3485	.3508	.3531	.3554	.3577	.3599	.3621
1.1	.3643	.3665	.3686	.3708	.3729	.3749	.3770	.3790	.3810	.3830
1.2	.3849	.3869	.3888	.3907	.3925	.3944	.3962	.3980	.3997	.4015
1.3	.4032	.4049	.4066	.4082	.4099	.4115	.4131	.4147	.4162	.4177
1.4	.4192	.4207	.4222	.4236	.4251	.4265	.4279	.4292	.4306	.4319
1.5	.4332	.4345	.4357	.4370	.4382	.4394	.4406	.4418	.4429	.4441
1.6	.4452	.4463	.4474	.4484	.4495	.4505	.4515	.4525	.4535	.4545
1.7	.4554	.4564	.4573	.4582	.4591	.4599	.4608	.4616	.4625	.4633
1.8	.4641	.4649	.4656	.4664	.4671	.4678	.4686	.4693	.4699	.4706
1.9	.4713	.4719	.4726	.4732	.4738	.4744	.4750	.4756	.4761	.4767
2.0	.4772	.4778	.4783	.4788	.4793	.4798	.4803	.4808	.4812	.4817
2.1	.4821	.4826	.4830	.4834	.4838	.4842	.4846	.4850	.4854	.4857
2.2	.4861	.4864	.4868	.4871	.4875	.4878	.4881	.4884	.4887	.4890
2.3	.4893	.4896	.4898	.4901	.4904	.4906	.4909	.4911	.4913	.4916
2.4	.4918	.4920	.4922	.4925	.4927	.4929	.4931	.4932	.4934	.4936
2.5	.4938	.4940	.4941	.4943	.4945	.4946	.4948	.4949	.4951	.4952
2.6	.4953	.4955	.4956	.4957	.4959	.4960	.4961	.4962	.4963	.4964
2.7	.4965	.4966	.4967	.4968	.4969	.4970	.4971	.4972	.4973	.4974
2.8	.4974	.4975	.4976	.4977	.4977	.4978	.4979	.4979	.4980	.4981
2.9	.4981	.4982	.4982	.4983	.4984	.4984	.4985	.4985	.4986	.4986
3.0	.49865	.4987	.4987	.4988	.4988	.4989	.4989	.4989	.4990	.4990
4.0	.49997									

[*]Z is the standard normal variable. Other variables can be transformed to Z as follows:

$$Z = \frac{X - \mu}{\sigma}$$

For Z = 1.96, the shaded area in the distribution is 0.4750 (found at the intersection of the 1.9 row and the .06 column).

Source: Adapted from Owen P. Hall, Jr., and Harvey M. Adelman, *Computerized Business Statistics* (Homewood, Ill.: Richard D. Irwin, 1987), p. 91.

Since the Z-distribution is symmetrical, negative values would be superfluous in Table 2–4. The area between $Z = 0$ and $Z = -2$ is identical to the area between $Z = 0$ and $Z = +2$. From Table 2–4, we see that this is 0.4772 (or 47.72 percent). Thus, 47.72 percent would lie between 30 and 50. Since 50 percent is always above the mean (i.e., $Z = 0$), the total that would be above $X = 30$ is 97.72 percent ($= 47.74$ percent $+ 50$ percent).

The Sampling Distribution of the Mean

Statistical theory tells us some very interesting and useful things about the *distribution of sample statistics*. For example, when the population is normally distributed or when the sample size is large, sample means are distributed normally. That means that a graph of the distribution of sample means ($\overline{X}$'s) would look like the bell-shaped curves in Figure 2–5. Second, the distribution of sample means is centered on the population mean μ. That is, the mean of the sample means is equal to the population mean. Third, the standard deviation of the sample means is equal to the standard deviation of the population divided by the square root of the sample size. The standard deviation of sample means is denoted $\sigma_{\overline{X}}$ and is usually called the *standard error of the mean*. It is:

$$\sigma_{\overline{X}} = \frac{\sigma}{\sqrt{n}}$$

We will use other types of standard errors as we work with regression models in Chapters 4 and 5.

When we select a sample, we get just one sample from a great many that could have been selected. Knowing that the distribution of sample means is normal with a mean equal to the population mean and a standard error equal to $\sigma/\sqrt{n}$ gives us a great deal of power in working with a sample. Suppose, for example, that a sample of $n = 100$ is selected and that it has a mean of 300. For now we will assume that the population standard deviation is known and is equal to 60. We can now answer a question such as, What is the probability that a sample of 100 elements with a mean of 300 or more would be selected if the true population mean were 288? To answer such a question, we have to transform this information from the distribution of sample means to the standard normal distribution (Z). This is done as follows:

$$Z = \frac{\overline{X} - \mu}{\sigma_{\overline{X}}}$$

where $\sigma_{\overline{X}} = \sigma/\sqrt{n}$. Notice that this is the same as the Z-transformation used earlier except that now the variable of interest is $\overline{X}$ (rather than X), and that we use the standard deviation of the mean ($\sigma_{\overline{X}}$ rather than σ).

$$Z = \frac{\overline{X} - \mu}{\sigma/\sqrt{n}}$$

$$Z = \frac{300 - 288}{60/\sqrt{100}} = \frac{12}{6} = 2$$

From Table 2–4 we see that the area between $Z = 0$ and $Z = 2$ is 0.4772. Since 0.5000 is the total area above $Z = 0$, the area beyond $Z = 2$ must be $0.5000 - 0.4772 = 0.0228$. Thus, there is a 2.28 percent chance of selecting a sample with a mean greater than 300 when the true population mean is 288 and the population standard deviation is 60.

The Student's t-Distribution

When the population standard deviation is not known, or when the sample size is small, the Student's *t*-distribution should be used rather than the normal distribution. The Student's *t*-distribution resembles the normal distribution but is somewhat more spread out for small sample sizes. As the sample size becomes very large, the two distributions become the same. The formula for standardizing the distribution of sample means to the *t*-distribution is similar to the *Z*-transformation except that the sample standard deviation (s) is used instead of the population standard deviation (σ). The formula is:

$$t = \frac{\overline{X} - \mu}{s/\sqrt{n}}$$

Like the normal distribution, the *t*-distribution is centered at zero (i.e., has a mean of zero) and is symmetrical.

Since the *t*-distribution depends on the number of degrees of freedom (df), there are many *t*-distributions. The number of degrees of freedom appropriate for a given application depends on the specific characteristics of the analysis. Throughout this text, we will specify the value for df in each application. In our present application there are $n - 1$ degrees of freedom. Table 2–5 has a *t*-distribution for 29 different degrees of freedom plus infinity. The body of this table contains *t*-values such that the shaded area in the graph is equal to the subscript on *t* at the top of the column, for each number of degrees of freedom (df).

To learn how to read the *t*-table, let us consider three examples. First, what value of *t* would correspond to 5 percent of the area in the shaded region if there are 15 degrees of freedom? To answer this, go to the row for 15 degrees of freedom, then to the column that has .050 for the subscript on *t*. The *t*-value at the intersection of that row and column is 1.753. Second, if there are 26 degrees of freedom and the *t*-value is 2.479, how much area would be in the shaded region? Looking across the row for 26 degrees of freedom we see that 2.479 is in the column for which *t* is subscripted with .010. Thus, 1 percent of the area would be in that tail.

For our third example, consider the following question: If there are 85 degrees of freedom, what value of *t* would be associated with finding 97.5 percent of the area in the unshaded portion of the curve? For any number of degrees of freedom greater than 29, we would use the infinity (Inf.) row of the table. If we want 97.5 percent in the clear area, then 2.5 percent must be in the shaded region. Thus, we need the column for which *t* is subscripted with .025. The *t*-value at the intersection of this row and column is found to be 1.960. (Note that this is the same as the *Z*-value for which 2.5 percent would be in the tail, or 0.4750 is in the shaded section of the normal distribution shown in Table 2–4.)

TABLE 2–5   Student's *t*-Distribution*

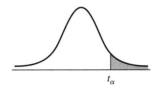

t_α

df	$t_{.100}$	$t_{.050}$	$t_{.025}$	$t_{.010}$	$t_{.005}$
1	3.078	6.314	12.706	31.821	63.657
2	1.886	2.920	4.303	6.965	9.925
3	1.638	2.353	3.182	4.541	5.841
4	1.533	2.132	2.776	3.747	4.604
5	1.476	2.015	2.571	3.365	4.032
6	1.440	1.943	2.447	3.143	3.707
7	1.415	1.895	2.365	2.998	3.499
8	1.397	1.860	2.306	2.896	3.355
9	1.383	1.833	2.262	2.821	3.250
10	1.372	1.812	2.228	2.764	3.169
11	1.363	1.796	2.201	2.718	3.106
12	1.356	1.782	2.179	2.681	3.055
13	1.350	1.771	2.160	2.650	3.012
14	1.345	1.761	2.145	2.624	2.977
15	1.341	1.753	2.131	2.602	2.947
16	1.337	1.746	2.120	2.583	2.921
17	1.333	1.740	2.110	2.567	2.898
18	1.330	1.734	2.101	2.552	2.878
19	1.328	1.729	2.093	2.539	2.861
20	1.325	1.725	2.086	2.528	2.845
21	1.323	1.721	2.080	2.518	2.831
22	1.321	1.717	2.074	2.508	2.819
23	1.319	1.714	2.069	2.500	2.807
24	1.318	1.711	2.064	2.492	2.797
25	1.316	1.708	2.060	2.485	2.787
26	1.315	1.706	2.056	2.479	2.779
27	1.314	1.703	2.052	2.473	2.771
28	1.313	1.701	2.048	2.467	2.763
29	1.311	1.699	2.045	2.462	2.756
Inf.	1.282	1.645	1.960	2.326	2.576

*The *t*-distribution is used for standardizing when the population standard deviation is unknown and the sample standard deviation is used in its place.

$$t = \frac{\overline{X} - \mu}{s/\sqrt{n}}$$

Source: Adapted from Owen P. Hall, Jr., and Harvey M. Adelman, *Computerized Business Statistics* (Homewood, Ill.: Richard D. Irwin, 1987), p. 93.

While *t*-tables are usually limited to four or five areas in the tail of the distribution and perhaps 30 levels for degrees of freedom, most statistical software incorporates the equation for the *t*-distribution and will give exact areas, given any *t*-value and the appropriate number of degrees of freedom. We will rely on the *t*-distribution extensively in Chapters 4 and 5 as part of the evaluation of statistical significance in regression models.

From Sample to Population: Statistical Inference

We are usually much less interested in a sample than in the population from which the sample is drawn. The reason for looking at a sample is almost always to provide a basis for making some inference about the whole population. For example, suppose we are interested in marketing a new service in Oregon and want to know something about the income per person in the state. Roughly 3 million people live in Oregon. Clearly, trying to contact all of them to determine the mean income per person would be impractical and very costly. Instead we might select a sample and make an inference about the population based on the responses of the people in that sample of Oregon residents.

A sample statistic is our best point estimate of the corresponding population parameter. While it is best, it is also likely to be wrong. Thus, in making an inference about a population it is usually desirable to make an interval estimate.

For example, an interval estimate of the population mean is one that is centered on the sample mean and extends above and below that value by an amount that is determined by how confident we want to be, by how large a sample we have, and by the variability in the data. These elements are captured in the following equation for a confidence interval:

$$\mu = \overline{X} \pm t(s/\sqrt{n})$$

Recall that $s/\sqrt{n}$ is the standard error of the sample mean. The *t*-value is determined from Table 2–5 after choosing the number of degrees of freedom ($n - 1$ in this case), and the level of confidence we desire as reflected by the area in the shaded tail of the distribution.

If we want a 95 percent confidence interval that is symmetrical around the mean, we would want a total of 5 percent in the two extreme tails of the distribution. Thus, 2.5 percent would be in each tail. The following diagram will help you see this:

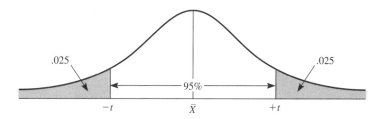

The *t*-value that would correspond to 2.5 percent in each tail can be determined from Table 2–5, given the appropriate number of degrees of freedom. Several examples follow:

Number of Degrees of Freedom	t-Value for 95% Confidence Interval
5	2.571
10	2.228
20	2.086
50	1.960
100	1.960

Suppose that a sample of 100 responses gives a mean of $15,000 and a standard deviation of $5,000. Our best point estimate for the population mean would be $15,000, and a 95 percent confidence interval would be:

$$\mu = 15{,}000 \pm 1.96(5{,}000/\sqrt{100})$$

$$= 15{,}000 \pm 980$$

that is,

$$14{,}020 \le \mu \le 15{,}980$$

See if you can correctly find the endpoints for a 90 percent confidence interval given this same set of sample results.[5]

Hypothesis Testing

Frequently we have a theory or hypothesis that we would like to evaluate statistically. For example, we might hypothesize that the mean expenditure on entertainment in some city is equal to the national average for all age groups. Or we may theorize that consumption of soft drinks by retired people is less than the national level. Or we may want to evaluate the assumption that women professionals work more than the standard 40-hour work week. All of these can be evaluated by using an appropriate hypothesis testing procedure.

The process begins by setting up two hypotheses, the null hypothesis (designated H_0:) and the alternative hypothesis (designated H_1:). These two hypotheses should be structured so that they are mutually exclusive and exhaustive. For example, if we hypothesize that the mean expenditure on entertainment by people in some city is different from the national average, the null and alternative hypotheses would be (let μ_0 = the national average and μ = this city's population mean):

Case I
$$\begin{cases} H_0: \quad \mu = \mu_0 \\ \text{i.e., } H_0: \quad \text{The city mean equals the national mean.} \\ H_1: \quad \mu \ne \mu_0 \\ \text{i.e., } H_1: \quad \text{The city mean is not equal to the national mean.} \end{cases}$$

The process begins by setting up two hypotheses, the null hypothesis (designated H_0:) and the alternative hypothesis (designated H_1:). These two hypotheses should be structured so that they are mutually exclusive and exhaustive.

[5]The lower bound is $14,177.5; the upper bound is $15,822.5. Notice that at this lower confidence level the value of *t* is smaller (other things equal) and thus the confidence interval is narrower.

If we theorize that the consumption of soft drinks by retired people is *less* than the national average, the null and alternative hypotheses would be (let μ_0 = national average and μ = the mean for retired people):

Case II $\begin{cases} H_0: & \mu \geq \mu_0 \\ \text{i.e., } H_0: & \text{The mean for retired people is greater than or equal} \\ & \text{to the national average.} \\ H_1: & \mu < \mu_0 \\ \text{i.e., } H_1: & \text{The mean for retired people is less than the} \\ & \text{national average.} \end{cases}$

If we want to evaluate the assumption that women professionals work *more* than the standard 40-hour work week, the null and alternative hypotheses would be (let μ_0 = the standard work week and μ = the mean for professional women):

Case III $\begin{cases} H_0: & \mu \leq \mu_0 \\ \text{i.e., } H_0: & \text{The mean for professional women is less than or} \\ & \text{equal to the standard.} \\ H_1: & \mu > \mu_0 \\ \text{i.e., } H_1: & \text{The mean for professional women is greater than} \\ & \text{the standard.} \end{cases}$

In each of these cases the null and alternative hypotheses are mutually exclusive and exhaustive.

In statistical hypothesis testing, the approach is to see whether you find sufficient evidence to reject the null hypothesis. If so, the alternative is found to have support. For questions of the type we are considering, this is done by using a *t*-test. To perform a *t*-test, we must first determine how confident we want to be in our decision regarding whether or not to reject the null hypothesis. In most business applications a 95 percent confidence level is used. A measure that is closely related to the confidence level is the significance level for the test. The significance level, often denoted α (alpha), is equal to 1 minus the confidence level. Thus, a 95 percent confidence level is the same as a 5 percent significance level. The significance level is the probability of rejecting the null hypothesis when in fact it is true.

In testing hypotheses, there are four possible outcomes, two of which are good and two of which are bad. These are summarized in Table 2–6. If we reject H_0: when in fact it is true, we have what is termed a *type I error*. The other possible error results when we fail to reject a null hypothesis that is in fact incorrect. This is a *type II error*. These two

TABLE 2–6   Type I and Type II Errors

Statistical Decision	**The Truth**	
	H_0: Is True	*H_0: Is Not True*
Reject H_0:	Type I error	No error
Fail to Reject H_0:	No error	Type II error

errors are related in that by reducing the chance of a type I error we increase the chance of a type II error and vice versa. Most of the time, greater attention is given to type I errors. The probability of making a type I error is determined by the significance level (α) we select for the hypothesis test. If the cost of a type I error is large, we would use a low α, perhaps 1 percent or less.

Hypothesis tests may be one- or two-tailed tests. When the sign in the alternative hypothesis is an unequal sign ($\neq$), the test is a two-tailed test. Otherwise, a one-tailed test is appropriate. For a two-tailed test the significance level (α) is split equally into the two tails of the distribution. For a one-tailed test the entire significance level (α) goes in the one tail of the distribution that is indicated by the direction of the inequality sign in the alternative hypothesis. Consider the three situations described a few paragraphs back. These are summarized in the following diagrams, which show where the significance level would be (a 5 percent significance level is used in all three cases).

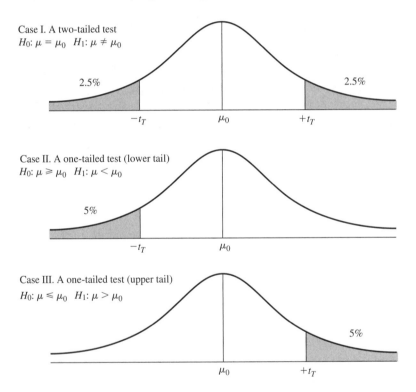

Case I. A two-tailed test
$H_0: \mu = \mu_0$ $H_1: \mu \neq \mu_0$

2.5%   2.5%

$-t_T$ μ_0 $+t_T$

Case II. A one-tailed test (lower tail)
$H_0: \mu \geq \mu_0$ $H_1: \mu < \mu_0$

5%

$-t_T$ μ_0

Case III. A one-tailed test (upper tail)
$H_0: \mu \leq \mu_0$ $H_1: \mu > \mu_0$

5%

μ_0 $+t_T$

The t_T values are determined from a t-distribution, such as that in Table 2–5, at the appropriate number of degrees of freedom ($n - 1$, in the examples used here) and for the tail areas indicated in these diagrams ($\alpha/2$ for two-tailed tests and α for one-tailed tests).

For each hypothesis test, a t-value is calculated (t_{calc}) and compared with the critical value from the t-distribution (t_T). If the calculated value is further into the tail of the distribution than the table value, we have an observation that is extreme, given the assumption inherent in H_0, and so H_0 is rejected. That is, we have sufficient evidence to reject the null hypothesis (H_0) when the *absolute value* of t_{calc} is greater than t_T. Otherwise we fail to reject the premise in H_0.

The calculated *t*-statistic is found as follows:

$$t_{calc} = \frac{\overline{X} - \mu_0}{s/\sqrt{n}}$$

where $\overline{X}$ is our sample mean and our best point estimate of μ. The value we are testing against is μ_0. The sample standard deviation is s and the sample size is n.

Let us now apply these concepts to our three situations. Starting with case I, let us assume that a sample of 49 people resulted in a mean of $200 per month with a standard deviation of $84. The national average is $220 per month. The hypotheses are:

$$H_0: \mu = 220$$
$$H_1: \mu \neq 220$$

The calculated value is:

$$t_{calc} = \frac{200 - 220}{84/\sqrt{49}} = \frac{-20}{12} = -1.67$$

If we want a 95 percent confidence level ($\alpha = 0.05$), the critical or table value of t is ± 1.96. Notice that the $t_{.025}$ column of Table 2–5 was used. This is because we have a two-tailed test, and the α of 0.05 is split equally between the two tails. Since our calculated *t*-value (t_{calc}) has an absolute value that is less than the critical value from the *t*-table (t_T), we fail to reject the null hypothesis. Thus, we conclude that the evidence from this sample is not sufficient to say that entertainment expenditures by people in this city are any different from the national average.

This result is summarized in the following diagram:

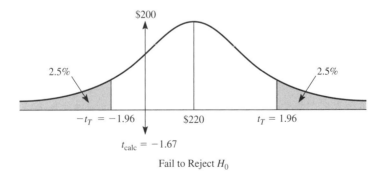

Fail to Reject H_0

We see here that the observed mean of $200 or its corresponding *t*-value (-1.67) is not extreme. That is, it does not fall into either of the shaded areas. These shaded areas taken together are often called the *rejection region*, because t_{calc} values in the shaded areas would call for rejection of H_0.

Let us now look at case II. Assume that for a sample of 25 retired people the mean was 1.2 six-packs per week with a standard deviation of 0.6. The national average (μ_0) is 1.5. The hypotheses are:

$$H_0: \mu \geq 1.5$$
$$H_1: \mu < 1.5$$

The calculated t-value is:

$$t_{\text{calc}} = \frac{1.2 - 1.5}{0.6/\sqrt{25}} = \frac{-0.3}{0.12} = -2.50$$

The critical value from the t-distribution in Table 2–5, assuming a 95 percent confidence level ($\alpha = 0.05$), is $t_T = -1.711$. Note that there are 24 degrees of freedom. Since the absolute value of t_{calc} is greater than the table value of t, we reject H_0. Thus, we conclude that there is sufficient evidence to support the notion that retired people consume fewer soft drinks than the national average.

This result is shown in graphic form as follows:

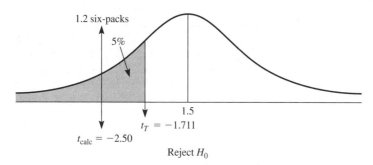

Here we see that the sample mean of 1.2 is extreme, given $\alpha = 0.05$ and $df = 24$, and so we reject H_0. The calculated value of t falls in the rejection region.

Finally, let us consider case III. We will assume that we have a sample of 144 professional women and that the mean number of hours per week worked for that sample is 45 with a sample standard deviation of 29. The national norm is the 40-hour work week. The hypotheses are:

$$H_0: \mu \leq 40$$
$$H_1: \mu > 40$$

Our calculated t-value is:

$$t_{\text{calc}} = \frac{45 - 40}{29/\sqrt{144}} = \frac{5}{2.42} = 2.07$$

The relevant table value is 1.645 ($\alpha = 0.05$ and $df = 143$). Since $T_{\text{calc}} > t_T$, we reject the null hypothesis and conclude that the mean for professional women is greater than 40 hours per week.

This result is shown graphically as follows:

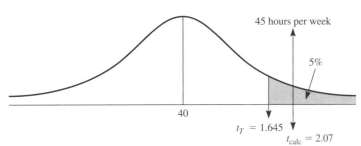

The calculated *t*-value lies in the shaded (or rejection) region, and so H_0 is rejected.

The *t*-tests illustrated in this section involved making judgments about a population mean based on information from a sample. In each *t*-test, the calculated value of *t* was determined by dividing some difference $(\bar{X} - \mu_0)$ by a standard error $(s/\sqrt{n})$. All *t*-statistics are calculated in this general way:

$$t = \frac{\text{the difference being evaluated}}{\text{the corresponding standard error}}$$

We will use this general form later in this chapter as well as in subsequent chapters of the text when *t*-tests are appropriate.

There are other statistical tests and other distributions that are applicable to forecasting. These include *F*-tests, Durbin-Watson tests, and chi-square tests, which will be discussed later in the text as they are applied. If you have a basic understanding of the use of *t*-tests, these other statistical tests will not be difficult to use.

Correlation

It is often useful to have a measure of the degree of association between two variables. For example, if you believe that sales may be affected by expenditures on advertising, you might want to measure the degree of association between sales and advertising. One measure of association that is often used is the Pearson product-moment correlation co efficient, which is designated ρ (rho) for a population and *r* for a sample. There are other measures of correlation, but Pearson's is the most common and the most useful for the type of data encountered in forecasting situations. Thus, when we refer to correlation or a correlation coefficient, we mean the Pearson product-moment correlation.

There are several alternative ways to write the algebraic expression for the correlation coefficient. For our purposes the following is the most instructive:

$$r = \frac{\sum(X - \bar{X})(Y - \bar{Y})}{\sqrt{[\sum(X - \bar{X})^2][\sum(Y - \bar{Y})^2]}}$$

where *X* and *Y* represent the two variables of interest (e.g., advertising and sales). This is the sample correlation coefficient. The calculation of the population correlation coefficient (ρ) is strictly analogous except that the population means for *X* and *Y* would be used rather than the sample means. It is important to note that the correlation coefficient defined here measures the degree of *linear* association between X and Y.

The correlation coefficient can have any value in the range from -1 to $+1$. A perfect positive correlation would be $r = +1$, while a perfect negative correlation would be $r = -1$. These cases are shown in scatterplots A and B of Figure 2–7. You can see that when there is a perfect correlation (positive or negative) all of the data points fall along a straight line.

In scatterplot C it appears that in general when X increases, Y_C increases as well. That is, there appears to be a positive (or direct) association between X and Y_C. However, all five points do not fall along a single straight line, and so there is not a perfect linear association. In this case the correlation coefficient is $+0.80$. Scatterplot D shows a negative (or inverse) association between X and Y_D, but one that is not perfectly linear. For scatterplot D, $r = -0.85$.

The remaining two scatterplots in Figure 2–7 illustrate cases for which the correlation coefficient is zero. In both cases there is no linear association between the variables. However, note that in panel F there is a clear nonlinear association between X and Y_F.

We could perform a hypothesis test to determine whether the value of a sample correlation coefficient (r) gives us reason to believe that the true population correlation coefficient (ρ) is significantly different from zero. If it is not, then there would be no linear association between the two measures. The hypothesis test would be:

$$H_0: \rho = 0$$
$$H_1: \rho \neq 0$$

and t would be calculated as:

$$t = \frac{r - 0}{\sqrt{(1 - r^2)/(n - 2)}}$$

where $\sqrt{(1 - r^2)/(n - 2)}$ is the standard error of r.

Let us apply this to the data in scatterplots D and F of Figure 2–7. In both of these cases, for a two-tailed test, with $\alpha = 0.05$ and $n = 5$, the table value of t_T is 3.182 (there are $n - 2$, or 3 degrees of freedom for this test). For panel D the calculated value of t is:

$$t_{\text{calc}} = \frac{0.85 - 0}{\sqrt{[1 - (-0.85)^2]/(5 - 2)}}$$

$$= \frac{-0.85}{\sqrt{0.2775/3}} = \frac{-0.85}{\sqrt{0.0925}} = -2.795$$

Since t_{calc} is in the interval between $\pm t_T$ (i.e., ± 3.182), we would fail to reject the null hypothesis on the basis of a sample of five observations at a 95 percent confidence level ($\alpha = 0.05$). Thus, we conclude that there is not enough evidence to say that ρ is different from zero. While the $r = -0.85$ is a fairly strong correlation, we are not able to say it is significantly different from zero in this case, largely because we have such a small

FIGURE 2–7

Representative Scatterplots with the Corresponding Correlation Coefficients

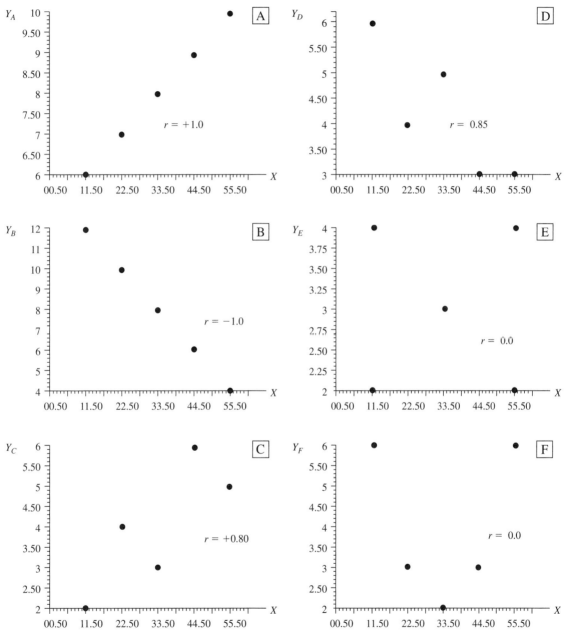

These scatterplots show correlation coefficients that range from a perfect positive correlation (A) and a perfect nega-tive correlation (B) to zero correlations (E and F).

sample. If $n = 50$ and $r = -0.85$, the calculated value for t would be -11.18, and the table value would be 1.96, so that the null hypothesis would be rejected.

For the data in panel F, the calculated value of t is:

$$t_{calc} = \frac{0 - 0}{\sqrt{(1 - 0^2)/(5 - 2)}} = 0$$

Since this t_{calc} is again in the interval between $\pm t_T$, we would fail to reject H_0 and would conclude that we do not have enough evidence to suggest that ρ is different from zero (at a 95 percent confidence level, or $\alpha = 0.05$, and on the basis of a sample of five observations).

Correlograms: An Alternative Method of Data Exploration

In evaluating a time series of data, it is useful to look at the correlation between successive observations over time. This measure of correlation is called an *autocorrelation* and may be calculated as follows:

$$r_k = \frac{\sum_{t=1}^{n-k}(Y_{t-k} - \bar{Y})(Y_t - \bar{Y})}{\sum_{t-1}^{n}(Y_t - \bar{Y})^2}$$

where:

$r_k =$ Autocorrelation for a k-period lag

$Y_t =$ Value of the time series at period t

$Y_{t-k} =$ Value of time series k periods before period t

$\bar{Y} =$ Mean of the time series

If the time series is stationary, the value of r_k should diminish rapidly toward zero as k increases. If, on the other hand, there is a trend, r_k will decline toward zero slowly. If a seasonal pattern exists, the value of r_k will be significantly different from zero at $k = 4$ for quarterly data, or $k = 12$ for monthly data. (For quarterly data, r_k for $k = 8$, $k = 12$, $k = 16, \ldots$ may also be large. For monthly data, a large r_k may also be found for $k = 24$, $k = 36$, etc.)

A k-period plot of autocorrelations is called an *autocorrelation function* (ACF), or a *correlogram*. We will look at a number of such graphics as we further analyze GDP, Leo Burnett U.S. billings, and private housing starts.

To determine whether the autocorrelation at lag k is significantly different from zero, the following hypothesis test and rule of thumb may be used:

$$H_0: \rho_k = 0$$
$$H_1: \rho_k \neq 0$$

FIGURE 2–8

Autocorrelation Structure of Real GDP (c2f8)

ACF Values for Real GDP

Obs	ACF	Obs	ACF
1	.9615	7	.7205
2	.9200	8	.6820
3	.8772	9	.6423
4	.8359	10	.6034
5	.7961	11	.5639
6	.7576	12	.5240

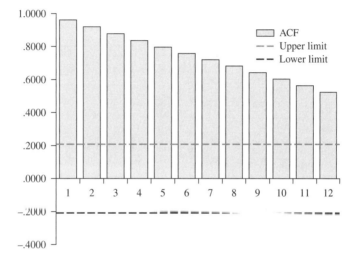

For any k, reject H_0 if $|r_k| > 2/\sqrt{n}$, where n is the number of observations. This rule of thumb is for a 95 percent confidence level.[6]

The use of autocorrelations and correlograms can be illustrated by looking at some of the data used earlier in this chapter. Let us begin with the gross domestic product data that were graphed in Figure 2–1. From that plot it was clear that GDP has a fairly strong positive trend, so that we might expect high autocorrelation coefficients. The autocorrelation structure of GDP is shown in Figure 2–8.

In this case 84 observations were used, from 1980Q1 through 2000Q4. Thus, $2/\sqrt{n} = 2/\sqrt{84} = 0.218$. Since all of the autocorrelation coefficients in Figure 2–8 are

---

[6]The complete t-test would be to reject H_0 if $|t_{calc}| > t_T$, where:

$$t_{calc} = \frac{(r_k - 0)}{(1/\sqrt{(n - k)}}$$

and t_T is from the t-table for $\alpha/2$ and $n - k$ degrees of freedom (n = number of observations, k = period of the lag).

greater than 0.218, we can conclude, by our rule of thumb, that they are all significantly different from zero. Therefore, we have additional evidence of a trend in the GDP data.[7] The actual 95 percent confidence interval is shown by the two horizontal lines labeled "Upper limit" and "Lower limit."

If we want to try a forecasting method for GDP that requires stationary data, we must first transform the GDP data to a stationary series. Often this can be done by using first differences. For GDP, the first differences can be calculated as:

$$\text{DGDP}_t = \text{GDP}_t - \text{GDP}_{t-1}$$

where DGDP_t is the first difference (or change) in GDP. Figure 2–9 shows a plot of GDP in the panel on this page (below) and of DGDP in the panel at the top of page 81. The series at the top of page 81 appears more stationary.

We can check for stationarity in DGDP by examining the autocorrelation structure for DGDP shown in Figure 2–10.

FIGURE 2–9

Real GDP and the Quarter-to-Quarter Change in Real GDP

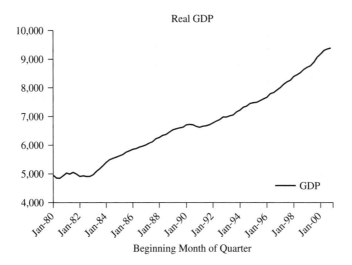

Real GDP

Beginning Month of Quarter

[7]The more formal hypothesis test is:

$$H_0: \rho_k = 0$$
$$H_1: \rho_k \neq 0$$

and the calculated *t*-ratio is:

$$t_{\text{calc}} = \frac{r_k - 0}{1/\sqrt{n-k}}$$

For example, for $k = 12$ where $r_k = 0.524$,

$$t_{\text{calc}} = \frac{0.524 - 0}{1/\sqrt{84 - 12}} = 4.446$$

which is greater than the table value of 1.96 at $\alpha/2 = 0.025$ (a 95 percent confidence level).

FIGURE 2–9

(Continued)

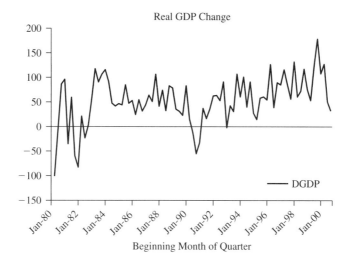

Real GDP Change

Beginning Month of Quarter

FIGURE 2–10

Autocorrelation Structure of DGDP (c2f10)

ACF Values for the Change in Real GDP

Obs	ACF	Obs	ACF
1	.4140	7	.0883
2	.3039	8	−.0192
3	.2101	9	.1232
4	.1369	10	.1100
5	.0254	11	−.0160
6	.1187	12	−.0811

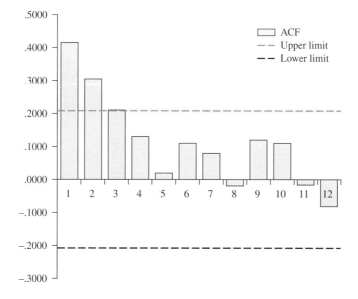

For 83 observations (one was lost in calculating DGDP), $2/\sqrt{n} = 2/\sqrt{83} = 0.220$. At the third-period lag, r_k has dropped below this ($0.210 < 0.220$), so we can conclude that for DGDP the autocorrelation coefficients do drop quickly toward zero. Note that after r_2, all the autocorrelations are within the 95 percent confidence bounds. Thus, DGDP can be considered stationary, and forecasting methods requiring stationarity could be used to forecast DGDP. Once DGDP is forecast, the transformation can be reversed to forecast GDP.

Let us now look at the U.S. billings of Leo Burnett advertising. As illustrated in Figure 2–3, there is an increasing positive trend to the LBB series. The first difference in LBB (defined as $\text{DLBB}_t = \text{LBB}_t - \text{LBB}_{t-1}$) also shows a positive trend. These trends can be confirmed by looking at the corresponding autocorrelation structures in Figure 2–11.

For LBB the autocorrelations are significant through r_{11}, and for DLBB all of the first eight r_s are significant, or nearly so. Thus, neither series is stationary.

In a case like this, we may do a further transformation to the second difference, that is, the difference in the first difference. In this case the second difference, DDLBB, is:

$$\text{DDLBB} = \text{DLBB}_t - \text{DLBB}_{t-1}$$

FIGURE 2–11

The Autocorrelation Structure of LBB, DLBB, and DDLBB

ACF Values for LBB

Obs	ACF	Obs	ACF
1	.9348	7	.5504
2	.8697	8	.4886
3	.8048	9	.4278
4	.7404	10	.3682
5	.6764	11	.3097
6	.6130	12	.2527

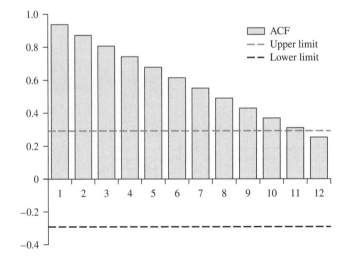

FIGURE 2–11

(Continued)

ACF Values for the First Difference in LBB (DLBB)

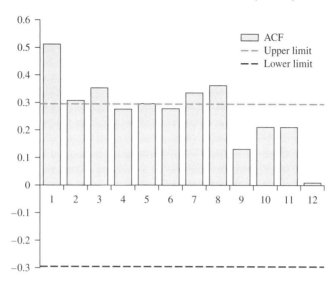

ACF Values for the Second Difference in LBB (DDLBB)

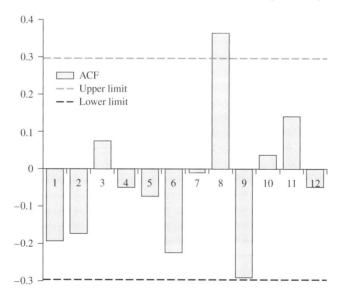

The autocorrelation structure of DDLBB is shown in the third panel of Figure 2–11. From the autocorrelation structure for DDLBB we can conclude that DDLBB is essentially stationary and could be forecast using methods that require stationarity.

Before leaving this section let us look at the autocorrelation structure for the private housing starts (PHS) data series. Recall from Figure 2–2 that this series exhibits all of the trend, seasonal, and cyclical components of a time series. When we look at the autocorrelation structure for the raw data for PHS we see a pattern that is somewhat mixed, as shown in the first graph of Figure 2–12. Note especially the high values for lags of 4, 8, and 12. These high values are caused by the seasonal pattern in the data. This seasonality in the PHS data may also cause some of the other autocorrelation coefficients to be understated. Therefore, before looking at the autocorrelation structure to evaluate the possibility of a significant trend in the data it is best to deseasonalize the data first. The deseasonalized data are shown graphically in Figure 2–2 along with the raw data and the trend. When we study the autocorrelation structure for the deseasonalized PHS series we get the results shown in the second graph of Figure 2–12. Here we see that the first seven values of r_k are significant. Thus, we can say that this provides strong statistical evidence for a trend in the PHS series.

FIGURE 2–12

Autocorrelation Structure for Private Housing Starts (PHS) (c2f12)

ACF Values for PHS

Obs	ACF	Obs	ACF
1	.4852	7	.1651
2	.1078	8	.5116
3	.3871	9	.0542
4	.7133	10	-.2427
5	.2062	11	.0377
6	-.1172	12	.3470

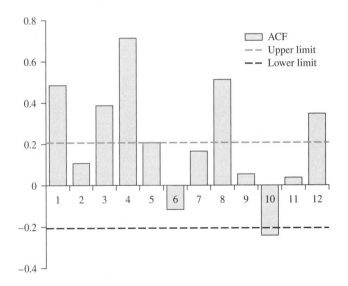

FIGURE 2–12

(Continued)

ACF Values for Deseasonalized PHS

Obs	ACF	Obs	ACF
1	.9487	7	.2267
2	.8544	8	.1466
3	.7303	9	.0833
4	.5898	10	.0335
5	.4517	11	−.0059
6	.3287	12	−.0411

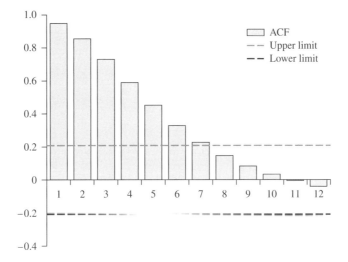

Domestic Car Sales: Exploratory Data Analysis and Model Selection

Let us apply exploratory data analysis techniques to the domestic car sales data that were introduced in Chapter 1 and that will be used as a running example throughout the text. Figure 2–13 shows the raw data for domestic car sales (DCS), a trend line, and the deseasonalized values of DCS. In this plot we see several things of interest. First, there appear to be fairly regular, sharp up-and-down movements that may be a reflection of seasonality in domestic car sales. Second, the long-term trend of domestic car sales appears only slightly positive. Finally, it looks as if there may be a cyclical pattern around the long-term trend. The autocorrelation structure of DCS is shown in Figure 2–14.

We see that the autocorrelations for DCS do not fall quickly to zero. For lags 1 through 5, the autocorrelation coefficients are significantly different from zero, except for r_2. We also show the ACF for seasonally adjusted domestic car sales in Figure 2–14.

FIGURE 2–13

Domestic Car Sales (DCS), Deseasonalized DCS, and the Long-Term Trend in DCS
(c2f13)

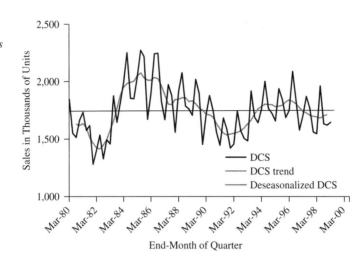

FIGURE 2–14

Autocorrelation Functions for Domestic Car Sales and Deseasonalized Domestic Car Sales

ACF for Domestic Car Sales

Obs	ACF	Obs	ACF
1	.4769	7	.0662
2	.1724	8	.3097
3	.3636	9	−.0006
4	.6376	10	−.3145
5	.3090	11	−.1216
6	−.0525	12	.0602

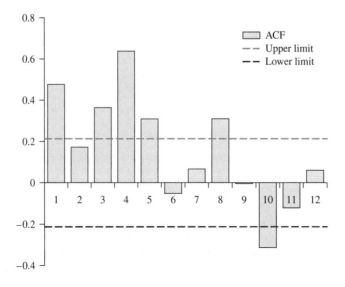

FIGURE 2–14
(Continued)

ACF for Seasonally Adjusted Domestic Car Sales

Obs	ACF	Obs	ACF
1	.9668	7	.2276
2	.8885	8	.0899
3	.7828	9	−.0321
4	.6580	10	−.1371
5	.5211	11	−.2279
6	.3752	12	−.3051

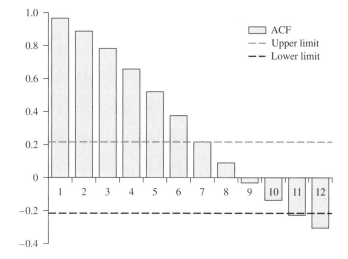

The noise created by the seasonality is removed in this graphic and we see that the first six ACF values are significant. Thus, we have evidence of a significant, albeit modest, trend in DCS.

From this exploratory analysis of the domestic car sales data, we can conclude that there is trend, seasonality, and some cycle. From Table 2–1 we can, therefore, suggest the following as potential forecasting methods for retail car sales:

Winters' exponential smoothing

Regression trend with seasonality

Causal regression

Time-series decomposition

ARIMA

Note that ARIMA is included, since the data could be transformed to a stationary state, as was demonstrated. If the cycle component of this time series proves to be important, the regression trend with seasonality would probably be less accurate than some of the other methods listed.

Business Forecasting: A Process, Not an Application

Charles W. Chase, Jr.

Current literature and experience dictate that the best forecasting system provides easy access, review, and modification of forecast results across all corporate disciplines; provides alternative modeling capabilities (multi-dimensional); includes the ability to create a knowledge base by which future forecasts can be refined; provides timely and accurate automated link/feed interfaces with other systems such as I.R.I. (Information Resources Inc.)/Nielsen syndicated databases and the mainframe shipment database. The present industry trend has been redirected away from mainframe systems toward PC-based software applications due to the lack of flexibility associated with mainframe access and reporting. Mainframes are being utilized primarily as storage bins for PC-based systems to extract and store information.

SOURCE: *Journal of Business Forecasting* 11, no. 3 (Fall 1992), pp. 12–13. Reprinted by permission.

INTEGRATIVE CASE
THE GAP

Part 2: Data Analysis of The Gap Sales Data

The sales of The Gap stores for the 56 quarters covering 1985Q1 through 1998Q4 are shown below.

(c2gap)

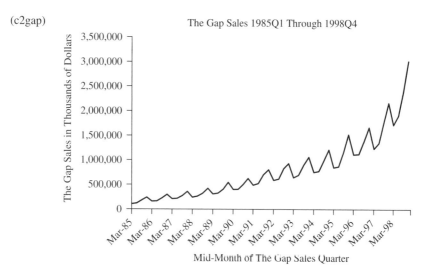

From this graph it is clear that The Gap sales are seasonal and increasing over time (a positive trend). There does not appear to be a cycle.

Case Questions

1. In 1998, The Gap sales by quarter were as given below:

Quarter	The Gap Sales in Thousands of Dollars
1998Q1	1,719,712
1998Q2	1,904,970
1998Q3	2,399,900
1998Q4	3,029,900

Based on these data, calculate a 95 percent confidence interval for quarterly sales of The Gap.

2. The Gap sales on an annual basis are shown in the following table.

Year	The Gap Sales ($000)
1985	647,333
1986	848,009
1987	1,062,020
1988	1,252,100
1989	1,586,600
1990	1,933,780
1991	2,518,890
1992	2,960,410
1993	3,295,680
1994	3,722,940
1995	4,395,250
1996	5,284,390
1997	6,507,825
1998	9,054,482

Plot these data in a time-series plot. Based on this graph, what pattern do you see in annual The Gap sales?

3. Using data for 1985Q1 through 1998Q4, calculate the autocorrelation coefficients for quarterly The Gap sales (the quarterly data are in Table 1–9 and in the C2Gap.xls data file) using twelve lags, and construct the corresponding correlogram (plot of the autocorrelations) for lags of 1 through 12. What do the autocorrelation coefficients and the correlogram tell you about the series?

4. Based on the plot of The Gap sales, on what you learned from question 3, as well as the information in Table 2–1, what forecasting methods might you suggest if you were to forecast The Gap's quarterly sales?

Solutions to Case Questions

1. The 95 percent confidence interval is calculated as:

Mean of The Gap Sales $\pm$ t(Standard Deviation of The Gap Sales $\div \sqrt{n}$)

In this case, $n = 4$ and $df = n - 1$, so $df = 3$ and the corresponding value of t is 3.182 (see Table 2–5).

$$2,263,620.5 \pm 3.182(586,010 \div \sqrt{4})$$

$$2,263,620.5 \pm 932,341.9$$

$$1,331,278.6 \text{ to } 3,195,962.4$$

2. The plot of annual The Gap sales shown below indicates that there is a positive trend to their sales over time.

3. The critical value of r_k for an n of 56 (14 years of quarterly data) is 0.267. As you see from the autocorrelations and correlogram on the next page, the first 12 values are all greater than the critical value at a 95 percent confidence level. Thus, we have further evidence of a trend in The Gap data.

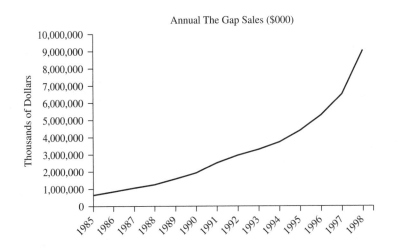

Annual The Gap Sales ($000)

ACF for The Gap Sales

Obs	ACF	Obs	ACF
1	.8116	7	.4446
2	.6827	8	.4709
3	.6631	9	.3660
4	.6768	10	.2932
5	.5407	11	.2956
6	.4445	12	.3124

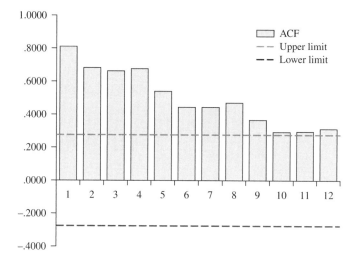

4. Based on the plot of The Gap's quarterly sales, as well as the data analysis from question 3, the following forecasting methods might be suggested from the information in Table 2–1:

    Winters' exponential smoothing

    Regression trend with seasonality

Causal regression

Time-series decomposition

ARIMA (if the series is transformed to stationarity and deseasonalized)

USING FORECASTX™ TO FIND AUTOCORRELATION FUNCTIONS

The most difficult calculations in this chapter were the autocorrelation coefficients. These can be calculated easily in the ForecastX™ software that accompanies your text. What follows is a brief discussion of how to use ForecastX™ for this purpose. This also serves as a good introduction to the ease of use of ForecastX™.

First, put your data into an Excel spreadsheet in column format such as the sample of The Gap data shown in Table 2–7. Once you have your data in this format, while in Excel highlight the data you want to use, then start ForecastX™. The following dialog box appears.

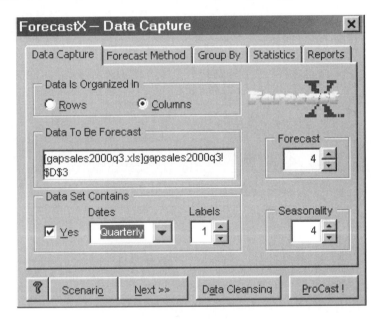

TABLE 2–7   A Sample of The Gap Data in Column Format

Date	The Gap Sales ($000)
Sep-1996	1,383,000
Dec-1996	1,667,900
Mar-1997	1,231,186
Jun-1997	1,345,221
Sep-1997	1,765,939
Dec-1997	2,165,479
Mar-1998	1,719,712
Jun-1998	1,904,970
Sep-1998	2,399,900
Dec-1998	3,029,900

Dates are the middle months of The Gap sales quarters.

Set the **Dates** window to the periodicity of your data (**Quarterly** for this example), then click the **Forecast Method** tab at the top and the following screen appears.

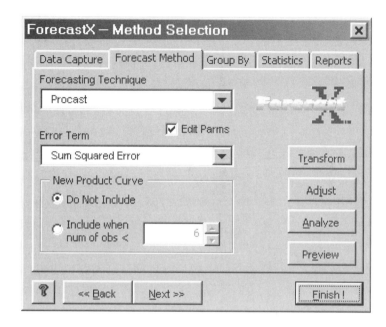

Click the down arrow in the **Forecasting Technique** window and select **Box Jenkins** to get the result shown on the following screen.

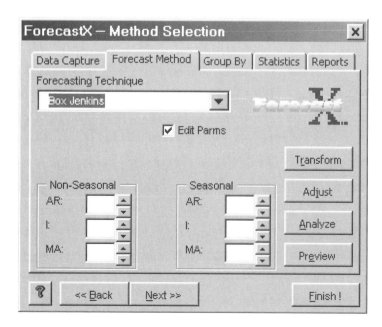

Now click the **Analyze** button and the following screen appears. Click **Export** and the results will be saved to a new Excel book.

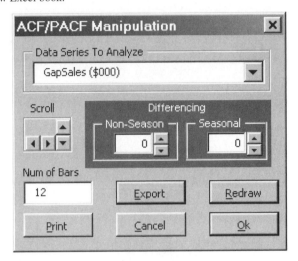

You will have the results shown below (along with some other results) in that new Excel book.

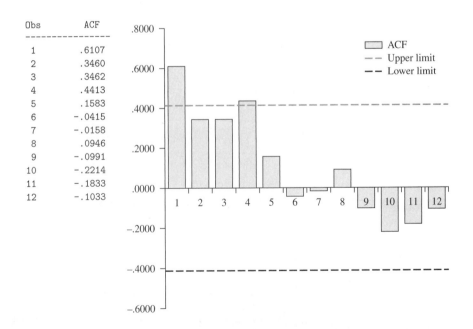

Obs	ACF
1	.6107
2	.3460
3	.3462
4	.4413
5	.1583
6	-.0415
7	-.0158
8	.0946
9	-.0991
10	-.2214
11	-.1833
12	-.1033

Suggested Readings

Aghazadeh, Seyed-Mahmoud; and Jane B. Romal. "A Directory of 66 Packages for Forecasting and Statistical Analyses." *Journal of Business Forecasting* 11, no. 2 (Summer 1992), pp. 14–20.

"Beyond the Business Cycle?" *The Economist* 353, no. 8142 (October 1999), p. 90.

Bowerman, Bruce L.; and Richard T. O'Connell. *Applied Statistics: Improving Business Processes*. Chicago: Richard D. Irwin, 1997. (Especially chapters 5 and 7.)

Chatterjee, Satyajit. "From Cycles to Shocks: Progress in Business-Cycle Theory." *Business Review,* Federal Reserve Bank of Philadelphia (March/April 2000), pp. 27–37.

Chen, Rong, et al. "Forecasting with Stable Seasonal Pattern Models with an Application to Hawaiian Tourism Data." *Journal of Business & Economic Statistics* 17, no. 4 (October 1999), pp. 497–504.

Drumm, William J. "Living with Forecast Error." *Journal of Business Forecasting* 11, no. 2 (Summer 1992), p. 23.

Ermer, Charles M. "Cost of Error Affects the Forecasting Model Selection." *Journal of Business Forecasting* 10, no. 1 (Spring 1991), pp. 10–11.

Huff, Darrell. *How to Lie with Statistics.* New York: W. W. Norton, 1954.

Makridakis, Spyros. "Forecasting: Its Role and Value for Planning and Strategy." *International Journal of Forecasting* 12, no. 4 (December 1996), pp. 513–37.

Mentzer, John T.; and Bienstock, Carol C. *Sales Forecasting Management,* Thousand Oaks, CA: Sage Publications, 1998.

Mentzer, John T.; and Kenneth B. Kahn. "Forecasting Technique Familiarity, Satisfaction, Usage, and Application." *Journal of Forecasting* 14, no. 5 (September 1995), pp. 465–76.

——. "State of Sales Forecasting Systems in Corporate America." *Journal of Business Forecasting* 16, no. 1 (Spring 1997), pp. 6–13.

O'Clock, George; and Priscilla M. O'Clock. "Political Realities of Forecasting." *Journal of Business Forecasting* 8, no. 1 (Spring 1989), pp. 2–6.

Sawhney, Mohanbir S., et al. "A Parsimonious Model for Forecasting Gross Box-Office Revenues of Motion Pictures." *Marketing Science* 15, no. 2 (1996), pp. 113–31.

Smith, Michael. "Modeling and Short-Term Forecasting of New South Wales Electricity System Load." *Journal of Business & Economic Statistics* 18, no. 4 (October 2000), pp. 465–78.

Tufte, Edward R. *Envisioning Information.* Cheshire, CT: Graphics Press, 1990.

——. *The Visual Display of Quantitative Information.* Cheshire, CT: Graphics Press, 1983.

Winklhofer, Heidi; Adamantios Diamantopoulos; and Stephen F. Witt. "Forecasting Practice: A Review of the Empirical Literature and an Agenda for Future Research." *International Journal of Forecasting* 12, no. 2 (June 1996), pp. 193–221.

Exercises

1. The mean volume of sales for a sample of 100 sales representatives is $25,350 per month. The sample standard deviation is $7,490. The vice president for sales would like to know whether this result is significantly different from $24,000 at a 95 percent confidence level. Set up the appropriate null and alternative hypotheses and perform the appropriate statistical test.

2. Larry Bomser has been asked to evaluate sizes of tire inventories for retail outlets of a major tire manufacturer. From a sample of 120 stores he has found a mean of 310 tires. The industry average is 325. If the standard deviation for the sample was 72, would you say that the inventory level maintained by this manufacturer is significantly different from the industry norm? Explain why. (Use a 95 percent confidence level.)

3. Twenty graduate students in business were asked how many credit hours they were taking in the current quarter. Their responses are shown as follows:

(c2p3)	*Student Number*	*Credit Hours*	*Student Number*	*Credit Hours*	*Student Number*	*Credit Hours*
	1	2	8	8	15	10
	2	7	9	12	16	6
	3	9	10	11	17	9
	4	9	11	6	18	6
	5	8	12	5	19	9
	6	11	13	9	20	10
	7	6	14	13		

a. Determine the mean, median, and mode for this sample of data. Write a sentence explaining what each means.

b. It has been suggested that graduate students in business take fewer credits per quarter than the typical graduate student at this university. The mean for all graduate students is 9.1 credit hours per quarter, and the data are normally distributed. Set up the appropriate null and alternative hypotheses and determine whether the null hypothesis can be rejected at a 95 percent confidence level.

4. Arbon Computer Corporation (ACC) produces a popular PC clone. The sales manager for ACC has recently read a report that indicated that sales per sales representative for other producers are normally distributed with a mean of $255,000. She is interested in knowing whether her sales staff is comparable. She picked a random sample of 16 salespeople and obtained the following results:

(c2p4)	*Person*	*Sales*	*Person*	*Sales*
	1	$177,406	9	$110,027
	2	339,753	10	182,577
	3	310,170	11	177,707
	4	175,520	12	154,096
	5	293,332	13	236,083
	6	323,175	14	301,051
	7	144,031	15	158,792
	8	279,670	16	140,891

At a 5 percent significance level, can you reject the null hypothesis that ACC's mean sales per salesperson was $255,000? Draw a diagram that illustrates your answer.

5. Assume that the weights of college football players are normally distributed with a mean of 205 pounds and a standard deviation of 30.

a. What percent of players would have weights greater than 205 pounds?

b. What percent of players would weigh less than 250 pounds?

c. Ninety percent of players would weigh more than what number of pounds?

d. What percent of players would weigh between 180 and 230 pounds?

6. Mutual Savings Bank of Appleton has done a market research survey in which people were asked to rate their image of the bank on a scale of 1 to 10, with 10 being the most favorable. The mean response for the sample of 400 people was 7.25, with a standard deviation of 2.51. On this same question a state association of mutual savings banks has found a mean of 7.01.

a. Clara Wharton, marketing director for the bank, would like to test to see whether the rating for her bank is significantly greater than the norm of 7.01. Perform the appropriate hypothesis test for a 95 percent confidence level.

b. Draw a diagram to illustrate your result.

c. How would your result be affected if the sample size had been 100 rather than 400, with everything else being the same?

7. In a sample of 25 classes, the following numbers of students were observed:

(c2p7)				
40	50	42	20	29
39	49	46	52	45
51	64	43	37	35
44	10	40	36	20
20	29	58	51	54

a. Calculate the mean, median, standard deviation, variance, and range for this sample.

b. What is the standard error of the mean based on this information?

c. What would be the best point estimate for the population class size?

d. What is the 95 percent confidence interval for class size? What is the 90 percent confidence interval? Does the difference between these two make sense?

8. CoastCo Insurance, Inc., is interested in forecasting annual larceny thefts in the United States using the following data:

(c2p8)

Year	Larceny Thefts*	Year	Larceny Thefts*
1972	4,151	1984	6,592
1973	4,348	1985	6,926
1974	5,263	1986	7,257
1975	5,978	1987	7,500
1976	6,271	1988	7,706
1977	5,906	1989	7,872
1978	5,983	1990	7,946
1979	6,578	1991	8,142
1980	7,137	1992	7,915
1981	7,194	1993	7,821
1982	7,143	1994	7,876
1983	6,713		

* Data are in thousands.
Source: U.S. Bureau of the Census, at http://www.census.gov.

a. Prepare a time-series plot of these data. On the basis of this graph, do you think there is a trend in the data? Explain.

b. Look at the autocorrelation structure of larceny thefts for lags of 1, 2, 3, 4, and 5. Do the autocorrelation coefficients fall quickly toward zero? Demonstrate that the critical value for r_k is 0.471. Explain what these results tell you about a trend in the data.

c. On the basis of what is found in parts *a* and *b*, suggest a forecasting method from Table 2–1 that you think might be appropriate for this series.

9. Use exploratory data analysis to determine whether there is a trend and/or seasonality in mobile home shipments (MHS). The data by quarter are shown in the following table:

(c2p9)

Year	Q1	Q2	Q3	Q4
1981	54.9	70.1	65.8	50.2
1982	53.3	67.9	63.1	55.3
1983	63.3	81.5	81.7	69.2
1984	67.8	82.7	79.0	66.2
1985	62.3	79.3	76.5	65.5
1986	58.1	66.8	63.4	56.1
1987	51.9	62.8	64.7	53.5
1988	47.0	60.5	59.2	51.6
1989	48.1	55.1	50.3	44.5
1990	43.3	51.7	50.5	42.6
1991	35.4	47.4	47.2	40.9
1992	43.0	52.8	57.0	57.6
1993	56.4	64.3	67.1	66.4
1994	69.1	78.7	78.7	77.5
1995	79.2	86.8	87.6	86.4

Data are in thousands.

On the basis of your analysis, do you think there is a significant trend in MHS? Is there seasonality? What forecasting methods might be appropriate for MHS according to the guidelines in Table 2–1?

10. Housing starts are often considered an important determinant of the future health of the economy. Thus, there is widespread interest in being able to forecast private housing starts (PHS). Quarterly data for PHS are shown in the following table in thousands of units:

(c2p10) **Quarterly Data for Private Housing Starts (In Thousands)**

Date	PHS	Date	PHS
Feb-1980	150.9	Nov-1982	184.1
May-1980	203.3	Feb-1983	202.9
Aug-1980	272.6	May-1983	322.3
Nov-1980	225.3	Aug-1983	307.5
Feb-1981	166.5	Nov-1983	234.8
May-1981	229.9	Feb-1984	236.5
Aug-1981	184.8	May-1984	332.6
Nov-1981	124.1	Aug-1984	280.3
Feb-1982	113.6	Nov-1984	234.7
May-1982	178.2	Feb-1985	215.3
Aug-1982	186.7	May-1985	317.9

(*continued*)

(c2p10) **Quarterly Data for Private Housing Starts (In Thousands)   (Continued)**

Date	PHS	Date	PHS
Aug-1985	295.0	Nov-1992	238.8
Nov-1985	244.1	Feb-1993	213.2
Feb-1986	234.1	May-1993	323.7
May-1986	369.4	Aug-1993	309.3
Aug-1986	325.4	Nov-1993	279.4
Nov-1986	250.6	Feb-1994	252.6
Feb-1987	241.4	May-1994	354.2
May-1987	346.5	Aug-1994	325.7
Aug-1987	321.3	Nov-1994	265.9
Nov-1987	237.1	Feb-1995	214.2
Feb-1988	219.7	May-1995	296.7
May-1988	323.7	Aug-1995	308.2
Aug-1988	293.4	Nov-1995	257.2
Nov-1988	244.6	Feb-1996	240.0
Feb-1989	212.7	May-1996	344.5
May-1989	302.1	Aug-1996	324.0
Aug-1989	272.1	Nov-1996	252.4
Nov-1989	216.5	Feb-1997	237.8
Feb-1990	217.0	May-1997	324.5
May-1990	271.3	Aug-1997	314.5
Aug-1990	233.0	Nov-1997	256.8
Nov-1990	173.6	Feb-1998	258.4
Feb-1991	146.7	May-1998	360.4
May-1991	254.1	Aug-1998	348.0
Aug-1991	239.8	Nov-1998	304.6
Nov-1991	199.8	Feb-1999	294.1
Feb-1992	218.5	May-1999	377.1
Ma-1992	296.4	Aug-1999	355.6
Aug-1992	276.4	Nov-1999	308.1

a. Prepare a time-series plot of PHS. Describe what you see in this plot in terms of trend and seasonality.

b. Calculate and plot the first eight autocorrelation coefficients for PHS. What does this autocorrelation structure suggest about trend and seasonality?

c. De-trend the data by calculating first differences:

$$DPHS_t = PHS_t - PHS_{t-1}$$

Calculate and plot the first eight autocorrelation coefficients for DPHS. Is there a trend in DPHS? Do the values of r_4 and r_8 suggest seasonality? Explain.

11. Exercise 9 of Chapter 1 includes data on the Japanese exchange rate (EXRJ) by month. On the basis of a time-series plot of these data and the autocorrelation structure of EXRJ, would you say the data are stationary? Explain your answer. (c2p11)

3 MOVING AVERAGES AND EXPONENTIAL SMOOTHING

Consider the situation facing a manager who must periodically forecast the inventories for hundreds of products. Each day, or week, or month, updated forecasts for the many inventories are required within a short time period. While it might well be possible to develop sophisticated forecasting models for each of the items, in many cases some very simple short-term forecasting tools are adequate for the job.

A manager facing such a task is likely to use some form of time-series *smoothing*. All the time-series smoothing methods use a form of weighted average of past observations to smooth up-and-down movements, that is, some statistical method of suppressing short-term fluctuations. The assumption underlying these methods is that the fluctuations in past values represent random departures from some smooth curve that, once identified, can plausibly be extrapolated into the future to produce a forecast or series of forecasts.

We will examine five basic smoothing techniques in this chapter. All five of these have the common characteristic that only a past history of the time series to be forecast is necessary to produce the forecast. Further, all are based on the concept that there is some underlying pattern to the data; that is, all time-series data to be forecast are assumed to have some cycles or fluctuations that tend to recur. The five methods, to be examined in turn, are:

1. Moving averages
2. Simple exponential smoothing
3. Holt's exponential smoothing
4. Winters' exponential smoothing
5. Adaptive–response-rate single exponential smoothing

Moving Averages

The simple statistical method of moving averages may mimic some data better than a complicated mathematical function.

The simple statistical method of moving averages may mimic some data better than a complicated mathematical function. Figure 3–1 shows the exchange rate between the Japanese yen and the U.S. dollar from 1983Q1 through 1998Q4. Figure 3–1 does not exhibit a simple linear, exponential, or quadratic trend similar to those we will examine in Chapters 4 and 5. Instead, the series appears to show substantial randomness, which we may be able to eliminate with a technique that averages the most recent values.

To illustrate how a moving average is used, consider Table 3–1, which displays the exchange rate between the Japanese yen and the U.S. dollar shown in Figure 3–1. To calculate the three-quarter moving average first requires that we sum the first three observations (239.3, 239.8, and 236.1). This three-quarter total is then divided by 3 to obtain 238.40, which is the first number in the "Three-Quarter Moving Average" column. This "smoothed" number, 238.40, becomes the forecast for 1983Q4.

The final value in the "Three-Quarter Moving Average" column (130.29) is the forecast for 1999Q1; it was arrived at by summing the final three values in the "Actual" column and then dividing by 3 ($390.87/3 = 130.29$).

The five-quarter moving averages displayed in the same table are calculated in like manner: the first moving average of 234.39 is calculated by summing the first five actual values and dividing by 5:

$$\frac{239.3 + 239.8 + 236.1 + 232 + 224.75}{5} = \frac{1,179.98}{5} = 234.39$$

Thus, 234.39 becomes the forecast for the next period (1984Q2). The five entries from Dec-1997 through Dec-1998 in the "Actual" column are averaged to give the final five-quarter moving average:

$$\frac{129.92 + 133.39 + 139.95 + 135.72 + 115.2}{5} = \frac{654.18}{5} = 130.84$$

FIGURE 3–1

Exchange Rate with Japan in Yen per U.S. Dollar (c3f2)

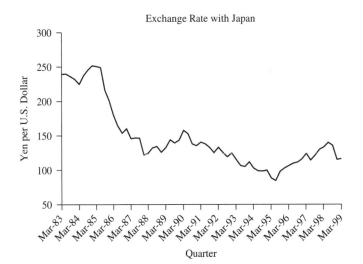

Exchange Rate with Japan

This final moving average serves as the forecast for 1999Q1.

Obviously, three- and five-quarter moving averages are not the only kinds of moving averages. We could calculate seven- or nine-quarter moving averages if we wished, or eight- or ten-quarter averages, and so on. The choice of the interval for the moving average depends on the length of the underlying cycle or pattern in the original data. If we believe the actual data to be exhibiting a cycle that recurs every four periods, we would choose a four-period moving average in order to best dampen the short-run fluctuation. The simplest naive model of Chapter 1 used each period's actual value as the forecast for the next period; you could correctly think of this model as a one-period moving average, that is, a special case of the model we are examining here.

The choice of the interval for the moving average depends on the length of the underlying cycle or pattern in the original data.

In order to compute whether the three-quarter or five-quarter moving average is the better forecasting model, it is useful to compute the root-mean-squared error (RMSE) as we calculated it in Chapter 1. Table 3–1 shows the RMSE for both forecasts at the bottom of the table. The RMSE of 13.47 for the three-quarter moving average is less than the 17.23 calculated for the five-quarter case, and so we might conclude that the better forecast in this particular case is generated by the three-quarter model.

In preparing the forecasts for 1999Q1 it was assumed that the actual value for that quarter was unknown. However, the actual value for that quarter is known in this

---

TABLE 3–1   Exchange Rate with Japan and Two Moving-Average Forecasts (c3f2)

Period	Actual	Three-Quarter Moving Average	Three-Quarter Moving-Average Forecast	Five-Quarter Moving Average	Five-Quarter Moving-Average Forecast
Mar-1983	239.3	Missing	Missing	Missing	Missing
Jun-1983	239.8	Missing	Missing	Missing	Missing
Sep-1983	236.10	238.40	Missing	Missing	Missing
Dec-1983	232.00	235.97	238.40	Missing	Missing
Mar-1984	224.75	230.95	235.97	234.39	Missing
Jun-1984	237.45	231.40	230.95	234.02	234.39
Sep-1984	245.40	235.87	231.40	235.14	234.02
Dec-1984	251.58	244.81	235.87	238.24	235.14
Mar-1985	250.70	249.23	244.81	241.98	238.24
Jun-1985	248.95	250.41	249.23	246.82	241.98
Sep-1985	216.00	238.55	250.41	242.53	246.82
Dec-1985	200.60	221.85	238.55	233.57	242.53
Mar-1986	179.65	198.75	221.85	219.18	233.57
Jun-1986	163.95	181.40	198.75	201.83	219.18
Sep-1986	153.63	165.74	181.40	182.77	201.83
Dec-1986	160.10	159.23	165.74	171.59	182.77
Mar-1987	145.65	153.13	159.23	160.60	171.59
Jun-1987	146.75	150.83	153.13	154.02	160.60
Sep-1987	146.35	146.25	150.83	150.50	154.02
Dec-1987	122.00	138.37	146.25	144.17	150.50
Mar-1988	124.50	130.95	138.37	137.05	144.17
Jun-1988	132.20	126.23	130.95	134.36	137.05
Sep-1988	134.30	130.33	126.23	131.87	134.36
Dec-1988	125.90	130.80	130.33	127.78	131.87
Mar-1989	132.55	130.92	130.80	129.89	127.78

(continued)

TABLE 3–1   *(Continued)*

Period	Actual	Three-Quarter Moving Average	Three-Quarter Moving-Average Forecast	Five-Quarter Moving Average	Five-Quarter Moving-Average Forecast
Jun-1989	143.95	134.13	130.92	133.78	129.89
Sep-1989	139.35	138.62	134.13	135.21	133.78
Dec-1989	143.40	142.23	138.62	137.03	135.21
Mar-1990	157.65	146.80	142.23	143.38	137.03
Jun-1990	152.85	151.30	146.80	147.44	143.38
Sep-1990	137.95	149.48	151.30	146.24	147.44
Dec-1990	135.40	142.07	149.48	145.45	146.24
Mar-1991	140.55	137.97	142.07	144.88	145.45
Jun-1991	138.15	138.03	137.97	140.98	144.88
Sep-1991	132.95	137.22	138.03	137.00	140.98
Dec-1991	125.25	132.12	137.22	134.46	137.00
Mar-1992	133.05	130.42	132.12	133.99	134.46
Jun-1992	125.55	127.95	130.42	130.99	133.99
Sep-1992	119.25	125.95	127.95	127.21	130.99
Dec-1992	124.65	123.15	125.95	125.55	127.21
Mar-1993	115.35	119.75	123.15	123.57	125.55
Jun-1993	106.51	115.50	119.75	118.26	123.57
Sep-1993	105.10	108.99	115.50	114.17	118.26
Dec-1993	111.89	107.83	108.99	112.70	114.17
Mar-1994	102.80	106.60	107.83	108.33	112.70
Jun-1994	98.95	104.55	106.60	105.05	108.33
Sep-1994	98.59	100.11	104.55	103.47	105.05
Dec-1994	99.83	99.12	100.11	102.41	103.47
Mar-1995	88.38	95.60	99.12	97.71	102.41
Jun-1995	84.77	90.99	95.60	94.10	97.71
Sep-1995	98.18	90.44	90.99	93.95	94.10
Dec-1995	102.91	95.29	90.44	94.81	93.95
Mar-1996	106.49	102.53	95.29	96.15	94.81
Jun-1996	109.88	106.43	102.53	100.45	96.15
Sep-1996	111.45	109.27	106.43	105.78	100.45
Dec-1996	115.98	112.44	109.27	109.34	105.78
Mar-1997	123.97	117.13	112.44	113.55	109.34
Jun-1997	114.30	118.08	117.13	115.12	113.55
Sep-1997	121.44	119.90	118.08	117.43	115.12
Dec-1997	129.92	121.89	119.90	121.12	117.43
Mar-1998	133.39	128.25	121.89	124.60	121.12
Jun-1998	139.95	134.42	128.25	127.80	124.60
Sep-1998	135.72	136.35	134.42	132.08	127.80
Dec-1998	115.20	130.29	136.35	130.84	132.08
Mar-1999	*116.48**	Missing	130.29	Missing	130.84

*Value assumed not to be known in developing moving-average forecasts.

	RMSE for Mar-1983–Dec-1998
Three-Quarter Moving-Average Model	13.47
Five-Quarter Moving-Average Model	17.23
	Mean Absolute Percentage Error for 1996Q1
Three-Quarter Moving-Average Model	7.05%
Five-Quarter Moving-Average Model	9.07%

situation and is shown in Table 3–1. Thus, we can see which of the two moving-average forecasts developed above was really the best for 1999Q1. The error for the three-quarter moving-average forecast was 7.05 percent, while for the five-quarter moving-average forecast the error was 9.07 percent.

The three- and five-quarter moving averages are shown graphically in Figures 3–2 and 3–3, respectively. Notice in Figures 3–2 and 3–3 that the peaks and troughs of the actual series are different from those for either moving average. This failure of the moving averages to predict peaks and troughs is one of the shortcomings of moving-average models.

FIGURE 3–2

Three-Quarter Moving-Average Forecast of the U.S. Exchange Rate with Japan (c3f2)

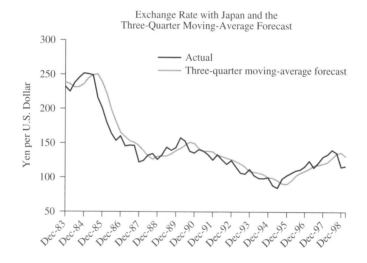

FIGURE 3–3

Five-Quarter Moving-Average Forecast of the U.S. Exchange Rate with Japan (c3f2)

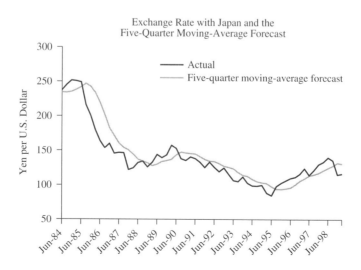

The moving-average forecasting method has fooled more than one forecaster by appearing to identify a cycle.

One final and important observation: The moving-average forecasting method has fooled more than one forecaster by appearing to identify a cycle when, in fact, no cycle was present in the actual data. Such an occurrence can be understood if you think of an actual data series as being simply a series of random numbers. Since any moving average is serially correlated, because a number of contiguous periods have been averaged, *any* sequence of random numbers could appear to exhibit cyclical fluctuation.[1]

Simple Exponential Smoothing

With exponential smoothing, the forecast value at any time is a weighted average of all the available previous values.

Simple exponential smoothing, like moving averages, uses only past values of a time series to forecast future values of the same series and is properly employed when there is no trend or seasonality present in the data. With exponential smoothing, the forecast value at any time is a weighted average of all the available previous values; the weights decline geometrically as you go back in time. Moving-average forecasting gives equal weights to the past values included in each average; exponential smoothing gives more weight to the recent observations and less to the older observations. The weights are made to decline geometrically with the age of the observation to conform to the argument that the most recent observations contain the most relevant information, so that they should be accorded proportionately more influence than older observations.

Exponential smoothing proceeds as do moving averages by smoothing past values of the series; the calculations for producing exponentially smoothed forecasts can be expressed as an equation. The weight of the most recent observation is assigned by multiplying the observed value by α, the next most recent observation by $(1 - \alpha)\alpha$, the next observation by $(1 - \alpha)^2\alpha$, and so on. The number we choose for α is called the *smoothing constant.*

The number we choose for α is called the *smoothing constant.*

The simple exponential smoothing model can be written in the following manner:

$$F_{t+1} = \alpha X_t + (1 - \alpha)F_t \tag{3.1}$$

where[2]

F_{t+1} = Forecast value for period $t + 1$

α = Smoothing constant $(0 < \alpha < 1)$

X_t = Actual value now (in period t)

F_t = Forecast (i.e., smoothed) value for period t

---

[1]This incorrect conclusion is sometimes called the *Slutsky-Yule effect,* named after Eugen Slutsky and G. Udny Yule, who first pointed out the possibility of making a mistake in this manner. See Eugen E. Slutsky, "The Summation of Random Causes as the Source of Cyclic Processes," *Econometrica* 5 (1937), pp. 105–46; and G. Udny Yule, "On a Method of Investigating Periodicities in Disturbed Series, with Special Reference to Wolfer's Sunspot Numbers," Royal Society of London, *Philosophical Transactions* (1927), pp. 267–98.

[2]Our notation throughout the chapter for exponential smoothing follows approximately the notation found in Everette S. Gardner, "Exponential Smoothing: The State of the Art," *Journal of Forecasting* 4, no. 1 (1985), pp. 1–28. This article contains a very complete description of different forms of smoothing that are in common use and explains (with advanced mathematics) that there may be theoretical advantages for employing smoothing in situations where it can be shown that certain assumptions concerning the probability distribution of the series are met.

In using this equation the forecaster does not need to deal with every actual past value at every step; only the exponentially smoothed value for the last period and the actual value for this period are necessary. An alternative way of writing Equation 3.1 results from rearranging the terms as follows:

$$F_{t+1} = \alpha X_t + (1 - \alpha)F_t \tag{3.2}$$

$$= \alpha X_t + F_t - \alpha F_t$$

$$= F_t + \alpha (X_t - F_t)$$

From this form we can see that the exponential smoothing model "learns" from past errors. The forecast value at period $t + 1$ is increased if the actual value for period t is greater than it was forecast to be, and it is decreased if X_t is less than F_t. Forecasting the value for the next period (F_{t+1}) requires us to know only the actual value for this period (X_t) and the forecast value for this period (F_t). However, all historical observations are included, as follows:

$$F_{t+1} = \alpha X_t + (1 - \alpha)F_t \tag{3.3}$$

and, $F_t = \alpha X_{t-1} + (1 - \alpha)F_{t-1}$

therefore, $F_{t+1} = \alpha X_t + (1 - \alpha)\alpha X_{t-1} + (1 - \alpha)^2 F_{t-1}$

and, $F_{t-1} = \alpha X_{t-2} + (1 - \alpha)F_{t-2}$

thus, $F_{t+1} = \alpha X_t + (1 - \alpha)\alpha X_{t-1} + (1 - \alpha)^2 \alpha X_{t-2} + (1 - \alpha)^3 F_{t-2}$

We could continue this expansion to include X terms as far back as we have data, but this is probably far enough to help you see how the weights for previous time periods become smaller and smaller at a rate that depends on the value of α, as will be shown in the following tables for two alternative values of α.

The value of the smoothing constant α must be between 0 and 1. The value of the smoothing constant cannot be *equal* to 0 or 1; if it is, the entire idea of exponential smoothing is negated. If a value close to 1 is chosen, recent values of the time series are weighted heavily relative to those of the distant past when the smoothed values are calculated. Likewise, if the value of α is chosen close to 0, then the values of the time series in the distant past are given weights comparable to those given the recent values. The rate at which the weights decrease can be seen from their values for an α of 0.1:

| | $\alpha = 0.1$ | |
Time	*Calculation*	*Weight*
t		0.1
$t - 1$	0.9×0.1	0.090
$t - 2$	$0.9 \times 0.9 \times 0.1$	0.081
$t - 3$	$0.9 \times 0.9 \times 0.9 \times 0.1$	0.073
$\vdots$		
Total		1.000

Regardless of the smoothing constant chosen, the weights will eventually sum to 1. Whether the sum of the weights converges on 1 quickly or slowly depends on the smoothing constant chosen. If, for example, we choose a smoothing constant of 0.9, the sum of the weights will approach 1 much more rapidly than when the smoothing constant is 0.1:

Time	$\alpha = 0.9$ Calculation	Weight
t		0.9
$t - 1$	0.1×0.9	0.09
$t - 2$	$0.1 \times 0.1 \times 0.9$	0.009
$t - 3$	$0.1 \times 0.1 \times 0.1 \times 0.9$	0.0009
⋮		
Total		1.000

As a guide in choosing α, select values close to 0 if the series has a great deal of random variation; select values close to 1 if you wish the forecast values to depend strongly on recent changes in the actual values. The root-mean-squared error (RMSE) is often used as the criterion for assigning an appropriate smoothing constant; the smoothing constant giving the smallest RMSE would be selected as the model likely to produce the smallest error in generating additional forecasts. In practice, relatively small values of alpha (α) generally work best when simple exponential smoothing is the most appropriate model.

In practice, relatively small values of alpha (α) generally work best when simple exponential smoothing is the most appropriate model.

The following example will demonstrate the technique. Suppose we wish to forecast the University of Michigan Index of Consumer Sentiment for September 2000 based on data from Jan-1995 through Aug-2000. These values are shown in the "Actual" column of Table 3–2 for Jan-1995 through Sep-2000. Since no previous forecast is available for the first period (January 1995), we have arbitrarily chosen to use 95.93; thus 95.93 becomes the first entry in the "Forecast" column. This process of choosing an initial value for the smoothed series is called *initializing* the model, or *warming up* the model.[3] All the other values in the "Forecast" column were calculated by using Equation 3.1 with a smoothing constant (α) of 0.60, which was selected by ForecastX™ to minimize the RMSE. The actual and forecast values are shown in Figure 3–4.

---

[3]The choice of a starting value in exponential smoothing models has been a matter of some discussion, with little empirical evidence favoring any particular approach. R. G. Brown first suggested using the mean of the data for the starting value, and this suggestion has been quite popular in actual practice. A linear regression (like that described in Chapter 4) is sometimes used when selecting starting values for seasonal factors, and time-series decomposition (as discussed in Chapter 6) has also been used. If the data include a trend, backcasting is sometimes used to select a starting value; but if the trend is erratic, this sometimes leads to negative starting values, which make little sense. A discussion of the various alternatives (including using the first value in the series or using the mean of the series, which are both popular in practice) appears in the Gardner article (footnote 2).

TABLE 3–2   Simple Exponential Smoothing Forecast of the University of Michigan Index of Consumer Sentiment (c3t2)

Date	Actual	Forecast	Error	Date	Actual	Forecast	Error
Jan-1995	97.60	95.93	1.67	Dec-1997	102.10	106.55	−4.45
Feb-1995	95.10	96.93	−1.83	Jan-1998	106.60	103.89	2.71
Mar-1995	90.30	95.83	−5.53	Feb-1998	110.40	105.51	4.89
Apr-1995	92.50	92.52	−0.02	Mar-1998	106.50	108.44	−1.94
May-1995	89.80	92.51	−2.71	Apr-1998	108.70	107.28	1.42
Jun-1995	92.70	90.89	1.81	May-1998	106.50	108.13	−1.63
Jul-1995	94.40	91.97	2.43	Jun-1998	105.60	107.15	−1.55
Aug-1995	96.20	93.42	2.78	Jul-1998	105.20	106.22	−1.02
Sep-1995	88.90	95.09	−6.19	Aug-1998	104.40	105.61	−1.21
Oct-1995	90.20	91.38	−1.18	Sep-1998	100.90	104.89	−3.99
Nov-1995	88.20	90.68	−2.48	Oct-1998	97.40	102.50	−5.10
Dec-1995	91.00	89.19	1.81	Nov-1998	102.70	99.45	3.25
Jan-1996	89.30	90.27	−0.97	Dec-1998	100.50	101.39	−0.89
Feb-1996	88.50	89.69	−1.19	Jan-1999	103.90	100.86	3.04
Mar-1996	93.70	88.98	4.72	Feb-1999	108.10	102.68	5.42
Apr-1996	92.70	91.80	0.90	Mar-1999	105.70	105.92	−0.22
May-1996	89.40	92.34	−2.94	Apr-1999	104.60	105.79	−1.19
Jun-1996	92.40	90.58	1.82	May-1999	106.80	105.08	1.72
Jul-1996	94.70	91.67	3.03	Jun-1999	107.30	106.11	1.19
Aug-1996	95.30	93.48	1.82	Jul-1999	106.00	106.82	−0.82
Sep-1996	94.70	94.57	0.13	Aug-1999	104.50	106.33	−1.83
Oct-1996	96.50	94.65	1.85	Sep-1999	107.20	105.23	1.97
Nov-1996	99.20	95.76	3.44	Oct-1999	103.20	106.41	−3.21
Dec-1996	96.90	97.82	−0.92	Nov-1999	107.20	104.49	2.71
Jan-1997	97.40	97.27	0.13	Dec-1999	105.40	106.11	−0.71
Feb-1997	99.70	97.35	2.35	Jan-2000	112.00	105.69	6.31
Mar-1997	100.00	98.75	1.25	Feb-2000	111.30	109.46	1.84
Apr-1997	101.40	99.50	1.90	Mar-2000	107.10	110.56	−3.46
May-1997	103.20	100.64	2.56	Apr-2000	109.20	108.49	0.71
Jun-1997	104.50	102.17	2.33	May-2000	110.70	108.92	1.78
Jul-1997	107.10	103.56	3.54	Jun-2000	106.40	109.98	−3.58
Aug-1997	104.40	105.68	−1.28	Jul-2000	108.30	107.84	0.46
Sep-1997	106.00	104.91	1.09	Aug-2000	107.30	108.11	−0.81
Oct-1997	105.60	105.56	0.04	Sep-2000		107.63	
Nov-1997	107.20	105.59	1.61				

Alpha = 0.60

Root-mean-squared error (RMSE) = 2.65

Historical data for Aug-2000 were used to forecast Sep-2000

Let us illustrate the calculation of the forecast value for March 1995 by using Equation 3.1 as follows:

$$F_{t+1} = \alpha X_t + (1 - \alpha)F_t$$
$$F_{2+1} = \alpha X_2 + (1 - \alpha)F_2$$
$$F_3 = 0.6(95.10) + (1 - 0.6)(96.93) = 95.832$$

FIGURE 3–4

*A Simple
Exponential
Smoothing
Forecast of the
University of
Michigan Index
of Consumer
Sentiment
(c3t2)*

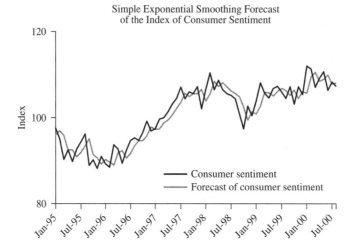

Simple Exponential Smoothing Forecast
of the Index of Consumer Sentiment

In this forecast an alpha of 0.6 was selected to minimize the root-mean-squared error (RMSE).

This smoothed value of 95.832 is the forecast for March ($t = 3$). Once actual data for March become available, the model is used to forecast April, and so on.

Taking this one step further, assume now that the actual sales figure for March 1995 has become available. In Table 3–2 we see that this figure is 90.3. We now wish to forecast the sales figure for $t = 4$ (April 1995). The technique applied before is repeated:

$$F_{t+1} = \alpha X_t + (1 - \alpha)F_t$$

$$F_{3+1} = \alpha X_3 + (1 - \alpha)F_3$$

$$F_4 = 0.6(90.3) + (1-0.6)(95.832) = 92.51$$

The error for the March 1995 forecast (rounded) is calculated as:

$$e_3 = X_3 - F_3 = 90.30 - 95.83 = -5.53$$

The error for the April 1995 forecast (rounded) is calculated as:

$$e_4 = X_4 - F_4 = 92.50 - 92.52 = -0.02$$

The predominant reason for using simple smoothing is that it requires a limited quantity of data and it is simpler than most other forecasting methods. Its limitations, however, are that its forecasts lag behind the actual data and it has no ability to adjust for any trend or seasonality in the data.

Holt's Exponential Smoothing

Two further extensions of the smoothing model can be used in order to bring the forecast values closer to the values observed if the data series exhibits a trend and/or seasonality (the first extension is discussed in this section, and the second in the following section). In real-world situations one or both of these techniques are often used because real-world data are not very often so simple in their patterns that simple exponential smoothing provides an accurate forecast.

The first extension is to adjust the smoothing model for any trend in the data; with a trend in the data the simple smoothing model will have large errors that usually tend from positive to negative or vice versa. When a trend exists, the forecast may then be improved by adjusting for this trend by using a form of smoothing named after its originator, C. C. Holt. Holt's two-parameter exponential smoothing method is an extension of simple exponential smoothing; it adds a growth factor (or trend factor) to the smoothing equation as a way of adjusting for the trend. Three equations and two smoothing constants are used in the model.

Holt's two-parameter exponential smoothing method is an extension of simple exponential smoothing; it adds a growth factor (or trend factor) to the smoothing equation as a way of adjusting for the trend

$$F_{t+1} = \alpha X_t + (1 - \alpha)(F_t + T_t) \qquad (3.4)$$

$$T_{t+1} = \beta(F_{t+1} - F_t) + (1 - \beta)T_t \qquad (3.5)$$

$$H_{t+m} = F_{t+1} + mT_{t+1} \qquad (3.6)$$

where:

F_{t+1} = Smoothed value for period $t + 1$

α = Smoothing constant for the data $(0 < \alpha < 1)$

X_t = Actual value now (in period t)

F_t = Forecast (i.e., smoothed) value for time period t

T_{t+1} = Trend estimate

β = Smoothing constant for the trend estimate $(0 < \beta < 1)$

m = Number of periods ahead to be forecast

H_{t+m} = Holt's forecast value for period $t + m$

Equation 3.4 adjusts F_{t+1} for the growth of the previous period, T_t, by adding T_t to the smoothed value of the previous period, F_t. The trend estimate is calculated in Equation 3.5, where the difference of the last two smoothed values is calculated. Because these two values have already been smoothed, the difference between them is assumed to be an estimate of trend in the data. The second smoothing constant, β in Equation 3.5, is arrived at by using the same principle employed in simple exponential smoothing. The most recent trend $(F_{t+1} - F_t)$, is weighted by β and the last previous smoothed trend, T_t, is weighted by $(1 - \beta)$. The sum of the weighted values is the new smoothed trend value T_{t+1}.

Equation 3.6 is used to forecast m periods into the future by adding the product of the trend component, T_{t+1}, and the number of periods to forecast, m, to the current value of the smoothed data F_{t+1}.

TABLE 3–3   Holt's Exponential Smoothing Forecast of Standard & Poor's 500 Returns (c3t3)

Date	Original Data	Fitted Data	Error	Date	Original Data	Fitted Data	Error
Mar-1970	88.58	86.25	2.33	Jun-1998	3,240.48	3,151.98	88.50
Jun-1970	78.13	91.01	−12.88	Sep-1998	3,017.14	3,391.08	−373.94
Sep-1970	83.37	84.09	−0.71	Dec-1998	3,417.08	3,277.53	139.55
Dec-1970	90.64	84.80	5.84	Mar-1999	3,735.15	3,512.80	222.36
Mar-1971	101.92	90.60	11.32	Jun-1999	3,949.49	3,835.32	114.17
Jun-1971	106.32	101.64	4.67	Sep-1999	3,885.27	4,106.61	−221.34
Sep-1971	103.52	109.18	−5.66	Dec-1999	4,184.12	4,129.80	54.31
Dec-1971	103.41	109.25	−5.84	Mar-2000	4,234.45	4,337.05	−102.60
Mar-1972	113.99	108.30	5.69	Jun-2000	4,315.00	4,428.41	−113.41
Jun-1972	117.20	115.58	1.62				
Sep-1972	119.76	120.52	−0.77				
Dec-1972	126.96	123.82	3.14	*Accuracy Measure*			*Value*
⋮	⋮	⋮	⋮	Mean absolute percentage error (MAPE)			5.51%
Mar-1996	1,788.77	1,714.45	74.32	R-squared			99.59%
Jun-1996	1,866.24	1,847.44	18.80	Root-mean-squared error			66.95
Sep-1996	1,863.32	1,947.97	−84.65				
Dec-1996	2,085.27	1,969.46	115.81	*Method Statistic*			*Value*
Mar-1997	2,219.67	2,136.63	83.04				
Jun-1997	2,422.28	2,295.81	126.47	Method selected	Double exponential smoothing—Holt		
Sep-1997	2,688.49	2,502.27	186.22	Alpha			0.64
Dec-1997	2,737.89	2,775.69	−37.79	Gamma			0.24
Mar-1998	3,029.98	2,900.51	129.47				

Please note carefully that the ForecastX™ package assigns the name *Gamma* to the smoothing factor for the trend estimate.

This method accurately accounts for any linear trend in the data.[4] Table 3–3 illustrates the application of Holt's model to the Standard & Poor's (S&P) 500 returns. The two smoothing constants are $\alpha = 0.64$ and $\beta = 0.24$. Two starting values are needed: one for the first smoothed value and another for the first trend value. The initial smoothed value is often a recent actual value available; the initial trend value is often 0.00 if no past data are available (see footnote 3).

For the S&P 500 data, Equations 3.4 through 3.6 can be used to calculate the Holt's forecast for Jun-1970. To do so we will arbitrarily select the first actual value as our initial smoothed value ($F_1 = 88.58$) and 4 as our initial trend ($T_1 = 4$). The smoothed

---

[4]All trends, of course, do not have to be linear, and there are smoothing models that can account for multiplicative trend. In this chapter we are examining only a subset of the number of possible smoothing models. For a listing of smoothing models, see Carl C. Pegels, "Exponential Forecasting: Some New Variations," *Management Science* 15, no. 12 (1969), pp. 311–15, or the Gardner article (1985). Both of these articles cover many smoothing models, including some that are very rarely used in actual practice.

value for period 2 (Jun-1970) is calculated by:

$$F_{t+1} = \alpha X_t + (1 - \alpha)(F_t + T_t)$$
$$F_2 = 0.64(X_1) + (1 - 0.64)(F_1 + T_1)$$
$$= 0.64(88.58) + (0.36)(88.58 + 4) = 90.02$$

The trend estimate for period 2 is calculated as:

$$T_{t+1} = \beta(F_{t+1} - F_t) + (1 - \beta)T_t$$
$$T_3 = 0.24(F_2 - F_1) + (1 - 0.24)T_1$$
$$= (0.24)(90.02 - 88.58) + 0.76(4) = 3.3856$$

The forecast for period 2 is calculated as:

$$H_{t+m} = F_{t+1} + mT_{t+1}$$
$$H_2 = F_2 + 1T_2$$
$$= 90.02 + (1)(3.3856) = 93.4056$$

Our calculated forecast for Jun-1970 differs from what you see in Table 3–3 by 2.4. This is because our arbitrary selection of seed values differs from those selected by ForecastX™. Over the course of 122 quarters the effect of differing seed values would diminish to almost nothing, and if we continued the hand calculations our final forecasts would be virtually identical to those in Table 3–3.

Figure 3–5 shows a plot of both the actual values and the forecast values generated by this model. Some commercially available forecasting packages allow the forecaster to minimize the value of RMSE (or some similar summary statistic) by automatically adjusting the smoothing constants (ForecastX™ automatically adjusts). This, of course, is preferable to making numerous adjustments by hand. We picked the smoothing constants here using ForecastX™.

FIGURE 3–5

Standard & Poor's 500 Return and a Holt's Forecast (Alpha = 0.64; Gamma = 0.24) (c3t3)

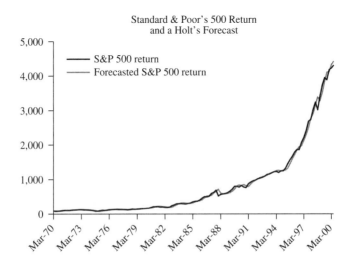

Standard & Poor's 500 Return and a Holt's Forecast

— S&P 500 return
— Forecasted S&P 500 return

Holt's form of exponential smoothing is then best used when the data show some linear trend but little or no seasonality. A descriptive name for Holt's smoothing might be *linear-trend smoothing*.

Winters' Exponential Smoothing

Winters' exponential smoothing model is the second extension of the basic smoothing model; it is used for data that exhibit both trend and seasonality.

Winters' exponential smoothing model is the second extension of the basic smoothing model; it is used for data that exhibit both trend and seasonality. It is a three-parameter model that is an extension of Holt's model. An additional equation adjusts the model for the seasonal component. The four equations necessary for Winters' model are:

$$F_t = \alpha X_t / S_{t-p} + (1 - \alpha)(F_{t-1} + T_{t-1}) \tag{3.7}$$

$$S_t = \beta X_t / F_t + (1 - \beta)S_{t-p} \tag{3.8}$$

$$T_t = \gamma(F_t - F_{t-1}) + (1 - \gamma)T_{t-1} \tag{3.9}$$

$$W_{t+m} = (F_t + mT_t)\, S_{t+m-p} \tag{3.10}$$

where:

F_t = Smoothed value for period t

α = Smoothing constant for the data $(0 < \alpha < 1)$

X_t = Actual value now (in period t)

F_{t-1} = Average experience of series smoothed to period $t - 1$

T_{t+1} = Trend estimate

S_t = Seasonality estimate

β = Smoothing constant for seasonality estimate $(0 < \beta < 1)$

γ = Smoothing constant for trend estimate $(0 < \gamma < 1)$

m = Number of periods in the forecast lead period

p = Number of periods in the seasonal cycle

W_{t+m} = Winters' forecast for m periods into the future

Equation 3.7 updates the smoothed series for both trend and seasonality; note that the equation is only slightly different from Equation 3.4 in Holt's model. In Equation 3.7, X_t is divided by S_{t-p} to adjust for seasonality; this operation deseasonalizes the data or removes any seasonal effects left in the data. It is easy to see how this deseasonalizes the data if you consider what happens when S_{t-p} is greater than 1, as it would be when the value in period $t - p$ is greater than average in its seasonality. Dividing X_t by S_{t-p} reduces the original value by a percentage equal to the percentage that the seasonality of the period was above the average. An opposite adjustment would take place if the period were below average in terms of seasonality.

The seasonality estimate itself is smoothed in Equation 3.8, and the trend estimate is smoothed in Equation 3.9; each of these processes is exactly the same as in simple exponential smoothing. The final equation, 3.10, is used to compute the forecast for m periods into the future; the procedure is almost identical to that in Holt's model (Equation 3.6).

FIGURE 3–6

Quarterly Light Truck Production in Units (TS) and a Winters' Exponential Smoothing Forecast of Light Truck Production (Alpha = 0.41, Beta = 0.37, and Gamma = 0.03) (c3t4)

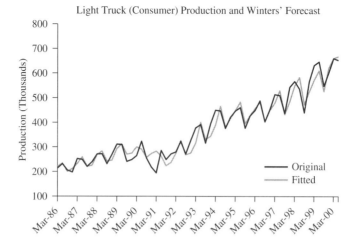

To illustrate Winters' exponential smoothing we will use data for the production of light trucks in the United States by quarter. Light truck production is quite seasonal, with quarter 2 typically being the strongest production quarter (this includes the months of April, May, and June). As you can see in Figure 3–6, there has been an overall upward trend in the data since our 1986Q1 starting point. You have seen above how to apply the equations to do a few of the calculations for simple and Holt's exponential smoothing. We will not repeat that process for the Winters' model.

Having ForecastX™ determine the parameters that would minimize the RMSE results in an alpha of 0.41, a beta of 0.37, and a gamma of 0.03.

As with simple and Holt's exponential smoothing, initial values must be selected to *initialize* or *warm up* the model. Over a long time period, such as in this example, the particular values selected have little effect on the forecast of light truck production for 2000. These initial values are also determined within the software.

The results of the Winters' exponential smoothing forecast of light truck production are shown in Table 3–4 and in Figure 3–6. You can see, especially in the graph, that the model works quite well. The root-mean-squared error (RMSE) of 16.33 for the forecast period is only about 2.6 percent of the average quarterly production for the last two quarters of 1999 and the first two quarters of 2000. (The average quarterly sales for these four quarters was 615.78.)

Adaptive–Response-Rate Single Exponential Smoothing

An interesting variant on simple smoothing called *adaptive–response-rate single exponential smoothing (ADRES)* has an important advantage over normal smoothing models because of the manner in which the smoothing constant is chosen. In ADRES smoothing there is no requirement to actually choose an α value! This is an attractive feature if what you need is a very low-cost method of forecasting requiring no

TABLE 3–4 **Winters' Three-Parameter Linear and Seasonal Exponential Smoothing for Light Truck Production** (c3t4)

Date	Original Data	Fitted Data	Error	Date	Original Data	Fitted Data	Error
Mar-1986	213.83	220.59	−6.76	Sep-1993	315.82	330.88	−15.07
Jun-1986	231.68	234.30	−2.62	Dec-1993	394.48	343.51	50.97
Sep-1986	205.90	200.72	5.19	Mar-1994	449.78	389.52	60.26
Dec-1986	197.82	211.83	−14.02	Jun-1994	447.02	465.95	−18.93
Mar-1987	252.45	232.49	19.95	Sep-1994	376.37	380.11	−3.73
Jun-1987	249.02	259.55	−10.53	Dec-1994	421.07	417.25	3.81
Sep-1987	220.37	220.94	−0.57	Mar-1995	446.75	448.00	−1.25
Dec-1987	239.85	225.35	14.49	Jun-1995	460.55	482.79	−22.24
Mar-1988	271.03	269.32	1.71	Sep-1995	377.20	395.11	−17.92
Jun-1988	271.92	282.98	−11.05	Dec-1995	427.25	428.41	−1.17
Sep-1988	231.70	242.69	−10.99	Mar-1996	448.99	455.79	−6.80
Dec-1988	269.23	246.17	23.06	Jun-1996	488.18	483.21	4.98
Mar-1989	311.13	293.63	17.50	Sep-1996	403.40	404.38	−0.98
Jun-1989	309.74	311.78	−2.04	Dec-1996	452.82	450.24	2.57
Sep-1989	240.94	270.41	−29.47	Mar-1997	513.58	479.05	34.54
Dec-1989	248.50	274.57	−26.07	Jun-1997	509.55	529.09	−19.54
Mar-1990	264.41	300.17	−35.76	Sep-1997	437.25	432.84	4.41
Jun-1990	322.82	290.63	32.19	Dec-1997	543.44	485.16	58.27
Sep-1990	254.99	257.40	−2.41	Mar-1998	566.82	548.40	18.42
Dec-1990	218.56	272.98	−54.42	Jun-1998	535.83	582.86	−47.03
Mar-1991	194.56	282.58	−88.02	Sep-1998	440.15	472.96	−32.82
Jun-1991	285.71	262.43	23.27	Dec-1998	565.61	524.00	41.60
Sep-1991	248.66	223.70	24.96	Mar-1999	632.32	572.19	60.12
Dec-1991	271.55	237.01	34.54	Jun-1999	646.66	609.86	36.79
Mar-1992	279.71	274.17	5.53	Sep-1999	547.793	*526.45*	
Jun-1992	322.26	326.10	−3.84	Dec-1999	601.651	*620.95*	
Sep-1992	271.39	268.52	2.87	Mar-2000	660.525	*660.37*	
Dec-1992	326.65	275.18	51.47	Jun-2000	653.024	*668.50*	
Mar-1993	378.13	315.74	62.39				
Jun-1993	391.59	400.91	−9.32				

Alpha = 0.41 Beta = 0.37 Gamma = 0.03
Historical root-mean-squared error (RMSE) = 30.5
Mean absolute percentage error (MAPE) = 6.64%
Please note carefully that the ForecastX™ package assigns the names *Alpha* to the simple smoothing factor, *Gamma* to the smoothing factor for the trend estimate, and *Beta* to the smoothing factor for the seasonality estimate.

Adaptive-response smoothing does not use one single α value like the simple exponential smoothing model.

sophisticated knowledge of the technique. Real-world situations requiring the frequent forecasting of many items (perhaps thousands) would be ideal candidates for ADRES smoothing forecasts.

Adaptive-response smoothing does not use one single α value like the simple exponential smoothing model. The word *adaptive* in its name gives a clue to how the model works. The α value in the ADRES model is not just a single number, but rather *adapts* to the data. When there is a change in the basic pattern of the data, the α value adapts.

For instance, suppose that some data to be forecast fluctuate around a mean value of *m*. The best estimate of the next observation of the data might then be that mean value (*m*). But suppose further that after some time an outside force changes the mean value of *m* and the new value is now *m'*. The data then fluctuate around the new mean value of *m'*. If we had a way of adapting to the new mean of *m'*, we could then use that adapted estimate as the forecast for future values of the data. In fact, we would like to be able to adapt each time the mean value of the data changed; sometimes we would adapt very often, if the mean changed frequently, and at other times we would adapt very rarely, if the data changed only infrequently.

Because of the simplicity of the ADRES smoothing model and its ability to adapt to changing circumstances, it is quite often used in actual practice. Keep in mind, however, that it is a variant of the simple smoothing model and so assumes that the data to be forecast have little trend or seasonality (or that the trend or seasonality in the data has been removed).

The ADRES model looks very much like the simple smoothing model presented earlier:

$$F_{t+1} = \alpha_t X_t + (1 - \alpha_t)F_t \qquad \text{(ADRES equation)} \qquad (3.11)$$

where:

$$\alpha_t = \left| \frac{S_t}{A_t} \right| \qquad (3.12)$$

$$S_t = \beta e_t + (1 - \beta)S_{t-1} \qquad \text{(Smoothed error)} \qquad (3.13)$$

$$A_t = \beta|e_t| + (1 - \beta)A_{t-1} \qquad \text{(Absolute smoothed error)} \qquad (3.14)$$

$$e_t = X_t - F_t \qquad \text{(Error)} \qquad (3.15)$$

Note carefully the subscripts on the α term! There may now be a different α value for each period.

The ADRES equation is the same as the one for simple exponential smoothing with the exception of the manner in which the α value is chosen. In the simple exponential smoothing model we chose the α value by selecting the value that minimized the root-mean-squared error associated with the model. But in simple smoothing we were allowed to choose only a single value for α. In the ADRES smoothing model we may allow the α value to adapt as the data change.

The smoothing value (α) is now given as the absolute value of the smoothed error divided by the absolute smoothed error. The smoothed error is itself a smoothed value, with a smoothing factor of β. The absolute smoothed error is also a smoothed value, again using the smoothing constant β. In most cases, β is assigned a value of either 0.1 or 0.2. Thus, the first term of both the smoothed error and absolute smoothed error equations has a lighter weight than the second term.

To explain ADRES smoothing, consider Table 3–5, which lists 12 values of an observed data series. We would like to model the series using an adaptive–response-rate smoothing model. Note that the first six values of the series average about 100; the last (c3t5)   **TABLE 3–5**   **Adaptive-Response Example** (c3t5)

Period	Observed	Forecast	Error	Smoothed Error	Absolute Smoothed Error	α
1	100					
2	96	100.000	−4.00	−0.800	0.800	1.000
3	107	96.000	11.00	1.560	2.840	0.549
4	98	102.042	−4.04	0.440	3.080	0.143
5	103	101.464	1.53	0.659	2.771	0.238
6	99	101.830	−2.83	−0.039	2.783	0.014
7	126	101.790	24.21	4.811	7.068	0.681
8	128	118.267	9.73	5.795	7.601	0.762
9	122	125.687	−3.69	3.899	6.818	0.572
10	130	123.579	6.42	4.403	6.739	0.653
11	125	127.774	−2.77	2.968	5.946	0.499
12	124	126.390	−2.39	1.896	5.235	0.362

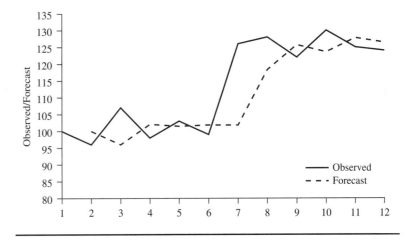

six values in the series average about 125. This is a situation similar to that described in the preceding paragraphs and one conducive to the use of this technique. An adaptive–response-rate model should do quite well in modeling these data.

For period 5 the computations are as follows (with some rounding difference in the third decimal place):

$$F_5 = \alpha_4 X_4 + (1 - \alpha_4)F_4$$

$$= (0.143)(98) + (1 - 0.143)(102.042)$$

$$= 14.014 + 87.450$$

$$= 101.464$$

Once the observed value of 103 becomes available for period 5, it is possible to make the following computations (assuming Beta = .2):

$$e_5 = 103 - 101.464 = 1.536$$

$$S_5 = (0.2)(1.536) + (1 - 0.2)(0.440) = 0.659$$

$$A_5 = (0.2)(|1.536|) + (1 - 0.2)(3.080) = 2.771$$

and finally

$$\alpha_5 = \left| \frac{0.659}{2.771} \right| = 0.238$$

The process continues iteratively for all the remaining values in the example. In ForecastX™ you will get somewhat different results due to their use of a somewhat different algorithm.

Perhaps the most important consideration in adaptive–response-rate single exponential smoothing is the selection of the appropriate β factor. The β factor is usually set near 0.1 or 0.2 because these values reduce the effects of previous errors (i.e., they allow adaptation) but the values are small enough that the adaptation takes place gradually.

The ADRES model has no explicit way to handle seasonality. There are ways of using the ADRES model, however, with seasonal data. In fact, simple smoothing, Holt's smoothing, and the ADRES smoothing model may all be used with seasonal data. An example follows in the next section.

Using Single, Holt's, or ADRES Smoothing to Forecast a Seasonal Data Series

When data have a seasonal pattern, the Winters' model provides an easy way to incorporate the seasonality *explicitly* into the model. An alternative method, however, is widely practiced. This alternative consists of first "deseasonalizing" the data. Deseasonalizing is a process that removes the effects of seasonality from the raw data before the forecasting model is employed.[5] The forecasting model is then applied to the deseasonalized data, and finally, the results are "reseasonalized" to provide accurate forecasts. In sum, the process consists of these steps:

1. Calculate seasonal indices for the series. This can be done in different ways, one of which is to use the HOLT WINTERS command routine in ForecastX™.

2. Deseasonalize the original data by dividing each value by its corresponding seasonal index.

3. Apply a forecasting method (such as simple, Holt's, or adaptive-response exponential smoothing) to the deseasonalized series to produce an intermediate forecast of the deseasonalized data.

4. Reseasonalize the series by multiplying each deseasonalized forecast by its corresponding seasonal index.

---

[5]A complete description of deseasonalizing and reseasonalizing data appears in Chapter 6. The results that follow here are computed with ForecastX™ using the HOLT WINTERS command routine.

Many forecasters
have found this
method more
accurate than using
Winters' smoothing
to incorporate
seasonality.

Many forecasters have found this method more accurate than using Winters' smoothing to incorporate seasonality. This method is more flexible than the Winters' method alone because it allows for the use of simple smoothing in situations without any trend whatsoever while allowing Holt's smoothing to be used if a trend is present. (Recall that Winters' model assumes that a trend is present.) Further, the ADRES model could be used in situations where some adaptation of the α factor is desirable.

To illustrate this approach to forecasting a seasonal series, let us return to the light truck production data used in our example of the application of Winters' exponential smoothing. Table 3–6 shows the first and last portions of the light truck production

TABLE 3–6   **Light Truck Production (TP), Seasonally Adjusted Light Truck Production (TPSA), Holt's Exponential Smoothing Forecast of Seasonally Adjusted Light Truck Production (TPSA_FCST), the Seasonal Indices (SI), and the Reseasonalized Forecast of Light Truck Production (TPF)** (c3t6)

Date	TP	TPSA_FCST	SI	TPF	Date	TP	TPSA_FCST	SI	TPF	
Mar-1986	206.38	210.70	1.04	218.303	Sep-1994	443.41	438.42	0.85	372.137	
Jun-1986	223.87	212.17	1.03	219.573	Dec-1994	426.39	440.94	0.99	435.439	
Sep-1986	242.58	229.70	0.85	194.969	Mar-1995	431.19	434.24	1.04	449.908	
Dec-1986	200.32	244.32	0.99	241.272	Jun-1995	445.02	441.44	1.03	456.855	
Mar-1987	243.65	204.11	1.04	211.479	Sep-1995	444.39	451.26	0.85	383.030	
Jun-1987	240.61	249.45	1.03	258.163	Dec-1995	432.65	441.55	0.99	436.034	
Sep-1987	259.63	246.93	0.85	209.599	Mar-1996	433.35	440.28	1.04	456.172	
Dec-1987	242.88	260.47	0.99	257.214	Jun-1996	471.71	443.44	1.03	458.916	
Mar-1988	261.59	247.42	1.04	256.345	Sep-1996	475.26	477.55	0.85	405.344	
Jun-1988	262.75	267.46	1.03	276.802	Dec-1996	458.54	471.91	0.99	466.022	
Sep-1988	272.97	269.46	0.85	228.722	Mar-1997	495.69	466.51	1.04	483.345	
Dec-1988	272.64	273.38	0.99	269.963	Jun-1997	492.36	506.94	1.03	524.641	
Mar-1989	300.29	277.43	1.04	287.441	Sep-1997	515.13	498.65	0.85	423.258	
Jun-1989	299.29	306.39	1.03	317.090	Dec-1997	550.31	510.90	0.99	504.522	
Sep-1989	283.85	306.77	0.85	260.384	Mar-1998	547.07	559.55	1.04	579.739	
Dec-1989	251.64	284.39	0.99	280.842	Jun-1998	517.76	559.70	1.03	579.244	
Mar-1990	255.20	256.51	1.04	265.763	Sep-1998	518.55	524.92	0.85	445.557	
Jun-1990	311.93	260.13	1.03	269.210	Dec-1998	572.76	514.51	0.99	508.082	Historical period
Sep-1990	300.41	318.18	0.85	270.071	Mar-1999	610.29	581.23	1.04	602.203	RMSE = 39.80698
Dec-1990	221.33	300.46	0.99	296.708	Jun-1999	624.84	623.21	1.03	644.970	
Mar-1991	187.78	226.44	1.04	234.609	Sep-1999	547.793	633.28	0.85	537.534	
Jun-1991	276.07	191.97	1.03	198.670	Dec-1999	601.651	629.27	0.99	621.415	← Holdout period
Sep-1991	292.96	279.92	0.85	237.599	Mar-2000	660.525	639.27	1.04	662.345	
Dec-1991	274.99	291.34	0.99	287.700	Jun-2000	653.024	652.76	1.03	675.549	
Mar-1992	269.96	280.27	1.04	290.384						
Jun-1992	311.39	276.76	1.03	286.421	**Holdout Period Forecast RMSE**					
Sep-1992	319.73	315.86	0.85	268.100						
Dec-1992	330.78	317.65	0.99	313.680	*Forecast*	*Actual*	$(A_t - F_t)$	$(A_t - F_t)^2$		
Mar-1993	364.95	336.57	1.04	348.716						
Jun-1993	378.38	374.07	1.03	387.133	537.534	547.793	10.26	105.25		
Sep-1993	372.07	384.08	0.85	326.009	621.415	601.651	−19.76	390.61		
Dec-1993	399.47	369.94	0.99	365.318	662.345	660.525	−1.82	3.31		
Mar-1994	434.11	406.33	1.04	420.994	675.549	653.024	−22.53	507.39		
Jun-1994	431.94	444.70	1.03	460.226	Holdout period RMSE = 15.86					

FIGURE 3–7

*Light Truck
Production and
Light Truck
Production
Forecast Based
on a Holt's
Exponential
Smoothing
Forecast of
Deseasonalized
Light Truck
Production
(c3t6)*

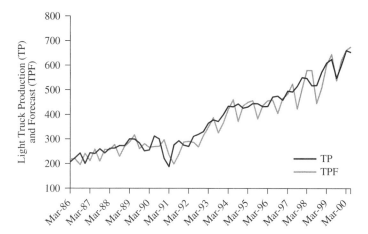

TP = Actual light truck production
TPF = Forecast of light truck production
   Historical period: RMSE = 39.80698
    Forecast period: RMSE = 15.86
*Light truck production was first deseasonalized, then a Holt's forecast
was done and the results were reseasonalized.*

series (TP), the deseasonalized light truck production data (TPSA), a Holt's exponential smoothing forecast of the deseasonalized light truck production (TPSAF), the seasonal indices (SI) that were obtained from the HOLT WINTERS command routine in ForecastX™, and the reseasonalized forecast of light truck production (TPF). In this table TPSA = TP ÷ SI, and TPF = TPSAF × SI. You may want to check a couple of these calculations to verify the process for yourself (you may get slightly different answers due to rounding effects).

The results of this forecast of light truck production are shown in Figure 3–7. The RMSE for the historical period is lower than that from the Winters' forecast (see Figure 3–6). For this approach the forecast period RMSE is about 2.5 percent of the average quarterly production for the forecast period compared to 2.6 percent for the Winters' forecast.

Event Modeling

When forecasting
sales or demand in
a highly promoted
market, using this
smoothing
technique will
significantly
improve forecast
accuracy.

Event modeling is a feature of some exponential smoothing programs such as ForecastX™. This feature allows the user to specify the time of one or more special events, such as irregular promotions and natural disasters, in the calibration data. For each type of special event, the effect is estimated and the data adjusted so that the events do not distort the trend and seasonal patterns of the time series.

When forecasting sales or demand in a highly promoted market, using this smoothing technique will significantly improve forecast accuracy. Consider the case of a manufacturer of a popular condiment (e.g., ketchup, mustard, steak sauce, and so on). This type of product tends to be highly seasonal and also tends to be aggressively promoted by marketers. Is there a method for modeling the effect of future promotions on the sales or demand for such a product?

The answer to this dilemma is *event modeling*. By using the basic smoothing models already developed earlier in the chapter as a base, an event model may be generated to replicate the effects of various promotions and combinations of promotions.

The method of event modeling follows in the same pattern for the smoothing models already examined: after the systematic patterns are identified in the historical data, the exponential smoothing method uses smoothing equations for each component in the series to estimate and build up structural patterns. The event model adds a smoothing equation for each of the "events" identified as being important. The weights for each smoothing equation are represented by a parameter.

Event models are analogous to seasonal models: just as each month is assigned its own index for seasonality, so, too, each event type is assigned its own index for a specific promotional activity. For example, when monthly data are used, the seasonal index for a particular month is updated at regular intervals, each time that month recurs. However, event adjustments are created through the use of an indicator variable that assigns an integer for each event type to the period during which it recurs. Thus, one example of integer value assignment would be that 0 indicates a period where no event has occurred, 1 indicates a period where a free-standing insert (FSI) was circulated, 2 indicates a period where instant redeemable coupons (IRC) were used, and so on. The event indicator variable must be defined for each historic period *and* future period in the forecast horizon. In this way, the event smoothing equation is used to calculate historical lift in sales above baseline that occurred as a result of a particular type of promotion, and applies that lift to the baseline forecast in the future period where the same promotion is planned.

To illustrate how this method is used in actual practice, we examine some actual demand data; because these data are from a particular company for a particular product, we neglect to specify the product precisely. The product, however, is a condiment commonly used in American households and found at every picnic (e.g., ketchup, mustard, or steak sauce). The company that produces and sells this condiment uses a number of marketing promotions to enhance sales and maintain market share. Free-standing inserts are perhaps the most common of the promotions for this type of product; these are the familiar coupons found in Sunday newspapers and redeemable when the item is purchased. These FSIs are often used in conjunction with themed advertising campaigns, especially during particular seasons of the year. Our condiment manufacturer uses a separate event value to stand for the combination of FSIs and a themed advertising campaign. Instant redeemable coupons (IRC) are a separate type of coupon usually attached to the product packaging itself and redeemed at the cash register at checkout.

The condiment manufacturer in addition to adjusting the price to the consumer through coupons also adjusts the price to the jobber by reducing case prices for a short period of time. When this takes place it is common for jobbers to stock up on the reduced price item and delay future purchase. Because of this, the manufacturer uses two event values called *load* and *deload* to signify periods of reduced prices and the periods immediately following such a promotion; these are actually two separate events.

Event models are analogous to seasonal models.

The event values for this particular condiment manufacturer are listed in the following table.

Event Indices Legend	
0	No event present
1	Free-standing inserts (FSIs)
2	FSI/radio, television, print campaign
3	Load (trade promotion)
4	Deload (month after effect of load)
5	Thematics (themed advertising campaign)
6	Instant redeemable coupon (IRC)

Figure 3–8 shows monthly historical demand of the condiment over time. Table 3–7 shows the events related to each of these historical months and the company's planned promotions for the next six months.

Using Winters' smoothing model on these data picks up the implied seasonality and trend quite well; the calculated alpha, beta, and gamma are 0.11, 1.00, and 0.45, respectively. This indicates that there is very little trend in the data but a high degree of seasonality. Actually, some of the apparent seasonality is not seasonality at all; instead, it is "induced seasonality" caused by the company's various promotions. Using the Winters' smoothing model again, but with six event smoothing factors added in as well, the alpha, beta, and gamma factors are 0.50, 1.00, and 0.00. By examining these factors we see that there is definitely little trend, but now the seasonality has also apparently disappeared.

FIGURE 3–8

Condiment Consumption as Reported by A. C. Nielsen (c3t7)

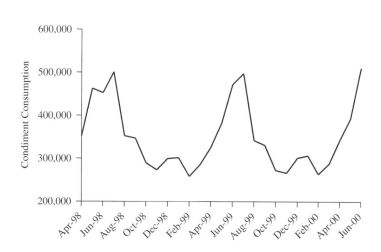

(c3t7) **TABLE 3–7   An Event Model Example**

Date	Condiment	Event Indices
Apr-1998	351,957.90	5
May-1998	462,520.90	2
Jun-1998	452,427.15	3
Jul-1998	500,727.27	3
Aug-1998	352,241.13	4
Sep-1998	346,972.63	0
Oct-1998	289,695.22	6
Nov-1998	273,470.71	0
Dec-1998	299,693.42	3
Jan-1999	301,837.47	4
Feb-1999	258,669.15	1
Mar-1999	285,772.66	0
Apr-1999	325,737.36	5
May-1999	382,745.83	1
Jun-1999	472,267.06	1
Jul-1999	497,796.59	1
Aug-1999	342,191.30	6
Sep-1999	331,274.72	0
Oct-1999	273,095.91	0
Nov-1999	266,740.56	1
Dec-1999	301,614.78	3
Jan-2000	307,126.61	4
Feb-2000	264,117.43	0
Mar-2000	287,866.92	0
Apr-2000	343,697.51	0
May-2000	393,994.53	1
Jun-2000	510,945.15	3
Jul-2000		4
Aug-2000		1
Sep-2000		0
Oct-2000		0	← Forecast period
Nov-2000		1
Dec-2000		3

Event Legend:
0 = No event present
1 = FSI
2 = FSI/Campaign
3 = Load
4 = Deload
5 = Thematics
6 = IRC

Definitions:
FSI = Free-standing inserts. These are cents-off coupons distributed in newspapers.
Thematics = Themed ad campaign
Load — Trade promotion usually involving a drop in the case price to a supplier
Deload = Month after effect of a "load"
Campaign = Radio, television, or print ad campaign
IRC = Instant redeemable coupons. These are cents-off coupons placed directly on the product packaging.

The seasonality has not disappeared; it was accounted for by the six event indices.

	Winters' Model	*Winters' Model with Event Indices*
Historical RMSE	16,813	12,897
Alpha	0.11	0.05
Beta	1.00	1.00
Gamma	0.45	0.00
Event index 1	NA	1.01
Event index 2	NA	1.00
Event index 3	NA	1.06
Event index 4	NA	1.03
Event index 5	NA	0.94
Event index 6	NA	0.99

Note that the RMSE for the event model is much lower (12,897 compared to 16,813) than the RMSE for the Winters' model. The addition of the events to the historical period caused a tighter fit between the actual condiment demand and predicted condiment demand. Using the knowledge of the planned company promotions for the next six months allows the forecaster to calculate a much better picture of predicted demand than the Winters' model alone.

In this particular case we used the Winters' model as a base because we believed the original data had both trend and seasonality. If the data had lacked trend or seasonality, we could have used simple smoothing as the base model. ForecastX™ allows any number of models to be used as the underlying basis for event forecasting.

Ignoring events (usually promotions) that a company has scheduled in advance will likely lead to poorer forecasts when those events have significant impacts. The events you specify need not be promotions, however. An event may be any occurrence that has taken place in the historical period that you believe will either be replicated in the forecast period (such as advertising promotions) or requires adjustment to the parameters because of its large effect (such as a natural disaster).

Summary

If the time series you are forecasting is a stationary one, the moving-average method of forecasting may accurately predict future values. The moving-average method calculates the average of the past observations, and this average becomes the forecast for the next period.

When recent-past observations are thought to contain more information than distant-past observations, some form of exponential smoothing may be appropriate. Exponential smoothing provides self-correcting forecasts that adjust so as to regulate the forecast values by changing them in the opposite direction from recent errors. It is a characteristic of smoothing models in general, however, that their forecasts lag behind movements in the original time-series data. Exponential smoothing requires the specification of a smoothing constant, which determines the relative weights accorded to recent as opposed to more distant historical observations.

A suggested method for choosing an optimal smoothing constant is to minimize the root-mean-squared error (RMSE); the RMSE is found by dividing the sum of the squared errors by the number of observations and then taking the square root of the result.

When some trend is observed in the original time series, simple exponential smoothing becomes less able to perform accurate prediction; adding a procedure to adjust for the trend results in Holt's two-parameter exponential smoothing. Holt's smoothing adds a growth factor to the smoothing model to account for trend; in a sense, the growth or trend factor itself is smoothed in the same manner as the original data.

When seasonality is also present in the original data, Winters' three-parameter exponential smoothing adds a correction factor to Holt's smoothing model to correct for the seasonality. The correction factor is provided by an additional equation.

Adaptive–response-rate single exponential smoothing provides another technique that can be useful when the "level" of the forecasted variable changes infrequently. Adaptive-response models adjust the smoothing factor for changing conditions rather than choosing a constant smoothing factor.

In addition to trying Winters' exponential smoothing for seasonal data, one might also deseasonalize the data and then use another forecasting tool to forecast the deseasonalized series. The deseasonalized forecast can then be reseasonalized by multiplying the deseasonalized forecast by the corresponding seasonal indices.

Forecasting Domestic Car Sales with Exponential Smoothing

You will recall that in Chapter 1 we presented quarterly data on domestic car sales (in thousands of units); these data were presented in order to provide a single series that could be used to compare the various forecasting techniques presented in this text. In Chapter 1, Figure 1–5, you saw that the DCS series shows a great deal of seasonality, some cycle, and only a very slight trend.

In this chapter Winters' exponential smoothing was the only method that we used in which seasonality was explicitly taken into account. Thus, Winters' would appear to be an excellent candidate as a forecasting technique for domestic car sales. You might want to go back to Table 2–1, which provided a guide to model selection, to see how this handy table would help you select Winters' for this series. The Holt's exponential smoothing model might also be a good candidate *if we first deseasonalize the DCS data*. You will note that we do not apply simple or Holt's exponential smoothing to the domestic car sales data because neither of those methods would be an appropriate model given the guidelines in Table 2–1.

Applying the Winters' model, the software found the optimum values for the weights to be: alpha = 0.45; beta = 0.17; and gamma = 0.00. The historical RMSE for this Winters' model was 144.45, while the RMSE for the forecast horizon was 61.79. This RMSE corresponds to about 3.5 percent of the average quarterly sales for the forecast period. In terms of total sales for the year, the forecast period actual was 7045.3, while the forecast was, 6934.94—an error for the yearly total of 1.5 percent.

When the DCS series is deseasonalized, the seasonal factors turn out to be: 0.95, 1.10, 0.99, and 0.91 for quarters one through four, respectively. From these we see that on average quarter two is the strongest season for domestic car sales, while quarter four is the weakest. Applying an optimal Holt's model to the deseasonalized series, then making the forecast, and finally reseasonalizing the data, we obtain another forecast of DCS. The RMSE for the historic period was 200.46 and for the forecast period the RMSE was 62.21.

Figure 3–9 shows both of these forecasts of domestic car sales in comparison to the actual data. The top panel shows the results from the Winters' model, while the lower panel is for the Holt's seasonally adjusted forecast.

FIGURE 3–9

Two Forecasts of Domestic Car Sales (c3f9)

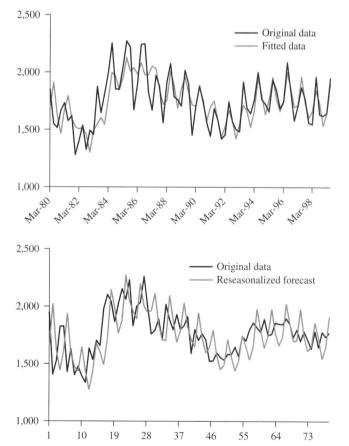

Actual values of DCS are shown along with the Winters' forecast in the top graph, while the actual and the Holt's seasonally adjusted forecast are shown in the bottom graph.

Table 3–8 provides a summary of root-mean-squared errors for various methods used to forecast domestic car sales. A similar table will appear at the end of the corresponding section of each chapter in which a new forecast of DCS is developed.

TABLE 3–8   Summary Table of RMSEs for Domestic Car Sales

Chapter	Method	Period	RMSE
1	Naive—with 4-period lag	Historical	187.13
		Holdout	112.26
2	Not applicable		
3	Winters' exponential smoothing	Historical	144.45
		Holdout	61.79
	Holt's with	Historical	200.46
	seasonal adjustment	Holdout	62.21

INTEGRATIVE CASE
THE GAP

(c3gap)

Part 3: Forecasting The Gap Sales Data with Exponential Smoothing

The sales of The Gap stores for the 60 quarters covering 1985Q1 through 1999Q4 are once again shown below. From this graph it is clear that The Gap sales are quite seasonal and are increasing over time. Recall that the 1999 data is used as a holdout period.

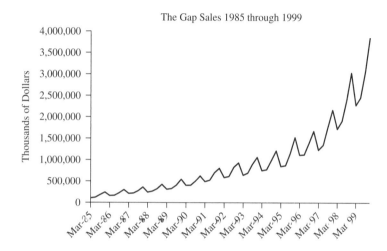

The Gap Sales 1985 through 1999

Case Questions

1. Using The Gap data, which are not adjusted to remove the seasonality, what exponential smoothing model do you think would be the most appropriate if you want to develop a quarterly forecast for 1999 sales? Explain why. Make a forecast for The Gap sales using the method you selected and use the RMSE to evaluate your historic fit and your forecast accuracy for the four quarters of 1999. For the entire year of 1999, what percent error is there in your forecast?

2. What are the seasonal indices for the The Gap sales and what do they tell you about this company's sales pattern?

3. If The Gap data are deseasonalized, what exponential smoothing model do you think would be the most likely to work well in preparing a forecast of sales for the four quarters of 1999? Apply that method and evaluate your results.

Solutions to Case Questions

1. Of the exponential smoothing models discussed in the text the one that is most appropriate for the non-seasonally adjusted data is Winters' exponential smoothing. This model takes both trend and seasonality into account. Allowing ForecastX™ to determine the optimal smoothing weights we obtain: alpha = 0.81; beta = 0.50; and gamma = 0.23. The RMSE using the historic period is 49,479.48, while for the four quarters of 1996 the RMSE is 99,493.20 (remember that our data are in thousands of dollars). If we compare the

RMSE for these last four quarters to the mean level of sales for those quarters (2,908,831), we find that the RMSE is about 3.4 percent of the mean actual quarterly sales. For the entire year of 1999 our forecast was for yearly sales of 11,296,646. This compares favorably with actual sales of 11,635,325 (an error for the year of about 2.9 percent).

The original Gap sales and the Winters' forecast (fitted) of The Gap sales (in thousands of dollars) are shown below for the four quarters of 1999.

	The Gap Sales	*Forecast*
Mar-1999	2,277,700	2,260,870
Jun-1999	2,453,300	2,361,384
Sep-1999	3,045,386	2,977,478
Dec-1999	3,858,939	3,696,913

The graph below shows actual The Gap sales and the Winters' forecast of The Gap sales for both the historical and forecast periods.

(c3gap)

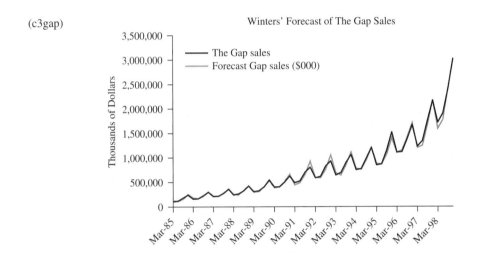

Winters' Forecast of The Gap Sales

2. The seasonal factors for The Gap sales in quarters one through four are: 0.88, 0.88, 1.05, and 1.25. This indicates strong sales during the fall back-to-school buying season (for The Gap, the third quarter includes the months of August, September, and October) followed by even stronger sales in their fourth quarter due to the Christmas season (the fourth quarter includes November, December, and January).

3. When The Gap sales are deseasonalized, about all that remains is the positive trend and some noise around that trend. Using Holt's exponential smoothing (alpha = 1.00 and beta = 0.30) to forecast the deseasonalized series for The Gap sales, then multiplying this forecast by the seasonal factors provides another forecast of The Gap sales. The RMSE for this forecast in the historical period was 42,388, while in the forecast period the resulting RMSE was 74,034. If we compare the RMSE for these last four quarters to the mean level of sales for

those quarters (11,635,325) we find that the RMSE is about 0.63 percent of the mean actual quarterly sales. For the entire year of 1999 our Holt's forecast was for yearly sales of 11,390,069. This compares even more favorably with actual sales of 11,635,325 (an error for the year of about 2.1 percent) than did the Winters' model.

The actual (The Gap sales) and Holt's forecast of The Gap sales (after reintroducing the seasonality) are shown below for the four quarters of 1999.

	The Gap Sales	*Forecast (Holt's)*
Mar-1999	2,277,700	2,269,430
Jun-1999	2,453,300	2,376,925
Sep-1999	3,045,386	3,004,607
Dec-1999	3,858,939	3,739,105

A time-series plot of this forecast, along with the actual data, is shown below. The following table provides a summary of root-mean-squared errors for various methods used to forecast The Gap sales. A similar table will appear along with the Integrative Case for each chapter in which a new forecast of The Gap sales is developed.

(c3gap)

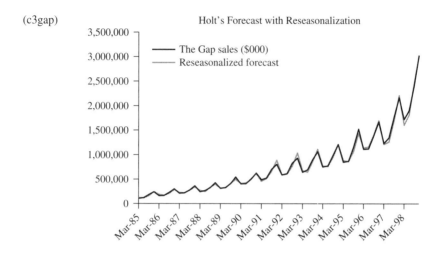

Holt's Forecast with Reseasonalization

Chapter	Method	Period	RMSE
1	Naive—with 4-period lag	Historical	233,092
		Holdout	654,976
2	Not applicable		
3	Winters' exponential smoothing	Historical	49,479
		Holdout	99,493
	Holt's exponential smoothing	Historical	42,388
	with seasonal readjustment	Holdout	74,034

USING FORECASTX™ TO MAKE EXPONENTIAL SMOOTHING FORECASTS

What follows is a brief discussion of how to use ForecastX™ for preparing an exponential smoothing forecast. This also serves as a further introduction to the ease of use of ForecastX™. The illustration used here is for a forecast of The Gap data that has trend and seasonality.

First, put your data into an Excel spreadsheet in column format, such as the sample of The Gap data shown in the table below. Once you have your data in this format, while in Excel highlight the data you want to use, then start ForecastX™. The dialog box to the right of the data table appears.

A Sample of The Gap Data in Column Format

Date	The Gap Sales ($000)
Mar-1994	751,670
Jun-1994	773,131
Sep-1994	988,346
Dec-1994	1,209,790
Mar-1995	848,688
Jun-1995	868,514
Sep-1995	1,155,930
Dec-1995	1,522,120
Mar-1996	1,113,150
Jun-1996	1,120,340
Sep-1996	1,383,000
Dec-1996	1,667,900
Mar-1997	1,231,186
Jun-1997	1,345,221
Sep-1997	1,765,939
Dec-1997	2,165,479
Mar-1998	1,719,712
Jun-1998	1,904,970
Sep-1998	2,399,900
Dec-1998	3,029,900

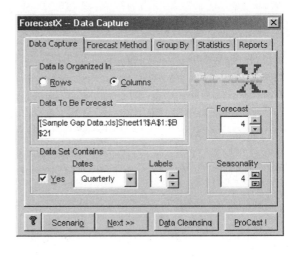

Set the **Dates** window to the periodicity of your data (quarterly for this example), then click the **Forecast Method** tab at the top. The following screen appears.

Click the down arrow in the **Forecasting Technique** window and select **Holt Winters,** which is what ForecastX™ calls what we have referred to as simply "Winters'" in this chapter. This

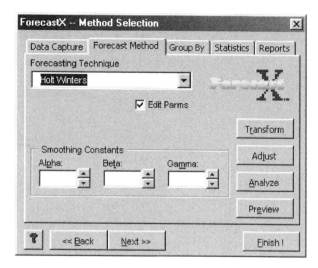

would be an appropriate method for data such as The Gap series. You can enter desired weights or you can leave those spaces blank and let ForecastX™ select the best set of values.

Next, click the **Statistics** tab and the following dialog box will appear.

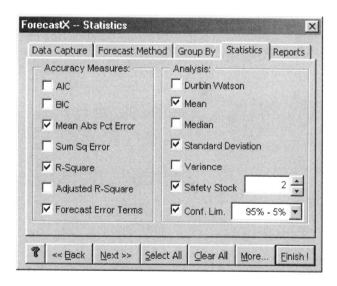

Here you select the statistics you want to have reported. You will want to experiment with various selections.

Next click the **Reports** tab and the **Report Options** dialog box will appear.

As you place a check next to each of the five boxes for various reports, the options available in that report will appear below. For example, in the **Standard** report box you will normally check **Output In Columns** and **Show Charts.**

Again you will want to experiment with the various reports to get a feel for the ones that will give you the output you want for your specific application. After you click **Finish!** in the lower right corner, reports will be put in new Excel workbooks—Book 2, Book 3, and so forth. The book numbers will vary depending on how many books have previously been opened.

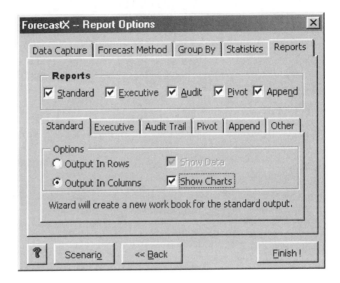

Deseasonalizing Data

To deseasonalize data in ForecastX™ we use a method called **Decomposition** in ForecastX™ (this method of forecasting will be discussed in detail in Chapter 6). For now we will simply look at the portion of the method and results that we need to take the seasonality out of a data series.

Begin by opening your data file in Excel and then start the ForecastX™ Wizard. Go through the data capture process. Then, in the **Method Selection** dialog box select **Decomposition** as the **Forecasting Technique,** check **Multiplicative,** and select **Linear Regression** as shown here.

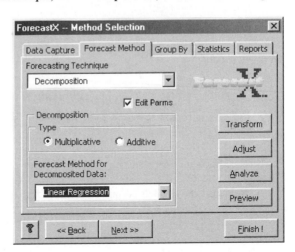

Click the **Statistics** tab. In the **Statistics** dialog box you can uncheck all boxes, because for this purpose we do not need any statistics. This will save computational time.

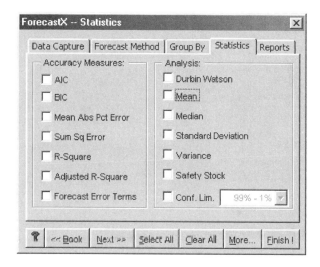

Then click the **Reports** tab and select only the **Audit** report.

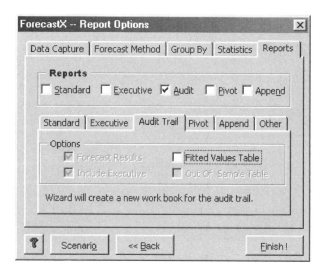

Now click **Finish!** and you will get results that will include the following:

Components of Decomposition

Date	Original Data	Forecasted Data	Centered Moving Average	CMA Trend	Seasonal Indices
Mar-1985	105,715.00	−109,539.43		−127,715.45	0.86
Jun-1985	120,136.00	−80,068.78		−94,038.87	0.85
Sep-1985	181,669.00	−62,989.93	168,616.38	−60,362.28	1.04
Dec-1985	239,813.00	−33,286.18	180,977.50	−27,685.70	1.25
Mar-1986	159,980.00	5,995.97	191,946.88	6,990.89	0.86
Jun-1986	164,760.00	34,626.06	204,670.25	40,667.48	0.85
Sep-1986	224,800.00	77,580.35	218,387.25	74,344.06	1.04
Dec-1986	298,469.00	134,738.66	231,396.38	108,020.65	1.25
Mar-1987	211,060.00	121,531.38	244,122.50	141,697.23	0.86
Jun-1987	217,753.00	149,320.90	257,864.88	175,373.82	0.85
Sep-1987	273,616.00	218,150.62	269,291.25	209,050.40	1.04
Dec-1987	359,592.00	302,763.51	278,899.13	242,726.99	1.25

The "Seasonal Indices" column is highlighted here but will not be highlighted in your output. These are the indices that you will use to deseasonalize the original data and to reseasonalize results. You should copy this column of seasonal indices and paste it into your Excel workbook along with your original data.

You can now calculate a deseasonalized series by dividing the original data by the seasonal indices.

$$\text{Deseasonalized Series} = \text{Original Series} \div \text{Seasonal Indices}$$

To reseasonalize results reverse the process.

$$\text{Reseasonalized Results} = \text{Deseasonalized Results} \times \text{Seasonal Indices}$$

NOTE: You may also calculate the seasonal indices by using the Winters' model in ForecastX™. This may give slightly different results than the decomposition method described above. In most cases, the decomposition method will produce superior results.

Suggested Readings

Gardner, Everette S. "Exponential Smoothing: The State of the Art." *Journal of Forecasting* 4, no. 1 (1985), pp. 1–28.

Holt, C. C. "Forecasting Seasonal and Trends by Exponentially Weighted Moving Averages." Office of Naval Research, Memorandum No. 52, 1957.

Makridakis, Spyros; and Steven C. Wheelwright. *Forecasting Methods for Management.* 5th ed. New York: John Wiley & Sons, 1989.

Makridakis, Spyros, et al. "The M2-Competition: A Real-Time Judgementally Based Forecasting Study." *International Journal of Forecasting* 9 (1), April 1993, pp. 5–22.

Makridakis, Spyros; Steven C. Wheelwright; and Victor E. McGee. *Forecasting: Methods and Applications.* 2nd ed. New York: John Wiley & Sons, 1983.

Pegels, Carl C. "Exponential Forecasting: Some New Variations." *Management Science* 15, no. 12 (January 1969), pp. 311–15.

West, Douglas C. "Number of Sales Forecast Methods and Marketing Management." *Journal of Forecasting* 13, no. 4 (August 1994), pp. 395–407.

Winters, P. R. "Forecasting Sales by Exponentially Weighted Moving Averages." *Management Science* 6 (1960), pp. 324–42.

Exercises

1. Assume you were to use α values of 0.1, 0.5, and 0.9 in a simple exponential smoothing model. How would these different α values weight past observations of the variable to be forecast? How would you know which of these α values provided the best forecasting model? If the $\alpha = 0.9$ value provided the best forecast for your data, would this imply that you should do anything else? Does exponential smoothing place more or less weight on the most recent data when compared with the moving-average method? What weight is applied to each observation in a moving-average model? Why is smoothing (simple, Holt's, and Winters') also called *exponential* smoothing?

2. Under what conditions would you choose to use simple exponential smoothing, Holt's exponential smoothing, and Winters' exponential smoothing? Are these the only smoothing models possible to construct? If there are other possible models, suggest one that might be useful.

3. Exponential smoothing is meant to be used with time-series data when the data are made up of some or all of the basic components of average, trend, seasonality, and error. If the data series only fluctuates about an average with no trend and no seasonality, which form of smoothing would you employ? If the data include all of these components, which form of smoothing would you employ? How should the correct smoothing factors be chosen?

4. The smoothing factor chosen in simple exponential smoothing determines the weight to be placed on different terms of time-series data. If the smoothing factor is high rather than low, is more or less weight placed on recent observations? If α is .3, what weight is applied to the observation four periods ago?

5. Consider the following rates offered on certificates of deposit at a large metropolitan bank during a recent year:

Month	Rate	Month	Rate
January	7.025%	July	7.575%
February	9.047%	August	8.612%
March	8.280%	September	8.985%
April	8.650%	October	9.298%
May	9.714%	November	7.454%
June	8.963%	December	8.461%

Use a three-month average to forecast the rate for the following January.

6. The following inventory pattern has been observed in the Zahm Corporation over 12 months:

Month	Inventory	Month	Inventory
January	1,544	July	1,208
February	1,913	August	2,467
March	2,028	September	2,101
April	1,178	October	1,662
May	1,554	November	2,432
June	1,910	December	2,443

Use both three-month and five-month moving-average models to forecast the inventory for the next January. Use root-mean-squared error (RMSE) to evaluate these two forecasts.

7. Consider the following data on mobile-home shipments. Calculate both the three-quarter and five-quarter moving averages for these data and compare the forecasts by calculating the root-mean-squared errors. The data are in thousands of units.

Mobile Homes: Manufacturers' Shipments (Thousands of Units), Not Seasonally Adjusted

Period	Shipments	Period	Shipments
1986Q1	58.1	1991Q1	35.4
1986Q2	66.8	1991Q2	47.4
1986Q3	63.4	1991Q3	47.2
1986Q4	56.1	1991Q4	40.9
1987Q1	51.9	1992Q1	43.0
1987Q2	62.8	1992Q2	52.8
1987Q3	64.7	1992Q3	57.0
1987Q4	53.5	1992Q4	57.6
1988Q1	47.0	1993Q1	56.4
1988Q2	60.5	1993Q2	64.3
1988Q3	59.2	1993Q3	67.1
1988Q4	51.6	1993Q4	66.4
1989Q1	48.1	1994Q1	69.1
1989Q2	55.1	1994Q2	78.7
1989Q3	50.3	1994Q3	78.7
1989Q4	44.5	1994Q4	77.5
1990Q1	43.3	1995Q1	79.2
1990Q2	51.7	1995Q2	86.8
1990Q3	50.5	1995Q3	87.6
1990Q4	42.6	1995Q4	86.4

8. Forecasters at Siegfried Corporation are using simple exponential smoothing to forecast the sales of its major product. They are trying to decide what smoothing constant will give the best results. They have tried a number of smoothing constants with the following results:

Smoothing Constant	RMSE
0.10	125
0.15	97
0.20	136
0.25	141

Which smoothing constant appears best from these results? Why? Could you perhaps get even better results given these outcomes? How would you go about improving the RMSE?

9. The number of tons of brake assemblies received at an auto parts distribution center last month was 670. The forecast tonnage was 720. The company uses a simple exponential smoothing model with a smoothing constant of 0.6 to develop its forecasts. What will be the company's forecast for the next month?

10. The number of service calls received at LaFortune Electric during four months is shown in the following table:

Month	Number of Service Calls
April	19
May	31
June	27
July	29

Forecast the number of service calls in August by using a simple exponential smoothing model with a smoothing constant of 0.1. (Assume the forecast for April was 21.)

11. *a.* Plot the data presented in Exercise 7 to examine the possible existence of trend and seasonality in the data.

b. Prepare four separate smoothing models to examine the mobile-home shipment data using those 10 years of quarterly data.

1. A simple smoothing model
2. Holt's model
3. Winters' model
4. Adaptive–response-rate model (Deseasonalize the data first then reseasonalize to get your forecasts.)

c. Examine the accuracy of each model by calculating the root-mean-squared error for each during the 10-year historical period. Explain carefully what characteristics of the original data led one of these models to minimize the root-mean-squared error.

d. Calculate the RMSE for each of the four models based on the four quarters of 1996 and explain your interpretation of the results. The actual values for 1996 were: Q1 = 84.4; Q2 = 97.2; Q3 = 94.9; Q4 = 86.9.

12. The data in the table below represent single-family houses sold (HS) in the United States on a quarterly basis in thousands of units from 1986Q1 through 1995Q4.

Period	HS	Period	HS
1986Q1	203	1991Q1	121
1986Q2	225	1991Q2	144
1986Q3	169	1991Q3	126
1986Q4	151	1991Q4	116
1987Q1	185	1992Q1	159
1987Q2	192	1992Q2	158
1987Q3	163	1992Q3	159
1987Q4	132	1992Q4	134
1988Q1	166	1993Q1	154
1988Q2	197	1993Q2	183
1988Q3	170	1993Q3	169
1988Q4	143	1993Q4	160
1989Q1	161	1994Q1	178
1989Q2	179	1994Q2	185
1989Q3	172	1994Q3	165
1989Q4	138	1994Q4	142
1990Q1	153	1995Q1	154
1990Q2	152	1995Q2	185
1990Q3	130	1995Q3	181
1990Q4	100	1995Q4	145

a. Prepare a time-series plot of the data and visually inspect that plot to determine the characteristics you see in this series.

b. Use a smoothing model to develop a forecast of HS for the four quarters of 1996 and explain why you selected that model. Plot the actual and forecast values. Determine the RMSE for your model during the historical period (prior to 1996).

c. The actual values for 1996 are: Q1 = 192; Q2 = 204; Q3 = 201; Q4 = 161. Based on these values determine the RMSE for the four quarters of 1996. Explain why you think your forecast was (or was not) a good forecast.

13. The data in the table below are for the college tuition consumers' price index (CTCPI) by quarter.

Period	CTCPI	Period	CTCPI
1986Q1	126.500	1991Q1	185.297
1986Q2	126.633	1991Q2	186.098
1986Q3	129.540	1991Q3	194.525
1986Q4	135.800	1991Q4	205.100
1987Q1	136.200	1992Q1	206.004
1987Q2	136.666	1992Q2	207.764
1987Q3	139.687	1992Q3	215.115
1987Q4	144.935	1992Q4	225.103
1988Q1	146.127	1993Q1	227.500
1988Q2	146.499	1993Q2	227.965
1988Q3	150.811	1993Q3	234.953
1988Q4	156.500	1993Q4	243.466
1989Q1	157.862	1994Q1	244.066
1989Q2	157.968	1994Q2	244.631
1989Q3	162.605	1994Q3	251.489
1989Q4	169.099	1994Q4	258.900
1990Q1	169.997	1995Q1	259.524
1990Q2	170.199	1995Q2	259.466
1990Q3	176.607	1995Q3	266.496
1990Q4	183.000	1995Q4	273.700

a. Plot these data and examine the plot. Does this view of the data suggest a particular smoothing model? Do the data appear to be seasonal? Explain.

b. Use a smoothing method to forecast the four quarters of 1996. Plot the actual and forecast values.

c. Calculate the RMSE for the historic period (prior to 1996) and again for just the four quarters of 1996, given the following actual values for 1996:

1996Q1	274.464
1996Q2	274.833
1996Q3	281.533
1996Q4	288.300

4 INTRODUCTION TO FORECASTING WITH REGRESSION METHODS

In this chapter the fundamentals of bivariate regression analysis are presented in the context of forecasting applications. Regression models are developed for retail sales (RS), private housing starts (PHS), and disposable personal income per capita (DPI), all based on 10 years of quarterly data starting with 1990Q1 and ending with 1999Q4. These regression models are then used to make forecasts of each series for the four quarters of 2000. At the end of the chapter, we return to our continuing example of forecasting domestic car sales and to the continuing The Gap case study.

The Bivariate Regression Model

Bivariate regression analysis (also called *simple regression*) is a statistical tool that gives us the ability to estimate the mathematical relationship between a dependent variable (usually called Y) and a single independent variable (usually called X).[1] The dependent variable is the variable for which we want to develop a forecast. While various nonlinear forms may be used, simple linear regression models are the most common. Nonlinear models will be discussed in Chapter 5.

In using regression analyses we begin by supposing that Y is a function of X. That is:

$$Y = f(X)$$

Since we most often begin by using linear functions, we may write the population regression model as:

$$Y = \beta_0 + \beta_1 X + \varepsilon$$

---

[1]For a more detailed discussion of the regression model, including underlying assumptions, see Bruce Bowerman and Richard T. O'Connell, *Applied Statistics,* (Chicago: Irwin, 1997).

where β_0 represents the intercept of the regression line on the vertical (or Y) axis and β_1 is the slope of the regression line. Thus, β_1 tells us the rate of change in Y per unit change in X. The intercept (β_0) is the value that the dependent variable would have if $X = 0$. While this is a correct interpretation from an algebraic perspective, such an interpretation is often not valid in applications, since a value of $X = 0$ is frequently not in the relevant range of observations on X. The ε in this model represents an error term. That is, every Y is not likely to be predicted exactly from the values of β_0 and $\beta_1 X$. The resulting error is ε.

We would like to estimate values of β_0 and β_1 such that the resulting equation best fits the data. To do so we need to decide on a criterion against which the fit of the estimated model can be evaluated. The most common such rule is called the *ordinary least-squares* (OLS) criterion. This rule says that the best model is the one that minimizes the sum of the squared error terms.

The unobserved model that describes the whole population of data is expressed as

$$Y = \beta_0 + \beta_1 X + \varepsilon$$

These values of the intercept (β_0) and slope (β_1) are population parameters that are typically estimated using sample data. The corresponding sample statistics are b_0 and b_1. The estimated regression model is expressed as

$$\hat{Y} = b_0 + b_1 X$$

Deviations of predicted values ($\hat{Y}$) from the actual values of Y are called *residuals* and are denoted by e, where

$$e = Y - \hat{Y}$$

or,

$$e = Y - b_0 - b_1 X$$

The ordinary least-squares method seeks to find estimates of the slope and intercept parameters that minimize the sum of squared residuals:

$$Minimize \sum e^2 = \sum (Y - b_0 - b_1 X)^2$$

By taking partial derivatives of the sum of squared residuals with respect to b_0 and b_1, setting the partial derivatives equal to zero, and solving the two equations simultaneously, we obtain estimating formulas:

$$b_1 = \left(\sum XY - n\overline{X}\,\overline{Y} \right) \Big/ \left(\sum X - n\overline{X}^2 \right)$$

$$b_0 = \overline{Y} - \beta_1 \overline{X}$$

These formulas could be used to calculate b_0 and b_1 by hand. However, even for simple regression, a computer program is normally used for such calculations.

Visualization of Data: An Important Step in Regression Analysis

There was a time when regression lines were estimated in a rather ad hoc manner, based solely on an analyst's visual interpretation of the data. The analyst would plot the data by hand and would "eyeball" the resulting scatter of points to determine the position of a straight line that was believed to "best" represent the general relationship between Y and X. Such a straight line was then drawn through the scatterplot, and by selecting two points from the line, its algebraic equation was calculated (i.e., values for b_0 and b_1 were estimated). One obvious problem with such a procedure is that different analysts would almost surely come up with differing estimates of b_0 and b_1.

Today it is doubtful that anyone would take this approach to estimating a regression equation. Modern computer technology makes it very easy to obtain the OLS equation without ever looking at the data. This equation is best, according to the ordinary least-squares criterion, and numerous evaluative statistics can be simultaneously determined. Every analyst obtains precisely the same results, and those results are easily replicated. Thus it may appear that computer-based regression analysis is a clearly superior method. However, something is lost. Analysts may just enter data, issue appropriate commands, get the corresponding statistical results, and run off to apply the model in some decision-based context such as forecasting. In the process, they would never have *looked* at the data. Such blind attention to statistical estimates can be dangerous.

To illustrate this point, consider the four data sets in Table 4–1. For all four of the data sets in Table 4–1, the regression results show an OLS equation of:

$$\hat{Y} = 3 + 0.5X$$

(c4t1) TABLE 4–1   **Four Dissimilar Data Sets with Similar Regression Results**

Set A		Set B		Set C		Set D	
X	Y	X	Y	X	Y	X	Y
10	8.04	10	9.14	10	7.46	8	6.58
8	6.95	8	8.14	8	6.77	8	5.76
13	7.58	13	8.74	13	12.74	8	7.71
9	8.81	9	8.77	9	7.11	8	8.84
11	8.33	11	9.26	11	7.81	8	8.47
14	9.96	14	8.10	14	8.84	8	7.04
6	7.24	6	6.13	6	6.08	8	5.25
4	4.26	4	3.10	4	5.39	19	12.50
12	10.84	12	9.13	12	8.15	8	5.56
7	4.82	7	7.26	7	6.42	8	7.91
5	5.68	5	4.74	5	5.73	8	6.89

SOURCE: F. J. Anscombe, "Graphs in Statistical Analysis," *American Statistician* 27 (February 1973), pp. 17–21; as reported in Edward R. Tufte, *The Visual Display of Quantitative Information* (Cheshire, CT: Graphics Press, 1983), p. 13.

It might also be noted that the mean of the X's is 9.0 and the mean of the Y's is 7.5 in all four cases. The standard deviation is 3.32 for all of the X variables and 2.03 for all of the Y variables. Similarly, the correlation for each pair of X and Y variables is 0.82.[2]

From these results, an analyst who looks only at these summary statistics would be likely to conclude that the four data sets are identical or, at the very least, quite similar. But oh, how wrong this conclusion would be. If one were to take the time to prepare a scattergram of each of the four data sets, dramatic differences would become apparent. In Figure 4–1 we have plotted each XY pair in a separate plot, along with the corresponding OLS regression lines (all four of the regression lines have the same equation: $\hat{Y} = 3 + 0.5X$).

Visualization of these data allows us to see stark differences that would not be apparent from the descriptive statistics we have reviewed. The regression line is most

FIGURE 4–1

Scatterplots of Four XY Data Sets That Have Very Similar Statistical Properties but Are Visually Quite Different
(c4f1)

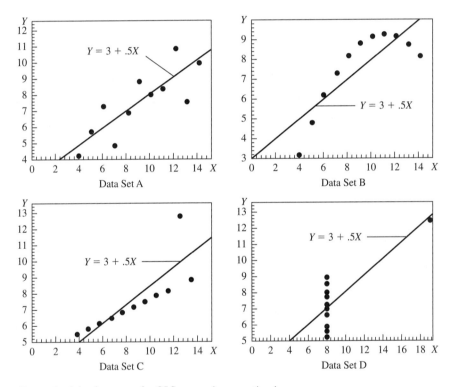

For each of the data sets, the OLS regression equation is

$$Y = 3 + 0.5X$$

---

[2]Many statistical diagnostics on the regression equations, which we will cover later in this chapter, are also equal. These include standard errors of the regression, t-ratios for the coefficients, R-squared, and the regression sum of squares. Statistics related to the evaluation of residuals, such as the Durbin-Watson statistic, show some differences.

clearly inappropriate for the data in the lower right plot. The lower left plot has, with the exception of one outlier, a perfectly linear relationship between *Y* and *X*, which is not so clear without visual inspection of the data. The upper right-hand plot of data suggests that a nonlinear model would fit the data better than a linear function. Only the plot on the upper left suggests a data set that is a good candidate for a linear regression model. Visually, these data sets are quite dissimilar even though they have some very similar statistical properties.

Forecasters can benefit from this example. It is important to *look* at the data before plunging into data analysis and the selection of an appropriate set of forecasting techniques.

A Process for Regression Forecasting

It is usually useful to have a plan at hand when approaching any task. And so it is with developing a regression-based forecast. In this section we suggest one such plan, or process, that helps to organize the task of preparing a regression forecast. What we say here is not separate from the forecast process discussed in Chapter 2. Rather, it complements that process, especially data considerations, model selection, model evaluation, and forecast preparation.

We begin with data considerations, which become somewhat more complex for regression models. Not only do we need to pay attention to the dependent variable, the series to be forecasted, but we must also consider the independent variable(s) that will drive the regression forecast. One should utilize graphic techniques to inspect the data, looking especially for trend, seasonal, and cyclical components, as well as for outliers. This will help in determining what type of regression model may be most appropriate (e.g., linear versus nonlinear, or trend versus causal).

> One should utilize graphic techniques to inspect the data, looking especially for trend, seasonal, and cyclical components, as well as for outliers.

Next one must make a forecast of the independent variable(s). This becomes a separate, yet related, forecasting effort. Each potential independent variable should be forecast using a method that is appropriate to that particular series, taking into account the model-selection guidelines discussed in Chapter 2 and summarized in Table 2–1.

Once the data have been thoroughly reviewed and the type of regression model has been selected, it is time to specify the model. By model specification, we mean the statistical process of estimating the regression coefficients (b_0 and b_1, in simple bivariate regression models). In doing so we recommend using a holdout period for evaluation. Thus, if you have 10 years of quarterly data ($n = 40$), you might use 9 years of data ($n = 36$) to estimate the regression coefficients. Initial evaluation of regression models (based on diagnostic statistics we will discuss shortly) can be done on this subsample of the historical data. However, the real test of a forecasting model is in the actual forecast. Thus, if you have set aside a holdout period of data, you can then test the model in this period to get a truer feel for how well the model meets your needs.

This relates to our discussion of fit versus accuracy in Chapter 2. When the model is evaluated in comparison with the data used in specifying the model, we are determining how well the model "fits" the data. This is a retrospective approach, often called an *in-sample* evaluation. By using a holdout period, we have an opportunity to evaluate the model "out of sample." That is, we can determine how "accurate" the model is for an actual forecast horizon. After an evaluation of fit and accuracy, a forecaster may respecify the best of the models using the entire span of data that are available. The newly specified model is then used to forecast beyond the frontier of what is known at the time of the forecast.

Forecasting with a Simple Linear Trend

It is sometimes possible to make reasonably good forecasts on the basis of a simple linear time trend. To do so we set up a time index (T) to use as the independent or X variable in the basic regression model, where T is usually set equal to 1 for the first observation and increased by 1 for each subsequent observation. The regression model is then:

$$\hat{Y} = b_0 + b_1(T)$$

where Y is the series we wish to forecast.

To illustrate this process, consider the data in Table 4–2. DPI is disposable personal income per capita in 1996 dollars and is given for the 40 quarters from 1990Q1 through

(c4t2&f2)   **TABLE 4–2   Disposable Personal Income Per Capita, 1990–1999**

Period	DPI*	Time (T)	Period	DPI*	Time (T)	
Mar-1990	18,035.00	1	Mar-1995	18,834.00	21	
Jun-1990	18,063.00	2	Jun-1995	18,798.00	22	
Sep-1990	18,031.00	3	Sep-1995	18,871.00	23	
Dec-1990	17,856.00	4	Dec-1995	18,942.00	24	
Mar-1991	17,748.00	5	Mar-1996	19,071.00	25	
Jun-1991	17,861.00	6	Jun-1996	19,081.00	26	
Sep-1991	17,816.00	7	Sep-1996	19,161.00	27	
Dec-1991	17,811.00	8	Dec-1996	19,152.00	28	
Mar-1992	18,000.00	9	Mar-1997	19,331.00	29	
Jun-1992	18,085.00	10	Jun-1997	19,315.00	30	
Sep-1992	18,036.00	11	Sep-1997	19,385.00	31	
Dec-1992	18,330.00	12	Dec-1997	19,478.00	32	
Mar-1993	17,975.00	13	Mar-1998	19,632.00	33	
Jun-1993	18,247.00	14	Jun-1998	19,719.00	34	
Sep-1993	18,246.00	15	Sep-1998	19,904.60	35	
Dec-1993	18,413.00	16	Dec-1998	20,194.00	36	
Mar-1994	18,154.00	17	Mar-1999	20,377.00	37	
Jun-1994	18,409.00	18	Jun-1999	20,472.00	38	← Holdout period
Sep-1994	18,493.00	19	Sep-1999	20,756.00	39	
Dec-1994	18,667.00	20	Dec-1999	21,124.00	40	

*DPI is disposable personal income per capita in constant 1996 dollars.

1999Q4. This is an important economic series, since income is an important determinant for many kinds of sales. The linear time-trend model for DPI is:

$$\widehat{DPI} = b_0 + b_1(T)$$

You see in Table 4–2 that T (time) equals 1 for 1990Q1 and 40 for 1999Q4.

It is usually a good idea to look at data such as those given in Table 4–2 in graphic form before beginning to do any regression analysis. A visual inspection of the data can be helpful in deciding whether a linear or nonlinear model would be most appropriate. A graph of DPI versus T is shown in Figure 4–2. From this graph one can get a good feel for how this important measure of income has increased over the 40 quarters presented. All 40 observations do not fall on a single straight line. However, it does appear that a linear trend line may fit the data reasonably well. The positive trend to DPI is more easily seen in the graphic form of Figure 4–2 than in the tabular form of Table 4–2.

Suppose that you are asked to forecast DPI for the four quarters of 1999, using a simple linear trend, based only on data through 1998. The first thing you would do is to use the linear regression part of your regression software to provide the estimates of b_0 and b_1 for the following model:

$$DPI = b_0 + b_1(T)$$

The regression results are shown at the bottom of Figure 4–3. From those results we see that the intercept (b_0) is 17,560.23 and that the coefficient on T (b_1, or the slope) is 61.87. Thus, the regression forecast model may be written as:

$$\widehat{DPI} = 17,498.40 + 61.87(T)$$

FIGURE 4–2

Graph of Disposable Personal Income Per Capita in 1996 Dollars (DPI) Versus a Time Index (T) for 1990 through 1999 (40 Quarters) (c4t2&f2)

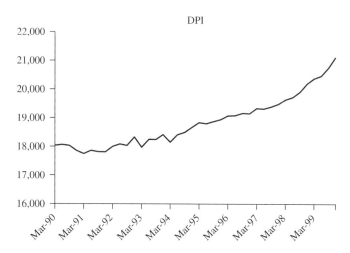

While DPI does not fall on a perfectly straight line, it does show a positive trend that is close to linear.

FIGURE 4–3

*DPI with a Linear
Trend Line*
(c4t3&f3)

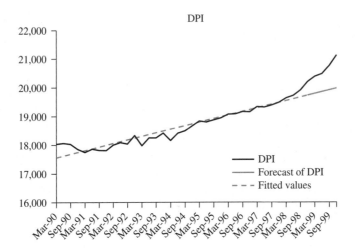

The linear trend follows the general upward movement in DPI quite
well. The trend equation is DPI = 17,498.40 + 61.87(T).

Audit Trail--ANOVA Table (Linear Regression Selected)

Source of Variation	SS	df	MS	SEE
Regression	14,870,026.73	1	14,870,026.73	
Error	1,350,406.34	34	39,717.83	199.29
Total	16,220,433.07	35		

Audit Trail--Coefficient Table (Linear Regression Selected)

Name	Value	Standard Error	T-test	P-value	Elasticity	Overall F-test
Intercept	17,498.40	67.84	257.94	0.00		374.39
Slope	61.87	3.20	19.35	0.00	0.06	

Audit Trail--Statistics

Accuracy Measure	Value	Forecast Statistic	Value
Mean absolute percentage error (MAPE)	0.74%	Durbin-Watson	0.53
R-squared	91.67%		
Adjusted R-squared	91.43%		

The slope term in this model tells us that, on average, disposable personal income per
capita in 1996 dollars increased by 61.87 per quarter. The other statistical results shown
at the bottom of Figure 4–3 are helpful in evaluating the usefulness of the model. Most
of these will be discussed in detail in the section "Statistical Evaluation of Regression
Models," later in this chapter. Our discussion of others will be held in abeyance until
Chapter 5. For now we will just comment that statistical evaluation suggests that this
linear equation provides a reasonably good fit to the data.

To use this equation to make a forecast for the four quarters of 1999, we need only substitute the appropriate values for time (T). These are 37, 38, 39, and 40 for 1999Q1, 1999Q2, 1999Q3, and 1999Q4, respectively. The trend estimates of DPI for 1999 are as follows:

$$1999Q1: DPI = 17,498.40 + 61.87(37) = 19,787.45$$

$$1999Q2: DPI = 17,498.40 + 61.87(38) = 19,849.31$$

$$1999Q3: DPI = 17,498.40 + 61.87(39) = 19,911.18$$

$$1999Q4: DPI = 17,498.40 + 61.87(40) = 19,973.05$$

You can see in Figure 4–3 that the simple linear trend line does fit the actual data reasonably well through the period from 1990 through 1998.

The actual values of DPI are shown in Table 4–3 along with the trend values in order to determine the root-mean-squared error (RMSE) for the historic and forecast periods. The calculation of the RMSE for the 1999 holdout period is illustrated below:

Period	Actual DPI	Trend Forecast of DPI	Actual Minus Forecast	Square of Actual Minus Forecast
1999Q1	20,377	19,787.45	589.55	347,572.65
1999Q2	20,472	19,849.31	622.69	387,737.52
1999Q3	20,736	19,911.18	844.82	713,718.38
1999Q4	21,124	19,973.05	1,150.95	1,324,689.04

Sum of squared errors = 2,773,717.59

Mean-squared error (MSE) = 2,773,717.59 ÷ 4 = 693,429.398

Root-mean-squared error (RMSE) = Square root of MSE = 832.72

In the above calculations, as well as in Table 4–3 and Figure 4–3, one can see that the linear trend forecast did not do well in picking up the increased growth rate in DPI at the end of the 1990s. However, the long-term linear trend forecasts of DPI are quite accurate overall. This RMSE is about 4.0 percent of the mean for DPI during the forecast period. The RMSE for this method could be compared with that of other techniques to determine the most appropriate method to use.[3]

Trend models such as this can sometimes be very helpful in forecasting, and, as you see, they are easy to develop and to implement. In such models we simply track the past time trend and project it forward for the forecast horizon of interest. Note that we do not

---

[3]For example, based on 1990 through 1998 data, the optimal Holt's exponential smoothing model for DPI (alpha = 0.59; gamma = 0.24) produces a forecast for the four quarters of 1999 that has an RMSE for that period of 286.55 (i.e., the smoothing model would be a better model because of the lower RMSE). If you think back to the discussion of the Holt's model in Chapter 3 you will realize that this model would have picked up the increased rate of growth in DPI during the late 1990s.

(c4t3&f3) | **TABLE 4–3   Disposable Personal Income with Linear Trend Forecast and Errors by Quarter**

Date	DPI	Forecast	Error	Squared Error	
Mar-1990	18,035.00	17,560.23	474.77	225,408.09	
Jun-1990	18,063.00	17,622.10	440.90	194,396.72	
Sep-1990	18,031.00	17,683.96	347.04	120,434.85	
Dec-1990	17,856.00	17,745.83	110.17	12,137.44	
Mar-1991	17,748.00	17,807.70	−59.70	3,563.75	
Jun-1991	17,861.00	17,869.56	−8.56	73.35	
Sep-1991	17,816.00	17,931.43	−115.43	13,324.43	
Dec-1991	17,811.00	17,993.30	−182.30	33,232.81	
Mar-1992	18,000.00	18,055.17	−55.17	3,043.27	
Jun-1992	18,085.00	18,117.03	−32.03	1,026.12	
Sep-1992	18,036.00	18,178.90	−142.90	20,420.48	
Dec-1992	18,330.00	18,240.77	89.23	7,962.45	
Mar-1993	17,975.00	18,302.63	−327.63	107,344.44	
Jun-1993	18,247.00	18,364.50	−117.50	13,806.67	
Sep-1993	18,246.00	18,426.37	−180.37	32,532.97	Historical
Dec-1993	18,413.00	18,488.24	−75.24	5,660.48	period
Mar-1994	18,154.00	18,550.10	−396.10	156,897.87	RMSE =
Jun-1994	18,409.00	18,611.97	−202.97	41,197.04	193.68
Sep-1994	18,493.00	18,673.84	−180.84	32,702.29	
Dec-1994	18,667.00	18,735.70	−68.70	4,720.37	
Mar-1995	18,834.00	18,797.57	36.43	1,326.99	
Jun-1995	18,798.00	18,859.44	−61.44	3,774.79	
Sep-1995	18,871.00	18,921.31	−50.31	2,530.74	
Dec-1995	18,942.00	18,983.17	−41.17	1,695.27	
Mar-1996	19,071.00	19,045.04	25.96	673.88	
Jun-1996	19,081.00	19,106.91	−25.91	671.23	
Sep-1996	19,161.00	19,168.78	−7.78	60.45	
Dec-1996	19,152.00	19,230.64	−78.64	6,184.63	
Mar-1997	19,331.00	19,292.51	38.49	1,481.51	
Jun-1997	19,315.00	19,354.38	−39.38	1,550.53	
Sep-1997	19,385.00	19,416.24	−31.24	976.19	
Dec-1997	19,478.00	19,478.11	−0.11	0.01	
Mar-1998	19,632.00	19,539.98	92.02	8,467.99	
Jun-1998	19,719.00	19,601.85	117.15	13,725.17	
Sep-1998	19,904.60	19,663.71	240.88	58,021.62	
Dec-1998	20,194.00	19,725.58	468.38	219,379.45	
Mar-1999	20,377.00	19,787.45	589.55	347,572.65	Holdout
Jun-1999	20,472.00	19,849.31	622.69	387,737.52	period
Sep-1999	20,756.00	19,911.18	844.82	713,718.38	RMSE =
Dec-1999	21,124.00	19,973.05	1,150.95	1,324,689.04	832.72

imply any sense of causality in such a model. Time does not cause income to rise. Income has increased over time at a reasonably steady rate for reasons not explained in our model.

Using a Causal Regression Model to Forecast

Trend models, such as the one we looked at in the previous section for real disposable personal income, use the power of regression analysis to determine the best linear trend line. However, such uses do not exploit the full potential of this powerful statistical tool. Regression analysis is especially useful for developing causal models.

In a causal model, expressed as $Y = f(X)$, a change in the independent variable (X) is assumed to cause a change in the dependent variable (Y). The selection of an appropriate causal variable (X) should be based on some insight that suggests that a causal relationship is reasonable. One does not arbitrarily select an X variable, but rather looks to past experience and understanding to identify potential causal factors. For example, suppose that you were attempting to develop a bivariate regression model that might be helpful in explaining and predicting the level of retail sales in the United States. What factors do you think might have an impact on retail sales? Some potential causal variables that might come to mind could include income, some measure of the level of interest rates, and the unemployment rate, among others.

Discussions with knowledgeable people in the retailing industry would help you determine other variables and would be helpful in prioritizing those that are identified. Library research in areas related to retail sales and to consumer behavior may turn up yet other potential X variables. One thing you would learn quickly is that there is a substantial seasonal aspect to retail sales.

It is important that the independent variable be selected on the basis of a logical construct that relates it to the dependent variable. Otherwise one might find a variable through an arbitrary search process that works well enough in a given historical period, more or less by accident, but then breaks down severely out of sample. Consider, for example, William Stanley Jevons' sunspot theory of business cycles. For a certain historical period a reasonably strong correlation appeared to support such a notion. Outside that period, however, the relationship was quite weak. In this case it is difficult to develop a strong conceptual theory tying business cycles to sunspot activity.

To illustrate the use of a causal model, we will consider how well retail sales (RS) can be forecast on the basis of two different causal variables: (1) disposable personal income per capita in 1996 dollars as a measure of overall purchasing power; and (2) the mortgage rate as one possible measure of the general level of interest rates, since many "big ticket" items such as cars and home appliances may be financed.

Before we start to develop a forecast of retail sales, we should take a look at a time-series plot of the series. In this example we will assume that we have quarterly data for retail sales from 1990Q1 through 1998Q4 and that we want to forecast RS for each of the four quarters of 1999. A time-series plot of RS is found in Figure 4–4 and the raw data are in Table 4–4.

FIGURE 4–4

Retail Sales in Millions of Dollars (c4t4&f4)

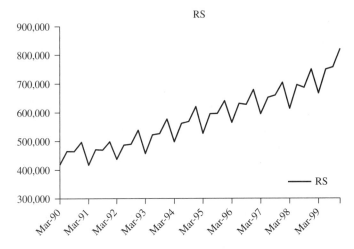

This graph of retail sales shows a clear positive trend and a reasonably consistent seasonal pattern.

Months shown are the end months of the quarters.

(c4t4&f4)   **TABLE 4–4   Retail Sales (RS) in Millions of Dollars**

Period*	RS	Period*	RS	
Mar-1990	418,436	Mar-1995	526,748	
Jun-1990	464,944	Jun-1995	595,468	
Sep-1990	464,490	Sep-1995	596,375	
Dec-1990	496,741	Dec-1995	640,422	
Mar-1991	417,357	Mar-1996	564,968	
Jun-1991	470,851	Jun-1996	631,151	
Sep-1991	469,494	Sep-1996	627,404	
Dec-1991	498,235	Dec-1996	678,842	
Mar-1992	437,388	Mar-1997	594,984	
Jun-1992	486,553	Jun-1997	651,881	
Sep-1992	489,541	Sep-1997	659,643	
Dec-1992	538,107	Dec-1997	704,054	
Mar-1993	456,913	Mar-1998	613,448	
Jun-1993	521,799	Jun-1998	695,875	
Sep-1993	526,234	Sep-1998	686,297	
Dec-1993	577,166	Dec-1998	749,973	
Mar-1994	497,770	Mar-1999	666,676	
Jun-1994	561,668	Jun-1999	749,668	← Holdout period
Sep-1994	568,419	Sep-1999	757,234	
Dec-1994	620,341	Dec-1999	821,351	

*Months shown are the end months of the quarters.

SOURCE: The Bureau of the Census (http://www.census.gov).

A Retail Sales Forecast Based on Disposable Personal Income Per Capita

If we hypothesize that disposable personal income per capita (DPI) is influential in determining RS, we might initially want to look at a scattergram of these two variables. This is shown in Figure 4–5, where RS is plotted on the vertical axis and DPI is on the horizontal axis. You see that higher values of RS appear to be associated with higher incomes. All 36 observations (for 1990 through 1998) do not fall on a single straight line,

FIGURE 4–5

Scatterplots of Retail Sales Versus Disposable Personal Income Per Capita (c4f5)

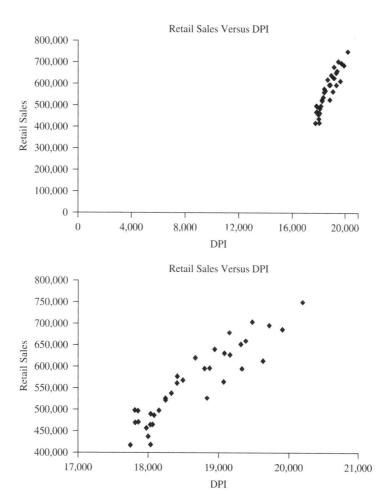

In this graph you see a fairly tight clustering of the 36 data points for RS and DPI. Note in the top panel that all the data are quite far from the origin. If you picture a straight line drawn through these points and extended clear to the vertical axis, you can see that the vertical intercept would be negative. The lower panel is constructed so the axes do not start at zero. This allows you to better see the pattern of the relationship between RS and DPI.

but a straight line through those points appears to provide a reasonably good fit to the data. You also see that all of these 36 observations are well away from the origin. The importance of this observation will be apparent as we discuss the regression results below.

The bivariate regression model for RS as a function of DPI may be written as:

$$RS = b_0 + b_1(DPI)$$

The RS data used to estimate values for b_0 and b_1 are given in Table 4–4 and the data for DPI are in Table 4–2. The basic regression results are shown in Figure 4–6, along with a graph of the actual and predicted values based on this model. To use this model in the holdout period a Holt's exponential smoothing forecast of DPI was used. On the basis of these results the forecast model (equation) for retail sales as a function of disposable personal income per capita is:

$$RS = -1,690,954.06 + 120.80(DPI)$$

Note the "large" negative value for the vertical (RS) intercept, as we expected based on the plot in Figure 4–5. The positive slope (120.80) indicates that on average, RS (in

FIGURE 4–6

Actual Retail Sales (RS) and Values Predicted by the Regression Model: RS = f(DPI), Without Accounting for Seasonality (c4f6)

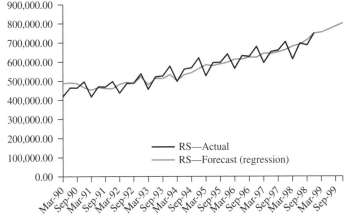

The regression equation is: RS = −1,690,954.06 + 120.80(DPI). Notice that the predicted values in the graph, based on this model, do not replicate the seasonal pattern in retail sales very well.

Audit Trail--Coefficient Table (Multiple Regression Selected)

Series Description	Included in Model	Coefficient	Standard Error	T-test	P-value
DPI	Yes	120.80	8.55	14.12	0.00
RS	Dependent	-1,690,954.06	159,570.60	-10.60	0.00

Multiple Regression--Result Formula

```
RS = -1,690,954.06 + ((DPI) * 120.80)
```

millions) increases by 120.80 for each additional \$1 increase in disposable personal income per capita. A major problem with this model is apparent in Figure 4–6. It is clear from the graph of actual and predicted retail sales that this model fails to deal with the seasonality in RS.

The failure of this model to deal well with the seasonal nature of retail sales suggests that either we should use a model that can account for seasonality directly or we should deseasonalize the data before developing the regression forecasting model. In Chapter 3 you learned how to forecast a seasonal series with Winters' exponential smoothing. In the next chapter you will see how regression methods can also incorporate seasonality, and in Chapter 6 you will see how a seasonal pattern can be modeled using time-series decomposition. For the remainder of this chapter we will develop models based on seasonally adjusted retail sales data (SARS), then reintroduce the seasonality as we develop forecasts.

When retail sales are seasonally adjusted, the following seasonal indices are found (arithmetically normalized to average 1): Q1 = 0.91; Q2 = 1.01; Q3 = 1.00; and Q4 = 1.07. From these we see that retail sales are highest in the fourth quarter (the Christmas season) and lowest in the first quarter.

When we regress the seasonally adjusted values of retail sales (SARS) as a function of disposable personal income, we get the results shown at the bottom of Figure 4–7 and summarized by the following equation:

$$\text{SARS} = -1{,}582{,}975.37 + 114.99(\text{DPI})$$

We can substitute values of DPI into this equation to get predictions for seasonally adjusted retail sales (SARS). Then, multiplying SARS by the seasonal index for each quarter, we obtain a prediction of the unadjusted retail sales for each quarter.

To forecast RS as a function of DPI, one must first forecast DPI. Forecasts for primary macroeconomic series such as DPI are often purchased from one of the econometric firms that provide such services. These causal variables may also be forecast "in-house" by using an appropriate method. If we want to use the above regression model to forecast RS for the four quarters of 1999, we must first develop forecast values for DPI for those same quarters. As indicated in footnote 3, Holt's exponential smoothing model provides a good forecast for DPI. That model generates the following forecast values of DPI for 1999: Q1 = 20,233.25; Q2 = 20,368.93; Q3 = 20,504.62; and Q4 = 20,640.30. Recall that the seasonal indices (SI) are: Q1 = 0.91; Q2 = 1.01; Q3 = 1.00; and Q4 = 1.07. Our retail sales forecasts (RS) for 1999 can now be calculated as follows:[4]

$$\text{RS} = (\text{Regression Prediction of SARS}) \times (\text{SI})$$
$$\text{RS} = [-1{,}582{,}975.37 + 114.99(\text{DPI})] \times (\text{SI})$$

1999Q1: RS = [−1,582,975.37 + 114.99(20,233.25)] × (0.91) = 679,039

1999Q2: RS = [−1,582,975.37 + 114.99(20,368.93)] × (1.01) = 768,797

1999Q3: RS = [−1,582,975.37 + 114.99(20,504.62)] × (1.00) = 777,343

1999Q4: RS = [−1,582,975.37 + 114.99(20,640.30)] × (1.07) = 846,420

---

[4]If you do these calculations by hand, you will get slightly different results due to the rounding and truncating done in the manual calculations compared to the computer-calculated results that are shown here.

FIGURE 4–7

Retail Sales and Forecasts Derived from a Regression Model of Seasonally Adjusted Retail Sales Based on Disposable Personal Income Per Capita (c4f7)

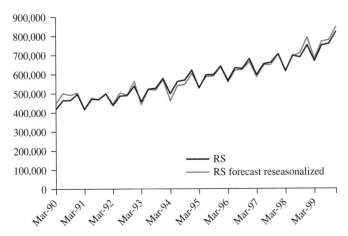

The regression equation is: SARS = −1,582,975.37 + 114.99(DPI). Values for DPI are substituted into this equation, and the results are multiplied by the seasonal indices to arrive at the predicted values for retail sales shown in the graph. That is: RS = (regression prediction of SARS) × (SI) = [−1,582,975.37 + 114.99(DPI)] × (SI)

Multiple Regression--Result Formula

SARS = -1,582,975.37 + ((DPI) * 114.99)

Audit Trail--Coefficient Table (Multiple Regression Selected)

Series Description	Included in Model	Coefficient	Standard Error	T-test	P-value
SARS	Dependent	-1,582,975.37	79,923.19	-19.81	0.00
DPI	Yes	114.99	4.28	26.84	0.00

Seasonal Indices

Q1	0.91
Q2	1.01
Q3	1.00
Q4	1.07

Audit Trail--Statistics

Accuracy Measure	Value	Forecast Statistic	Value
Mean absolute percentage error (MAPE)	2.30%	Durbin-Watson	0.69
Sum squared error (SSE)	10,122,718,223		
R-squared	95.49%		
Adjusted R-squared	95.36%		

These values, as well as the values the model predicts for the historical period, are plotted in Figure 4–7, along with the actual data for 1990Q1 through 1999Q4. During the historical period, actual values of DPI were used to calculate RS, while in the forecast period (1999Q1 to 1999Q4) forecast values of DPI were used as described.

Actual and predicted values of retail sales for 1999 are shown in the following table, along with the calculation of the root-mean-squared error (RMSE) for the forecast period:

Period	Actual RS	Forecast RSF	$(RS - RSF)^2$
1999Q1	666,676	679,039	152,852,575
1999Q2	749,668	768,797	365,935,211
1999Q3	757,234	777,343	404,362,890
1999Q4	821,351	846,420	628,457,772

Sum of squared errors = 1,551,608,448

Mean-squared error: MSE = 1,551,608,448 ÷ 4 = 387,902,112

Root-mean-squared error: RMSE = $\sqrt{387,902,112}$ = 19,695

This RMSE is about 2.6 percent of the mean for RS during these four holdout quarters.

A Retail Sales Forecast Based on the Mortgage Rate

As mentioned above, a portion of retail sales involves "big ticket" items that are financed by many consumers, and thus we might expect that interest rates would influence purchasing decisions. Examples of products that may be bought on credit would include dishwashers, washing machines, dryers, refrigerators, home computers, home entertainment centers, and, of course, cars. To measure the influence of interest rates on retail sales, what we would really like is a weighted average of all different interest rates used for consumer purchases.

In reality we often find that the measure we most want is not available and so we use a "proxy" variable. That is, we use another variable that is available and that is closely related to the variable we want. We will show an example of this in the forecasting of retail sales. Because all interest rates tend to be closely related, we will use the mortgage rate as a proxy measure of the effect that interest rates may have on retail sales. We are not suggesting that people take out a mortgage to buy a car or a new washer and dryer, but rather that this rate may be indicative of the actual rate used for such purchases. It might be noted in passing that some people do get a new, or additional, mortgage on their home to borrow money that is then used to purchase a car or other consumer good.

Figure 4–8 shows a scatterplot of the relationship between retail sales and the mortgage rate. In general it appears in that graph that these two variables have an inverse relationship. Higher levels of retail sales appear to be related to lower mortgage rates, and vice versa.

Of the two causal variables we are considering, a measure of income per person and an interest rate, which do you think would be of the most help in forecasting retail sales? Most people would probably pick the income measure, since it takes money for

FIGURE 4–8

*Scatterplot of
Retail Sales
Versus the
Mortgage Rate
(c4f8)*

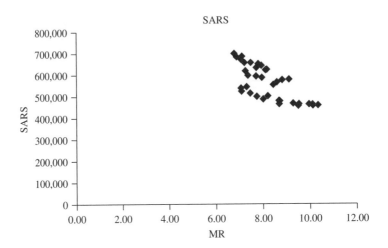

*In this graph you see an inverse relationship between retail sales and the
mortgage rate.*

all consumer purchases but only some retail sales are purchased using credit. Let's see
how our models compare.

To develop the forecast model, seasonally adjusted retail sales were first regressed
on the mortgage rate using data from 1990Q1 through 1998Q4. This resulted in the following model:

$$SARS = 1{,}033{,}403.26 - 57{,}676.74(MR)$$

The negative coefficient for the mortgage rate is consistent with the idea that higher
interest rates make credit purchases more expensive and should therefore reduce sales.
The full regression model of seasonally adjusted retail sales as a function of the mortgage rate is given in Figure 4–9.

To get a forecast of SARS for the four quarters of 1999, we needed to have a forecast of the mortgage rate for 1999Q1 through 1999Q4. This forecast was done using a
simple exponential smoothing model. The predictions of SARS from the model are multiplied by the seasonal indices to arrive at the forecasts of retail sales.[5] These forecast
values, along with actual retail sales, are plotted in the time-series graph of Figure 4–9.
A visual inspection of this time-series plot in comparison with the results shown in
Figure 4–7 supports the notion that DPI is a more important determinant of retail sales
than is MR.

Actual and predicted values of retail sales for 1999, based on the mortgage
rate model, are shown at the bottom of page 157, along with the root-mean-squared
error (RMSE) for the forecast period.

---

[5]The seasonal indices are: Q1 = 0.91; Q2 = 1.01; Q3 = 1.00; and Q4 = 1.07. These are the same
indices used for our model involving DPI.

FIGURE 4–9

Retail Sales and Forecasts Derived from a Regression Model of Seasonally Adjusted Retail Sales Based on the Mortgage Rate (c4f9)

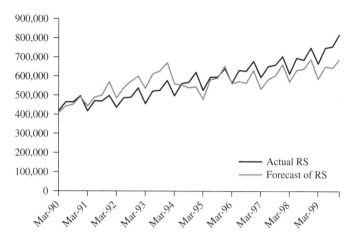

The regression equation is: SARS = 1,033,403.26 − 57,676.74(MR). Values for MR are substituted into this equation and the results are multiplied by the seasonal indices to arrive at the predicted values for retail sales shown in the graph. That is: RS = (regression prediction of SARS) × (SI) = [1,033,403.26 − 57,676.74(MR)] × (SI)

Multiple Regression--Result Formula

SARS = 1,033,403.26 + ((MR) * -57,676.74)

Audit Trail--Coefficient Table (Multiple Regression Selected)

Series Description	Included in Model	Coefficient	Standard Error	T-test	P-value
MR	Yes	-57,676.74	9,187.25	-6.28	0.00
SARS	Dependent	1,033,403.26	75,854.84	13.62	0.00

Seasonal Indices	
Q1	0.91
Q2	1.01
Q3	1.00
Q4	1.07

Audit Trail--Statistics

Accuracy Measure	Value	Forecast Statistic	Value
Mean absolute percentage error (MAPE)	8.32%	Durbin-Watson	0.21
Sum squared error (SSE)	104,016,708,347		
R-squared	53.69%		
Adjusted R-squared	52.32%		

Period	Actual RS	Predicted RS
1999Q1	666,676	587,468.10
1999Q2	749,668	651,453.35
1999Q3	757,234	645,430.47
1999Q4	821,351	688,913.16

Root-mean-squared error = 107,191

Note that this RMSE is greater than the RMSE for the DPI model (19,695). This supports our conclusion that the DPI is the better predictor of retail sales.

In the next chapter we will investigate the possibility of using the influence of both disposable personal income per capita and the mortgage rate in the same model. This will take us into the realm of multiple regression.

Statistical Evaluation of Regression Models

Now that you have a basic understanding of how simple bivariate regression models can be applied to forecasting, let us look more closely at some things that should be considered in evaluating regression models. Three of the regression models developed above will be used as the basis for our initial discussion. These are reproduced in Table 4–5. After evaluating these models in more detail we will turn our attention to the use of bivariate regression models to forecast domestic car sales and the sales of The Gap.

Basic Diagnostic Checks for Evaluating Regression Results

There are several things you should consider when you look at regression results. First, ask yourself whether the sign on the slope term makes sense. There is almost always an economic or business logic that indicates whether the relationship between the dependent variable (Y) and the independent variable (X) should be positive or negative.

In two of the examples considered so far in this chapter, a positive sign makes sense. In the first model we know that real disposable personal income per capita in the United States has generally increased over time. There have been some short periods of decline but such periods have been exceptions. Thus, we would expect the positive sign on the coefficient for the time index in the trend model for DPI. In the second example, where seasonally adjusted retail sales (SARS) are modeled as a function of real disposable personal income per capita (DPI), a positive sign is also logical. For most goods and services, sales can be expected to increase as income increases. In the third model, for which seasonally adjusted retail sales is a function of the mortgage rate, the negative coefficient for MR is also to be expected. The mortgage rate is used as a proxy for the rate of interest on consumer installment loans, and as that rate increases we would expect consumers to borrow less. Thus, retail sales should decrease as interest rates rise.

What if the signs do not make sense? This is a clear indication that something is wrong with the regression model. It may be that the model is incomplete and that more than one independent variable is needed. In such a case the model is said to be *under-specified*. If so, a multiple-regression model may be appropriate. (Such models will be discussed in Chapter 5.) It would not be wise to use regression models that have coefficients with signs that are not logical.

It would not be wise to use regression models that have coefficients with signs that are not logical.

The second thing that should be considered in an initial evaluation of a regression model is whether or not the slope term is significantly positive or negative. If not, then there is probably no statistical relationship between the dependent and independent variables. If the slope is zero, the regression line is perfectly horizontal, indicating that the value of Y is independent of the value of X (i.e., there is probably no relationship between X and Y).

TABLE 4–5   Basic Regression Results for Three Bivariate Models   (c4t6)

Model 1. Linear (Trend) Regression—Result Formula

SEE

199.29

DPI = 17,498.40 + 61.87* (Time Index)

Audit Trail--Coefficient Table (Linear Regression Selected)

Name	Value	Standard Error	T-test	P-value
Intercept	17,498.40	67.84	257.94	0.00
Slope	61.87	3.20	19.35	0.00

Audit Trail--Statistics

Accuracy Measure	Value	Forecast Statistic	Value
Mean absolute percentage error (MAPE)	0.74%	Durbin-Watson	0.53
R-squared	91.67%		

Model 2. Multiple Regression—Result Formula

SEE

17,254.77

SARS = -1,582,975.37 + ((DPI) * 114.99)

Audit Trail--Coefficient Table (Multiple Regression Selected)

Series Description	Included in Model	Coefficient	Standard Error	T-test	P-value		Seasonal Indices	
						Q1	0.91
						Q2	1.01
SARS	Dependent	-1,582,975.37	79,923.19	-19.81	0.00	Q3	1.00
DPI	Yes	114.99	4.28	26.84	0.00	Q4	1.07

Audit Trail--Statistics

Accuracy Measure	Value	Forecast Statistic	Value
Mean absolute percentage error (MAPE)	2.30%	Durbin-Watson	0.69
R-squared	95.49%		

Model 3. Multiple Regression—Result Formula

SEE

55,311.07

SARS = 1,033,403.26 + ((MR) * -57,676.74)

Audit Trail--Coefficient Table (Multiple Regression Selected)

Series Description	Included in Model	Coefficient	Standard Error	T-test	P-value		Seasonal Indices	
						Q1	0.91
						Q2	1.01
MR	Yes	-57,676.74	9,187.25	-6.28	0.00	Q3	1.00
SARS	Dependent	1,033,403.26	75,854.84	13.62	0.00	Q4	1.07

Audit Trail--Statistics

Accuracy Measure	Value	Forecast Statistic	Value
Mean absolute percentage error (MAPE)	8.32%	Durbin-Watson	0.21
R-squared	53.69%		

But how far from zero need the slope term be? In the first example in Table 4–5 the slope is 61.87, in the second it is 114.99, and in the third model the coefficient is −57,676.74. These are relatively large numbers in terms of how much above or below zero they are, but we must be cautious about evaluating just the size of the slope term. To determine if the slope is significantly greater or less than zero, we must test a hypothesis concerning the true slope. Remember that our basic regression model is:

$$Y = \beta_0 + \beta_1 X + \varepsilon$$

If $\beta_1 = 0$, then $Y = \beta_0$ regardless of the value of X.

When we have a predisposition about whether the coefficient should be positive or negative based on our knowledge of the relationship, a one-tailed hypothesis test is appropriate. If our belief suggests a positive coefficient, the hypothesis would be set up as follows:

$$H_0: \beta \leq 0$$
$$H_1: \beta > 0$$

This form would be correct for the first two cases in Table 4–5, since in both cases a direct (positive) relationship is expected.

When our belief suggests a negative coefficient, the hypothesis would be set up as follows:

$$H_0: \beta \geq 0$$
$$H_1: \beta < 0$$

This form would be correct for the third case in Table 4–5 because an inverse (negative) relationship is expected.

In some situations we may not have a specific expectation about the direction of causality, in which case a two-tailed hypothesis test is used. The hypothesis would be set up as follows:

$$H_0: \beta = 0$$
$$H_1: \beta \neq 0$$

The appropriate statistical test is a *t*-test, where the calculated value of t (t_{calc}) is equal to the slope term minus zero, divided by the standard error of the slope.[6] That is:

$$t_{calc} = (b_1 - 0)/(\text{s.e. of } b_1)$$

It is typical to use a 95 percent confidence level (an α, or significance level, of 5 percent) in testing this type of hypothesis. The appropriate number of degrees of freedom in bivariate regression is always $n - 2$, where n is the number of observations used in estimating the model. As described above, when we have a greater-than or less-than sign in the alternative hypothesis, a one-tailed test is appropriate.

---

[6]The standard error of the estimated regression coefficient measures the sampling variability of b_1 about its expected value β_1, the true population parameter.

For our present examples there are 34 degrees of freedom $(36 - 2)$. From the t-table on page 68 we find the critical value of t (such that 0.05 is in one tail) to be 1.645 (using the infinity row). The calculated values of t are:

For the DPI Trend Model	For the SARS = $f(DPI)$ Causal Model	For the SARS = $f(MR)$ Causal Model
$t_{calc} = (61.87 - 0)/3.20$ $= 19.35$	$t_{calc} = (114.99 - 0)/4.28$ $= 26.84$	$t_{calc} = (-57{,}676.74 - 0)/9{,}187.25$ $= -6.28$

The t-values shown here are from Table 4–5. If you do these calculations by hand, results will differ slightly due to rounding.

For the first two cases the calculated values are larger (more positive) than the critical, or table, value so we can reject H_0 in both cases and conclude that the regression coefficients are significantly greater than zero. In the third case the calculated t is more negative than the negative of the table value, and so once again we can reject H_0. In this case we conclude that the coefficient on MR is significantly negative. If this statistical evaluation of the coefficients in a regression analysis results in failure to reject the null hypothesis, then it is probably not wise to use the model as a forecasting tool.[7] However, it is not uncommon to relax the criterion for evaluation of the hypothesis test to a 90 percent confidence level (a 10 percent significance level).

In determining whether or not to reject H_0, an alternative to comparing t-values is to consider the significance level (often called the P-value) given in most computer output. Let us assume that we desire a 95 percent confidence level. This is the equivalent of saying that we desire a 5 percent significance level.[8]

For a two-tailed hypothesis test $(H_1: \beta_1 \neq 0)$, we can then reject H_0 if the reported two-tailed significance level[9] in our output is less than 0.05. For a one-tailed hypothesis test $(H_1: \beta_1 < 0$ or $H_1: \beta_1 > 0)$, we can reject H_0 if one-half of the reported two-tailed significance level is less than 0.05.

In all three of the examples in Table 4–5 the two-tailed significance levels associated with the calculated t-ratios are 0.00. Clearly, one-half of 0.00 is less than 0.05, so it is appropriate to reject H_0 in all three cases. Note that we reach the same conclusion whether we evaluate the hypotheses by comparing the calculated and table t-ratios or by looking at the significance levels.

The third check of regression results is to evaluate what percent of the variation (i.e., up-and-down movement) in the dependent variable is explained by variation in the independent variable. This is evaluated by interpreting the R-squared value that is reported in regression output. R-squared is the coefficient of determination, which tells

---

[7]A phenomenon known as *serial correlation* (which we will discuss shortly) may cause coefficients to appear significantly different from zero (as measured by the t-test) when in fact they are not.

[8]Remember that the confidence level and the significance level add to one. Thus, if we know one of these we can easily determine the other.

[9]In ForecastX™, as well as most other statistical packages, two-tailed significance levels are reported. These are frequently referred to as *P-values*, as is the case in ForecastX™.

us the fraction of the variation in the dependent variable that is explained by variation in the independent variable. Thus, R-squared can range between zero and one. Zero would indicate no explanatory power, while one would indicate that all of the variation in Y is explained by the variation in X. (A related statistic, adjusted R-squared, will be discussed in Chapter 5.)

Our trend model for disposable personal income per capita (DPI) has an R-squared of .9167. Thus, 91.67 percent of the variation in real disposable personal income per capita is accounted for by this simple linear-trend model. The causal model for retail sales as a function of DPI has an R-squared of .9549, which suggests that 95.49 percent of the variation in retail sales is explained by variations in real disposable personal income per capita. The model for retail sales as a function of the mortgage rate has the lowest R-squared of the three models in Table 4–5: $R^2 = .5369$. Thus, variations in the mortgage rate explain only 53.69 percent of the variation in retail sales.

It is possible to perform a statistical test to determine whether the the coefficient of determination (R^2) is significantly different from zero. The hypothesis test may be stated as:

$$H_0: R^2 = 0$$
$$H_1: R^2 \neq 0$$

The appropriate statistical test is an F-test, which will be presented in Chapter 5. With bivariate regression it turns out that the t-test for the slope term in the regression equation is equivalent to the F-test for R-squared. Thus, we will wait until we explore multiple-regression models to discuss the application of the F-test.

Before considering other statistical diagnostics, let us summarize these three initial evaluative steps for bivariate regression models:

1. Ask whether the sign for the slope term makes sense.
2. Check to see whether the slope term is statistically positive or negative at the desired significance level by using a t-test.
3. Evaluate how much of the variation in the dependent variable is explained by the regression model using the R-squared (R^2) value.

These three items can be evaluated from the results presented in standard computer output, such as those shown in Table 4–5.

Using the Standard Error of the Estimate

The forecasts we made in the preceding pages—using a simple linear-trend model and the two causal regression models—were point estimates. In each case we substituted a value for the independent variable into the regression equation to obtain a single number representing our best estimate (forecast) of the dependent variable. It is sometimes useful to provide an interval estimate rather than a point estimate.

The standard error of the estimate (SEE) can be used to generate *approximate* confidence intervals with relative ease. The SEE is often also called the *standard error of the regression.* The confidence intervals we present here are approximate because the

FIGURE 4–10

*Confidence
Bands around a
Regression Line*

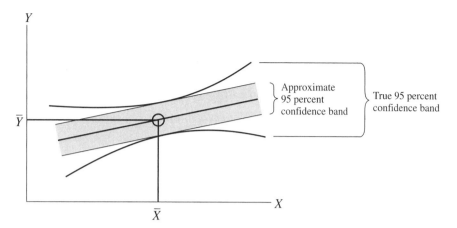

*The true confidence band bows away from the regression line. An approximate 95 percent
confidence band can be calculated by taking the point estimate for each X, plus or minus 2
times the standard error of the estimate.*

true confidence band is not parallel to the regression line but rather bows away from the
regression line at values of Y and X far from the means. This is illustrated in Figure 4–10.
The approximate 95 percent confidence interval can be calculated as follows.[10]

$$\text{Point estimate} \pm 2 \text{ (standard error of the estimate)}$$

The value of 2 is used as an easy approximation for the correct t-value. Recall that if
there is a large number of degrees of freedom, $t = 1.96$.

Representative calculations of approximate 95 percent confidence bands for the
regression forecasts developed for DPI and SARS are shown in Table 4–6. The standard
errors of the regressions are taken from Table 4–5, while the point estimates for each
model and each quarter are those that were found in the sections "Forecasting with a
Simple Linear Trend" and "Using a Causal Regression Model to Forecast."

Serial Correlation

Business and economic data used in forecasting are most often time-series data. The
retail sales data and the real disposable personal income data used in this chapter are
typical of such time series. In using regression analysis with time-series data, the problem known as *serial correlation* can cause some difficulty.

---

[10]The true 95 percent confidence band for predicting Y for a given value of X (X_0) can be found as
follows:

$$\hat{Y} \pm t(\text{SEE})\sqrt{1 + (1/n) + [(X_0 + \overline{X})^2/\textstyle\sum(X - \overline{X})^2]}$$

where t is the appropriate value from the t-distribution at $n - 2$ degrees of freedom and the desired
significance level; SEE is the standard error of the estimate; and $\hat{Y}$ is the point estimate determined from the
estimated regression equation.

TABLE 4–6   **Representative Calculations of Approximate 95 Percent Confidence Intervals: Point Estimate ± 2 × Standard Error of the Estimate (SEE)***

	For DPI: 2 × SEE = 2 × 199.29 = 398.58	
Period	*95 Percent Confidence Interval*	*Actual DPI*
1999Q4	19,787 ± 398.58 = 19,388 to 20,186	20,377

	For SARS: 2 × SEE = 2 × 17,254.77 = 34,509.54	
Period	*95 Percent Confidence Interval*	*Actual SARS***
1999Q4	791,047 ± 34,509.54 = 756,537 to 825,557	767,618

*Point estimates have been rounded to integers.
**Note that this is for retail sales seasonally adjusted.

One of the assumptions of the ordinary least-squares regression model is that the error terms are independent and normally distributed, with a mean of zero and a constant variance. If this is true for a particular case, we would not expect to find any regular pattern in the error terms. When a significant time pattern that violates the independence assumption is found in the error terms, serial correlation is indicated.

Figure 4–11 illustrates the two possible cases of serial correlation. In the left-hand graph, the case of negative serial correlation is apparent. Negative serial correlation exists when a negative error is followed by a positive error, then another negative error, and so on. The error terms alternate in sign. Positive serial correlation is shown in the right-hand graph in Figure 4–11. In positive serial correlation, positive errors tend to be followed by other positive errors, while negative errors are followed by other negative errors.

When serial correlation exists, problems can develop in using and interpreting the OLS regression function. The existence of serial correlation does not bias the coefficients that are estimated, but it does make the estimates of the standard errors smaller than the true standard errors. This means that the *t*-ratios calculated for each coefficient will be overstated, which in turn may lead to the rejection of null hypotheses that should not have been rejected. That is, regression coefficients may be deemed statistically significant when indeed they are not. In addition, the existence of serial correlation causes the *R*-squared and *F*-statistics to be unreliable in evaluating the overall significance of the regression function (the *F*-statistic will be discussed in Chapter 5).

There are a number of ways to test statistically for the existence of serial correlation. The method most frequently used is the evaluation of the Durbin-Watson statistic (DW). This statistic is calculated as follows:

$$\text{DW} = \frac{\sum (e_t - e_{t-1})^2}{\sum e_t^2}$$

FIGURE 4–11

Negative and Positive Serial Correlation

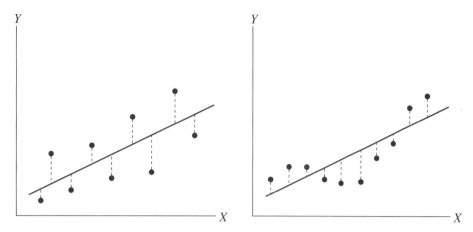

The left-hand graph shows an example of negative serial correlation; the right-hand graph illustrates positive serial correlation. The latter is common when dealing with business data.

where e_t is the residual for the time period t, and e_{t-1} is the residual for the preceding time period ($t - 1$). Almost all computer programs for regression analysis include the Durbin-Watson statistic, so you are not likely to have to calculate it directly.

The DW statistic will always be in the range of 0 to 4. As a rule of thumb, a value close to 2 (e.g., between 1.75 and 2.25) indicates that there is no serial correlation. As the degree of negative serial correlation increases, the value of the DW statistic approaches 4. If positive serial correlation exists, the value of DW approaches 0.

To be more precise in evaluating the significance and meaning of the calculated DW statistic, we must refer to a Durbin-Watson table, such as Table 4–7. Note that for each number of independent variables (k), two columns of values labeled d_l and d_u are given. The values in these columns for the appropriate number of observations (N) are used in evaluating the calculated value of DW according to the criteria shown in Figure 4–12.

To illustrate, let us consider the simple trend regression for real disposable personal income per capita (DPI). From Table 4–5 (see page 159) you see that the calculated Durbin-Watson statistic is 0.53. Using Table 4–5, we find for $k = 1$ and $N = 36$ that:

$$d_l = 1.41$$
$$d_u = 1.52$$

Using these values and our calculated value, we can evaluate the criteria in Figure 4–12:

Region	Comparison	Result
A	$4 > 0.53 > (4 - 1.41)$	False
B	$(4 - 1.41) > 0.53 > (4 - 1.52)$	False
C	$(4 - 1.52) > 0.53 > 1.52$	False
D	$1.52 > 0.53 > 1.41$	False
E	$1.41 > 0.53 > 0$	True

TABLE 4–7   The Durbin-Watson Statistic

N	k = 1		k = 2		k = 3		k = 4		k = 5	
	d_l	d_u	d_l	d_u	d_l	d_u	d_l	d_u	d_l	d_u
15	1.08	1.36	0.95	1.54	0.82	1.75	0.69	1.97	0.56	2.21
16	1.10	1.37	0.98	1.54	0.86	1.73	0.74	1.93	0.62	2.15
17	1.13	1.38	1.02	1.54	0.90	1.71	0.78	1.90	0.67	2.10
18	1.16	1.39	1.05	1.53	0.93	1.69	0.82	1.87	0.71	2.06
19	1.18	1.40	1.08	1.53	0.97	1.68	0.86	1.85	0.75	2.02
20	1.20	1.41	1.10	1.54	1.00	1.68	0.90	1.83	0.79	1.99
21	1.22	1.42	1.13	1.54	1.03	1.67	0.93	1.81	0.83	1.96
22	1.24	1.43	1.15	1.54	1.05	1.66	0.96	1.80	0.86	1.94
23	1.26	1.44	1.17	1.54	1.08	1.66	0.99	1.79	0.90	1.92
24	1.27	1.45	1.19	1.55	1.10	1.66	1.01	1.78	0.93	1.90
25	1.29	1.45	1.21	1.55	1.12	1.66	1.04	1.77	0.95	1.89
26	1.30	1.46	1.22	1.55	1.14	1.65	1.06	1.76	0.98	1.88
27	1.32	1.47	1.24	1.56	1.16	1.65	1.08	1.76	1.01	1.86
28	1.33	1.48	1.26	1.56	1.18	1.65	1.10	1.75	1.03	1.85
29	1.34	1.48	1.27	1.56	1.20	1.65	1.12	1.74	1.05	1.84
30	1.35	1.49	1.28	1.57	1.21	1.65	1.14	1.74	1.07	1.83
31	1.36	1.50	1.30	1.57	1.23	1.65	1.16	1.74	1.09	1.83
32	1.37	1.50	1.31	1.57	1.24	1.65	1.18	1.73	1.11	1.82
33	1.38	1.51	1.32	1.58	1.26	1.65	1.19	1.73	1.13	1.81
34	1.39	1.51	1.33	1.58	1.27	1.65	1.21	1.73	1.15	1.81
35	1.40	1.52	1.34	1.53	1.28	1.65	1.22	1.73	1.16	1.80
36	1.41	1.52	1.35	1.59	1.29	1.65	1.24	1.73	1.18	1.80
37	1.42	1.53	1.36	1.59	1.31	1.66	1.25	1.72	1.19	1.80
38	1.43	1.54	1.37	1.59	1.32	1.66	1.26	1.72	1.21	1.79
39	1.43	1.54	1.38	1.60	1.33	1.66	1.27	1.72	1.22	1.79
40	1.44	1.54	1.39	1.60	1.34	1.66	1.29	1.72	1.23	1.79
45	1.48	1.57	1.43	1.62	1.38	1.67	1.34	1.72	1.29	1.78
50	1.50	1.59	1.46	1.63	1.42	1.67	1.38	1.72	1.34	1.77
55	1.53	1.60	1.49	1.64	1.45	1.68	1.41	1.72	1.38	1.77
60	1.55	1.62	1.51	1.65	1.48	1.69	1.44	1.73	1.41	1.77
65	1.57	1.63	1.54	1.66	1.50	1.70	1.47	1.73	1.44	1.77
70	1.58	1.64	1.55	1.67	1.52	1.70	1.49	1.74	1.46	1.77
75	1.60	1.65	1.57	1.68	1.54	1.71	1.51	1.74	1.49	1.77
80	1.61	1.66	1.59	1.69	1.56	1.72	1.53	1.74	1.51	1.77
85	1.62	1.67	1.60	1.70	1.57	1.72	1.55	1.75	1.52	1.77
90	1.63	1.68	1.61	1.70	1.59	1.73	1.57	1.75	1.54	1.78
95	1.64	1.69	1.62	1.71	1.60	1.73	1.58	1.75	1.56	1.78
100	1.65	1.69	1.63	1.72	1.61	1.74	1.59	1.76	1.57	1.78

k = the number of independent variables; N = the number of observations used in the regression.

Source: J. Durbin and G. S. Watson, "Testing for Serial Correlation in Least Squares Regression," *Biometrika* 38 (June 1951), p. 173.

FIGURE 4–12

A Schematic for Evaluating Serial Correlation Using the Durbin-Watson Statistic

Value of Calculated Durbin-Watson	Result	Region Designator
4		
	Negative serial correlation (reject H_0)	A
$4 - d_l$		
	Indeterminate	B
$4 - d_u$		
2	No serial correlation (do not reject H_0)	C
d_u		
	Indeterminate	D
d_l		
	Positive serial correlation (reject H_0)	E
0		

d_u = Upper value of Durbin-Watson from Table 4–7
d_l = Lower value of Durbin-Watson from Table 4–7
H_0: $\rho = 0$ (i.e., no serial correlation)
H_1: $\rho \neq 0$ (i.e., serial correlation exists)

Since our result is in region E, we can conclude that positive serial correlation exists in this case.[11] You can see evidence of this positive serial correlation if you look in Figure 4–3 at how the regression line (fitted) is at first below, then above, and then below the actual data in a recurring pattern.

You might well ask: What causes serial correlation and what can be done about it? A primary cause of serial correlation is the existence of long-term cycles and trends in economic and business data. Such trends and cycles are particularly likely to produce positive serial correlation. Serial correlation can also be caused by a misspecification of the model. Either leaving out one or more important variables or failing to include a nonlinear term when one is called for can be a cause.

We can try several relatively simple things to reduce serial correlation. One is to use first differences of the variables rather than the actual values when performing the regression analysis. That is, use the change in each variable from period to period in the regression. For example, we could try the following:

$$\Delta Y = b_0 + b_1(\Delta X)$$

where Δ means "change in" and is calculated as follows:

$$\Delta Y_t = Y_t - Y_{t-1}$$
$$\Delta X_t = X_t - X_{t-1}$$

A primary cause of serial correlation is the existence of long-term cycles and trends in economic and business data.

---

[11]Check for serial correlation in the regression of SARS as a function of DPI. You should find that with a calculated Durbin-Watson statistic of 0.69, with $k = 1$, and with $N = 36$, the criterion in region E is satisfied, indicating positive serial correlation.

This process of "first-differencing" will be seen again in Chapter 7, when we discuss ARIMA forecasting models.

Other approaches to solving the serial-correlation problem often involve moving into the realm of multiple regression, where there is more than one independent variable in the regression model. For example, it may be that other causal factors account for the differences between the actual and predicted values. For example, in the retail sales regression, we might add the interest rate and the unemployment rate as additional independent variables.

A third, and somewhat related, approach to dealing with serial correlation is to introduce the square of an existing causal variable as another independent variable. Also, we might introduce a lag of the dependent variable as an independent variable. Such a model might look as follows:

$$Y_t = b_0 + b_1 X_t + b_2 Y_{t-1}$$

where t represents the current time period and $t - 1$ represents the previous time period.

There are other procedures, based on more sophisticated statistical models, that are helpful in dealing with the problems created by serial correlation. These are typically based on an extension of the use of first differences in that they involve the use of generalized differencing to alter the basic linear regression model into one for which the error terms are independent of one another (i.e., $\rho = 0$, where ρ (rho) is the correlation between successive error terms).

The basic regression model is:

$$Y_t = \beta_0 + \beta_1 X_t + \varepsilon_t$$

and since this is true for all time periods, it follows that:

$$Y_{t-1} = \beta_0 + \beta_1 X_{t-1} + \varepsilon_{t-1}$$

Multiplying the second of these equations by ρ and subtracting the result from the first yields the following generalized-differencing transformed equation:

$$Y_t^* = (1 - \rho)\beta_0 + \beta_1 X_t^* + v_t$$

where:

$$Y_t^* = Y_t - \rho Y_{t-1}$$
$$X_t^* = X_t - \rho X_{t-1}$$
$$v_t = \varepsilon_t - \rho \varepsilon_{t-1}$$

It can be shown that the resulting error term, v_t, is independently distributed with a mean of zero and a constant variance.[12] The problem with this generalized-differencing model is that we do not know the correct value for ρ. Two common methods for estimating ρ

---

[12]Most econometrics books describe the underlying statistical theory as well as the two correction procedures we include herein. For example, see Pindyck and Rubinfeld, *Econometric Models and Economic Forecasts*, 3rd ed., 1991, pp. 137–47.

and the corresponding regression model are the Cochrane-Orcutt procedure and the Hildreth-Lu procedure.[13]

The Cochrane-Orcutt procedure uses an iterative approach to estimate the value for ρ, starting with the standard OLS regression model, from which the residuals (e_t) are used to estimate the equation $e_t = \rho e_{t-1} + v_t$. The estimated value of ρ is then used to perform the generalized-differencing transformation, and a new regression is run. New error terms result and are used to make another estimate of ρ. This process continues until the newest estimate of ρ differs from the previous one by a prescribed amount (such as 0.01).

Heteroscedasticity

One of the assumptions of regression analysis is that the error terms in the population regression (ε_i) have a constant variance across all values of the independent variable (X). When this is true, the model is said to be *homoscedastic,* and if this assumption is violated the model is termed *heteroscedastic.* With heteroscedasticity, the standard errors of the regression coefficients may be underestimated, causing the calculated *t*-ratios to be larger than they should be, which may lead us to conclude incorrectly that a variable is statistically significant.

We can evaluate a regression model for heteroscedasticity by looking at a scatterplot of the residuals (on the vertical axis) versus the independent variable (on the horizontal axis). In an ideal model, the plot of the residuals would fall within a horizontal band, as shown in the top graph of Figure 4–13. This graph illustrates a residual pattern representative of homoscedasticity. A typical heteroscedastic situation is shown by the funnel-shaped pattern of residuals in the lower graph of Figure 4–13.

One common way to reduce or eliminate a problem of heteroscedasticity is to use the logarithm of the dependent variable in the estimation of the regression model. This often works because the logarithms will have less overall variability than the raw data. A second possible solution would be to use a form of regression analysis other than the ordinary least-squares method. Discussion of such methods is beyond the scope of this text but can be found in many econometric texts.

To illustrate the evaluation of a specific model for heteroscedasticity, let us look at the model of seasonally adjusted retail sales (SARS) as a function of disposable personal income per capita (DPI). Figure 4–14 shows a scattergram of the residuals from that model. There does not appear to be a systematic pattern to the residuals that would lead us to suspect heteroscedasticity in this case.

Cross-Sectional Forecasting

While most forecasting is based on time-series data, there are situations in which cross-sectional analysis is useful. In cross-sectional analysis the data all pertain to one time period rather than a sequence of periods. Suppose, for example, that you are the sales manager for a firm that sells small specialty sandwiches through convenience stores.

---

[13]While these methods help solve the serial-correlation problem, they are not often used in practice for forecasting, largely due to their added complexity.

FIGURE 4–13

*Residual Patterns
Indicative of
Homoscedasticity
(Top Graph) and
Heteroscedasticity
(Bottom Graph)*

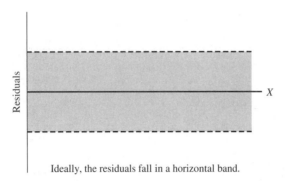

Ideally, the residuals fall in a horizontal band.

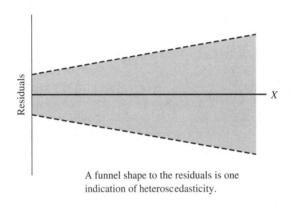

A funnel shape to the residuals is one
indication of heteroscedasticity.

FIGURE 4–14

*Scatterplot of the
Residuals from
the Regression of
SARS with DPI
(c4f14)*

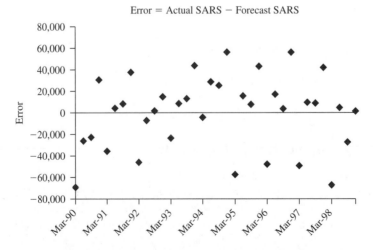

Error = Actual SARS − Forecast SARS

*This scatterplot does not show a pattern that would suggest
heteroscedasticity.*

While most forecasting is based on time-series data, there are situations in which cross-sectional analysis is useful. In cross-sectional analysis the data all pertain to one time period rather than a sequence of periods.

You currently operate in eight cities and are considering expanding into another. You have the data shown at the top of Table 4–8 for the most recent year's sales and the population of each city. You may try to predict sales based on population by using a bivariate regression model. The model may be written as:

$$\text{Sales} = b_0 + b_1(\text{POP})$$

Regression results for this model, given the eight data points just shown, are presented in Table 4–8.

These results show the expected positive sign for the coefficient of population. The critical value of t from the t-table at six degrees of freedom ($n - 2 = 6$) and a 5 percent significance level (one-tailed test) is 1.943. Since the calculated value for population is greater ($8.00 > 1.943$), we conclude that there is a statistically significant positive relationship between sales and population. The coefficient of determination (R-squared) is 0.914, which tells us that 91.4 percent of the variation in sales is explained by the variation in population.

Now suppose that the city that you are considering expanding into has a population of 155,000. You can use the regression results to forecast sales as follows:

$$\text{Sales} = 37.02 + 0.67(\text{POP})$$
$$= 37.02 + 0.67(155)$$
$$= 140.87$$

(c4t8) **TABLE 4–8　Regression Results for Sales as a Function of Population**

Population (000)	Sales (000)
505	372
351	275
186	214
175	135
132	81
115	144
108	90
79	97

Regression Statistic	
Multiple R	0.956
R-squared	0.914
Standard error	32.72
Observations	8

	Coefficient	Standard Error	t-Stat	P-Value
Intercept	37.02	20.86	1.77	0.126
Population (000)	0.67	0.08	8.00	0.000

The Durbin-Watson statistic is not shown because it is not relevant for cross-sectional data.

Remember that sales are in thousands, so this is a point estimate of 140,870 sandwiches. An approximate 95 percent confidence band could be constructed as follows:

$$\text{Point estimate} \pm 2(\text{standard error of regression}) = 140.870 \pm 2(32.72)$$
$$= 140.870 \pm 65.44$$
$$= 75.43 \text{ to } 206.31$$

That is, about 75,430 to 206,310 sandwiches.

Forecasting Domestic Car Sales with Bivariate Regression

You may recall that the domestic car sales series (DCS) that we forecast in Chapters 1 and 3 shows quite a bit of variability, including a substantial seasonal component. Therefore, you might expect that it would be difficult to forecast such a series based on a simple regression equation with one causal variable. One thing that would make the process more workable would be to deseasonalize DCS prior to attempting to build a regression model.

What are the causal factors that you think would influence the sales of domestic cars? You might come up with a fairly long list. Some of the variables that might be on such a list are:

Income

Unemployment rate

Interest rates

Consumer attitudes[14]

Domestic car prices

Foreign car prices

In this section we will focus on disposable personal income.

---

[14]Consumer attitudes are often measured by the University of Michigan's Index of Consumer Sentiment. This is an index that is released each month by the University of Michigan Survey Research Center. Each month 500 respondents in a national survey are interviewed about a variety of topics. There are five specific questions in the survey that go into the calculation of the Index of Consumer Sentiment, which has been adjusted to a base of 100 for 1966. Those five questions are:

1. We are interested in how people are getting along financially these days. Would you say that you (and your family living there) are better off or worse off financially than you were a year ago?
2. Now looking ahead—do you think that a year from now you (and your family living there) will be better off financially, or worse off, or about the same as now?
3. Now turning to business conditions in the country as a whole—do you think that during the next twelve months we'll have good times financially, or bad times, or what?
4. Looking ahead, which would you say is more likely—that in the country as a whole we'll have continuous good times during the next five years or so, or that we will have periods of widespread unemployment or depression, or what?
5. About the big things people buy for their homes—such as furniture, a refrigerator, stove, television, and things like that. Generally speaking, do you think now is a good or bad time for people to buy major household items?

The way in which the index is computed makes it higher when people's responses to these questions are more positive.

When seasonally adjusted quarterly data for domestic car sales (SADCS) are regressed as a function of disposable personal income (DPI), the results are as shown in Figure 4–15. Data used to develop the model and forecast were from 1990Q1 through 1998Q4. The forecast was made through the four quarters of 1999. The equation for

FIGURE 4–15

Domestic Car Sales and a Simple Regression Forecast (c4f15)

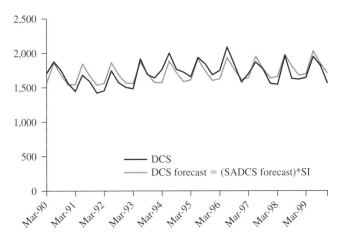

To develop this forecast, DCS were first deseasonalized, then those values were regressed as a function of disposable personal income. The resulting model was used to predict deseasonalized values for DCS, which were multiplied by the seasonal indices to arrive at the forecast shown in the graph.

```
SADCS = 484.06 + ((DPI) * 0.0655)
DCS Forecast = (SADCS) times (Seasonal Index)
```

Audit Trail for SADCS--Coefficient Table (Multiple Regression Selected)

Series Description	Included in Model	Coefficient	Standard Error	T-test	SEE
SADCS	Dependent	484.06	466.18	1.04	100.65
DPI	Yes	0.0655	0.02	2.62	----------

Audit Trail for SADCS--Statistics

Accuracy Measure	Value	Forecast Statistic	Value
Mean absolute percentage error (MAPE)	5.03%	Durbin-Watson	0.69
R-squared	16.80%		

Q1 Seasonal Index	Q2 Seasonal Index	Q3 Seasonal Index	Q4 Seasonal Index
0.94	1.12	1.01	0.93

seasonally adjusted domestic car sales is:

$$\text{SADCS} = 484.06 + 0.0655(\text{DPI})$$

The positive coefficient (.0655) for DPI is logical, and from the *t*-ratio (2.62) we see that DPI is quite statistically significant in this model (the significance level is .000— even at a two-tailed level). The *R*-squared (R^2) tells us that 16.8 percent of the variation in seasonally adjusted retail car sales is explained by this model. From Figure 4–12 we see that the Durbin-Watson test for serial correlation indicates positive serial correlation.

To make a forecast of SADCS for the four quarters of 1999 with this model we first need a forecast of DPI for those quarters. A Holt's exponential smoothing forecast was used in this instance. The forecast values of DPI were substituted into the above model to obtain a forecast of SADCS for the four quarters of 1999. These forecasts were then multiplied by the seasonal indices to obtain the following forecasts for domestic car sales:

Period	Actual DCS	Forecast DCS
1999Q1	1,646.3	1,698.5
1999Q2	1,951.0	2,029.9
1999Q3	1,821.6	1,851.4
1999Q4	1,562.8	1,708.0

These results are shown in the graph at the top of Figure 4–15.

The root-mean-squared errors for this model in the historic period and in the 1999 forecast horizon are shown in Table 4–9.

TABLE 4–9   Summary Table of RMSEs for DCS

Chapter	Method	Period	RMSE
1	Naive—with 4-period lag	Historical	187.13
		Holdout	112.26
2	Not applicable		
3	Winters' exponential smoothing	Historical	144.45
		Holdout	61.79
	Holt's with	Historical	200.46
	seasonal adjustment	Holdout	62.21
4	Simple regression model using seasonally	Historical	96.98
	adjusted DCS as a function of disposable	Holdout	87.93
	personal income		

Comments from the Field

While working for Dow Plastics, a business group of the Dow Chemical Company, Jan Neuenfeldt received on-the-job training while assisting others in developing forecasts. This led her to enroll in an MBA forecasting class in which she obtained formal training in quantitative forecasting methods.

The methodology that Jan uses most is regression analysis. On occasion she also uses exponential smoothing models, such as Winters'. However, the marketing and product managers who use the forecasts usually are interested in *why* as well as in the forecast values. Most of the forecasts Jan prepares are on a quarterly basis. It is fairly typical for annual forecasts one year out to be within a 5 percent margin of error. For large-volume items in mature market segments the annual margin for error is frequently only about 2 percent.

Each quarter, Jan reports forecast results to management, using a newsletter format. She begins with an exposition of the results, followed by the supporting statistical information and a graphic presentation of the forecast. She finds that graphics are extremely useful as she prepares forecasts, as well as when she communicates results to end users.

This comment is based on an interview with Jan Neuenfeldt.

INTEGRATIVE CASE
THE GAP

Part 4: Forecasting The Gap Sales Data with a Simple Regression Model

The sales of The Gap stores for the 56 quarters covering 1985Q1 through 1998Q4 are shown in the graph below. From this graph it is clear that The Gap sales are quite seasonal and are increasing over time.

(c4gap)

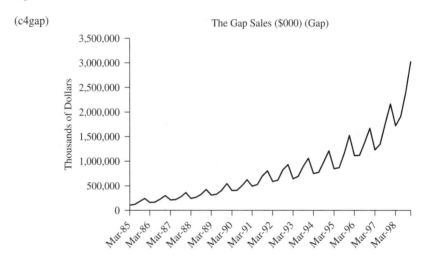

The Gap Sales ($000) (Gap)

Case Questions

1. Do you think that the general growth path of The Gap sales has followed a linear path over the period shown? As part of your answer, show a graph of the deseasonalized The Gap sales along with a linear-trend line. What does this graph suggest to you about the results you might expect from using a linear trend as the basis of a forecast of The Gap sales for 1999?

2. Use a trend regression of deseasonalized The Gap sales as the basis for a forecast of The Gap sales for 1999. Be sure to reseasonalize your forecast, then graph the actual The Gap sales along with your forecast. What do you think would happen to the accuracy of your forecast if you extended it out through 2000? Why?

3. Calculate the root-mean-squared errors for both the historical period and for the 1999Q1 through 1999Q4 forecast horizon.

Solutions to Case Questions

1. When The Gap sales data are deseasonalized and a linear trend is plotted through the deseasonalized series, it becomes clear that the trend in sales was increasing at an increasing rate during the 1985Q1 through 1998Q4 pe-riod. This can be seen in the graph on page 177, in which actual sales (seasonally adjusted) are at first above the trend line, then fall below the linear trend, and finally are again greater than the trend. The trend would fall below

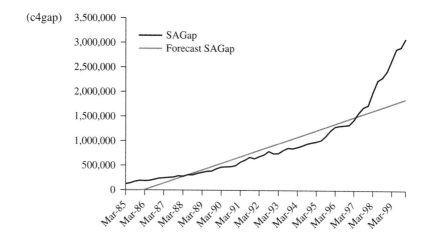

Audit Trail--Coefficient Table (Linear Regression Selected)

Name	Value	Standard Error	T-test	P-Value
Intercept	-161,392.04	57,300.93	-2.82	0.00
Slope	33,676.59	1,748.88	19.26	0.00

Audit Trail--Statistics

Accuracy Measure	Value	Forecast Statistic	Value
Mean absolute percentage error (MAPE)	27.39%	Durbin-Watson	0.07
R-squared	87.91%		

zero for the four quarters of 1985, but because negative sales do not make sense we have them as zero. It might be expected based on this graph that a forecast based on a linear trend would underestimate sales for the coming quarters. This graph also suggests that a regression-trend model would have positive serial correlation.

2. The Gap sales data were deseasonalized using the following seasonal indices: Q1 = 0.858, Q2 = 0.851, Q3 = 1.044, and Q4 = 1.247. The deseasonalized sales data for 1985Q1 through 1998Q4 were then regressed against a time index, where $T = 1$ for 1985Q1 through $T = 56$ for 1998Q4. The regression results are shown above.

The trend equation is: SAGap = $-161,392.04 + 33,676.59(T)$. All of the diagnostic statistics for this model look good (t-ratio = 19.26 and R-squared = 87.91%) except for the Durbin-Watson statistic (DW = 0.07). From the tests in Figure 4–12 it is determined that this model does exhibit positive serial correlation. In this situation the positive serial correlation looks to be caused by the nonlinearity in the data. (In Chapter 5 you will learn how to account for such a nonlinearity using more advanced regression methods.)

The predicted values of SAGap were multiplied by the seasonal indices to get the forecast values graphed at the top of the next page.

(c4gap)

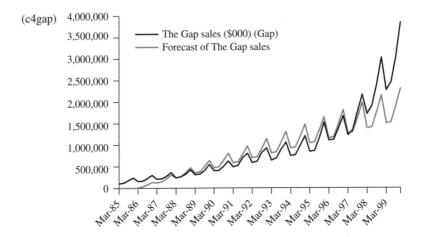

The actual and forecast Gap sales (in thousands of dollars) are shown below for the four quarters of 1999.

	Actual	Forecast
1999Q1	2,277,700	1,507,956
1999Q2	2,453,300	1,525,659
1999Q3	3,045,386	1,904,994
1999Q4	3,858,939	2,319,062

Notice that in the forecast horizon (1999) the forecast is below the actual in all four quarters. This is because the linear trend that underlies this forecast fails to take into account the fact that The Gap sales have been increasing at an increasing rate. If this model was used to forecast through 2000, it is likely that this tendency for low forecasts would continue and probably become worse.

3. The RMSEs for the historical period and the 1999 forecast horizon are:

1985Q1–1998Q4   Root-mean-squared error $= 212,016$

1999Q1–1999Q4   Root-mean-squared error $= 1,131,894$

If we compare the RMSE for these last four quarters to the mean level of sales for those quarters (2,908,831.25), we find that the RMSE is about 39 percent of the mean actual quarterly sales.

This is clearly not a very good model.

TABLE 4–10   Summary Table of RMSEs for The Gap Sales

Chapter	Method	Period	RMSE
1	Naive—with 4-period lag	Historical	233,092
		Holdout	654,976
2	Not applicable		
3	Winters' exponential smoothing	Historical	49,479
		Holdout	99,493
	Holt's exponential smoothing	Historical	42,388
	with seasonal readjustment	Holdout	74,034
4	Linear trend of deseasonalized	Historical	212,016
	data with forecast reseasonalized	Holdout	1,131,894

USING FORECASTX™ TO MAKE REGRESSION FORECASTS

What follows is a brief discussion of how to use ForecastX™ for making a forecast based on a regression model. This will increase your familiarity with the of use of ForecastX™. The illustration used here is for a trend forecast.

First, put your data into an Excel spreadsheet in column format, such as the sample of The Gap data shown in the table below. Once you have your data in this format, while in Excel highlight the data you want to use, then start ForecastX™. The following dialog box appears.

A Sample of The Gap Data in Column Format

Date	The Gap Sales ($000)
Mar-1994	751,670
Jun-1994	773,131
Sep-1994	988,346
Dec-1994	1,209,790
Mar-1995	848,688
Jun-1995	868,514
Sep-1995	1,155,930
Dec-1995	1,522,120
Mar-1996	1,113,150
Jun-1996	1,120,340
Sep-1996	1,383,000
Dec-1996	1,667,900
Mar-1997	1,231,186
Jun-1997	1,345,221
Sep-1997	1,765,939
Dec-1997	2,165,479
Mar-1998	1,719,712
Jun-1998	1,904,970
Sep-1998	2,399,900
Dec-1998	3,029,90

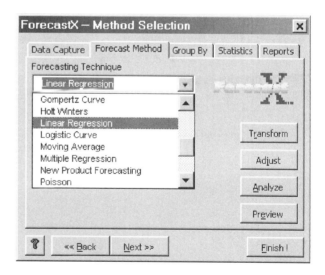

Set the **Dates** window to the periodicity of your data (**Quarterly** for this example), then click the **Forecast Method** tab at the top and the following screen appears.

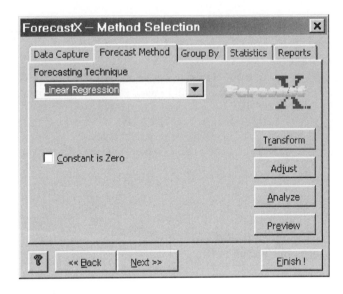

Click the down arrow in the **Forecasting Technique** window and select **Linear Regression.** In the terminology used by ForecastX, *linear regression* refers to a method that makes a regression trend forecast. If you want to develop a causal regression model you will want to select **Multiple Regression.** (See "Further Comments on Regression Models" on page 182.)

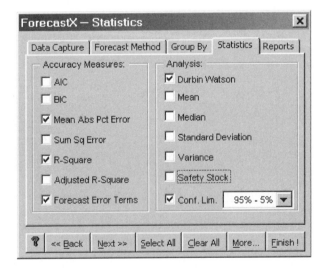

After selecting **Linear Regression,** the dialog box will then look like the one above. Now you are ready to click the **Statistics** tab, which will take you to the next dialog box.

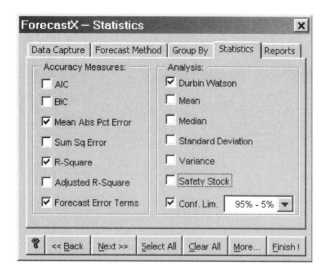

Here you want to select the desired statistics. Often the ones selected in this example would be what you would want for simple regression models.

In addition, you will want to click the **More** button at the bottom and check the box for **P-value** (in **Coeff table**) under the **Matrix Level** tab. Look at the other tabs in this box and select desired statistics such as the RMSE. Then click **OK** and you return to the **Statistics** box.

Next click the **Reports** tab to get the **Report Options** dialog box.

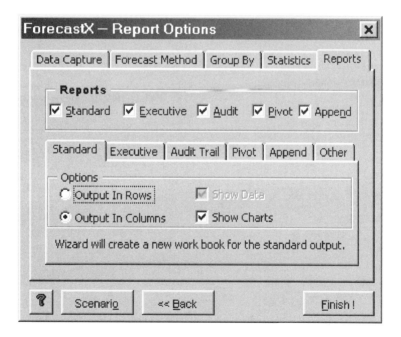

As you saw in Chapter 3 this is where you select the particular reports and report contents that you want. Some exploration and experimentation with these options will help you see what each option leads to in terms of results.

After you click **Finish!** in the lower right corner, reports will be put in new Excel workbooks—Book 2, Book 3, and so forth. The numbers will vary depending on what you have been doing in Excel up to that point.

FURTHER COMMENTS ON REGRESSION MODELS

Causal Models

To do a *causal regression model* and forecast, select the columns in the data file with the period, the independent variable (DPI in this example), and the dependent variable you want to forecast (RS, retail sales, in this example). Then open ForecastX™.

Period	DPI	RS
Mar-1990	18,035	418,436
Jun-1990	18,063	464,944
Sep-1990	18,031	464,490
Dec-1990	17,856	496,741
Mar-1991	17,748	417,357
Jun-1991	17,861	470,851
Sep-1991	17,816	469,494
Dec-1991	17,811	498,235

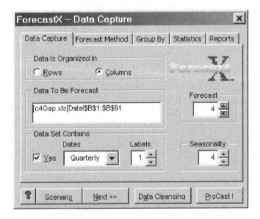

In the **Data Capture** window look at the selection. If it is not the three columns you want, click inside the **Data To Be Forecast** window and the following appears.

Click the _ button to the right of the window. Highlight the data columns you want, then click **Done.**

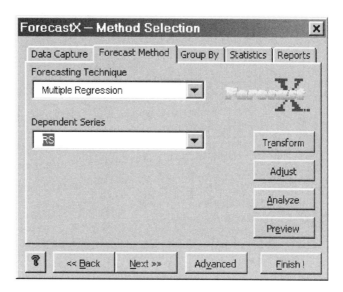

Next click the **Forecast Method** tab and select **Multiple Regression** in the **Forecasting Technique** window. In the **Dependent Series** window select the variable you want to forecast (RS in this example).

From this point on you follow the same selections as described above for regression trend forecasts.

You are probably wondering how you forecast the independent variable into the future and unknown forecast horizon. One can use any acceptable method to do this, but ForecastX™ makes it easy by doing an automated forecast using a procedure called "ProCast™."

Deseasonalizing Data

The following is a review of what was covered in Chapter 3. To deseasonalize data in ForecastX™ we use a method called "Decomposition" (this method of forecasting will be discussed in detail in Chapter 6). For now we will simply look at the portion of the method and results that we need to take the seasonality out of a data series.

Begin by opening your data file in Excel, then start the ForecastX™ software and capture the desired data. In the **Method Selection** dialog box select **Decomposition** as the **Forecasting Technique,** check **Multiplicative,** and select **Linear Regression,** as shown at the top of page 184.

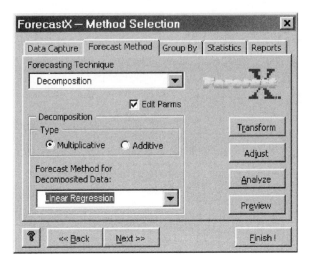

Then click the **Statistics** tab.

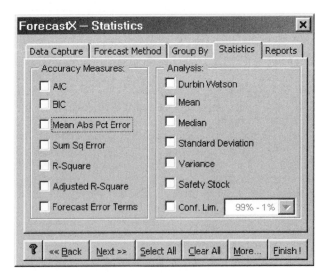

In the **Statistics** dialog box you can uncheck all, because for this purpose we do not need any statistics. This will save computational time. Then click the **Reports** tab and select only the **Audit** report.

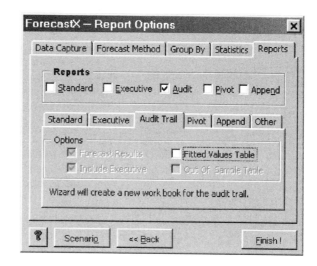

Now click **Finish!** and you will get results that will include the following:

Components of Decomposition

Date	Original Data	Forecasted Data	Centered Moving Average	CMA Trend	Seasonal Indices
Mar-1985	105,715.00	−109,539.43		−127,715.45	0.86
Jun-1985	120,136.00	−80,068.78		−94,038.87	0.85
Sep-1985	181,669.00	−62,989.93	168,616.38	−60,362.28	1.04
Dec-1985	239,813.00	−33,286.18	180,977.50	−26,685.70	1.25
Mar-1986	159,980.00	5,995.97	191,946.88	6,990.89	0.86
Jun-1986	164,760.00	34,626.06	204,670.25	40,667.48	0.85
Sep-1986	224,800.00	77,580.35	218,387.25	74,344.06	1.04
Dec-1986	298,469.00	134,738.66	231,396.38	108,020.65	1.25
Mar-1987	211,060.00	121,531.38	244,122.50	141,697.23	0.86
Jun-1987	217,753.00	149,320.90	257,864.88	175,373.82	0.85
Sep-1987	273,616.00	218,150.62	269,291.25	209,050.40	1.04
Dec-1987	359,592.00	302,763.51	278,899.13	242,726.99	1.25

The "Seasonal Indices" column is highlighted here but will not be highlighted in your output. These are the indices that you will use to deseasonalize the original data and to reseasonalize results. You should copy this column of seasonal indices and paste it into your Excel workbook along with your original data.

You can now calculate a deseasonalized series by dividing the original data by the seasonal indices.

$$\text{Deseasonalized series} = \text{Original series} \div \text{Seasonal indices}$$

To reseasonalize results, reverse the process.

$$\text{Reseasonalized results} = \text{Deseasonalized results} \times \text{Seasonal indices}$$

Suggested Readings

Bassin, William M. "How to Anticipate the Accuracy of a Regression Based Model." *Journal of Business Forecasting* 6, no. 4 (Winter 1987–88), pp. 26–28.

Bowerman, Bruce L.; and Richard T. O'Connell. *Applied Statistics: Improving Business Processes.* Chicago: Irwin, 1997.

Dalrymple, Douglas J.; William M. Strahle; and Douglas B. Bock. "How Many Observations Should Be Used in Trend Regression Forecasts?" *Journal of Business Forecasting* 8, no. 1 (Spring 1989), pp. 7–9.

Harris, John L.; and Lon-Mu Liu. "GNP as a Predictor of Electricity Consumption." *Journal of Business Forecasting* (Winter 1990–91), pp. 24–27.

Lapide, Larry. "Do You Need to Use Causal Forecasting?" *Journal of Business Forecasting,* Summer 1999, pp. 13–14.

Lind, Douglas A.; Robert D. Mason; and William G. Marchal. *Basic Statistics for Business and Economics,* 3rd ed. New York: Irwin/McGraw-Hill, 2000.

Meade, Nigel; and Towhidul Islam. "Forecasting with Growth Curves: An Empirical Comparison," *International Journal of Forecasting* 11, no. 2 (June 1995), pp. 199–215.

Monaco, Ralph M. "MEXVAL: A Simple Regression Diagnostic Tool." *Journal of Business Forecasting* (Winter 1989–90), pp. 23–27.

Morrison, Jeffrey S. "Target Marketing with Logit Regression," *Journal of Business Forecasting* 14, no. 4 (Winter 1995–96), pp. 10–12.

Pindyck, Robert S.; and Daniel L. Rubinfeld. *Econometric Models and Economic Forecasts,* 3rd ed. New York: McGraw-Hill, 1991.

Wang, George C. S.; and Charles K. Akabay. "Heteroscedasticity: How to Handle in Regression Modeling." *Journal of Business Forecasting* 13, no. 2 (Summer 1992), pp. 11–17.

West, Kenneth D.; et al. "Regression-Based Tests of Predictive Ability." *International Economic Review* 39, no. 4 (November 1998), pp. 817–40.

Exercises

1. What are the steps that should be used in evaluating regression models? Write each step in the order it should be evaluated, and following each one write a sentence or two in your own words to explain its importance.

2. In this chapter a number of graphic displays have been presented. What advantage(s) do you see in showing data in graphic form rather than, or in addition to, tabular form?

3. In evaluating regression models we have tested a hypothesis to determine whether the slope term is significantly different from zero. Why do we test this hypothesis? Why do we not test the comparable hypothesis for the intercept?

4. The following regression results relate to a study of the salaries of public school teachers in a midwestern city:

Variable	Coefficient	Standard Error	t-ratio
Constant	20,720	6,820	3.04
EXP	805	258	

R-squared $= 0.684$; $n = 105$.

Standard error of the estimate $= 2,000$.

EXP is the experience of teachers in years of full-time teaching.

a. What is the *t*-ratio for EXP? Does it indicate that experience is a statistically significant determinant of salary if a 95 percent confidence level is desired?

b. What percentage of the variation in salary is explained by this model?

c. Determine the point estimate of salary for a teacher with 20 years of experience.

d. What is the approximate 95 percent confidence interval for your point estimate from part (*c*)?

5. Nelson Industries manufactures a part for a type of aircraft engine that is becoming obsolete. The sales history for the last 10 years is as follows:

(c4p5)	Year	Sales	Year	Sales
	1991	945	1996	420
	1992	875	1997	305
	1993	760	1998	285
	1994	690	1999	250
	1995	545	2000	210

a. Plot sales versus time.

b. Estimate the regression model for a linear time trend of sales.

c. What is the root-mean-squared error of the linear regression estimates for these 10 years?

d. Using this model, estimate sales for year 11.

6. Mid-Valley Travel Agency (MVTA) has offices in 12 cities. The company believes that its monthly airline bookings are related to the mean income in those cities and has collected the following data:

(c4p6)	Location	Bookings	Income
	1	1,098	$43,299
	2	1,131	45,021
	3	1,120	40,290
	4	1,142	41,893
	5	971	30,620
	6	1,403	48,105
	7	855	27,482
	8	1,054	33,025
	9	1,081	34,687
	10	982	28,725
	11	1,098	37,892
	12	1,387	46,198

a. Develop a linear regression model of monthly airline bookings as a function of income.

b. Use the process described in the chapter to evaluate your results.

c. Make a point and approximate 95 percent confidence interval estimate of monthly airline bookings

for another city in which MVTA is considering opening a branch, given that income in that city is $39,020.

7. Barbara Lynch is the product manager for a line of skiwear produced by HeathCo Industries and privately branded for sale under several different names, including Northern Slopes and Jacque Monri. A new part of Ms. Lynch's job is to provide a quarterly forecast of sales for the northern United States, a region composed of 27 states stretching from Maine to Washington. A 10-year sales history is shown:

	Sales ($000)			
Year	1st Quarter	2nd Quarter	3rd Quarter	4th Quarter
1988	$ 72,962	$ 81,921	$ 97,729	$142,161
1989	145,592	117,129	114,159	151,402
1990	153,907	100,144	123,242	128,497
1991	176,076	180,440	162,665	220,818
1992	202,415	211,780	163,710	200,135
1993	174,200	182,556	198,990	243,700
1994	253,142	218,755	225,422	253,653
1995	257,156	202,568	224,482	229,879
1996	289,321	266,095	262,938	322,052
1997	313,769	315,011	264,939	301,479

(c4p7)

a. Because Ms. Lynch has so many other job responsibilities, she has hired you to help with the forecasting effort. First, she would like you to prepare a time-series plot of the data and to write her a memo indicating what the plot appears to show and whether it seems likely that a simple linear trend would be useful in preparing forecasts.

b. In addition to plotting the data over time, you should estimate the least-squares trend line in the form:

$$SALES = a + b(TIME)$$

Set TIME = 1 for 1988Q1 through TIME = 40 for 1997Q4. Write the trend equation:

$$SALES = \underline{\hspace{1cm}} +/- \underline{\hspace{1cm}} (TIME)$$

(Circle + or − as appropriate)

c. Do your regression results indicate to you that there is a significant trend to the data? Explain why or why not.

d. On the basis of your results, prepare a forecast for the four quarters of 1998.

Period	TIME	Sales Forecast (F1)
1998Q1	41	_____
1998Q2	42	_____
1998Q3	43	_____
1998Q4	44	_____

e. A year later, Barbara gives you a call and tells you that the actual sales for the four quarters of 1998 were: Q1 = 334,271; Q2 = 328,982; Q3 = 317,921; and Q4 = 350,118. How accurate was your model? What was the root-mean-squared error?

8. Dick Staples, another product manager with HeathCo (see Exercise 7), has mentioned to Barbara Lynch that he has found both the unemployment rate and the level of income to be useful predictors for some of the products under his responsibility.

a. Suppose that Ms. Lynch provides you with the following unemployment data for the northern region she is concerned with:

Year	\multicolumn{4}{c}{Unemployment Rate (%)}
	1st Quarter	2nd Quarter	3rd Quarter	4th Quarter
1988	8.4%	8.2%	8.4%	8.4%
1989	8.1%	7.7%	7.5%	7.2%
1990	6.9%	6.5%	6.5%	6.4%
1991	6.3%	6.2%	6.3%	6.5%
1992	6.8%	7.9%	8.3%	8.0%
1993	8.0%	8.0%	8.0%	8.9%
1994	9.6%	10.2%	10.7%	11.5%
1995	11.2%	11.0%	10.1%	9.2%
1996	8.5%	8.0%	8.0%	7.9%
1997	7.9%	7.9%	7.8%	7.6%

(c4p8)

b. Plot a scattergram of SALES versus northern-region unemployment rate (NRUR). Does there appear to be a relationship? Explain.

c. Prepare a bivariate regression model of sales as a function of NRUR in the following form:

$$SALES = a + b(NRUR)$$

Write your answer in the following equation:

SALES = _____ +/− _____(NRUR)

(Circle + or − as appropriate)

d. Write a memo to Ms. Lynch in which you evaluate these results and indicate how well you think this model would work in forecasting her sales series.

e. Use the model to make a forecast of sales for each quarter of 1998, given the forecast for unemployment (FNRUR) that HeathCo has purchased from a macroeconomic consulting firm (MacroCast):

Period	FNRUR	Sales Forecast (F2)
1998Q1	7.6%	_____
1998Q2	7.7%	_____
1998Q3	7.5%	_____
1998Q4	7.4%	_____

f. For the actual sales given in Exercise 7(e), calculate the root-mean-squared error for this model. How does it compare with what you found in Exercise 7(e)?

g. Barbara Lynch also has data on income (INC), in billions of dollars, for the region as follows:

Year	\multicolumn{4}{c}{Income ($Billions)}
	1st Quarter	2nd Quarter	3rd Quarter	4th Quarter
1988	$ 218	$ 237	$ 263	$ 293
1989	318	359	404	436
1990	475	534	574	622
1991	667	702	753	796
1992	858	870	934	1,010
1993	1,066	1,096	1,162	1,187
1994	1,207	1,242	1,279	1,318
1995	1,346	1,395	1,443	1,528
1996	1,613	1,646	1,694	1,730
1997	1,755	1,842	1,832	1,882

Plot a scattergram of SALES with INCOME. Does there appear to be a relationship? Explain.

h. Prepare a bivariate regression model of SALES as a function of income (INC) and write your results in the equation:

$$SALES = a + b(INC)$$

$$SALES = \underline{\hspace{1.5cm}} +/- \underline{\hspace{1.5cm}}(INC)$$

(Circle + or − as appropriate)

i. Write a memo to Ms. Lynch in which you explain and evaluate this model, indicating how well you think it would work in forecasting sales.

j. HeathCo has also purchased a forecast of income from MacroCast. Use the following income forecast (INCF) to make your own forecast of SALES for 1998:

Period	INCF	Sales Forecast (F3)
1998Q1	$1,928	\underline{\hspace{2cm}}
1998Q2	1,972	\underline{\hspace{2cm}}
1998Q3	2,017	\underline{\hspace{2cm}}
1998Q4	2,062	\underline{\hspace{2cm}}

k. On the basis of the actual sales given in Exercise 7(e), calculate the root-mean-squared error for this model. How does it compare with the other two models you have used to forecast sales?

l. Prepare a time-series plot with actual sales for 1988Q1 through 1997Q4 along with the sales forecast you found in part (j) of this exercise. To accompany this plot, write a brief memo to Ms. Lynch in which you comment on the strengths and weaknesses of the forecasting model.

9. Carolina Wood Products, Inc., a major manufacturer of household furniture, is interested in predicting expenditures on furniture (FURN) for the entire United States. It has the following data by quarter for 1988 through 1997:

FURN (in Billions of Dollars)

Year	1st Quarter	2nd Quarter	3rd Quarter	4th Quarter
1988	$ 98.1	$ 96.8	$ 96.0	$ 95.0
1989	93.2	95.1	96.2	98.4
1990	100.7	104.4	108.1	111.1
1991	114.3	117.2	119.4	122.7
1992	125.9	129.3	132.2	136.6
1993	137.4	141.4	145.3	147.7
1994	148.8	150.2	153.4	154.2
1995	159.8	164.4	166.2	169.7
1996	173.7	175.5	175.0	175.7
1997	181.4	180.0	179.7	176.3

(c4p9)

a. Prepare a naive forecast for 1998Q1 based on the following model (see Chapter 1):

$$NFURN_t = FURN_{t-1}$$

Period	Naive Forecast
1998Q1	\underline{\hspace{2cm}}

b. Estimate the bivariate linear-trend model for the data where TIME = 1 for 1988Q1 through TIME = 40 for 1997Q4.

$$FURN = a + b(TIME)$$

$$FURN = \underline{\hspace{1.5cm}} +/- \underline{\hspace{1.5cm}}(TIME)$$

(Circle + or − as appropriate)

c. Write a paragraph in which you evaluate this model, with particular emphasis on its usefulness in forecasting.

d. Prepare a time-trend forecast of furniture and household equipment expenditures for 1998 based on the model in part (b).

Period	TIME	Trend Forecast
1998Q1	41	\underline{\hspace{2cm}}
1998Q2	42	\underline{\hspace{2cm}}
1998Q3	43	\underline{\hspace{2cm}}
1998Q4	44	\underline{\hspace{2cm}}

e. Suppose that the actual values of FURN for 1998 were as shown in the following table. Calculate the RMSE for both of your forecasts and interpret the results. (For the naive forecast, there will be only one observation, for 1998Q1.)

Period	Actual FURN ($Billions)
1998Q1	177.6
1998Q2	180.5
1998Q3	182.8
1998Q4	178.7

10. Fifteen midwestern and mountain states have united in an effort to promote and forecast tourism. One aspect of their work has been related to the dollar amount spent per year on domestic travel (DTE) in each state. They have the following estimates for disposable personal income per capita (DPI) and DTE:

(c4p10)	State	DPI	DTE ($Millions)
	Minnesota	$17,907	$4,933
	Iowa	15,782	1,766
	Missouri	17,158	4,692
	North Dakota	15,688	628
	South Dakota	15,981	551
	Nebraska	17,416	1,250
	Kansas	17,635	1,729
	Montana	15,128	725
	Idaho	15,974	934
	Wyoming	17,504	778
	Colorado	18,628	4,628
	New Mexico	14,587	1,724
	Arizona	15,921	3,836
	Utah	14,066	1,757
	Nevada	19,781	6,455

a. From these data estimate a bivariate linear regression equation for domestic travel expenditures (DTE) as a function of income per capita (DPI):

$$DTE = a + b(DPI)$$

$$DTE = \underline{\hspace{1cm}} +/- \underline{\hspace{1cm}}(DPI)$$

(Circle + or − as appropriate)

Evaluate the statistical significance of this model.

b. Illinois, a bordering state, has asked that this model be used to forecast DTE for Illinois under the assumption that DPI will be $19,648. Make the appropriate point and approximate 95 percent interval estimates.

c. Given that actual DTE turned out to be $7,754 (million), calculate the percentage error in your forecast.

11. Collect data on population for your state (http://www.economagic.com may be a good source for these data) over the past 20 years and use a bivariate regression trend line to forecast population for the next five years. Prepare a time-series plot that shows both actual and forecast values. Do you think the model looks as though it will provide reasonably accurate forecasts for the five-year horizon? (c4p11)

12. AmerPlas, Inc., produces 20-ounce plastic drinking cups that are embossed with the names of prominent beers and soft drinks. It has been observed that sales of the cups match closely the seasonal pattern associated with beer production, but that, unlike beer production, there has been a positive trend over time. The sales data, by month, for 1994 through 1997 are as follows:

Period	T	Sales	Period	T	Sales
1994M01	1	857	1996M01	25	1,604
1994M02	2	921	1996M02	26	1,643
1994M03	3	1,071	1996M03	27	1,795
1994M04	4	1,133	1996M04	28	1,868
1994M05	5	1,209	1996M05	29	1,920
1994M06	6	1,234	1996M06	30	1,953
1994M07	7	1,262	1996M07	31	1,980
1994M08	8	1,258	1996M08	32	1,989
1994M09	9	1,175	1996M09	33	1,897
1994M10	10	1,174	1996M10	34	1,910
1994M11	11	1,123	1996M11	35	1,854
1994M12	12	1,159	1996M12	36	1,957
1995M01	13	1,250	1997M01	37	1,955
1995M02	14	1,289	1997M02	38	2,008
1995M03	15	1,448	1997M03	39	2,171
1995M04	16	1,497	1997M04	40	2,202
1995M05	17	1,560	1997M05	41	2,288
1995M06	18	1,586	1997M06	42	2,314
1995M07	19	1,597	1997M07	43	2,343
1995M08	20	1,615	1997M08	44	2,339
1995M09	21	1,535	1997M09	45	2,239
1995M10	22	1,543	1997M10	46	2,267
1995M11	23	1,493	1997M11	47	2,206
1995M12	24	1,510	1997M12	48	2,226

(c4p12)

a. Use these data to estimate a linear time trend as follows:

$$SALES = a + b(T)$$

$$SALES = \underline{\hspace{2cm}} +/- \underline{\hspace{2cm}}(T)$$

(Circle + or − as appropriate)

Do your regression results support the notion that there has been a positive time trend in the SALES data? Explain.

b. Use your equation to forecast SALES for the 12 months of 1998:

Period	SALES Forecast	Period	SALES Forecast
1998M01	_____	1998M07	_____
M02	_____	M08	_____
M03	_____	M09	_____
M04	_____	M10	_____
M05	_____	M11	_____
M06	_____	M12	_____

c. Actual SALES for 1998 are:

Period	Actual SALES	Period	Actual SALES
1998M01	2,318	1998M07	2,697
M02	2,367	M08	2,702
M03	2,523	M09	2,613
M04	2,577	M10	2,626
M05	2,646	M11	2,570
M06	2,674	M12	2,590

On the basis of your results in part (*b*) in comparison with these actual sales, how well do you think your model works? What is the RMSE for 1998?

d. Prepare a time-series plot of the actual sales and the forecast of sales for 1994M01 through 1998M12. Do the same for just the last two years (1997M01 to 1998M12). Do your plots show any evidence of seasonality in the data? If so, how might you account for it in preparing a forecast?

13. Alexander Enterprises manufactures plastic parts for the automotive industry. Its sales (in thousands) for 1993Q1 through 1997Q4 are as follows:

Period	Sales	Period	Sales
1993Q1	3,816.5	1996Q1	4,406.4
Q2	3,816.7	Q2	4,394.6
Q3	3,978.8	Q3	4,422.3
Q4	4,046.6	Q4	4,430.8
1994Q1	4,119.1	1997Q1	4,463.9
Q2	4,169.4	Q2	4,517.8
Q3	4,193.0	Q3	4,563.6
Q4	4,216.4	Q4	4,633.0
1995Q1	4,238.1	1998Q1	NA
Q2	4,270.5	Q2	NA
Q3	4,321.8	Q3	NA
Q4	4,349.5	Q4	NA

(c4p13)

You are asked to forecast sales for 1998Q1 through 1998Q4.

a. Begin by preparing a time-series plot of sales. Does it appear from this plot that a linear-trend model might be appropriate? Explain.

b. Use a bivariate linear regression-trend model to estimate the following trend equation:

$$SALES = a + b(TIME)$$

Is the sign for *b* what you would expect? Is *b* significantly different from zero? What is the coefficient of determination for this model? Is there a potential problem with serial correlation? Explain.

c. Based on this model, make a trend forecast of sales (SALESFT) for the four quarters of 1998.

d. Given that actual sales (SALESA) for the four quarters of 1998 are:

1998Q1	4,667.1
1998Q2	4,710.3
1998Q3	4,738.7
1998Q4	4,789.0

calculate the root-mean-squared error for this forecast model in the historical period (1993Q1–1997Q4) as well as for the forecast horizon (1998Q1–1998Q4). Which of these measures accuracy and which measures fit?

5 FORECASTING WITH MULTIPLE REGRESSION

In this chapter we will build on the introduction to the use of regression in forecasting developed in Chapter 4. The model used to forecast retail sales (RS) will be extended to include the interest rate as an explanatory variable, in addition to real disposable personal income. We will also forecast private housing starts (PHS). We will examine the mortgage rate as a causal factor. In addition we will add variables to account for seasonality in the data and also consider the effect that disposable personal income has on our ability to forecast PHS. We will also continue with our ongoing example of forecasting domestic car sales and the continuing The Gap case study at the end of this chapter. These extensions of the bivariate regression model take us into the realm of multiple regression, so let us begin by looking at the general multiple-regression model.

The Multiple-Regression Model

Multiple regression is a statistical procedure in which a dependent variable (Y) is modeled as a function of more than one independent variable $(X_1, X_2, X_3, \ldots, X_n)$.[1] The population multiple-regression model may be written as:

$$Y = f(X_1, X_2, X_3, \ldots, X_n)$$
$$= \beta_0 + \beta_1 X_1 + \beta_2 X_2 + \beta_3 X_3 + \cdots + \beta_k X_k + \varepsilon$$

where β_0 is the intercept and the other β_i's are the slope terms associated with the respective independent variables (i.e., the X_i's). In this model ε represents the

---

[1]For more-detailed discussions of the multiple-regression model, see the following: John Neter, William Wasserman, and Michael H. Kutner, *Applied Linear Statistical Models* (Homewood, Ill.: Richard D. Irwin, 1990); and George O. Wesolowsky, *Multiple Regression and Analysis of Variance: An Introduction for Computer Users in Management and Economics* (New York: John Wiley & Sons, 1976). The latter is particularly recommended for readers whose statistical background is limited.

population error term, which is the difference between the actual Y and that predicted by the regression model ($\hat{Y}$).

The ordinary least-squares (OLS) criterion for the best multiple-regression model is that the sum of the squares of all the error terms be minimized. That is, we want to minimize $\sum \varepsilon^2$, where

$$\sum \varepsilon^2 = \sum (Y - \hat{Y})^2$$

Thus, the ordinary least-squares criterion for multiple regression is to minimize:

$$\sum (Y - \beta_0 - \beta_1 X_1 - \beta_2 X_2 - \beta_3 X_3 - \cdots - \beta_k X_k)^2$$

The process of achieving this is more complicated than in the bivariate regression case and involves the use of matrix algebra.

Values of the true regression parameters (β_i) are typically estimated from sample data. The resulting sample regression model is:

$$\hat{Y} = b_0 + b_1 X_1 + b_2 X_2 + b_3 X_3 + \cdots + b_k X_k$$

where b_0, b_1, b_2, b_3, and so on, are sample statistics that are estimates of the corresponding population parameters β_0, β_1, β_2, β_3, and so on. Deviations between the predicted values based on the sample regression ($\hat{Y}$) and the actual values (Y) of the dependent variable for each observation are called *residuals* and are equal to ($Y - \hat{Y}$). The values of the sample statistics b_0, b_1, b_2, b_3, and so on, are almost always determined for us by a computer software package. Standard errors, t-ratios, the coefficient of determination, the Durbin-Watson statistic, and other evaluative statistics, as well as a table of residuals, are also found in most regression output.

Selecting Independent Variables

As with bivariate regression, the process of building a multiple-regression model begins by identifying the dependent variable.

As with bivariate regression, the process of building a multiple-regression model begins by identifying the dependent variable. In our context, that is the variable that we are most interested in forecasting. It may be some "prime mover" such as disposable personal income or another macroeconomic variable, or it may be total company sales, or sales of a particular product line, or the number of patient-days for a hospital, or state tax revenues.

Once the dependent variable is determined, we begin to think about what factors contribute to its changes. In our bivariate example of retail sales (RS) we first thought of real disposable personal income (DPI) as an explanatory variable. In this chapter, as we think of other potential independent variables that might improve that model, we want to think of other things that influence RS but that do not measure the same basic relationship that is being measured by DPI. Think, for example, of the possibility of adding GDP to the model. Both GDP and DPI are measures of aggregate income in the economy, so there would be a lot of overlap in the part of the variation in RS they explain. In fact, the correlation between real GDP and real disposable personal income is +0.99. A similar overlap would result if population and DPI were used in the same model. There is a high correlation between population size and real disposable personal income (approximately $+0.95$), and so they would have a lot of overlap in their ability to explain variations in RS. Such overlaps can cause a problem known as *multicollinearity*, which we will discuss in this chapter (see "Multicollinearity").[2]

Thus, in considering the set of independent variables to use, we should find ones that are not highly correlated with one another. For example, suppose that we hypothesize that at least some portion of RS may be influenced by the mortgage interest rate, since many purchases are financed. It seems less likely that there would be a stronger correlation between real personal income and the mortgage interest rate than between real personal income and either real GDP or population size. The correlation between the mortgage interest rate and real disposable personal income turns out to be just -0.67, so there is less overlap between those two variables.

Sometimes it is difficult, or even impossible, to find a variable that measures exactly what we want to have in our model. For example, in the RS model we might like to have as a measure of the interest rate a national average of the rate charged on installment loans. However, a more readily available series, the mortgage rate (MR), may be a reasonable proxy for what we want to measure, since all interest rates tend to be closely related.

In our model of private housing starts (PHS), we will begin by looking at the relationship between PHS and the mortgage rate. However, in plotting the data we notice that there is a regular seasonal pattern in PHS that is not accounted for by the mortgage rate (see Figure 5–5). We would like to consider adding another variable (or set of variables) to account for the seasonality in PHS. But how do we measure spring, or fall, or summer, or winter? The seasons are qualitative attributes that have no direct quantitative counterpart. We will see (in the section "Accounting for Seasonality in a Multiple-Regression Model") that a special kind of variable, known as a *dummy variable*, can be used to measure such a qualitative attribute as spring.

Forecasting with a Multiple-Regression Model

Our first example of a multiple-regression model in forecasting will involve retail sales (RS).

The data for RS from 1990Q1 through 1998Q4 are shown in Figure 5–1. Our beginning bivariate regression forecasting model is:

$$\text{RSF} = b_0 + b_1(\text{MR})$$

$$= 1{,}052{,}224 - 59{,}926(\text{MR})$$

where RSF stands for the forecast of retail sales (RS) and (MR) is the mortgage interest rate.

---

[2]Note that multicollinearity in regression analysis is really just strong correlation between two or more independent variables. Correlation here is measured just as we did in Chapter 2 with the Pearson product-moment correlation coefficient.

FIGURE 5–1

*Retail Sales (RS)
Unadjusted in
Millions of Dollars
(c5t1)*

SOURCE: The Bureau of the Census (http://www.census.gov)

Now we will expand this model to include disposable personal income per capita (DPI) as a second independent variable. We will let RSF2 represent the second forecasting model for RS.

$$RSF2 = b_0 + b_1(DPI) + b_2(MR)$$

Before running the regression, one should think about what signs should be expected for b_1 and b_2. Business and economic logic would suggest that b_1 should be positive ($b_1 > 0$) and that b_2 should be negative ($b_2 < 0$). As shown in Table 5–1, the regression results support this notion. The model estimate is:

$$RSF2 = 1,422,517 + 110(DPI) - 9,945(MR)$$

The raw data for this model, along with the complete regression results, are shown in Table 5–1. Statistical evaluation of this model, based on the information provided in Table 5–1, will be considered in the next section. For now, we can see that at least the signs for the coefficients are consistent with our expectations.

To use this model to forecast retail sales for 1999, one must first forecast the independent variables: real disposable personal income (DPI) and the mortgage rate (MR). Forecasts for the four quarters of 1999 for these two independent variables, based on Holt's exponential smoothing models, are:

Period	MR	DPI
1999Q1	6.71	20,230.20
1999Q2	6.66	20,365.07
1999Q3	6.60	20,500.84
1999Q4	6.55	20,637.51

TABLE 5–1   **Data and Regression Results for Retail Sales (RS) as a Function of Disposable Income Per Capita (DPI) and the Mortgage Interest Rate (MR)** (c5t1)

Period	RS	DPI	MR
Mar-1990	418436	18035	10.1202
Jun-1990	464944	18063	10.3372
Sep-1990	464490	18031	10.1033
Dec-1990	496741	17856	9.9547
Mar-1991	417357	17748	9.5008
Jun-1991	470851	17861	9.5265
Sep-1991	469494	17816	9.2755
Dec-1991	498235	17811	8.6882
Mar-1992	437388	18000	8.7098
Jun-1992	486553	18085	8.6782
Sep-1992	489541	18036	8.0085
Dec-1992	538107	18330	8.2052
Mar-1993	456913	17975	7.7332
Jun-1993	521799	18247	7.4515
Sep-1993	526234	18246	7.0778
Dec-1993	577166	18413	7.0537
Mar-1994	497770	18154	7.2958
Jun-1994	561668	18409	8.4370
Sep-1994	568419	18493	8.5882
Dec-1994	620341	18667	9.0977
Mar-1995	526748	18834	8.8123
Jun-1995	595468	18798	7.9470
Sep-1995	596375	18871	7.7012
Dec-1995	610422	18942	7.3508
Mar-1996	564968	19071	7.2430
Jun-1996	631151	19081	8.1050
Sep-1996	627404	19161	8.1590
Dec-1996	678842	19152	7.7102
Mar-1997	594984	19331	7.7905
Jun-1997	651881	19315	7.9255
Sep-1997	659643	19385	7.4692
Dec-1997	704054	19478	7.1980
Mar-1998	613448	19632	7.0547
Jun-1998	695875	19719	7.0938
Sep-1998	686297	19905	6.8657
Dec-1998	749973	20194	6.7633
Mar-1999	666676	20377	6.8805
Jun-1999	749668	20472	7.2037
Sep-1999	757234	20756	7.7990
Dec-1999	821351	21124	7.8338

←Holdout period

(continued)

TABLE 5–1   *(Continued)*

Audit Trail--ANOVA Table (Multiple Regression Selected)

Source of Variation	SS	df	MS	SEE
Regression	238,653,389,578.20	2	119,326,694,789.10	
Error	38,397,208,756.69	33	1,163,551,780.51	34,110.87
Total	277,050,598,334.89	35		

Audit Trail--Coefficient Table (Multiple Regression Selected)

Series Description	Included in Model	Coefficient	Standard Error	T-test	F-test	Elasticity	Overall F-test
RS	Dependent	-1,422,517.59	260,520.55	-5.46	29.81		102.55
DPI	Yes	110.77	11.47	9.66	93.24	3.68	
MR	Yes	-9,945.15	7,674.22	-1.30	1.68	-0.15	

Audit Trail--Statistics

Accuracy Measure	Value	Forecast Statistic	Value
AIC	852.52	Durbin-Watson	2.60
BIC	854.11	Mean	561,110.56
Mean absolute percentage error (MAPE)	4.80%	Max	749,973.00
Sum squared error (SSE)	38,397,208,756.69	Min	417,357.00
R-squared	86.14%	Sum squared deviation	277,050,598,334.89
Adjusted R-squared	85.30%	Range	332,616.00
Root-mean-squared error	32,658.68		

Our second forecasts of retail sales (RSF2) can be found as follows:

$$RSF2 = -1,422,517.59 - 9,945.15(MR) + 110.77(DPI)$$

1999Q1:

$$RSF2 = -1,422,517.59 - 9,945.15(6.71) + 110.77(20,230.20) = 751,649.70$$

1999Q2:

$$RSF2 = -1,422,517.59 - 9,945.15(6.66) + 110.77(20,365.07) = 767,086.51$$

1999Q3:

$$RSF2 = -1,422,517.59 - 9,945.15(6.60) + 110.77(20,500.84) = 782,722.47$$

1999Q4:

$$RSF2 = -1,422,517.59 - 9,945.15(6.55) + 110.77(20,637.51) = 798,358.66$$

These values are plotted in Figure 5–2 along with the values predicted by the equation for the historical period. The forecasts here were produced in ForecastX™ and the calculations involve more significant digits than shown here.

Date	RS	Forecasted RS
Mar-1990	418,436.00	474,628.38
Jun-1990	464,944.00	475,571.92
Sep-1990	464,490.00	474,352.69
Dec-1990	496,741.00	456,445.92
Mar-1991	417,357.00	448,995.87
Jun-1991	470,851.00	461,257.97
Sep-1991	469,494.00	458,769.41
Dec-1991	498,235.00	464,056.67
Mar-1992	437,388.00	484,777.30
Jun-1992	486,553.00	494,507.94
Sep-1992	489,541.00	495,740.00
Dec-1992	538,107.00	526,351.40
Mar-1993	456,913.00	491,721.07
Jun-1993	521,799.00	524,652.57
Sep-1993	526,234.00	528,257.97
Dec-1993	577,166.00	546,997.42
Mar-1994	497,770.00	515,898.80
Jun-1994	561,668.00	532,796.86
Sep-1994	568,419.00	540,598.42
Dec-1994	620,341.00	554,805.89
Mar-1995	526,748.00	576,142.67
Jun-1995	595,468.00	580,760.72
Sep-1995	596,375.00	591,292.00
Dec-1995	640,422.00	602,641.01
Mar-1996	564,968.00	618,003.16
Jun-1996	631,151.00	610,538.16
Sep-1996	627,404.00	618,862.97
Dec-1996	678,842.00	622,329.73
Mar-1997	594,984.00	641,359.19
Jun-1997	651,881.00	638,244.22
Sep-1997	659,643.00	650,536.64
Dec-1997	704,054.00	663,535.33
Mar-1998	613,448.00	682,019.86
Jun-1998	695,875.00	691,267.60
Sep-1998	686,297.00	714,095.07
Dec-1998	749,973.00	747,167.20
Mar-1999	666,676.00	751,649.70
Jun-1999	749,668.00	767,086.51	←Holdout period
Sep-1999	757,234.00	782,722.47
Dec-1999	821,351.00	798,358.66

In Figure 5–2 one line shows actual values of retail sales (RS) for 1990Q1 through 1999Q4. The other line shows the values predicted by this model for 1990Q1 through 1999Q4 (RSF2). For the historical period, actual values for the independent variables were used in determining RSF2. In the holdout period, forecast values (from smoothing models) for DPI and MR, as shown in the preceding computations, were used to calculate RSF2.

FIGURE 5–2

*Retail Sales (RS)
and Forecasted
Retail Sales (RSF2)
in Millions of
Dollars*

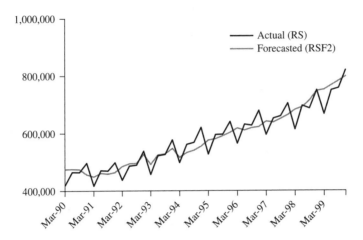

Actual and forecast values of retail sales for the four quarters of 1999 are shown, along with the calculation of the root-mean-squared error (RMSE) for the forecast period:

Holdout Period Forecast RMSE

Forecast	*Actual*	$(A_t - F_t)$	$(A_t - F_t)^2$
751,649.70	666,676.00	−84,973.70	7,220,529,691.69
767,086.51	749,668.00	−17,418.51	303,404,490.62
782,722.47	757,234.00	−25,488.47	649,662,102.94
798,358.66	821,351.00	22,992.34	528,647,698.68

RMSE = 46,642.91

This RMSE is about 5 percent of the mean for RS during these four quarters. The total for RS in 1999 was 2,994,929, and the total of the four quarterly forecasts was 3,099,817, so the error for the year was −104,888, or about 3.5 percent.

The Regression Plane

In our three-variable case (with RS as the dependent variable and with DPI and MR as independent variables), three observations are made for each sample point (i.e., for each quarter). Table 5–1 shows these three observations for every quarter. In the period 1990Q1, for instance, the three values are 418,436 for RS, 18,035 for DPI, and 10.1202 for MR. These observations can be depicted in a scatter diagram like those of Chapter 2, but the scatter diagram must be three-dimensional. Figure 5–3 shows the retail sales (RS) of any observation as measured vertically from the origin (labeled as RS in Figure 5–3). The value of MR is measured along the "MR" axis and the value of

FIGURE 5–3

Retail Sales (RS) in Millions of Dollars Viewed in Three Dimensions

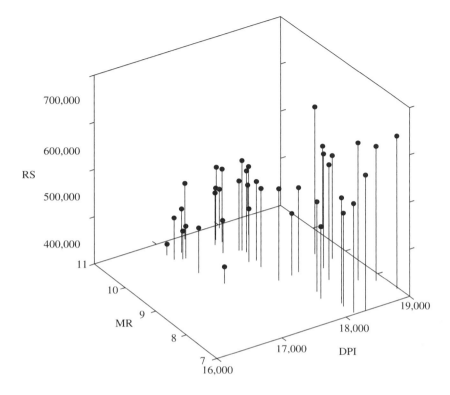

DPI is measured along the "DPI" axis. All 40 observations are represented as points in the diagram.

In multiple-regression analysis, our task is to suspend a three-dimensional plane (called the *regression plane*) among the observations in such a way that the plane best represents the observations. Multiple-regression analysis estimates an equation ($Y = a + b_1X + b_2Z$) in such a manner that all the estimates of Y made with the equation fall on the surface of the linear plane. The exact equation we estimated for retail sales,

$$RS = -1,422,517 - 9,945(MR) + 110.77(DPI)$$

is graphed as the plane shown in Figure 5–4. This regression plane, like the simple bivariate regression line of Chapter 4, is drawn in such a way as to minimize the sum of the squared vertical deviations between the sample points and the estimated plane. Some of the actual points lie above the regression plane, while other actual points lie below the regression plane.

Note that the b_1 estimate indicates how RS changes with respect to MR *while DPI is held constant*. If the sign of b_1 is negative, as it is in this example, then RS must decrease as MR increases. Looking at Figure 5–4 again, note that the plane "tilts down" as you move from 10 to 20 along the MR axis. Clearly, the regression plane is reacting to the negative relationship between MR and RS.

FIGURE 5–4

*Retail Sales (RS)
Viewed in Three
Dimensions with
Regression Plane
Superimposed*

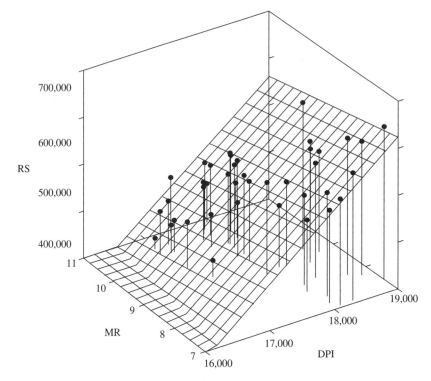

*Regression plane has the equation: RS = −1,422,517 − 9,945(MR) + 110.77(DPI).
See Table 5–2 for the estimation of this equation.*

Similarly, the sign for b_2 in this regression represents the relationship between DPI and RS *while MR is held constant.* Since the estimated sign of b_2 is positive, we should expect that as DPI increases in value, all else being equal, RS will increase. This is also easily seen by examining the regression plane. Note that the plane is tilted in such a way that higher incomes (DPI) are associated with higher retail sales (RS) values.

If all the actual data points were to lie very close to the regression plane, the *R*-squared of the equation would be very high. If, on the other hand, most of the actual points were far above and below the regression plane, the *R*-squared would be lower than it otherwise would be. Normally, regression packages do not have a provision for the graphing of output in three-dimensional form. This is because relatively few of the problems faced in the real world involve exactly three variables. Sometimes you are working with only two variables, while at other times you will be working with more than three. Thus, while the three-dimensional diagram will be useful only in a few cases, it is instructive to see it once in order to understand that a regression package is simply estimating the equation of a plane in three-space when multiple regression is used. The plane is a normal plane when there are two independent variables, and it is called a *hyperplane* (more than three-dimensional) when there are more than two independent variables.

Sidebar: If all the actual data points were to lie very close to the regression plane, the *R*-squared of the equation would be very high.

Statistical Evaluation of Multiple-Regression Models

The statistical evaluation of multiple-regression models is similar to that discussed in Chapter 4 for simple bivariate regression models. However, some important differences will be brought out in this section. In addition to evaluating the multiple-regression model, we will be comparing these results with the corresponding bivariate model. Thus, in Table 5–2 you see the regression results for both models. The multiple-regression results appear at the bottom of the table.

Three Quick Checks in Evaluating Multiple-Regression Models

The first thing one should do in reviewing regression results is to see whether the signs on the coefficients make sense.

As suggested in Chapter 4, the first thing one should do in reviewing regression results is to see whether the signs on the coefficients make sense. For our current model, that is,

$$RS = b_0 + b_1(MR) + b_2(DPI)$$

we have said that we expect a negative relationship between RS and the interest rate, and a positive relationship between real disposable personal income and RS. Our expectations are confirmed, since:

$$b_1 = -9,945.15 < 0$$
$$b_2 = +110.77 > 0$$

The second thing to consider is whether these results are statistically significant at our desired level of confidence.

The second thing to consider is whether these results are statistically significant at our desired level of confidence. We will follow the convention of using a 95 percent confidence level, and thus a 0.05 significance level. The hypotheses to be tested are summarized as follows:

For DPI	*For MR*
$H_0: \beta_1 \leq 0$	$H_0: \beta_2 \geq 0$
$H_1: \beta_1 > 0$	$H_1: \beta_2 < 0$

These hypotheses are evaluated using a *t*-test where, as with bivariate regression, the calculated *t*-ratio is found by dividing the estimated regression coefficient by its standard error (i.e., $t_{calc} = b_i/\text{s.e. of } b_i$). The table value of t (t_T) can be found from Table 2–5 at $n - (K + 1)$ degrees of freedom, where n = the number of observations and K = the number of independent variables. For our current problem $n = 36$ and $K = 2$, so df = $36 - (2 + 1) = 33$. We will follow the rule that if df ≥ 30 the infinity row of the *t*-table will be used. Thus, the table value is 1.645. Note that we have used the 0.05 column, since we have one-tailed tests, and in such cases the entire significance level (0.05) goes in one tail.

TABLE 5–2   **Regression Results for Multiple- and Bivariate-Regression Models of Retail Sales (RS)**

Bivariate Regression

Audit Trail--Coefficient Table (Multiple Regression Selected)

Series Description	Included in Model	Coefficient	Standard Error	T-test	F-test	Elasticity	Overall F-test
RS	Dependent	1,052,224.43	90,141.74	11.67	136.26		30.13
MR	Yes	-59,926.04	10,917.63	-5.49	30.13	-0.88	

Audit Trail--Statistics

Accuracy Measure	Value	Forecast Statistic	Value
AIC	900.82	Durbin-Watson	0.97
BIC	902.41	Mean	561,110.56
Mean absolute percentage error (MAPE)	9.70%	Max	749,973.00
Sum squared error (SSE)	146,888,677,848.55	Min	417,357.00
R-squared	46.98%	Sum squared deviation	277,050,598,334.89
Adjusted R-squared	45.42%	Range	332,616.00
Root-mean-squared error	63,876.76		

Multiple Regression

Audit Trail--Coefficient Table (Multiple Regression Selected)

Series Description	Included in Model	Coefficient	Standard Error	T-test	F-test	Elasticity	Overall F-test
RS	Dependent	-1,422,517.59	260,520.55	-5.46	29.81		102.55
DPI	Yes	110.77	11.47	9.66	93.24	3.68	
MR	Yes	-9,945.15	7,674.22	-1.30	1.68	-0.15	

Audit Trail--Statistics

Accuracy Measure	Value	Forecast Statistic	Value
AIC	852.52	Durbin-Watson	2.60
BIC	854.11	Mean	561,110.56
Mean absolute percentage error (MAPE)	4.80%	Max	749,973.00
Sum squared error (SSE)	38,397,208,756.69	Min	417,357.00
R-squared	86.14%	Sum squared deviation	277,050,598,334.89
Adjusted R-squared	85.30%	Range	332,616.00
Root-mean-squared error	32,658.68		

Remember that since the *t*-distribution is symmetrical, we compare the absolute value of t_{calc} with the table value. For our hypothesis tests, the results can be summarized as follows:

For MR	For DPI
$t_{calc} = -1.3$	$t_{calc} = 9.66$
$|t_{calc}| > t_T$	$|t_{calc}| > t_T$
$+1.3 < 1.645$	$9.66 > 1.645$
$\therefore$ Accept H_0	$\therefore$ Reject H_0

In one case (DPI), the absolute value of t_{calc} is greater than the table value at $\alpha = .05$ and df $= 33$. In the other case (MR), the absolute value of t_{calc} is less than the table value at $\alpha = .05$ but it is greater than the table value at $\alpha = .10$ (the table value here is 1.282). Thus we reject the null hypothesis at the .05 level for the DPI coefficient and we are also able to reject the null hypothesis at the .10 level for the MR coefficient. We are not able to reject the null hypothesis at the .05 level for the coefficient of MR.

By setting the 95 percent confidence level as our criterion, we are at the same time saying that we are willing to accept a 5 percent chance of error, or, alternatively, we set a 5 percent desired significance level.

In this particular case only one of the variable coefficients (the DPI coefficient) passes the stronger test of the 95 percent confidence level. The other coefficient (the MR coefficient) fails to pass at the 95 percent confidence level but does pass at the 90 percent confidence level.

If we are willing to accept the use of the 90 percent confidence level, we can then conclude that the coefficients on MR and DPI are statistically significant.

The third part of our quick check of regression results involves an evaluation of the coefficient of determination, which, you may recall, measures the percentage of the variation in the dependent variable that is explained by the regression model. In Chapter 4 we designated the coefficient of determination as *R*-squared. If you look at the second ForecastX™ output in Table 5–2, you will see that in addition to *R*-squared there is another measure called the *adjusted R*-squared. (See "Adjusted *R*-squared = 85.30%.") In evaluating multiple-regression equations, you should always consider the adjusted *R*-squared value. The reason for the adjustment is that adding another independent variable will always increase *R*-squared even if the variable has no meaningful relation to the dependent variable. Indeed, if we added enough independent variables, we could get very close to an *R*-squared of 1.00—a perfect fit for the historical period. However, the model would probably work very poorly for values of the independent variables other than those used in estimation. To get around this and to show only meaningful changes in *R*-squared, an adjustment is made to account for a decrease in the number of degrees of freedom.[3] The adjusted *R*-squared is often denoted $\bar{R}^2$ (called *R*-bar-squared).

The third part of our quick check of regression results involves an evaluation of the coefficient of determination.

---

[3]These concepts are expanded in J. Scott Armstrong, *Long-Range Forecasting* (New York: John Wiley & Sons, 1978), pp. 323–25, 466.

For our multiple-regression model of retail sales (RS), we see, in Table 5–2, that the adjusted R-squared is 85.30 percent. Thus, this model explains 85.30 percent of the variation in retail sales. This compares with an adjusted R-squared of 45.42 percent for the bivariate model.

In looking at regression output, you often see an F-statistic. This statistic can be used to test the following hypothesis:

$$H_0: \beta_1 = \beta_2 = \beta_3 = \cdots \beta_k = 0$$

(i.e., all slope terms are simultaneously equal to zero);

$$H_1: \text{All slope terms are not simultaneously equal to zero}$$

If the null hypothesis is true, it follows that none of the variation in the dependent variable would be explained by the regression model. It follows that if H_0 is true, the true coefficient of determination would be zero.

The F-statistic is calculated as follows:

$$F = \frac{\text{Explained variation}/K}{\text{Unexplained variation}/[n - (K + 1)]}$$

To test the hypothesis, this calculated F-statistic is compared with the F-value from Table 5–3 at K degrees of freedom for the numerator and $n - (K + 1)$ degrees of freedom for the denominator.[4] For our current regression, $K = 2$ and $[n - (K + 1)] = 33$, so the table value of F is 3.23 (taking the closest value). In using an F-test, the criterion for rejection of the null hypothesis is that $F_{calc} > F_T$ (the calculated F must be greater than the table value). In this case the calculated value is 102.55, so we would reject H_0 (i.e., our equation passes the F-test).

Multicollinearity

In multiple-regression analysis, one of the assumptions that is made is that the independent variables are not highly correlated with each other or with linear combinations of other independent variables. If this assumption is violated, a problem known as *multicollinearity* results. If your regression results show that one or more independent variables appear not to be statistically significant when theory suggests that they should be, and/or if the signs on coefficients are not logical, multicollinearity may be indicated. Sometimes it is possible to spot the cause of the multicollinearity by looking at a correlation matrix for the independent variables.

To illustrate the multicollinearity problem, suppose that we model retail sales (RS) as a function of real disposable personal income (DPI), the mortgage rate (MR), and the utility bond interest rate (BI). The model would be:

$$RS = b_0 + b_1(MR) + b_2(DPI) + b_3(BI)$$

In multiple-regression analysis, one of the assumptions that is made is that the independent variables are not highly correlated with each other or with linear combinations of other independent variables. If this assumption is violated, a problem known as *multicollinearity* results.

---

[4]This F-table corresponds to a 95 percent confidence level ($\alpha = 0.05$). One could use any α value and the corresponding F-distribution.

TABLE 5–3   Critical Values of the *F*-Distribution at a 95 Percent Confidence Level ($\alpha = .05$)

	1*	2	3	4	5	6	7	8	9
1†	161.40	199.50	215.70	224.60	230.20	234.00	236.80	238.90	240.50
2	18.51	19.00	19.16	19.25	19.30	19.33	19.35	19.37	19.38
3	10.13	9.55	9.28	9.12	9.01	8.94	8.89	8.85	8.81
4	7.71	6.94	6.59	6.39	6.26	6.16	6.09	6.04	6.00
5	6.61	5.79	5.41	5.19	5.05	4.95	4.88	4.82	4.77
6	5.99	5.14	4.76	4.53	4.39	4.28	4.21	4.15	4.10
7	5.59	4.74	4.35	4.12	3.97	3.87	3.79	3.73	3.68
8	5.32	4.46	4.07	3.84	3.69	3.58	3.50	3.44	3.39
9	5.12	4.26	3.86	3.63	3.48	3.37	3.29	3.23	3.18
10	4.96	4.10	3.71	3.48	3.33	3.22	3.14	3.07	3.02
11	4.84	3.98	3.59	3.36	3.20	3.09	3.01	2.95	2.90
12	4.75	3.89	3.49	3.26	3.11	3.00	2.91	2.85	2.80
13	4.67	3.81	3.41	3.18	3.03	2.92	2.83	2.77	2.71
14	4.60	3.74	3.34	3.11	2.96	2.85	2.76	2.70	2.65
15	4.54	3.68	3.29	3.06	2.90	2.79	2.71	2.64	2.59
16	4.49	3.63	3.24	3.01	2.85	2.74	2.66	2.59	2.54
17	4.45	3.59	3.20	2.96	2.81	2.70	2.61	2.55	2.49
18	4.41	3.55	3.16	2.93	2.77	2.66	2.58	2.51	2.46
19	4.38	3.52	3.13	2.90	2.74	2.63	2.54	2.48	2.42
20	4.35	3.49	3.10	2.87	2.71	2.60	2.51	2.45	2.39
21	4.32	3.47	3.07	2.84	2.68	2.57	2.49	2.42	2.37
22	4.30	3.44	3.05	2.82	2.66	2.55	2.46	2.40	2.34
23	4.28	3.42	3.03	2.80	2.64	2.53	2.44	2.31	2.32
24	4.26	3.40	3.01	2.78	2.62	2.51	2.42	2.36	2.30
25	4.24	3.39	2.99	2.76	2.60	2.49	2.40	2.34	2.28
26	4.23	3.37	2.98	2.74	2.59	2.47	2.39	2.32	2.27
27	4.21	3.35	2.96	2.73	2.57	2.46	2.37	2.31	2.25
28	4.20	3.34	2.95	2.71	2.56	2.45	2.36	2.29	2.24
29	4.18	3.33	2.93	2.70	2.55	2.43	2.35	2.28	2.22
30	4.17	3.32	2.92	2.69	2.53	2.42	2.33	2.27	2.21
40	4.08	3.23	2.84	2.61	2.45	2.34	2.25	2.18	2.12
60	4.00	3.15	2.76	2.53	2.37	2.25	2.17	2.10	2.04
120	3.92	3.07	2.68	2.45	2.29	2.17	2.09	2.02	1.96
∞	3.84	3.00	2.60	2.37	2.21	2.10	2.01	1.94	1.88

*Degrees of freedom for the numerator = K †Degrees of freedom for the denominator = $n - (K + 1)$

Business and economic logic would tell us to expect a negative sign for b_1, a positive sign for b_2, and a negative sign for b_3. The actual regression results are:

		Coefficient	t-Ratio
(c5t1)	Constant	−1,354,134	−4.39
	MR	8,018	0.19
	DPI	108	8.30
	BI	−20,490	−0.43

We see that the coefficient for MR is positive, which does not make sense. It would be difficult to argue persuasively that RS would rise as MR rises.

If we look at the correlations between these variables, we can see the source of the problem. The correlations are:

	DPI	*MR*	*BI*
DPI	1		
MR	−0.6745	1	
BI	−0.7154	0.989759	1

Clearly there is a very strong linear association between MR and BI. In this case both of these variables are measuring essentially the same thing. There are no firm rules in deciding how strong a correlation is too great. Two rules of thumb, however, provide some guidance. First, we might avoid correlations between independent variables that are close to 1 in absolute value. Second, we might try to avoid situations in which the correlation between independent variables is greater than the correlation of those variables with the dependent variable. One thing to do when multicollinearity exists is to drop all but one of the highly correlated variables. The use of first differences can also help when there is a common trend in the two highly correlated independent variables.

Serial Correlation: A Second Look

The problem known as *serial correlation* (or autocorrelation) was introduced in Chapter 4, where we indicated that serial correlation results when there is a significant time pattern in the error terms of a regression analysis that violates the assumption that the errors are independent over time. Positive serial correlation, as shown in the right-hand graph of Figure 4–11, is common in business and economic data.

Serial correlation results when there is a significant time pattern in the error terms of a regression analysis.

A test involving six comparisons between table values of the Durbin-Watson statistic and the calculated Durbin-Watson statistic is commonly used to detect serial correlation. These six comparisons are repeated here, where d_l and d_u represent the lower and upper bounds of the Durbin-Watson statistic from Table 4–8 and DW is the calculated value:

Test	Value of Calculated DW	Conclusion
1	$d_l < DW < d_u$	Result is indeterminate
2	$0 < DW < d_l$	Positive serial correlation exists
3	$2 < DW < (4 - d_u)$	No serial correlation exists
4	$d_u < DW < 2$	
5	$(4 - d_l) < DW < 4$	Negative serial correlation exists
6	$(4 - d_u) < DW < (4 - d_l)$	Result is indeterminate

Earlier in this chapter we indicated that for the bivariate regression of RS with MR, the DW of 0.97 indicated positive serial correlation.

For the multiple regression of RS with DPI and MR, the calculated Durbin-Watson statistic is approximately 2.6. (See Table 5–2, which has DW for both the bivariate and the multiple regressions.) This satisfies test 6:

$$4 - d_u < \text{DW} < d_l$$

$$(4 - 1.59) < 2.6 < 4 - 1.35$$

where d_u was found from Table 4–8 for $k = 2$ and $N = 36$. Thus, we conclude that the result is indeterminate. This illustrates one possible solution to the serial-correlation problem. Our bivariate model was underspecified: an important independent variable was missing. In this case it was disposable personal income (DPI). While the addition of this variable did not solve the problem in this case, the DW statistic did move in the correct direction.

Serial Correlation and the Omitted-Variable Problem

Table 5–4 presents data for a firm's sales, the price the firm charges for its product, and the income of potential purchasers. The most common reason for serial correlation is that an important explanatory variable has been omitted. To address this situation it will be necessary at times to add an additional explanatory variable to the equation to correct for serial correlation.

In the first regression displayed in Table 5–4, price is used as the single independent variable to explain the firm's sales. The results are somewhat less than satisfactory on a number of accounts. First, the R-squared is quite low, explaining only about 39 percent of the variation in sales. More importantly, the sign on the price coefficient is positive, indicating that as price increases, sales also increase. This does not seem to follow economic theory. Finally, the Durbin-Watson statistic is only 0.34, indicating a serious case of serial correlation.

The problem may be that an important variable that could account for the correlation of the error terms has been omitted from the regression. The second regression in Table 5–4 adds income as a second explanatory variable. The results are dramatic. The adjusted R-squared shows that the model now accounts for about 95 percent of the variation in sales. The signs of both the explanatory variable coefficients are as expected. The price coefficient is negative, indicating that sales decrease as price increases, while the income coefficient is positive, indicating that sales of the good rise as incomes increase (which would be reasonable for a "normal" economic good).

The Durbin-Watson statistic has risen to 1.67 and is within the rule of thumb 1.5 to 2.5 range. There does not seem to be serial correlation (and so the R-squared and t-statistics are probably accurate). The formal test for serial correlation requires us to look for the upper and lower values in the Durbin-Watson table (Table 4–8). Note carefully that the appropriate values are 0.95 and 1.54 (i.e., $N = 15$ and column $k = 2$).

TABLE 5–4   Data for a Firm's Sales, the Price the Firm Charges for Its Product, and the Income of Potential Purchasers (c5t4)

Period	Sales	Price	Income
Mar-1993	80	5.00	2620
Jun-1993	86	4.87	2733
Sep-1993	93	4.86	2898
Dec-1993	99	4.79	3056
Mar-1994	106	4.79	3271
Jun-1994	107	4.87	3479
Sep-1994	109	5.01	3736
Dec-1994	110	5.31	3868
Mar-1995	111	5.55	4016
Jun-1995	113	5.72	4152
Sep-1995	110	5.74	4336
Dec-1995	112	5.59	4477
Mar-1996	131	5.50	4619
Jun-1996	136	5.48	4764
Sep-1996	137	5.47	4802
Dec-1996	139	5.49	4916

Bivariate Regression

Audit Trail--Coefficient Table (Multiple Regression Selected)

Series Description	Included in Model	Coefficient	Standard Error	T-test	F-test	Elasticity	Overall F-test
Sales	Dependent	-51.24	54.32	-0.94	0.89		8.98
Price	Yes	30.92	10.32	3.00	8.98	1.46	

Audit Trail--Statistics

Accuracy Measure	Value	Forecast Statistic	Value
AIC	130.02	Durbin-Watson	0.34
BIC	130.80	Mean	111.19
Mean absolute percentage error (MAPE)	10.67%	Max	139.00
Sum squared error (SSE)	2,796.82	Min	80.00
R-squared	39.07%	Sum squared deviation	4,590.44
Adjusted R-squared	34.72%	Range	59.00
Root-mean-squared error	13.22		

(*continued*)

TABLE 5–4 *(Continued)*

Multiple Regression

Audit Trail--Coefficient Table (Multiple Regression Selected)

Series Description	Included in Model	Coefficient	Standard Error	T-test	F-test	Elasticity	Overall F-test
Sales	Dependent	123.47	19.40	6.36	40.51		154.86
Price	Yes	-24.84	4.95	-5.02	25.17	-1.17	
Income	Yes	0.03	0.0023	13.55	183.62	1.06	

Audit Trail--Statistics

Accuracy Measure	Value	Forecast Statistic	Value
AIC	86.56	Durbin-Watson	1.67
BIC	87.34	Mean	111.19
Mean absolute percentage error (MAPE)	2.22%	Max	139.00
Sum squared error (SSE)	184.92	Min	80.00
R-squared	95.97%	Sum squared deviation	4,590.44
Adjusted R-squared	95.35%	Range	59.00
Root-mean-squared error	3.40		

Using these values and our calculated value, we can evaluate each of the 6 tests explained earlier.

Test	Value	Conclusion
1	$.95 < 1.67 < 1.54$	False
2	$0 < 1.67 < 0.95$	False
3	$2 < 1.67 < 2.46$	False
4	$1.54 < 1.67 < 2$	True
5	$3.05 < 1.67 < 4$	False
6	$2.46 < 1.67 < 3.05$	False

Since our result is true for test number 4, we conclude that no serial correlation is present. Apparently, the addition of the second explanatory variable explained the pattern in the residuals that the Durbin-Watson statistic identified.

Alternative-Variable Selection Criteria

There is a strong tendency for forecasters to use a single criterion for deciding which of several variables ought to be used as independent variables in a regression. The criterion most people use appears to be the coefficient of multiple determination, or *R*-squared. Recall that *R*-squared is a measure of the proportion of total variance accounted for by the linear influence of the explanatory variables (only *linear* influence is accounted for, since we are using linear least-squares regression). The *R*-squared measure has at least one obvious fault when used in this manner: it can be increased by simply increasing the number of independent variables. Because of this, we proposed the corrected or adjusted R-squared, which uses unbiased estimators of the respective variances. Most forecasters use the adjusted R-squared to lead them to the correct model by selecting the model that maximizes adjusted R-squared. The adjusted R-squared measure is based on selecting the correct model by using a quadratic form of the residuals or squared errors in which the true model minimizes those squared errors. But the adjusted R-squared measure may not be the most powerful of the measures involving the squared errors.

There are two other model-specification statistics reported by ForecastX™ and other statistical packages that can be of use in selecting the "correct" independent variables.

There are two other model-specification statistics reported by ForecastX™ and other statistical packages that can be of use in selecting the "correct" independent variables. These are the Akaike information criterion (AIC) and the Bayesian information criterion (BIC).[5]

The Akaike information criterion selects the best model by considering the accuracy of the estimation and the "best" approximation to reality. The statistic (which is minimized by the best model) involves both the use of a measure of the accuracy of the estimate *and* a measure of the principle of parsimony (i.e., the concept that fewer independent variables are better than more, all other things being equal). The calculation of the AIC is detailed in Judge et al.[6] We can say that the statistic is constructed so that as the number of independent variables increases, the AIC has a tendency to increase as well; this means that there is a penalty for "extra" independent variables that must be sufficiently offset by an increase in estimation accuracy to keep the AIC from increasing. In actual practice, a decrease in the AIC as a variable is added indicates that accuracy has increased after adjustment for the rule of parsimony.

The Bayesian criterion is quite similar to the AIC. The BIC uses Bayesian arguments about the prior probability of the true model to suggest the correct model. While the calculation routine for the BIC is quite different from that for the AIC, the results are usually quite consistent.[7] The BIC is also to be minimized, so that if the BIC decreases after the addition of a new independent variable, the resulting model specification is seen as superior to the prior model specification. Often, AIC and BIC lead to the same model choice.

In a study of the model-selection process, Judge and coauthors created five independent variables that were to be used to estimate a dependent variable. Two of the five independent variables were actually related to the dependent variable, while the remaining three were extraneous variables. Various combinations of the five independent variables were used to estimate the dependent variable, and three measures were used to select the "best" model. The three measures used were the adjusted R-squared, the AIC, and the BIC.

The correct model containing only the two variables actually related to the dependent variable was chosen 27 percent of the time in repeated experiments by the

---

[5]The Bayesian information criterion is also called the Schwarz criterion, after its creator.

[6]For a complete description of the calculation routine, see George G. Judge, R. Carter Hill, William E. Griffiths, Helmut Lutkepohl, and Tsoung-Chao Lee, *Introduction to the Theory and Practice of Econometrics,* 2nd ed. (New York: John Wiley & Sons, 1988), Chapter 20.

[7]Again see Judge et al. for a complete description of the calculation routine.

adjusted *R*-squared criterion. The AIC chose the correct model in 45 percent of the cases, and the BIC chose the correct model in 46 percent of the cases. The results should make the forecaster wary of accepting only the statistical results of what constitutes the best model without some economic interpretation of why a variable is included. It should be clear, however, that the adjusted *R*-squared criterion is actually quite a poor judge to use in model selection; either the AIC or the BIC is far superior. The same study also showed that in 9 percent of the repeated trials the adjusted *R*-squared criterion chose the model with all five variables (i.e., the two "correct" ones and the three extraneous ones). The AIC and the BIC made the same incorrect choice in only 3 percent of the cases.

Examine the ForecastX™ output in Table 5–2, which includes the calculated Akaike and Schwarz criteria. In the upper half of Table 5–2, the retail sales (RS) regression includes only the mortgage rate (MR) as an independent variable. For this specification of the model, the AIC is 900.82, while the BIC is 902.41. When the disposable personal income (DPI) variable is added to the regression, the AIC (in absolute terms) decreases to 852.52 and the BIC decreases (again in absolute terms) to 854.11. These changes in the AIC and BIC indicate that the addition of MR to the model was a correct choice.

In Table 5–4 we added a second variable to a regression. When both price and income were included, the AIC (again in absolute terms) decreased to 86.56 from 130.02 and the BIC decreased to 87.34 from 130.80. Apparently, the inclusion of income as a variable was also a correct choice.

Accounting for Seasonality in a Multiple-Regression Model

Many business and economic data series display pronounced seasonal patterns that recur with some regularity year after year. The pattern may be associated with weather conditions typical of four seasons of the year. For example, sales of ski equipment would be expected to be greater during the fall and winter (the fourth and first quarters of the calendar year, respectively) than during the spring and summer (quarters 2 and 3).

Other regular patterns that would be referred to as seasonal patterns may have nothing to do with weather conditions. For example, jewelry sales tend to be high in November and December because of Christmas shopping, and turkey sales are also highest in these months because of traditions surrounding Thanksgiving and Christmas dinners.

Patterns such as these are not easily accounted for by the typical causal variables that we use in regression analysis. However, a special type of variable known as a *dummy variable* can be used effectively to account for seasonality or any other qualitative attribute. A dummy variable has a value of either 0 or 1. It is 0 if the condition does not exist for an observation, and it is 1 if the condition does exist.

A special type of variable known as a *dummy variable* can be used effectively to account for seasonality or any other qualitative attribute.

Suppose that we were studying monthly data on turkey sales at grocery stores and that we would like to include the November and December seasonality in our model. We could define a dummy variable called M11, for the eleventh month, to be equal to 1 for November observations and 0 otherwise. Another dummy variable, M12, could be defined similarly for December. Thus, for every year these variables would be as follows:

Month	M11	M12	Month	M11	M12
January	0	0	July	0	0
February	0	0	August	0	0
March	0	0	September	0	0
April	0	0	October	0	0
May	0	0	November	1	0
June	0	0	December	0	1

In the regression results, the coefficients for M11 and M12 would reveal the degree of difference in sales for November and December, respectively. In both of these cases we would expect the coefficients to be positive.

To illustrate very specifically the use of dummy variables to account for and measure seasonality, let us use private housing starts in the United States measured in thousands of units. These data are plotted for 1990Q1 through 1999Q4 in Figure 5–5. To help you see the seasonality, each first quarter is marked with the number 1. You see in this figure that through the nine years, there are typically few housing starts during the first quarter of the year (January, February, March); there is usually a big increase in the second quarter (April, May, June), followed by some decline in the third quarter (July, August, September), and further decline in the fourth quarter (October, November, December). The first quarter is almost always the lowest quarter for the year. This pattern is reasonably consistent, although there is variability in the degree of seasonality and some deviation from the overall pattern.

FIGURE 5–5

Private Housing Starts (PHS) in Thousands of Units (c5t6)

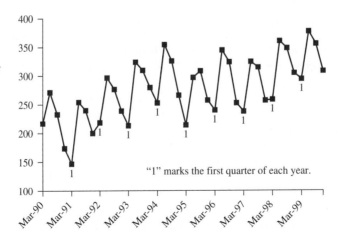

"1" marks the first quarter of each year.

To account for and measure this seasonality in a regression model, we will use three dummy variables: Q2 for the second quarter, Q3 for the third quarter, and Q4 for the fourth quarter. These will be coded as follows:

Q2 = 1 for all second quarters and zero otherwise

Q3 = 1 for all third quarters and zero otherwise

Q4 = 1 for all fourth quarters and zero otherwise

Data for private housing starts (PHS), the mortgage rate (MR), and these seasonal dummy variables are shown in Table 5–5. Look at the data carefully to verify your understanding of the coding for Q2, Q3, and Q4.

Since we have assigned dummy variables for the second, third, and fourth quarters, the first quarter is the base quarter for our regression model. Any quarter could be used as the base, with dummy variables to adjust for differences in other quarters. The number of seasonal dummy variables to use depends on the data. There is one important rule, however:

> *If we have P periods in our data series, we cannot use more than P − 1 seasonal dummy variables.*

In our current example $P = 4$, since we have quarterly data, and so we would use only three seasonal dummy variables. We could use fewer than three if we found that all three were unnecessary by evaluating their statistical significance by *t*-tests.

Let us now add these variables to the regression model for private housing starts (PHS). Our regression model will include the mortgage rate (MR) and the three dummy variables for seasonality (Q2, Q3, and Q4) as independent variables. The model is:

$$PHS = b_0 + b_1(MR) + b_2(Q2) + b_3(Q3) + b_4(Q4)$$

In this model we would expect b_1 to have a negative sign, and we would expect b_2, b_3, and b_4 all to have positive signs, since the first quarter of the year has been seen to be the lowest (see Figure 5–5).

Regression results for this model are shown in Table 5–6 along with the results for $PHS = f(MR)$, where the mortgage rate is the only independent variable. The bivariate model was discussed in Chapter 4, but the results are shown here to facilitate comparison. Looking at the output at the top of Table 5–6, you see that the signs for the coefficients are all consistent with our expectations. Further, from the *t*-statistics you can see that all of the coefficients are statistically significant.

A comparison of the two sets of regression results shown in Table 5–6 shows that important improvements result from adding the seasonal dummy variables. Note that the model with the dummy variables explains about 78.56 percent of the variation in private housing starts (see the adjusted *R*-squared), which is a considerable improvement over the bivariate model. The AIC and BIC both reflect the improvement from the addition of the seasonal dummy variables. Also, the standard error of the regression has fallen from 46 to 24.03. The Durbin-Watson statistic shows serial correlation for the multiple-regression model, while the test was indeterminate for the bivariate model. In

TABLE 5–5   Data for Private Housing Starts (PHS), the Mortgage Rate (MR), and Seasonal Dummy Variables for the Second, Third, and Fourth Quarters (Q2, Q3, Q4)

(c5t6)

Period	PHS	MR	Q2	Q3	Q4	
Mar-1990	217.0	10.1202	0	0	0	
Jun-1990	271.3	10.3372	1	0	0	
Sep-1990	233.0	10.1033	0	1	0	
Dec-1990	173.6	9.9547	0	0	1	
Mar-1991	146.7	9.5008	0	0	0	
Jun-1991	254.1	9.5265	1	0	0	
Sep-1991	239.8	9.2755	0	1	0	
Dec-1991	199.8	8.6882	0	0	1	
Mar-1992	218.5	8.7098	0	0	0	
Jun-1992	296.4	8.6782	1	0	0	
Sep-1992	276.4	8.0085	0	1	0	
Dec-1992	238.8	8.2052	0	0	1	
Mar-1993	213.2	7.7332	0	0	0	
Jun-1993	323.7	7.4515	1	0	0	
Sep-1993	309.3	7.0778	0	1	0	
Dec-1993	279.4	7.0537	0	0	1	
Mar-1994	252.6	7.2958	0	0	0	
Jun-1994	354.2	8.4370	1	0	0	
Sep-1994	325.7	8.5882	0	1	0	
Dec-1994	265.9	9.0977	0	0	1	
Mar-1995	214.2	8.8123	0	0	0	
Jun-1995	296.7	7.9470	1	0	0	
Sep-1995	308.2	7.7012	0	1	0	
Dec-1995	257.2	7.3508	0	0	1	
Mar-1996	240.0	7.2430	0	0	0	
Jun-1996	344.5	8.1050	1	0	0	
Sep-1996	324.0	8.1590	0	1	0	
Dec-1996	252.4	7.7102	0	0	1	
Mar-1997	237.8	7.7905	0	0	0	
Jun-1997	324.5	7.9255	1	0	0	
Sep-1997	314.6	7.4692	0	1	0	
Dec-1997	256.8	7.1980	0	0	1	
Mar-1998	258.4	7.0547	0	0	0	
Jun-1998	360.4	7.0938	1	0	0	
Sep-1998	348.0	6.8657	0	1	0	
Dec-1998	304.6	6.7633	0	0	1	
Mar-1999	294.1	6.8805	0	0	0	
Jun-1999	377.1	7.2037	1	0	0	
Sep-1999	355.6	7.7990	0	1	0	←Holdout period
Dec-1999	308.1	7.8338	0	0	1	

TABLE 5–6 **Regression Results for Private Housing Starts (PHS) as a Function of the Mortgage Rate (MR) Both with and without Seasonal Dummy Variables** (c5t6)

Bivariate Regression

Audit Trail--ANOVA Table (Multiple Regression Selected)

Source of Variation	SS	df	MS	SEE
Regression	22,317.89	1	22,317.89	
Error	71,948.82	34	2,116.14	46.00
Total	94,266.71	35		

Audit Trail--Coefficient Table (Multiple Regression Selected)

Series Description	Included in Model	Coefficient	Standard Error	T-test	F-test	Elasticity	Overall F-test
PHS	Dependent	473.69	63.09	7.51	56.38		10.55
MR	Yes	-24.81	7.64	-3.25	10.55	-0.75	

Audit Trail--Statistics

Accuracy Measure	Value	Forecast Statistic	Value
AIC	377.77	Durbin-Watson	1.79
BIC	379.35	Mean	270.33
Mean absolute percentage error (MAPE)	15.10%	Max	360.40
Sum squared error (SSE)	71,948.82	Min	146.70
R-squared	23.68%	Sum squared deviation	94,266.71
Adjusted R-squared	21.43%	Range	213.70
Root-mean-squared error	44.71		

Multiple Regression

Audit Trail--ANOVA Table (Multiple Regression Selected)

Source of Variation	SS	df	MS	SEE
Regression	76,364.02	4	19,091.00	
Error	17,902.69	31	577.51	24.03
Total	94,266.71	35		

Audit Trail--Coefficient Table (Multiple Regression Selected)

Series Description	Included in Model	Coefficient	Standard Error	T-test	F-test	Elasticity	Overall F-test
PHS	Dependent	448.97	34.22	13.12	172.11		33.06
MR	Yes	-27.50	4.03	-6.82	46.52	-0.83	
Q2	Yes	95.73	11.34	8.44	71.23	0.09	
Q3	Yes	72.53	11.34	6.40	40.93	0.07	
Q4	Yes	18.73	11.37	1.65	2.71	0.02	*(continued)*

TABLE 5–6   *(Continued)*

Audit Trail--Statistics

Accuracy Measure	Value	Forecast Statistic	Value
AIC	327.69	Durbin-Watson	0.77
BIC	329.28	Mean	270.33
Mean absolute percentage error (MAPE)	7.02%	Max	360.40
Sum squared error (SSE)	17,902.69	Min	146.70
R-squared	81.01%	Sum squared deviation	94,266.71
Adjusted R-squared	78.56%	Range	213.70
Root-mean-squared error	22.30		

the next section, we will work further with the PHS model and see some improvement in the serial-correlation problem.

Let us now use this model to make a forecast for each of the four quarters of 1999. The mortgage rate (MR) was forecast for 1999 earlier in this chapter as follows:

Period	MR Forecast
1999Q1	6.71%
1999Q2	6.66%
1999Q3	6.60%
1999Q4	6.55%

Our forecasts for private housing starts (PHS) are:

1999Q1:

$$PHSF2 = 448.97 - 27.50(6.71) + 95.73(0) + 72.53(0) + 18.73(0) = 264.445$$

1999Q2:

$$PHSF2 = 448.97 - 27.50(6.66) + 95.73(1) + 72.53(0) + 18.73(0) = 361.55$$

1999Q3:

$$PHSF2 = 448.97 - 27.50(6.60) + 95.73(0) + 72.53(1) + 18.73(0) = 340$$

1999Q4:

$$PHSF2 = 448.97 - 27.50(6.55) + 95.73 + 72.53(0) + 18.73(1) = 287.575$$

These forecasts are plotted in Figure 5–6 along with the actual and predicted values and the simple bivariate forecast for the historical period. If you examine Figure 5–6, you will see how much better the multiple regression model appears to be in comparison with the model of private housing starts as a function of only the mortgage rate.

FIGURE 5–6

*Private Housing
Starts (PHS) with a
Simple-Regression
Forecast (PHSF1)
and a Multiple-
Regression
Forecast (PHSF2)
in Thousands
of Units*
(c5t6)

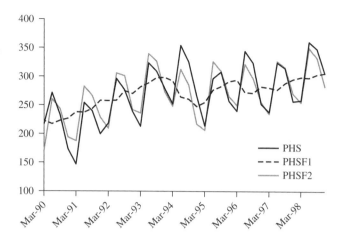

*PHSF1 uses only the mortgage interest rate as an explanatory
variable while PHSF2 uses the mortgage interest rate as well as
three dummy variables accounting for seasonality.*

To see whether this model actually did provide better forecasts for the four quarters
of 1999, let us look at the root-mean-squared error (RMSE):

Holdout Period Forecast RMSE—PHSF1

Date	Forecast	Actual	$(A_t - F_t)$	$(A_t - F_t)^2$
1999Q1	307.21	294.1	−13.11	172.00
1999Q2	308.46	377.1	68.64	4712.08
1999Q3	309.94	355.6	45.66	2084.47
1999Q4	311.18	308.1	−3.08	9.51

RMSE (PHSF1) = 41.77

Holdout Period Forecast RMSE—PHSF2

Date	Forecast	Actual	$(A_t - F_t)$	$(A_t - F_t)^2$
1999Q1	264.45	294.1	29.66	879.42
1999Q2	361.55	377.1	15.55	241.80
1999Q3	340.00	355.6	15.60	243.36
1999Q4	287.58	308.1	20.53	421.28

RMSE (PHSF2) = 21.13

The RMSE of 21.13 compares with an RMSE of 41.77 for the bivariate model using the
mortgage rate as the only independent variable.

Extensions of the Multiple-Regression Model

In some situations, nonlinear terms may be called for as independent variables in a regression analysis. Why? Business or economic logic may suggest that some nonlinearity is expected. A graphic display of the data may be helpful in determining whether nonlinearity is present. One common economic cause for nonlinearity is diminishing returns. For example, the effect of advertising on sales may diminish as increased advertising is used. In this section we will add real disposable personal income per capita (DPI) as an independent variable to the model for private housing starts and will investigate to see whether there are diminishing returns in the effect of DPI on private housing starts.

Some common forms of nonlinear functions are the following:

$$Y = b_0 + b_1(X) + b_2(X^2)$$
$$Y = b_0 + b_1(X) + b_2(X^2) + b_3(X^3)$$
$$Y = b_0 + b_1(1/X)$$
$$Y = B_0 X^{b_1} \quad \text{where } B_0 = e^{b_0}$$
$$\text{based on the regression of } \ln Y = f(\ln X) = b_0 + b_1(\ln X)$$

The first of these will be illustrated later in this section. In these examples only one explanatory variable (X) is shown. Other explanatory variables could be used in each model as well.

To illustrate the use and interpretation of a nonlinear term, let us return to the problem of developing a forecasting model for private housing starts (PHS). So far we have estimated the following two models:

$$\text{PHS} = b_0 + b_1(\text{MR})$$

$$\text{PHS} = b_0 + b_1(\text{MR}) + b_2(\text{Q2}) + b_3(\text{Q3}) + b_4(\text{Q4})$$

where MR = mortgage rate and Q2, Q3, and Q4 are dummy variables for quarters 2, 3, and 4, respectively. Our results have been encouraging, the best of these—in terms of adjusted R-squared and RMSE (the second model)—explains about 88 percent of the variation in PHS during the historical period and has been shown to have positive serial correlation.

Results for three additional regression models for PHS are summarized in Table 5–7 along with the results for the first two models that have been discussed previously. Models 1 and 2 are those we have already discussed. Model 3 adds real disposable personal income per capita (DPI) as an independent variable. In comparison with model 2 we see that the adjusted R-squared is slightly better.

It is in model 4 that we introduce a nonlinear term into the regression. The square of disposable personal income per capita (DPI^2) is included in the regression model. The t-statistic for DPI^2 in this model is -1.77. Inclusion of DPI^2 increases the adjusted R-squared to 85.86, reduces the standard error of the estimate to 19.49, and increases DW to 0.8.

The values for private housing starts predicted by model 4 are plotted in Figure 5–7 along with the original data. The forecast values (PHSF4) are shown by the lighter line, which follows the actual data quite well throughout the historical period. If you compare

TABLE 5–7 Estimated Regression Coefficients and Other Statistics for Five Models of Private Housing Starts (PHS)

Independent Variable	Model				
	1	2	3	4	5
Intercept	471.08	467.92	24.38	−4,861.35	−163.99
MR	−24.47	−30.59	−21.18	−20.12	−14.12
DPI			0.02	0.54	0.03
DPI-squared				−0.002751	−0.0002
Lagged PHS					0.64
Q2		102.67	98.65	97.00	108.26
Q3		78.70	76.23	75.81	29.28
Q4		24.47	21.31	21.77	−12.41
Adj. *R*-squared	21.27	81.86	84.83	85.86	93.6
SEE	46.68	22.5	20.19	19.49	13.11
DW	1.74	0.88	0.78	0.8	2.32
RMSE	45.33	20.83	18.38	17.43	11.52

MR = Mortgage rate

DPI = Real disposable personal income per capita

DPI-squared = Square of real disposable personal income per capita

LPHS = Private housing starts lagged one quarter

Q2 = Dummy variable for quarter 2

Q3 = Dummy variable for quarter 3

Q4 = Dummy variable for quarter 4

NOTE: In this table only data from 1990Q2 through 1998Q4 are used for calculation. This is one less data point than was used to estimate the previous models. This is done so that a fair comparison may be made with the model that includes PHS lagged on period.

FIGURE 5–7

Private Housing Starts (PHS) with Forecast Values (PHSF4) Using Model 4 from Table 5–7
(c5t7)

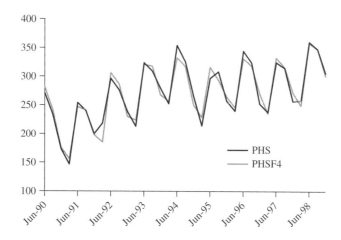

the forecast values in Figures 5–6 and 5–7, you can see the improvement between model 2 and model 4 visually (the forecast series are PHSF2 and PHSF4, respectively). This graphic comparison should reinforce the statistical findings for the two models presented in Table 5–7.

Model 5, in Table 5–7, is the same as model 4 except that the dependent variable, lagged one quarter, is added as an independent variable. You may recall that such a procedure was suggested as a way to help reduce serial correlation. As shown in Table 5–7, the Durbin-Watson statistic increases enough to rule out positive serial correlation. The adjusted R-squared increases, and the standard error of the estimate is further reduced. The root-mean-squared errors (RMSEs) are shown in Table 5–7 for models 1 through 5. You see that model 5 worked best for 1990Q1 to 1998Q4.

Data that were used in all of the regression models for private housing starts (PHS) are shown in Table 5–8.

Advice on Using Multiple Regression in Forecasting

Multiple-regression models are a very important part of the set of tools available to anyone interested in forecasting. Apart from their use in generating forecasts, they have considerable value in helping us to uncover structural relationships between the dependent variable and some set of independent variables. Knowing such relationships helps the forecaster understand the sensitivity of the variable to be forecast to other factors. This enhancement of our understanding of the business environment can only serve to improve our ability to make judgments about the future course of events. It is important not to downplay the role of judgments in forecasting. No one should ever rely solely on some quantitative procedure in developing a forecast. Expert judgments are crucial, and multiple-regression analyses can be helpful in improving one's level of expertise.

In developing forecasts with regression models, perhaps the best advice is to follow the "KIS" principle: keep it simple.[8] The more complex the model becomes, the more difficult it is to use. As more causal variables are used, the cost of maintaining the needed database increases in terms of both time and money. Further, complex models are more difficult to communicate to others who may be the actual users of the forecast. They are less likely to trust a model that they do not understand than a simpler model that they do understand.

In evaluating alternative multiple-regression models, is it better to compare adjusted R-squared values, or root-mean-squared errors? Remember that R-squared relates to the in-sample period, that is, to the past. A model may work well for the in-sample period but not work nearly so well in forecasting. Thus, it is usually best to focus on RMSE for actual forecasts (note that we say "focus on" and not "use exclusively"). You might track the RMSE for several alternative models for some period to see whether any one model consistently outperforms others in the forecast horizon. Use the AIC and BIC measures to help select appropriate independent variables. It is also desirable periodically to update the regression models to reflect possible changes in the parameter estimates.

---

[8]This is also called the *principle of parsimony* by Box and Jenkins. G. E. P. Box and G. M. Jenkins, *Time Series Analysis: Forecasting and Control,* 2nd ed. (San Francisco: Holden Day, 1976).

(c5t7)   TABLE 5–8   **Data for Regression Models of Private Housing Starts**

Period	PHS	MR	LPHS	Q2	Q3	Q4	DPI	DPI-Squared
Jun-1990	271.3	10.3372	217.0	1	0	0	18063	1,631,359.85
Sep-1990	233.0	10.1033	271.3	0	1	0	18031	1,625,584.81
Dec-1990	173.6	9.9547	233.0	0	0	1	17856	1,594,183.68
Mar-1991	146.7	9.5008	173.6	0	0	0	17748	1,574,957.52
Jun-1991	254.1	9.5265	146.7	1	0	0	17861	1,595,076.61
Sep-1991	239.8	9.2755	254.1	0	1	0	17816	1,587,049.28
Dec-1991	199.8	8.6882	239.8	0	0	1	17811	1,586,158.61
Mar-1992	218.5	8.7098	199.8	0	0	0	18000	1,620,000.00
Jun-1992	296.4	8.6782	218.5	1	0	0	18085	1,635,336.13
Sep-1992	276.4	8.0085	296.4	0	1	0	18036	1,626,486.48
Dec-1992	238.8	8.2052	276.4	0	0	1	18330	1,679,944.50
Mar-1993	213.2	7.7332	238.8	0	0	0	17975	1,615,503.13
Jun-1993	323.7	7.4515	213.2	1	0	0	18247	1,664,765.05
Sep-1993	309.3	7.0778	323.7	0	1	0	18246	1,664,582.58
Dec-1993	279.4	7.0537	309.3	0	0	1	18413	1,695,192.85
Mar-1994	252.6	7.2958	279.4	0	0	0	18154	1,647,838.58
Jun-1994	354.2	8.4370	252.6	1	0	0	18409	1,694,456.41
Sep-1994	325.7	8.5882	354.2	0	1	0	18493	1,709,955.25
Dec-1994	265.9	9.0977	325.7	0	0	1	18667	1,742,284.45
Mar-1995	214.2	8.8123	265.9	0	0	0	18834	1,773,597.78
Jun-1995	296.7	7.9470	214.2	1	0	0	18798	1,766,824.02
Sep-1995	308.2	7.7012	296.7	0	1	0	18871	1,780,573.21
Dec-1995	257.2	7.3508	308.2	0	0	1	18942	1,793,996.82
Mar-1996	240.0	7.2430	257.2	0	0	0	19071	1,818,515.21
Jun-1996	344.5	8.1050	240.0	1	0	0	19081	1,820,422.81
Sep-1996	324.0	8.1590	344.5	0	1	0	19161	1,835,719.61
Dec-1996	252.4	7.7102	324.0	0	0	1	19152	1,833,995.52
Mar-1997	237.8	7.7905	252.4	0	0	0	19331	1,868,437.81
Jun-1997	324.5	7.9255	237.8	1	0	0	19315	1,865,346.13
Sep-1997	314.6	7.4692	324.5	0	1	0	19385	1,878,891.13
Dec-1997	256.8	7.1980	314.6	0	0	1	19478	1,896,962.42
Mar-1998	258.4	7.0547	256.8	0	0	0	19632	1,927,077.12
Jun-1998	360.4	7.0938	258.4	1	0	0	19719	1,944,194.81
Sep-1998	348.0	6.8657	360.4	0	1	0	19905	1,980,963.41
Dec-1998	304.6	6.7633	348.0	0	0	1	20194	2,038,980.00
Mar-1999	294.1	6.8805	304.6	0	0	0	20377	2,076,010.87
Jun-1999	377.1	7.2037	294.1	1	0	0	20472	2,095,440.74
Sep-1999	355.6	7.7990	377.1	0	1	0	20756	2,153,982.23
Dec-1999	308.1	7.8338	355.6	0	0	1	21124	2,231,020.37

PHS = Private housing starts in thousands of units

MR = Mortgage rate (conventional fixed-rate) percent

DPI = Disposable personal income per capita per year

LPHS = PHS lagged one period

Q2, Q3, Q4 = Dummy variables for quarters 2, 3, and 4

DPI-squared = The square of the DPI variable

Note that the models estimated in Table 5–7 use a historical estimation period of 1990Q1 through 1998Q4. This table, however, also includes the forecast period of 1999Q1 through 1999Q4.

Forecasting Domestic Car Sales with Multiple Regression

In this section we apply the concepts covered in this chapter to the problem of forecasting domestic car sales by using a multiple-regression model. The explanatory variables selected are based on business logic and are ones for which data are readily available, should you want to look up the most recent data to update the results shown here. The model used here builds on the model in Chapter 4, in which domestic car sales (DCS) was a function of the disposable personal income (DPI). Explanatory variables used in the multiple regression are:

$$DPI = \text{Disposable personal income in constant 1996 dollars (expected sign of coefficient is positive)}$$

$$DPI^2/100 = \text{Square of DPI divided by 100}$$

$$PR = \text{Prime interest rate (expected sign negative)}$$

$$Q2 = \text{Dummy variable equal to 1 for second quarters and zero otherwise (expected sign positive because of spring car buying)}$$

$$Q3 = \text{Dummy variable equal to 1 for third quarters and zero otherwise (expected sign negative because of anticipation of new models)}$$

$$Q4 = \text{Dummy variable equal to 1 for fourth quarters and zero otherwise (expected sign positive because of introduction of new models)}$$

$$INDEX = \text{Univ. of Michigan Index of Consumer Sentiment}$$

$$TIME = \text{Time index}$$

$$TIME^2 = \text{Square of TIME}$$

Two regressions for domestic car sales (DCS) are presented in Table 5–9. The data used to generate both regressions appear in Table 5–10.

TABLE 5–9 Regression Results for Domestic Car Sales (c5t11)

Audit Trail--ANOVA Table (Multiple Regression Selected)

Source of Variation	SS	df	MS	SEE
Regression	161,225.75	2	80,612.87	
Error	3,678,089.19	75	49,041.19	221.45
Total	3,839,314.93	77		

Audit Trail--Coefficient Table (Multiple Regression Selected)

Series Description	Included in Model	Coefficient	Standard Error	T-test	F-test	Elasticity	Overall F-test
DCS	Dependent	2,175.97	443.76	4.90	24.04		1.64
DPI	Yes	-0.01	0.02	-0.69	0.47	-0.14	
PR	Yes	-18.67	11.39	-1.64	2.69	-0.11	

(continued)

TABLE 5–9 (*Continued*)

Audit Trail--Statistics

Accuracy Measure	Value	Forecast Statistic	Value
AIC	1,062.73	Durbin-Watson	1.11
BIC	1,065.08	Mean	1,748.21
Mean absolute percentage error (MAPE)	10.14%	Standard deviation	223.30
R-squared	4.20%	Ljung-Box	82.45
Adjusted R-squared	1.64%		
Root-mean-squared error	217.15		
Theil	0.97		

Audit Trail--ANOVA Table (Multiple Regression Selected)

Source of Variation	SS	df	MS	SEE
Regression	2,931,365.60	9	325,707.29	
Error	907,949.33	68	13,352.20	115.55
Total	3,839,314.93	77		

Audit Trail--Coefficient Table (Multiple Regression Selected)

Series Description	Included in Model	Coefficient	Standard Error	T-test	F-test	Elasticity	Overall F-test
DCS	Dependent	-25,409.19	4,191.37	-6.06	36.75		24.39
DPI	Yes	2.80	0.45	6.22	38.74	30.96	
$DPI^2/100$	Yes	-0.01	0.00	-6.07	36.89	-15.13	
Index	Yes	9.53	1.54	6.18	38.16	0.48	
PR	Yes	-18.59	8.14	-2.28	5.22	-0.11	
Q2	Yes	246.94	36.73	6.72	45.21	0.04	
Q3	Yes	73.75	37.13	1.99	3.95	0.01	
Q4	Yes	-50.06	37.17	-1.35	1.81	-0.01	
Time	Yes	-64.83	11.06	-5.86	34.38	-1.46	
$Time^2$	Yes	0.64	0.12	5.48	30.05	0.75	

Audit Trail--Statistics

Accuracy Measure	Value	Forecast Statistic	Value
AIC	953.61	Durbin-Watson	1.79
BIC	955.97	Mean	1,748.21
Mean absolute percentage error (MAPE)	5.25%	Standard deviation	223.30
R-squared	76.35%	Ljung-Box	13.58
Adjusted R-squared	73.22%		
Root-mean-squared error	107.89		
Theil	0.47		

TABLE 5–10   Domestic Car Sales Data Used for Regressions in Table 5–9 (c5t11)

Date	DCS	DPI	$DPI^2/100$	Index	PR	Q2	Q3	Q4	Time	$Time^2$
Mar-1980	1849.9	16088.4	2588366.15	63.3912	16.4135	0	0	0	1	1
Jun-1980	1550.8	15765.6	2485541.43	54.3374	16.326	1	0	0	2	4
Sep-1980	1515.3	15837.7	2508327.41	67.7022	11.6033	0	1	0	3	9
Dec-1980	1665.4	16086.1	2587626.13	72.0163	16.7407	0	0	1	4	16
Mar-1981	1733	16088.2	2588301.79	68.3122	19.2061	0	0	0	5	25
Jun-1981	1576	15980.8	2553859.69	73.9593	18.9375	1	0	0	6	36
Sep-1981	1618.5	16290.5	2653803.90	74.8185	20.326	0	1	0	7	49
Dec-1981	1281.3	16257.5	2643063.06	65.7348	17.0152	0	0	1	8	64
Mar-1982	1401.4	16208.6	2627187.14	66.5	16.2603	0	0	0	9	81
Jun-1982	1535.3	16273.6	2648300.57	66.2473	16.5	1	0	0	10	100
Sep-1982	1327.9	16266.3	2645925.16	66.6717	14.7299	0	1	0	11	121
Dec-1982	1493.6	16251.3	2641047.52	72.4707	11.9578	0	0	1	12	144
Mar-1983	1456.9	16306.8	2659117.26	75.2889	10.8767	0	0	0	13	169
Jun-1983	1875.8	16378.2	2682454.35	91.5527	10.5	1	0	0	14	196
Sep-1983	1646.2	16631.3	2766001.40	91.5848	10.7945	0	1	0	15	225
Dec-1983	1814.1	16935.1	2867976.12	91.538	11	0	0	1	16	256
Mar-1984	1994.6	17300.5	2993073.00	99.5462	11.0715	0	0	0	17	289
Jun-1984	2251.8	17602.3	3098409.65	96.5835	12.3076	1	0	0	18	324
Sep-1984	1854.3	17881.7	3197551.95	98.8446	12.9902	0	1	0	19	361
Dec-1984	1851	17957.1	3224574.40	94.9587	11.8037	0	0	1	20	400
Mar-1985	2042.2	17931.4	3215351.06	94.4922	10.5379	0	0	0	21	441
Jun-1985	2272.6	18234.7	3325042.84	94.2725	10.1979	1	0	0	22	484
Sep-1985	2217.7	18095	3274290.25	92.8413	9.5	0	1	0	23	529
Dec-1985	1672.2	18224.6	3321360.45	91.0685	9.5	0	0	1	24	576
Mar-1986	1898.7	18421.3	3393442.94	95.5211	9.36222	0	0	0	25	625
Jun-1986	2242.2	18568.8	3448003.33	96.7451	8.60879	1	0	0	26	676
Sep-1986	2246.9	18603.7	3460976.54	94.8652	7.85717	0	1	0	27	729
Dec-1986	1827.2	18550.9	3441358.91	92.0402	7.5	0	0	1	28	784
Mar-1987	1669.3	18740.3	3511988.44	90.4756	7.5	0	0	0	29	841
Jun-1987	1972.8	18528.7	3433127.24	91.7923	8.04769	1	0	0	30	900
Sep-1987	1878.2	18846.8	3552018.70	93.9033	8.39674	0	1	0	31	961
Dec-1987	1560.6	19045.7	3627386.88	86.4359	8.86761	0	0	1	32	1024
Mar-1988	1914	19271.5	3713907.12	92.3495	8.58835	0	0	0	33	1089
Jun-1988	2076	19374.6	3753751.25	93.5802	8.78066	1	0	0	34	1156
Sep-1988	1787.1	19497.2	3801408.08	96.0196	9.70685	0	1	0	35	1225
Dec-1988	1762.3	19647.4	3860203.27	93	10.1848	0	0	1	36	1296
Mar-1989	1707.4	19814.6	3926183.73	95.8822	10.9782	0	0	0	37	1369
Jun-1989	2018.6	19715.2	3886891.11	90.9308	11.3582	1	0	0	38	1444
Sep-1989	1898.5	19704.3	3882594.38	92.4304	10.6617	0	1	0	39	1521
Dec-1989	1453.6	19750.7	3900901.50	91.7761	10.5	0	0	1	40	1600
Mar-1990	1706.2	19989.4	3995761.12	91.3256	10.0379	0	0	0	41	1681
Jun-1990	1878.2	20039.4	4015775.52	90.9297	10	1	0	0	42	1764
Sep-1990	1752.1	20015.2	4006082.31	79.2022	10	0	1	0	43	1849
Dec-1990	1560.4	19824.2	3929989.06	65.1239	10	0	0	1	44	1936
Mar-1991	1445.1	19810.1	3924400.62	75.1189	9.19467	0	0	0	45	2025
Jun-1991	1683.9	19912.3	3964996.91	80.7066	8.66484	1	0	0	46	2116
Sep-1991	1586.6	19922.9	3969219.44	82.6293	8.40217	0	1	0	47	2209
Dec-1991	1421.3	19921.4	3968621.78	71.8967	7.59685	0	0	1	48	2304

(continued)

TABLE 5–10 (*Continued*)

Date	DCS	DPI	DPI²/100	Index	PR	Q2	Q3	Q4	Time	Time²
Mar-1992	1455.4	20241.7	4097264.19	70.8099	6.5	0	0	0	49	2401
Jun-1992	1746.1	20331.2	4133576.93	78.9363	6.5	1	0	0	50	2500
Sep-1992	1571.7	20275.2	4110837.35	76.1054	6.00674	0	1	0	51	2601
Dec-1992	1503.4	20587.8	4238575.09	83.1772	6	0	0	1	52	2704
Mar-1993	1483.5	20145.7	4058492.28	87.2889	6	0	0	0	53	2809
Jun-1993	1917.9	20378.6	4152873.38	82.4429	6	1	0	0	54	2916
Sep-1993	1690.3	20337.8	4136261.09	77.3946	6	0	1	0	55	3025
Dec-1993	1642.3	20555.4	4225244.69	84.0641	6	0	0	1	56	3136
Mar-1994	1762.3	20345.8	4139515.78	92.9933	6.02067	0	0	0	57	3249
Jun-1994	2001.5	20640.2	4260178.56	92.2066	6.89769	1	0	0	58	3364
Sep-1994	1766.6	20740.3	4301600.44	90.725	7.50065	0	1	0	59	3481
Dec-1994	1724.8	20970.3	4397534.82	93.15	8.13315	0	0	1	60	3600
Mar-1995	1658.2	21012.2	4415125.49	94.3078	8.82778	0	0	0	61	3721
Jun-1995	1938.4	20944.9	4386888.36	91.6462	9	1	0	0	62	3844
Sep-1995	1845.3	21036	4425132.96	93.213	8.76685	0	1	0	63	3969
Dec-1995	1686.9	21135.6	4467135.87	89.8174	8.7163	0	0	1	64	4096
Mar-1996	1749.4	21234.4	4508997.43	90.544	8.33516	0	0	0	65	4225
Jun-1996	2087.7	21300.2	4536985.20	91.4769	8.25	1	0	0	66	4356
Sep-1996	1837.1	21482.2	4614849.17	94.9022	8.25	0	1	0	67	4489
Dec-1996	1579.5	21520.1	4631147.04	97.5152	8.25	0	0	1	68	4624
Mar-1997	1704.1	21609.2	4669575.25	99.0111	8.26722	0	0	0	69	4761
Jun-1997	1870.6	21744.4	4728189.31	103.035	8.5	1	0	0	70	4900
Sep-1997	1769.7	21893.8	4793384.78	105.832	8.5	0	1	0	71	5041
Dec-1997	1561.8	22101.6	4884807.23	104.942	8 5	0	0	1	72	5184
Mar-1998	1547.3	22412	5022977.44	107.748	8.5	0	0	0	73	5329
Jun-1998	1961.6	22615	5114382.25	106.929	8.5	1	0	0	74	5476
Sep-1998	1633.1	22755.6	5178173.31	103.528	8.49674	0	1	0	75	5625
Dec-1998	1621.9	22901.6	5244832.83	100.173	7.92033	0	0	1	76	5776
Mar-1999	1646.3	23022.2	5300216.93	109.581	7.75	0	0	0	77	5929
Jun-1999	1951	23132.8	5351264.36	106.24	7.75	1	0	0	78	6084
Sep-1999	1821.6	23203.8	5384163.34	105.886	8.10174	0	1	0	79	6241
Dec-1999	1562.8	23403.7	5477331.74	105.246	8.37337	0	0	1	80	6400
Mar-2000	1746.5	23472.3	5509488.67	110.108	8.68571	0	0	0	81	6561
Jun-2000	1914.4	23617.2	5577721.36	108.788	9.24659	1	0	0	82	6724

←Holdout period

At the top of Table 5–9 is the regression of DCS with only disposable personal income (DPI) and the prime rate (PR) used as independent variables. The overall regression has an adjusted R-squared of only 1.64. The Durbin-Watson statistic is also quite low at 1.1. The signs of the coefficients are not, however, as expected. DCS falls as DPI increases and as PR increases. We show this regression because it is again possible to examine a figure showing the data points with the regression plane superimposed.

Figure 5–8 depicts the data points for the 78 observations and the estimated regression plane. It is easy to see in the figure that as the prime rate increases, domestic car sales decrease. This can clearly be seen by looking at the edge of the regression plane along which DPI equals 14,000; as PR increases from 0 to 30, the regression plane

FIGURE 5–8

Regression Plane for DCS = *f*(DPI, PR) (c5t11)

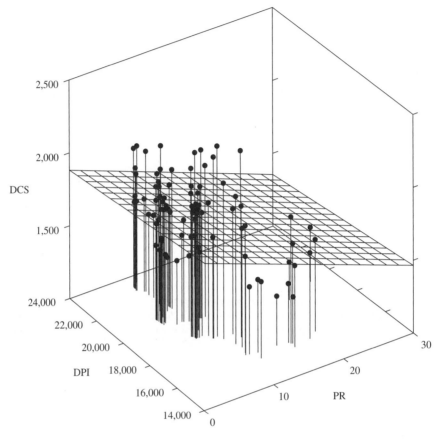

This figure shows the data points and the estimated regression plane for the two-independent variable model estimated in the upper half of Table 5–9. The regression plane has the equation:

$$DCS = 2,175.97 - 0.01(DPI) - 18.67(PR)$$

slopes downward. Remember that the "height" of the regression plane is the measure of domestic car sales, so that as the plane slopes downward, DCS is decreasing. Thus, as PR increases (while DPI is held constant), DCS decreases.

It is more difficult to see the effect of disposable personal income (DPI) on DCS. Look at the edge of the plane along which PR equals 0; as DPI decreases from 24,000 to 14,000, the regression plane tilts slightly downward. Thus, as DPI decreases (while PR is held constant at 0), DCS decreases.

It is obvious why the adjusted *R*-squared for the regression is quite low: many of the data points are quite a distance above or below the estimated regression plane. Because the adjusted *R*-squared is quite low and also because the Durbin-Watson statistic suggests that we may have left out an important explanatory variable, the regression presented in the lower half of Table 5–9 was estimated.

This equation (in the lower half of Table 5–9) adds dummy variables for the last three quarters of each year, the Index of Consumer Sentiment, DPI squared, TIME, and squared TIME squared. Recall that the DCS time series is quite seasonal (which would suggest the use of seasonal dummies) with a mild trend (which might suggest the use of a trend variable). The forecasting equation is improved in a number of ways by the addition of these independent variables. Note that the adjusted *R*-squared has increased from 1.64 to 73.22. The standard error of the regression has fallen, both the BIC and Akaike criteria show improvement, the *F*-statistic has increased, and the Durbin-Watson statistic now indicates that no serial correlation is present. Note that it is impossible to graph the data points and the regression plane for this estimate (which has six independent variables) because it would require a drawing in seven dimensions. In fact, the regression plane would now be referred to as a *hyperplane.*

This last regression can be used to forecast for the next four quarters (1999Q3 to 2000Q2). In making our forecasts, we again used estimates of DPI and PR for the period 1999Q3 through 2000Q2 that were the results of a Holt's smoothing model. The Index of Consumer Sentiment forecast uses a Winters' model. This approximates a forecast that might have actually been done with only the information available at the end of 1999Q2.

The results of the forecasting efforts are presented in Table 5–11. In the second column the root-mean-squared error (RMSE) for each of our previous models is presented along with the results for this model for the in-sample period of 1980Q1 through 1999Q2. The RMSE for the most recent model of 107.89 is the best yet for the in-sample period. In the fourth column of the table, the RMSEs for the forecast, or out-of-sample, period are presented. The RMSE for the most recent model of 162.59 is worse than the RMSE for Winters' model in Chapter 3. In most cases, the better test of a model's forecasting accuracy is the RMSE for the forecast period (i.e., the numbers in the fourth column of Table 5–11).

Figure 5–9 presents the actual and predicted DCS using the nine–independent variable regression presented in the bottom half of Table 5–9. The forecast results for 1999Q3 through 2000Q2 were estimated using the DPI and PR estimates from a Holt's

TABLE 5–11   **Summary Table of RMSEs for DCS**

Chapter	Method	Period	RMSE
1	Naive—with 4-period lag	Historical	187.13
		Holdout	112.26
2	Not applicable		
3	Winters' exponential smoothing	Historical	144.45
		Holdout	61.79
	Holt's with seasonal adjustment	Historical	200.46
		Holdout	62.21
4	Simple regression model using seasonally adjusted DCS as a function of disposable personal income	Historical	96.98
		Holdout	87.93
5	Multiple regression	Historical	107.89
		Holdout	162.59

FIGURE 5–9

Domestic Car Sales (DCS) and Multivariate Regression Forecast (DCSF) in Thousands of Units (c5t11)

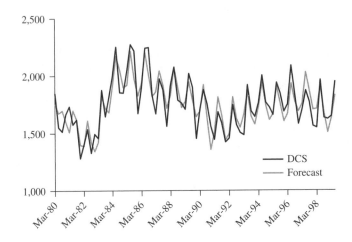

smoothing model. The Index of Consumer Sentiment forecast was done with a Winters' model. Comparing this figure with the bivariate regressions presented in Figure 4–9 shows graphically the improvement in model specification achieved with the use of additional variables.

Forecasting Consumer Products

Charles W. Chase, Jr.
Reckitt & Colman

The job of a practicing forecaster is very different from that of the academic one. He has to prepare forecasts for thousands of different items on a monthly, quarterly, or annual basis, versus one or two products, as is usually the case with an academic forecaster. Unlike an academic forecaster, he has deadlines to meet. If forecasts are not prepared at a set time, the entire planning process comes to a halt. His concern for bringing the error down to the last decimal point is not as great as that of an academic forecaster. He constantly weighs the costs and benefits of reducing the error further. In some cases, any further reduction in the error may not have any effect on the decision. Plus, each time a practicing forecaster prepares forecasts, his job is at stake. If the forecasts go awry, so does his future. The stake of an academic forecaster, on the other hand, is whether or not his article on forecasting is accepted for publication. The objective of this article is to explain how forecasts of consumer products are prepared in a business situation where thousands of items are involved, and deadlines are for real.

Forecasting Consumer Products continued

Procedure

Here is a step-by-step procedure for forecasting the sales demand for consumer products:

Step 1. Establish an objective, which in this case is to forecast the sales of consumer products. For the purposes of simplicity we will refer to these products as Brand X. Aggregate forecasts are generally more accurate than individual forecasts. "Aggregate forecasts" in this case refer to the forecasts of all the products of Brand X. Individual forecasts, then, will be the forecasts of each item (product code) of this brand.

Step 2. Decide on the method to be used for forecasting the sales of Brand X. There are several considerations that have to be made in the selection of a method. How much error is the company willing to tolerate? In this case, 10 percent error at the brand level was the chosen target. The industry average is much higher according to several recent studies. Next, consider the time horizon (how far ahead we want to forecast—one month, one quarter, or one year). This certainly has a bearing on the selection of a method, because some methods are good for short-term forecasting and others for long-term forecasting. In the consumer products industry the time horizon is generally three to twelve months out into the future. This is necessary to accommodate the long lead times of several of the components used in producing various consumer products. Components include such things as plastic bottles, labels, and cartons.

Forecasting is 80 percent mathematics and 20 percent judgment. Within mathematical methods, there are two categories: (1) time-series and (2) cause-and-effect. In time-series methods, forecasts are made simply by extrapolating the past data. They assume that the sales are related to time and nothing else. Time-series methods include simple moving averages, exponential smoothing, decomposition, and Box-Jenkins. Cause-and-effect methods use causal relationships. For example, sales are a function of advertising expenditures, price, trade and consumer promotions, and inventory levels. Sales, in this case, are a dependent variable, and advertising expenditures, price, and so forth, are independent variables. These methods assume that there exists a constant relationship between dependent and independent variables. Such methods are simple and multiple regressions, and econometrics.

The consumer products industry in recent years has encountered a shift in power from manufacturers to the trade. Today, the dominant players in the markets are not manufacturers but big chains such as Wal-Mart, Kmart, Kroger, CVS, and Walgreen. As a result, manufacturers have reduced their expenditures on national advertising and increased them on consumer and trade promotions. This shift has played havoc with forecasting, as it has made time-series methods obsolete. Constant changes in amount and period of promotions have disrupted the seasonality and trend of the historical data. Thus, forecasting with time-series methods is like driving down a highway in your car with the windshield blacked out. It's all well and good if you are driving in a desert with no bends in the road. However, if you are driving on a normal highway, sooner or later you will hit a turn. When you do, you won't see it until it's in your rearview mirror. At that point, it would be too late to react.

Taking this information into consideration, multiple regression was chosen as the forecasting method. There are several reasons for this. First, multiple regression has the ability to incorporate all the variables that impact the demand for a brand. Second, it produces extremely accurate forecasts for periods anywhere from three months to one year out into the future. Finally, multiple regression has the ability to measure the relationships of each independent variable with the demand for a brand. (The latter attribute has important implications for making managerial decisions. It helps management to determine how much to spend on national advertising, what should be the appropriate pricing strategy, and what are the most effective promotional programs.)

Step 3. Choose proper independent variables and gather proper data. This is an important step in the forecasting process for two reasons: (1) judgmental influence comes into play; (2) it involves the users in the process. We found that the best way to make the users accept our forecasts is to use the variables they believe have strong impact on their products, and to use the source of data that they are most comfortable with. In the consumer products industry, the marketing department, in most cases, is the primary user of sales forecasts. In fact, those same forecasts ultimately become the marketing plan. Since they are the main users, we chose from their variables—the variables they believe had a strong impact on their products. We used Nielsen syndicated data (Scantrack and Audit), as well as the data furnished by the marketing department. The Nielsen syndicated data was used because the marketing people were most comfortable with it. When Step 3 is completed, the best possible match has been made between the situation and the method.

In the consumer products industry, trade shipments are forecasted—shipments to the brokers, food and drug chains, and mass merchandisers who sell the products to the consumer. The relationship between the trade and retail consumption plays a significant role in predicting trade shipments. Most users (brand managers) agree that retail consumption has some impact on trade shipments. For Brand X, ten variables were selected to predict retail consumption (see Table 1). Several dummy variables were used to capture the impact of consumer promotions along with average retail price, national advertising expenditures, and Nielsen shipment data of the category for Brand X. Dummy variables are used where the variable is defined in terms of yes (when a certain element exists) and no (when it doesn't exist). It is used in the form of "1" for yes and "0" for no. For example, for FSI (free-standing insert) coupon 1, we used "1" in the equation when this coupon was used, and "0" when it was not.

Step 4. Compute the predictive regression equation for retail consumption of Brand X. The equation gives an excellent fit with an R-squared of 0.96. (See Table 1 for this and other statistics.) The ex post forecasts had a MAPE (mean absolute percentage error) of less than 1 percent (see Table 2). (Ex post forecasts are those for which actuals are known.)

Step 5. Forecast the retail consumption by plugging the values of independent variables into the predictive equation computed above. To do so, we need the values of the independent variables for the periods we want to forecast. For example, if we want to develop a forecast for Brand X for 2000 we need the values of average retail price, Nielsen shipment data of that category, national advertising expenditures, and so forth, for those periods. As for the dummy variables, we have no problem because we control them. However, for Nielsen shipment data we have to forecast the value, which we do by extrapolating the historical data.

Forecasting Consumer Products continued

TABLE 1 Variables and Statistics of Consumption Model

R-squared = 0.96	F-stat = 24.55
Adj. R-squared = 0.92	DW = 2.26

Variable	t-Stat
1. Time	−0.72
2. Average retail price	−2.70
3. National advertising expenditures	2.52
4. Nielsen shipment data in units	6.48
5. FSI 1	4.38
6. FSI 2	2.31
7. Direct mail coupon	1.93
8. FSI 3	1.25
9. FSI 4	2.15
10. FSI 5	2.81

NOTES: (1) Dummy variables are used to capture the effects of variables that have no quantitative data.
(2) FSI stands for "free-standing insert."

TABLE 2 Forecasts versus Actuals: Consumption Model

Brand X

Month	Actuals	Forecasts	Absolute Error
January	2578	2563	1%
February	2788	2783	0%
March	2957	2957	0%
April	2670	2758	3%
May	2447	2466	1%
June	3016	3016	0%

NOTE: Mean absolute percentage error (MAPE) = 0.81%

Step 6. Compute the predictive regression equation for trade shipments. The equation included retail consumption as the primary variable along with Nielsen inventory, trade price, and several dummy variables to capture trade promotions (see Table 3). Again, the fit was excellent with an R-squared of 0.96. The ex post forecasts had a MAPE of 3 percent, which is significantly lower than the original target of 10 percent (see Table 4). Those familiar with the rule of thumb for the t-statistic (variables are not significant if their value is less than 2) may feel that several of the variables should have been excluded from the

TABLE 3   Variables and Statistics of Trade Shipment Model

R-squared = 0.96	*F*-stat = 36.93
Adj. *R*-squared = 0.93	DW = 2.41

Variable	t-Stat
1. Time	2.40
2. Retail consumption	3.59
3. Trade inventory	1.87
4. Trade price	−1.55
5. Trade promotion 1 early shipment	5.82
6. Trade promotion 1 sell in	16.01
7. Trade promotion 1 post shipment	4.19
8. Trade promotion 2 early shipment	9.57
9. Trade promotion 2 sell in	1.18
10. Trade promotion 3 early shipment	2.62
11. Trade promotion 3 sell in	7.29
12. Trade promotion 3 post shipment	13.55

NOTE: Dummy variables are used to capture the effects of variables that have no quantitative data.

TABLE 4   Forecasts versus Actuals: Trade Shipment Model

Brand X

Month	Actuals	Forecasts	Absolute Error
January	69,158	69,190	0%
February	45,927	47,216	3%
March	40,183	40,183	0%
April	56,427	54,841	3%
May	81,854	72,788	12%
June	50,505	52,726	4%
July	37,064	36,992	0%
August	58,212	57,347	2%
September	96,566	95,112	2%

NOTE: Mean absolute percentage error (MAPE) = 3.0%

SOURCE: *Journal of Business Forecasting* 10, no. 1 (Spring 1991), pp. 2–6. Reprinted by permission.

---

model. I found through experience that if the forecasts are more accurate with the variables whose *t*-statistics are less than 2, then they should be left in the model. As you know, as a practitioner, our primary objective is to produce good forecasts.

Step 7. Forecast trade shipments by plugging the values of the independent variables (retail consumption, Nielsen inventory, and so forth) into the predictive equation computed above. Here again, we need the values of independent variables for the period we want to forecast. The only independent variable over which we have no control is the Nielsen inventory, which we estimate by extrapolating its historical data.

Step 8. Prepare item-by-item forecasts for all the products of Brand X. This is achieved by using the past-six-month rolling average ratio of each item. If item 1 represents 5 percent of the total, then the forecast of item 1 will be 5 percent of the trade total of Brand X; if item 2 represents 10 percent of the total, then 10 percent of the total will be the forecast of item 2; and so on.

Clearly, the main challenge to a business forecaster is to improve the quality of forecasts and consequently the decisions. This can best be achieved by sharing our forecasting experience with others.

234

234Chapter 5

INTEGRATIVE CASE
THE GAP

Part 5: Forecasting The Gap Sales Data with a Multiple-Regression Model

The sales of The Gap stores in thousands of dollars for the 44 quarters covering 1985Q1 through 1998Q4 are again shown in the graph below. Recall that The Gap sales data are quite seasonal and are increasing over time.

(c5gap)

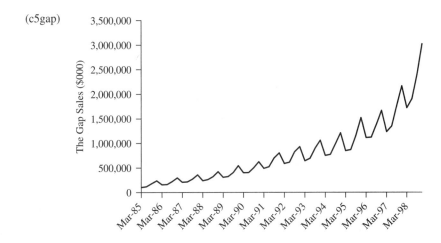

Case Questions

1. Have The Gap sales generally followed a linear path over time? Does the graph suggest to you that some accommodation for seasonality should be used in any forecast? Does the graph suggest that some nonlinear term should be used in any forecast model?

2. Use a multiple regression of raw (i.e., non-seasonally adjusted Gap sales) as the basis to forecast sales for

1999. What would happen to the accuracy of the model if your forecast is extended through 2000? Why?

3. Calculate the root-mean-squared errors both for the historical period and for the 1999Q1 through 1999Q4 forecast horizon.

Solutions to Case Questions

1. The Gap sales appear to have followed a highly seasonal pattern over time; in addition, the sales pattern appears to show an increase in the rate of sales over time. In other words, the pattern over time appears to be nonlinear and may require some accommodation in a forecasting model.

2. The raw (or non-seasonally adjusted) Gap sales were used as a dependent variable in a multiple regression that includes the following explanatory (or independent) variables:

TIME = The index of time

$TIME^2$ = The index of time squared (to account for the nonlinearity)

Q2 = A seasonal dummy variable for quarter 2

Q3 = A seasonal dummy variable for quarter 3

Q4 = A seasonal dummy variable for quarter 4

SP500 = The Standard & Poor's 500 stock index

The regression results follow:

```
Audit Trail--ANOVA Table (Multiple Regression Selected)
```

Source of Variation	SS	df	MS	SEE
Regression	20,966,785,166,782.70	6	3,494,464,194,463.78	
Error	740,029,583,949.28	49	15,102,644,570.39	122,892.82
Total	21,706,814,750,732.10	55		

```
Audit Trail--Coefficient Table (Multiple Regression Selected)
```

Series Description	Included in Model	Coefficient	Standard Error	T-test	F-test	Elasticity	Overall F-test
The Gap Sales ($000)	Dependent	-166,176.36	83,259.91	-2.00	3.98		231.38
Time	Yes	374.88	4,802.89	0.08	0.01	0.01	
Time squared	Yes	171.86	136.60	1.26	1.58	0.23	
Q2	Yes	-6,195.11	46,504.27	-0.13	0.02	0.0	
Q3	Yes	160,024.28	46,497.90	3.44	11.84	0.05	
Q4	Yes	324,646.92	46,565.00	6.97	48.61	0.10	
S&P 500	Yes	537.02	95.82	5.60	31.41	0.82	

```
Audit Trail--Statistics
```

Accuracy Measure	Value	Forecast Statistic	Value
AIC	1,465.98	Durbin-Watson	1.11
BIC	1,468.00	Mean	804,816.13
Mean absolute percentage error (MAPE)	16.45%	Standard deviation	628,227.16
Sum squared error (SSE)	740,029,583,949.28	Max	3,029,900.00
R-squared	96.59%	Min	105,715.00
Adjusted R-squared	96.17%	Range	2,924,185.00
Mean absolute error	82,467.71	Ljung-Box	41.42
Mean error	0.00		
Mean-squared error	13,214,813,999.09		
Root-mean-squared error	114,955.70		
Theil	1.01		

Since the $TIME^2$ variable is significant at less than the 95 percent level, it appears that The Gap sales have indeed been increasing *at an increasing rate* over time. Our impressions are confirmed by the regression equation. Two of the seasonal dummy variables are statistically significant; this confirms our impression of the seasonality of the data. The SP500 variable was included to account for the general level of economic activity in the economy over time; it is also significant.

Overall, the regression appears to be a reasonable fit, as seen in the graph of actual and predicted values on the following page.

The equation for The Gap sales here takes seasonality into account in a very different manner than the one in Chapter 4 (which seasonally adjusted the data before running the model). The results, however, are quite similar.

In this model we have also added $TIME^2$ as a variable to take into account that sales seem to be increasing at an increasing rate over time. The Standard & Poor's 500 stock index adds some further explanatory power. The results do not seem much different from the simple regression results of Chapter 4, but the difference lies in the explanatory power of this model in the forecast horizon.

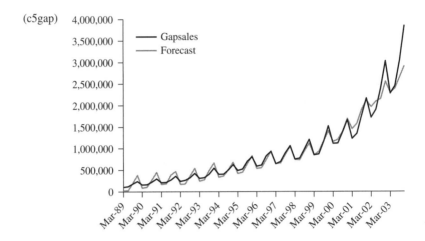

(c5gap)

3. The SP500 variable was forecast for the four quarters of 1999 with a simple trend equation. The results are as follows:

Holdout Period Forecast RMSE			
Forecast	*Actual*	$(A_t - F_t)$	$(A_t - F_t)^2$
2,299,849.16	2,277,700	−22,149.16	490,585,490
2,391,621.94	2,453,300	61,678.06	3,804,183,046
2,655,809.23	3,045,386	389,576.77	151,770,063,596
2,918,399.75	3,858,939	940,539.25	884,614,079,432

RMSE = 510,068.36

The RMSEs for the historical period and the 1999 forecast horizon are:

1985Q1–1999Q4 root-mean-squared error = 114,995

1999Q1–1999Q4 root-mean-squared error = 510,068

If we compare these results with the results presented at the end of Chapter 4, we find that the historical period forecast has much the same RMSE, but the forecast horizon RMSE is much lower with the multiple regression. This is due in part to the explanatory power of the nonlinear $TIME^2$ variable. For the present multiple-regression model, the RMSE is only 55 percent of the RMSE for the simple regression in the forecast horizon.

TABLE 5–12   Summary Table of RMSEs for The Gap Sales

Chapter	*Method*	*Period*	*RMSE*
1	Naive—with 4-period lag	Historical	233,092
		Holdout	654,976
2	Not applicable		
3	Winters' exponential smoothing	Historical	49,479
		Holdout	99,493
	Holt's exponential smoothing	Historical	42,388
	with seasonal readjustment	Holdout	74,034
4	Linear trend of deseasonalized	Historical	212,016
	data with forecast	Holdout	1,131,894
5	Multiple regression	Historical	114,995
		Holdout	510,068

USING FORECASTX™ TO MAKE MULTIPLE-REGRESSION FORECASTS

As usual, begin by opening your data file in Excel and start ForecastX™. In the **Data Capture** box identify the data you want to use, as shown below. Then click the **Forecast Method** tab.

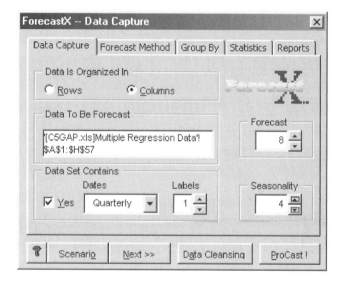

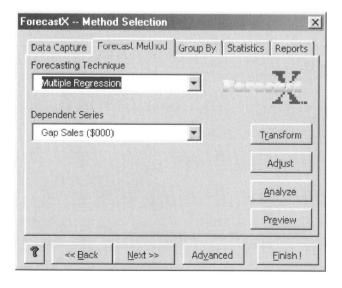

In the Method Selection box, click the down arrow in the **Forecasting Technique** box and select **Multiple Regression.** Make sure the desired variable is selected as the **Dependent Series,** which is **Gap Sales** in this example. Then click the **Statistics** tab.

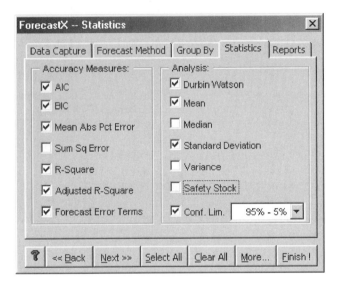

In this box, select the statistics that you desire. Do not forget that there are more choices if you click the **More** button at the bottom.

After selecting the statistics you want to see, click the **Reports** tab.

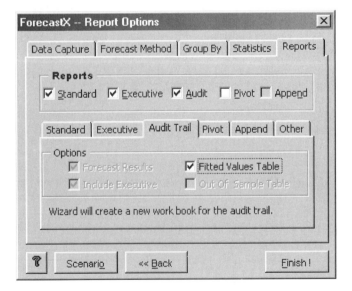

In the **Report Options** box, select those you want. Typical selections might be those shown here. When you click the **Standard** tab you will want to be sure to select the **Show Charts** box. In the **Audit Trail** tab (the active tab shown here) click the **Fitted Values Table.**

Then click the **Finish!** button.

ForecastX™ will automatically apply a time-series method to forecast the independent variables. The methods used are identified in the **Standard Report** that results.

Suggested Readings

Aykac, Ahmed; and Antonio Borges. "Econometric Methods for Managerial Applications." In *The Handbook of Forecasting: A Managers Guide.* Eds. Spyros Makridakis and Steven C. Wheelwright. New York: John Wiley & Sons, 1982, pp. 185–203.

Bassin, William M. "How to Anticipate the Accuracy of a Regression Based Model." *Journal of Business Forecasting* 6, no. 4 (Winter 1987–88), pp. 26–28.

Brennan, Michael J.; and Thomas M. Carroll. *Preface to Quantitative Economics & Econometrics.* Cincinnati: South-Western Publishing, 1987. Especially Part III, "Econometrics."

Doran, Howard; and Jan Kmenta. "Multiple Minima in the Estimation of Models with Autoregressive Disturbances." *Review of Economics and Statistics* 24 (May 1992), pp. 354–57.

Jarrell, Stephen B. *Basic Business Statistics.* Boston: Allyn & Bacon, 1988. Especially Chap. 23, "Regression," and Chap. 24, "Evaluating and Forecasting: Two Variable Regression Models."

Johnson, Aaron C., Jr.; Marvin B. Johnson; and Reuben C. Buse. *Econometrics: Basic and Applied.* New York: Macmillan, 1987.

Judge, George G.; R. Carter Hill; William E. Griffiths; Helmut Lutkepohl; and Tsoung-Chao Lee. *Introduction to the Theory and Practice of Econometrics.* 2nd ed. New York: John Wiley & Sons, 1988.

Lewis-Beck, Michael S. *Applied Regression: An Introduction.* Beverly Hills, CA: Sage Publications, 1980.

Neter, John; William Wasserman; and Michael H. Kutner. *Applied Linear Statistical Models.* Homewood, IL: Richard D. Irwin, 1990.

Ostrom, Charles W., Jr. *Time Series Analysis: Regression Techniques.* Beverly Hills, CA: Sage Publications, 1978.

Wesolowsky, George O. *Multiple Regression and Analysis of Variance: An Introduction for Computer Users in Management and Economics.* New York: John Wiley & Sons, 1976.

Exercises

1. Explain why the adjusted R-squared should be used in evaluating multiple-regression models rather than the unadjusted value.

2. Review the three quick checks that should be used in evaluating a multiple-regression model. Apply these to the model for domestic car sales discussed in this chapter, using your own words to describe each step and the conclusions you reach.

3. Explain what dummy variables are and how they can be used to account for seasonality. Give an example of how you might use dummy variables to measure seasonality for a good or service of your choice. Explain the signs you would expect on each. Assume that you are working with quarterly data.

4. The following regression results relate to a study of fuel efficiency of cars as measured by miles per gallon of gas (adjusted R-squared = 0.569; $n = 120$).

Variable*	Coefficient	Standard Error	t-Ratio
Intercept	6.51	1.28	
CID	0.031	0.012	
D	9.46	2.67	
M4	14.64	2.09	
M5	14.86	2.42	
US	4.64	2.48	

*CID = Cubic-inch displacement (engine size)

   D = 1 for diesel cars and 0 otherwise

   M4 = 1 for cars with a four-speed manual transmission and 0 otherwise

   M5 = 1 for cars with a five-speed manual transmission and 0 otherwise

   US = 1 for cars made in the United States and 0 otherwise

   a. Calculate the *t*-ratios for each explanatory variable.

   b. Use the three quick-check regression-evaluation procedures to evaluate this model.

5. Develop a multiple-regression model for auto sales as a function of population and household income from the following data for 10 metropolitan areas (c5p5):

Area	Auto Sales (AS)($000)	Household Income (INC)($000)	Population (POP)(000s)
1	$185,792	$23,409	133.17
2	85,643	19,215	110.86
3	97,101	20,374	68.04
4	100,249	16,107	99.59
5	527,817	23,432	289.52
6	403,916	19,426	339.98
7	78,283	18,742	89.53
8	188,756	18,553	155.78
9	329,531	21,953	248.95
10	91,944	16,358	102.13

a. Estimate values for b_0, b_1, and b_2 for the following model:

$$AS = b_0 + b_1(INC) + b_2(POP)$$

b. Are the signs you find for the coefficients consistent with your expectations? Explain.

c. Are the coefficients for the two explanatory variables significantly different from zero? Explain.

d. What percentage of the variation in AS is explained by this model?

e. What point estimate of AS would you make for a city where INC = $23,175 and POP = 128.07? What would the approximate 95 percent confidence interval be?

6. In Exercises 7 and 8 of Chapter 4 you worked with data on sales for a line of skiwear that is produced by HeathCo Industries. Barbara Lynch, product manager for the skiwear, has the responsibility of providing forecasts to top management of sales by quarter one year ahead. One of Ms. Lynch's colleagues, Dick Staples, suggested that unemployment and income in the regions in which the clothes are marketed might be causally connected to sales. If you worked the exercises in Chapter 4, you have developed three bivariate regression models of sales as a function of time (TIME), unemployment (NRUR), and income (INC). Data for these variables and for sales are as follows (c5p6):

Period	TIME	SALES	INC	NRUR
1988Q1	1	72,962	218	8.4
1988Q2	2	81,921	237	8.2
1988Q3	3	97,729	263	8.4
1988Q4	4	142,161	293	8.4
1989Q1	5	145,592	318	8.1
1989Q2	6	117,129	359	7.7
1989Q3	7	114,159	404	7.5
1989Q4	8	151,402	436	7.2
1990Q1	9	153,907	475	6.9
1990Q2	10	100,144	534	6.5
1990Q3	11	123,242	574	6.5
1990Q4	12	128,497	622	6.4
1991Q1	13	176,076	667	6.3
1991Q2	14	180,440	702	6.2
1991Q3	15	162,665	753	6.3
1991Q4	16	220,818	796	6.5
1992Q1	17	202,415	858	6.8
1992Q2	18	211,780	870	7.9
1992Q3	19	163,710	934	8.3
1992Q4	20	200,135	1,010	8.0
1993Q1	21	174,200	1,066	8.0
1993Q2	22	182,556	1,096	8.0
1993Q3	23	198,990	1,162	8.0
1993Q4	24	243,700	1,187	8.9
1994Q1	25	253,142	1,207	9.6
1994Q2	26	218,755	1,242	10.2
1994Q3	27	225,422	1,279	10.7
1994Q4	28	253,653	1,318	11.5
1995Q1	29	257,156	1,346	11.2
1995Q2	30	202,568	1,395	11.0
1995Q3	31	224,482	1,443	10.1
1995Q4	32	229,879	1,528	9.2
1996Q1	33	289,321	1,613	8.5
1996Q2	34	266,095	1,646	8.0
1996Q3	35	262,938	1,694	8.0
1996Q4	36	322,052	1,730	7.9
1997Q1	37	313,769	1,755	7.9
1997Q2	38	315,011	1,842	7.9
1997Q3	39	264,939	1,832	7.8
1997Q4	40	301,479	1,882	7.6

a. Now you can expand your analysis to see whether a multiple-regression model would work well. Estimate the following model:

$$SALES = b_0 + b_1(INC) + b_2(NRUR)$$

$$SALES = \_\_\_ +/- \_\_\_(INC) +/- \_\_\_(NRUR)$$

(Circle + or − as appropriate for each variable)

Do the signs on the coefficients make sense? Explain why.

b. Test to see whether the coefficients you have estimated are statistically different from zero, using a
95 percent confidence level and a one-tailed test.

c. What percentage of the variation in sales is explained by this model?

d. Use this model to make a sales forecast (SF1) for
1998Q1 through 1998Q4, given the previously
forecast values for unemployment (NRURF) and
income (INCF) as follows:

Period	NRURF	INCF	SF1
1998Q1	7.6	1,928	___
1998Q2	7.7	1,972	___
1998Q3	7.5	2,017	___
1998Q4	7.4	2,062	___

e. Actual sales for 1998 were: Q1 = 334,271; Q2 =
328,982; Q3 = 317,921; Q4 = 350,118. On the
basis of this information, how well would you say
the model worked? What is the root-mean-squared
error (RMSE)?

f. Plot the actual data for 1998Q1 through 1998Q4
along with the values predicted for each quarter
based on this model, for 1998Q1 through 1998Q4.

7. *a.* If you have not looked at a time-series graph of the
sales data for HeathCo's line of skiwear (see data in
Exercise 6), do so now. On this plot write a 1 next
to the data point for each first quarter, a 2 next to
each second quarter, and so forth for all four quarters. Does there appear to be a seasonal pattern in
the sales data? Explain why you think the results
are as you have found. (c5p6)

b. It does seem logical that skiwear would sell better
from October through March than from April
through September. To test this hypothesis, begin
by adding two dummy variables to the data:
dummy variable Q2 = 1 for each second quarter
(April, May, June) and Q2 = 0 otherwise; dummy
variable Q3 = 1 for each third quarter (July,
August, September) and Q3 = 0 otherwise. Once
the dummy variables have been entered into your
data set, estimate the following trend model:

$$\text{SALES} = b_0 + b_1(\text{TIME}) + b_2\text{Q2} + b_3\text{Q3}$$

$$\text{SALES} = \_\_\_\_ +/- \_\_\_\_ \text{ TIME}$$

$$+/- \_\_\_\_ \text{ Q2} +/- \_\_\_\_ \text{ Q3}$$

(Circle + or − as appropriate for each variable)

Evaluate these results by answering the following:
- Do the signs make sense?
- Are the coefficients statistically different from
  zero at a 95 percent confidence level (one-tailed
  test)?
- What percentage of the variation in SALES is
  explained by this model?

c. Use this model to make a forecast of SALES (SF2)
for the four quarters of 1998 and calculate the
RMSE for the forecast period.

Period	SALES	SF2
1998Q1	334,271	___
1998Q2	328,982	___
1998Q3	317,921	___
1998Q4	350,118	___

d. Prepare a time-series plot of SALES (for 1988Q1
through 1997Q4) and SF2 (for 1988Q1 through
1988Q4) to illustrate how SALES and SF2 compare.

8. Consider now that you have been asked to prepare a
forecast of wholesale furniture sales for the entire
United States. You have been given the monthly time-
series data in the accompanying table:

Data for Exercise 8

	WFS	UR	PHS
1990M1	1,226.00	8.60000	843.000
1990M2	1,287.00	8.90000	866.000
1990M3	1,473.00	9.00000	931.000
1990M4	1,383.00	9.30000	917.000
1990M5	1,208.00	9.40000	1,025.00
1990M6	1,344.00	9.60000	902.000
1990M7	1,161.00	9.80000	1,166.00
1990M8	1,221.00	9.80000	1,046.00
1990M9	1,367.00	10.1000	1,144.00
1990M10	1,380.00	10.4000	1,173.00
1990M11	1,310.00	10.8000	1,372.00
1990M12	1,302.00	10.8000	1,303.00
1991M1	1,344.00	10.4000	1,586.00
1991M2	1,362.00	10.4000	1,699.00
1991M3	1,694.00	10.3000	1,606.00
1991M4	1,611.00	10.2000	1,472.00
1991M5	1,648.00	10.1000	1,776.00

(continued)

Data for Exercise 8

	WFS	UR	PHS
1991M6	1,722.00	10.1000	1,733.00
1991M7	1,488.00	9.40000	1,785.00
1991M8	1,776.00	9.50000	1,910.00
1991M9	1,839.00	9.20000	1,710.00
1991M10	2,017.00	8.80000	1,715.00
1991M11	1,920.00	8.50000	1,785.00
1991M12	1,778.00	8.30000	1,688.00
1992M1	1,683.00	8.00000	1,897.00
1992M2	1,829.00	7.80000	2,260.00
1992M3	2,012.00	7.80000	1,663.00
1992M4	2,033.00	7.70000	1,851.00
1992M5	2,305.00	7.40000	1,774.00
1992M6	2,007.00	7.20000	1,843.00
1992M7	1,941.00	7.50000	1,732.00
1992M8	2,027.00	7.50000	1,586.00
1992M9	1,922.00	7.30000	1,698.00
1992M10	2,173.00	7.40000	1,590.00
1992M11	2,097.00	7.20000	1,689.00
1992M12	1,687.00	7.30000	1,612.00
1993M1	1,679.00	7.40000	1,711.00
1993M2	1,696.00	7.20000	1,632.00
1993M3	1,826.00	7.20000	1,800.00
1993M4	1,985.00	7.30000	1,821.00
1993M5	2,051.00	7.20000	1,680.00
1993M6	2,027.00	7.30000	1,676.00
1993M7	2,107.00	7.40000	1,684.00
1993M8	2,138.00	7.10000	1,743.00
1993M9	2,089.00	7.10000	1,676.00
1993M10	2,399.00	7.20000	1,834.00
1993M11	2,143.00	7.00000	1,698.00
1993M12	2,070.00	7.00000	1,942.00
1994M1	1,866.00	6.70000	1,938.00
1994M2	1,843.00	7.20000	1,869.00
1994M3	2,001.00	7.10000	1,873.00
1994M4	2,165.00	7.20000	1,947.00
1994M5	2,211.00	7.20000	1,847.00
1994M6	2,321.00	7.20000	1,845.00
1994M7	2,210.00	7.00000	1,789.00
1994M8	2,253.00	6.90000	1,804.00
1994M9	2,561.00	7.00000	1,685.00
1994M10	2,619.00	7.00000	1,683.00
1994M11	2,118.00	6.90000	1,630.00
1994M12	2,169.00	6.70000	1,837.00
1995M1	2,063.00	6.60000	1,804.00
1995M2	2,032.00	6.60000	1,809.00
1995M3	2,349.00	6.50000	1,723.00
1995M4	2,218.00	6.40000	1,635.00
1995M5	2,159.00	6.30000	1,599.00
1995M6	2,240.00	6.20000	1,583.00

Data for Exercise 8

	WFS	UR	PHS
1995M7	2,335.00	6.10000	1,594.00
1995M8	2,388.00	6.00000	1,583.00
1995M9	2,865.00	5.90000	1,679.00
1995M10	2,829.00	6.00000	1,538.00
1995M11	2,432.00	5.90000	1,661.00
1995M12	2,395.00	5.80000	1,399.00
1996M1	1,995.00	5.70000	1,382.00
1996M2	2,232.00	5.70000	1,519.00
1996M3	2,355.00	5.70000	1,529.00
1996M4	2,188.00	5.50000	1,584.00
1996M5	2,177.00	5.60000	1,393.00
1996M6	2,333.00	5.40000	1,465.00
1996M7	2,124.00	5.50000	1,477.00
1996M8	2,463.00	5.60000	1,461.00
1996M9	2,435.00	5.40000	1,467.00
1996M10	2,688.00	5.30000	1,533.00
1996M11	2,604.00	5.30000	1,558.00
1996M12	2,393.00	5.30000	1,524.00
1997M1	2,171.00	5.40000	1,678.00
1997M2	2,136.00	5.20000	1,465.00
1997M3	2,428.00	5.00000	1,409.00
1997M4	2,264.00	5.30000	1,343.00
1997M5	2,402.00	5.20000	1,308.00
1997M6	2,320.00	5.30000	1,406.00
1997M7	2,258.00	5.30000	1,420.00
1997M8	2,675.00	5.30000	1,329.00
1997M9	2,676.00	5.30000	1,264.00
1997M10	2,629.00	5.30000	1,428.00
1997M11	2,610.00	5.30000	1,361.00

(c5p8)

WFS is wholesale furniture sales in millions of dollars. It is not seasonally adjusted. PHS measures new private housing starts in thousands. UR is the unemployment rate as a percent. You believe that furniture sales are quite probably related to the general state of the economy and decide to test whether the unemployment rate affects furniture sales. You expect that as the unemployment rate rises (and the economy thus shows some sign of difficulty), furniture sales will decline.

a. Summarize the results of your bivariate regression by completing the following table:

Independent Variable	Intercept	Slope	t-Ratio	R-squared
UR				
	R-squared =			
	Durbin-Watson =			

b. After discussing the results at a staff meeting, someone suggests that you fit a multiple-regression model of the following form:

$$WFS = b_0 + b_1(UR) + b_2(M1) + b_3(M2) + b_4(M4) + b_5(M9) + b_6(M10)$$

where

M1 = A dummy variable for January
M2 = A dummy variable for February
M4 = A dummy variable for April
M9 = A dummy variable for September
M10 = A dummy variable for October

Summarize the results in the following table:

Independent Variable	Intercept	Slope	t-Ratio
UR			
M1			
M2			
M4			
M9			
M10			
	Adjusted *R*-squared =		
	Durbin-Watson =		

- Do the signs of the coefficients make sense?
- Are the coefficients statistically significant at a 95 percent confidence level (one-tailed test)?
- What percentage of the variation in WFS is explained by the model?

c. After a staff meeting where these results were presented, another analyst suggested that serial correlation can cause problems in such regression models. Interpret the Durbin-Watson statistic in part (*b*) and suggest what problems could result if serial correlation is a problem.

Add PHS lagged three months and time-squared (T^2) to the model and again examine the results for serial correlation. Summarize the results:

Independent Variable	Intercept	Slope	t-Ratio	R-squared
UR				
M1				
M2				
M4				
M9				
M10				
T^2				
PHS(-3)				
	Adjusted *R*-squared =			
	Durbin-Watson =			

Have the additional two variables affected the existence of serial correlation?

9. AmeriPlas, Inc., produces 20-ounce plastic drinking cups that are embossed with the names of prominent beers and soft drinks. In Chapter 4, Exercise 12, you may have developed a trend model for the company's sales from the following data:

Period	T	SALES	Period	T	SALES
1994M1	1	857	1996M1	25	1,604
1994M2	2	921	1996M2	26	1,643
1994M3	3	1,071	1996M3	27	1,795
1994M4	4	1,133	1996M4	28	1,868
1994M5	5	1,209	1996M5	29	1,920
1994M6	6	1,234	1996M6	30	1,953
1994M7	7	1,262	1996M7	31	1,980
1994M8	8	1,258	1996M8	32	1,989
1994M9	9	1,175	1996M9	33	1,897
1994M10	10	1,174	1996M10	34	1,910
1994M11	11	1,123	1996M11	35	1,854
1994M12	12	1,159	1996M12	36	1,957
1995M1	13	1,250	1997M1	37	1,955
1995M2	14	1,289	1997M2	38	2,008
1995M3	15	1,448	1997M3	39	2,171
1995M4	16	1,497	1997M4	40	2,202
1995M5	17	1,560	1997M5	41	2,288
1995M6	18	1,586	1997M6	42	2,314
1995M7	19	1,597	1997M7	43	2,343
1995M8	20	1,615	1997M8	44	2,339
1995M9	21	1,535	1997M9	45	2,239
1995M10	22	1,543	1997M10	46	2,267
1995M11	23	1,493	1997M11	47	2,206
1995M12	24	1,510	1997M12	48	2,226

(c5p9)

a. Prepare a time-series plot of the sales data. Does there appear to be a regular pattern of movement in the data that may be seasonal? Ronnie Newton, the product manager for this product line, believes that her brief review of sales data for the four-year period indicates that sales are slower in the colder months of November through February than in other months. Do you agree?

b. Since production is closely related to orders for current shipment, Ronnie would like to have a monthly sales forecast that incorporates monthly fluctuations. She has asked you to develop a trend model that includes dummy variables, with January as the base period (i.e., 11 dummy variables for February through December). Use M2 for the February dummy variable, which will equal 1 for each February and zero otherwise; M3 for the March dummy variable, which will equal 1 for each March and zero otherwise; and so forth to M12 for the December dummy variable, which will equal 1 for each December and zero otherwise. Summarize your results:

Variable	Coefficient	t-Ratio
Intercept		
T		
M2		
M3		
M4		
M5		
M6		
M7		
M8		
M9		
M10		
M11		
M12		
Adjusted R-squared =		
Durbin-Watson =		

Do these results support Ronnie Newton's observations? Explain.

c. While sales of this new product have experienced considerable growth in the first four years, Ronnie believes that there has been some decrease in the rate of growth. To test this and to include such a possibility in the forecasting effort, she has asked

that you add the square of the time index (T) to your model (call this new term $T2$). Summarize the new results:

Variable	Coefficient	t-Ratio
Intercept		
T		
T2		
M2		
M3		
M4		
M5		
M6		
M7		
M8		
M9		
M10		
M11		
M12		
Adjusted R-squared =		
Durbin-Watson =		

Is there any evidence of a slowing of sales growth? Compare the results of this model with those found in part (*b*).

d. Use the model in part (*c*) to forecast sales for 1993 and calculate the RMSE for the forecast period. Actual sales are as follows:

Month	Actual Sales	Forecast Sales	Squared Error
Jan	2,318		
Feb	2,367		
Mar	2,523		
Apr	2,577		
May	2,646		
Jun	2,674		
Jul	2,697		
Aug	2,702		
Sep	2,613		
Oct	2,626		
Nov	2,570		
Dec	2,590		
Sum of squared errors = _____			
RMSE = _____			

How does this model compare with the model developed in Exercise 12 of Chapter 4?

10. Norm Marks has recently been assigned the responsibility of forecasting the demand for P2CL, a coating produced by ChemCo that is used to line beer cans. He has decided to begin by trying to forecast beer production and has hired you as an outside consultant for this purpose.

    a. Go to the *Survey of Current Business* and/or *Business Statistics* and gather data on monthly beer production in millions of barrels for a recent four-year period. Prepare a time-series plot of the data.

    b. Develop a multiple-regression trend model with monthly dummy variables for February (M2) through December (M12) for beer production (i.e., use January as the base period). Summarize your findings:

Variable	Coefficient	t-Ratio
Intercept		
T		
M2		
M3		
M4		
M5		
M6		
M7		
M8		
M9		
M10		
M11		
M12		
	Adjusted R-squared =	
	Durbin-Watson =	

Write a paragraph in which you communicate your findings to Norm Marks.

    c. Prepare a forecast for the year following the four years for which you collected data.

6 TIME-SERIES DECOMPOSITION

Many business and economic time series contain underlying components that, when examined individually, can help the forecaster better understand data movements and therefore make better forecasts. As discussed in Chapter 2, these components include the long-term trend, seasonal fluctuations, cyclical movements, and irregular or random fluctuations. Time-series decomposition models can be used to identify such underlying components by breaking the series into its component parts and then reassembling the parts to construct a forecast.

These models are among the oldest of the forecasting techniques available and yet remain very popular today. Their popularity is due primarily to three factors. First, in many situations, time-series decomposition models provide excellent forecasts. Second, these models are relatively easy to understand and to explain to forecast users. This enhances the likelihood that the forecasts will be correctly interpreted and properly used. Third, the information provided by time-series decomposition is consistent with the way managers tend to look at data, and often helps them to get a better handle on data movements by providing concrete measurements for factors that are otherwise not quantified.

The information provided by time-series decomposition is consistent with the way managers tend to look at data and often helps them to get a better handle on data movements by providing concrete measurements for factors that are otherwise not quantified.

There are a number of different methods for decomposing a time series. The one we will use is usually referred to as *classical time-series decomposition* and involves the ratio-to-moving-average technique. The classical time-series decomposition model uses the concepts of moving averages presented in Chapter 3 and trend projections discussed in Chapter 4. It also accounts for seasonality in a multiplicative way that is similar to what you have seen in Winters' exponential smoothing and to the way we used seasonal indices in Chapters 3 and 4.[1]

---

[1]Remember that you have also accounted for seasonality using dummy variables in regression models. That method uses additive factors rather than multiplicative ones to account for seasonal patterns.

The Basic Time-Series Decomposition Model

Look at the data on private housing starts (PHS) that are shown in Table 6–1 and Figure 6–1. While the series appears quite volatile, there is also some pattern to the movement in the data. The sharp increases and decreases in housing starts appear to follow one another in a reasonably regular manner, which may reflect a seasonal component. There also appears to be some long-term wavelike movement to the data as well as

(c6t1&f1)   **TABLE 6–1   Private Housing Starts (PHS), 1965–1999 (000s)**

Period	PHS	Period	PHS	Period	PHS	Period	PHS
Feb-1965	181.5	Feb-1974	177.8	Feb-1983	202.9	Feb-1992	218.5
May-1965	296.7	May-1974	297.8	May-1983	322.3	May-1992	296.4
Aug-1965	266.2	Aug-1974	243.9	Aug-1983	307.5	Aug-1992	276.4
Nov-1965	219.4	Nov-1974	168.4	Nov-1983	234.8	Nov-1992	238.8
Feb-1966	180.2	Feb-1975	142.3	Feb-1984	236.5	Feb-1993	213.2
May-1966	258.8	May-1975	260.9	May-1984	332.6	May-1993	323.7
Aug-1966	197.9	Aug-1975	268.0	Aug-1984	280.3	Aug-1993	309.3
Nov-1966	141.7	Nov-1975	221.0	Nov-1984	234.7	Nov-1993	279.4
Feb-1967	147.1	Feb-1976	219.0	Feb-1985	215.3	Feb-1994	252.6
May-1967	254.7	May-1976	339.6	May-1985	317.9	May-1994	354.2
Aug-1967	244.2	Aug-1976	333.6	Aug-1985	295.0	Aug-1994	325.7
Nov-1967	197.8	Nov-1976	270.1	Nov-1985	244.1	Nov-1994	265.9
Feb-1968	179.9	Feb-1977	268.7	Feb-1986	234.1	Feb-1995	214.2
May-1968	266.2	May-1977	440.1	May-1986	369.4	May-1995	296.7
Aug-1968	249.0	Aug-1977	410.3	Aug-1986	325.4	Aug-1995	308.2
Nov-1968	204.2	Nov-1977	331.8	Nov-1986	250.6	Nov-1995	257.2
Feb-1969	171.1	Feb-1978	257.5	Feb-1987	241.4	Feb-1996	240.0
May-1969	259.0	May-1978	449.1	May-1987	346.5	May-1996	344.5
Aug-1969	214.5	Aug-1978	403.9	Aug-1987	321.3	Aug-1996	324.0
Nov-1969	165.9	Nov-1978	322.9	Nov-1987	237.1	Nov-1996	252.4
Feb-1970	136.7	Feb-1979	226.6	Feb-1988	219.7	Feb-1997	237.8
May-1970	231.6	May-1979	386.9	May-1988	323.7	May-1997	324.5
Aug-1970	228.8	Aug-1979	342.9	Aug-1988	293.4	Aug-1997	314.6
Nov-1970	215.8	Nov-1979	237.7	Nov-1988	244.6	Nov-1997	256.8
Feb-1971	204.8	Feb-1980	150.9	Feb-1989	212.7	Feb-1998	258.4
May-1971	348.5	May-1980	203.3	May-1989	302.1	May-1998	360.4
Aug-1971	321.5	Aug-1980	272.6	Aug-1989	272.1	Aug-1998	348.0
Nov-1971	276.2	Nov-1980	225.3	Nov-1989	216.5	Nov-1998	304.6
Feb-1972	263.9	Feb-1981	166.5	Feb-1990	217.0	Feb-1999	294.1
May-1972	386.9	May-1981	229.9	May-1990	271.3	May-1999	377.1
Aug-1972	370.9	Aug-1981	184.8	Aug-1990	233.0	Aug-1999	355.6
Nov-1972	287.6	Nov-1981	124.1	Nov-1990	173.6	Nov-1999	308.1
Feb-1973	255.8	Feb-1982	113.6	Feb-1991	146.7		
May-1973	366.9	May-1982	178.2	May-1991	254.1		
Aug-1973	306.0	Aug-1982	186.7	Aug-1991	239.8		
Nov-1973	203.3	Nov-1982	184.1	Nov-1991	199.8		

Shaded quarters are holdout periods and are not included in developing the forecast.

FIGURE 6–1

*Private Housing
Starts in Thousands
of Units by
Quarter:
1965Q1–1998Q4
(c6t1&f1)*

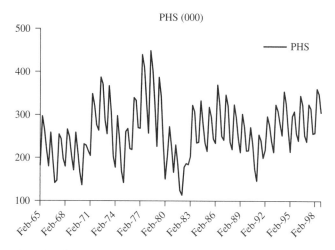

*This plot of private housing starts shows the volatility in the data.
There are repeated sharp upward and downward movements that
appear regular and may be of a seasonal nature. There also
appears to be some wavelike cyclical pattern and perhaps a slight
positive trend.*

a slight positive trend. Patterns such as these are relatively common and can best be understood if they can each be isolated and examined individually. The classical time-series decomposition forecasting technique is a well-established procedure for accomplishing this end.

The model can be represented by a simple algebraic statement, as follows:

$$Y = T \times S \times C \times I$$

where Y is the variable that is to be forecast, T is the long-term (or secular) trend in the data, S is a seasonal adjustment factor, C is the cyclical adjustment factor, and I represents irregular or random variations in the series. Our objective will be to find a way to decompose this series into the individual components.

Deseasonalizing the Data and Finding Seasonal Indexes

The first step in working with this model is to remove the short-term fluctuations from the data so that the longer-term trend and cycle components can be more clearly identified. These short-term fluctuations include both seasonal patterns and irregular variations. They can be removed by calculating an appropriate moving average (MA) for the series. The moving average should contain the same number of periods as there are in the seasonality that you want to identify. Thus, if you have quarterly data and suspect seasonality on a quarterly basis, a four-period moving average is appropriate. If you have monthly data and want to identify the monthly pattern in the data, a 12-period moving average should be used. The moving average for time period t (MA_t) is calculated as follows:

For quarterly data:

$$MA_t = (Y_{t-2} + Y_{t-1} + Y_t + Y_{t+1})/4$$

For monthly data:

$$MA_t = (Y_{t-6} + Y_{t-5} + \cdots + Y_t + Y_{t+1} + \cdots + Y_{t+5})/12$$

The moving average for each time period contains one element from each of the seasons. For example, in the case of quarterly data, each moving average would contain a first-quarter observation, a second-quarter observation, a third-quarter observation, and a fourth-quarter observation (not necessarily in that order). The average of these four quarters should therefore not have any seasonality. Thus, the moving average represents a "typical" level of Y for the year that is centered on that moving average. When an even number of periods are used in calculating a moving average, however, it is really not centered in the year. The following simple example will make that clear and also help you verify your understanding of how the moving averages are calculated.

The moving average represents a "typical" level of Y for the year that is centered on that moving average.

Let Y be the sales of a line of swimwear for which we have quarterly data (we will look at only six quarters of the data stream). MA_3 is the average of quarters 1 through 4. To be centered in the first year it should be halfway between the second and third quarters, but the convention is to place it at the third quarter ($t = 3$). Note that each of the three moving averages shown in the following example contains a first, second, third, and fourth quarter observation. Thus, seasonality in the data is removed. Irregular fluctuations are also largely removed, since such variations are random events that are likely to offset one another over time.

	Time Index	Y	Moving Average	Centered Moving Average
Year 1:				
First quarter	1	10	MISSING	MISSING
Second quarter	2	18	MISSING	MISSING
Third quarter	3	20	15.0(MA_3)	15.25(CMA_3)
Fourth quarter	4	12	15.5(MA_4)	15.75(CMA_4)
Year 2:				
First quarter	5	12	16.0(MA_5)	MISSING
Second quarter	6	20	MISSING	MISSING

$$MA_3 = (10 + 18 + 20 + 12)/4 = 15.0$$
$$MA_4 = (18 + 20 + 12 + 12)/4 = 15.5$$
$$MA_5 = (20 + 12 + 12 + 20)/4 = 16.0$$

As was noted, when an even number of periods are used, the moving averages are not really centered in the middle of the year. To center the moving averages, a two-period moving average of the moving averages is calculated.[2] This is called a *centered moving average*. The centered moving average for time period t (CMA_t) is found as follows:

$$CMA_t = (MA_t + MA_{t+1})/2$$

For the swimwear data used in our example we have:

$$CMA_3 = (15.0 + 15.5)/2 = 15.25$$

$$CMA_4 = (15.5 + 16.0)/2 = 15.75$$

This second moving average further helps to smooth out irregular or random fluctuations in the data.

Note the "MISSING"s that appear under the moving average and centered moving average columns in the data table. With just six data points, we could not calculate four-period moving averages for the first, second, or sixth time period. We then lose one more time period in calculating the centered moving average. Thus, the smoothing process has a cost in terms of the loss of some data points. If an n-period moving average is used, $n/2$ points will be lost at each end of the data series by the time the centered moving averages have been calculated. This cost is not without benefit, however, since the process will eventually provide clarification of the patterns in the data.

By comparing the actual value of the series in any time period (Y_t) with the deseasonalized value (CMA_t), you can get a measure of the degree of seasonality.

The centered moving averages represent the deseasonalized data (i.e., seasonal variations have been removed through an averaging process). By comparing the actual value of the series in any time period (Y_t) with the deseasonalized value (CMA_t), you can get a measure of the degree of seasonality. In classical time-series decomposition this is done by finding the ratio of the actual value to the deseasonalized value. The result is called a *seasonal factor* (SF_t). That is:

$$SF_t = Y_t/CMA_t$$

A seasonal factor greater than 1 indicates a period in which Y is greater than the yearly average, while the reverse is true if SF is less than 1. For our brief swimwear sales example, we can calculate seasonal factors for the third and fourth time periods as follows:

$$SF_3 = Y_3/CMA_3 = 20/15.25 = 1.31$$

$$SF_4 = Y_4/CMA_4 = 12/15.75 = 0.76$$

We see that the third period (third quarter of year 1) is a high-sales quarter while the fourth period is a low-sales quarter. This makes sense, since swimwear would be expected to sell well in July, August, and September, but not in October, November, and December.

When we look at all of the seasonal factors for an extended time period, we generally see reasonable consistency in the values for each season. We would not expect all

---

[2]If the number of periods used is odd, the moving averages will automatically be centered, and no further adjustment is usually made.

first-quarter seasonal factors to be exactly the same, but they are likely to be similar. To establish a seasonal index (SI), we average the seasonal factors for each season. This will now be illustrated for the private housing starts data shown initially in Table 6–1 and Figure 6–1.

The data for private housing starts are reproduced in part in Table 6–2. Only the first and last two years of the entire 34-year period are shown, but that is sufficient to illustrate all of the necessary calculations. The moving average for private housing starts is denoted as PHSMA (private housing starts moving average) and is shown in the fourth column of Table 6–2. The elements included in two values of PHSMA are shown with brackets in the table and are calculated as follows:

$$\text{For 1965Q3: PHSMA} = (181.5 + 296.7 + 266.2 + 219.4)/4 = 240.95$$

$$\text{For 1998Q3: PHSMA} = (258.4 + 360.4 + 348.0 + 304.6)/4 = 317.85$$

TABLE 6–2   Time-Series Decomposition of Private Housing Starts   (c6t2)

1	2	3	4	5	6	7	8	9
Period	*Time Index*	*PHS*	*PHSMA*	*PHSCMA*	*PHSCMAT*	*CF*	*SF*	*SI*
Feb-1965	1	181.5	MISSING	MISSING	237.819	MISSING	MISSING	0.797
May-1965	2	296.7	MISSING	MISSING	238.132	MISSING	MISSING	1.202
Aug-1965	3	266.2	240.950	240.788	238.446	1.010	1.106	1.113
Nov-1965	4	219.4	240.625	235.888	238.759	0.988	0.930	0.888
Feb-1966	5	180.2	231.150	222.613	239.073	0.931	0.809*	0.797
May-1966	6	258.8	214.075	204.363	239.386	0.854	1.266	1.202
Aug-1966	7	197.9	194.650	190.513	239.700	0.795	1.039	1.113
Nov-1966	8	141.7	186.375	185.863	240.013	0.774	0.762	0.888
⋮	⋮	⋮	⋮	⋮	⋮	⋮	⋮	⋮
Feb-1997	129	237.8	284.675	283.500	277.945	1.020	0.839	0.797
May-1997	130	324.5	282.325	282.875	278.259	1.017	1.147	1.202
Aug-1997	131	314.6	283.425	286.000	278.572	1.027	1.100	1.113
Nov-1997	132	256.8	288.575	293.063	278.886	1.051	0.876	0.888
Feb-1998	133	258.4	297.550	301.725	279.199	1.081	0.856	0.797
May-1998	134	360.4	305.900	311.875	279.512	1.116	1.156*	1.202
Aug-1998	135	348.0	317.850	MISSING	279.826	MISSING	MISSING	1.113
Nov-1998	136	304.6	MISSING	MISSING	280.139	MISSING	MISSING	0.888

PHS = Private housing starts (in thousands)
PHSMA = Private housing starts moving average
PHSCMA = Private housing starts centered moving average
PHSCMAT = Private housing starts centered moving-average trend (trend component)
CF = Cycle factor (PHSCMA/PHSCMAT)
SF = Seasonal factor (PHS/PHSCMA)
SI = Seasonal indices (normalized mean of seasonal factors)
*The seasonal factors for 1966Q1 and 1998Q2 are calculated as follows:
1966Q1: SF = 180.2 ÷ 222.613 = 0.809
1998Q2: SF = 360.4 ÷ 311.875 = 1.156

The centered moving average (PHSCMA) is shown in the next column. The calculations of PHSCMA for 1965Q3 and 1998Q2 are:

$$\text{For 1965Q3: PHSCMA} = (240.950 + 240.625)/2 = 240.788$$

$$\text{For 1998Q2: PHSCMA} = (305.900 + 317.850)/2 = 311.875$$

Notice that for PHSCMA there is a "MISSING" for each of the first two and last two quarters. This loss of four quarters of data over 34 years (136 quarters) is not too severe. The two lost quarters that are most critical are 1998Q3 and 1998Q4, since they are the closest to the period to be forecast (1999Q1 through 1999Q4).

Figure 6–2 shows a plot of the original private housing starts (PHS) data (dashed line) along with the deseasonalized data (solid line) represented by the centered moving averages (PHSCMA). Notice how much smoother the data appear once seasonal variations and random fluctuations have been removed.

The process of deseasonalizing the data has two useful results:

The deseasonalized data allow us to see better the underlying pattern in the data.

1. The deseasonalized data allow us to see better the underlying pattern in the data, as illustrated in Figure 6–2.
2. It provides us with measures of the extent of seasonality in the form of seasonal indexes.

The seasonal factors for each quarter are shown in the eighth column of Table 6–2. Recall that the seasonal factors measure the extent to which the observed value for each quarter is above or below the deseasonalized value (SF > 1 and SF < 1, respectively). For this example:

$$SF_i = PHS_i/PHSCMA_t$$

For the first two and the last two quarters, seasonal factors cannot be calculated, since

FIGURE 6–2

Private Housing Starts (PHS) with the Centered Moving Average of Private Housing Starts (PHSCMA) in Thousands of Units
(c6f2)

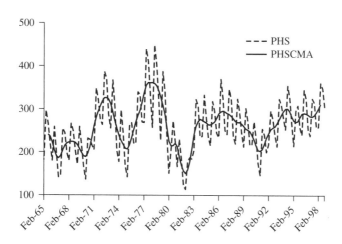

The centered moving-average series, shown by the solid line, is much smoother than the original series of private housing starts data (dashed line) because the seasonal pattern and the irregular or random fluctuations in the data are removed by the process of calculating the centered moving averages.

(c6t2&f2)   **TABLE 6–3   Seasonal Factors for Private Housing Starts (Selected Years)**

Obs	Q1	Q2	Q3	Q4
1965	MISSING	MISSING	1.106	0.930
1966	0.809	1.081	1.039	0.762
⋮	⋮	⋮	⋮	⋮
1997	0.839	1.149	1.100	0.876
1998	0.856	1.156	MISSING	MISSING

This table is abbreviated to save space. All of the SFs are in the data file c6t2&f2.

there are no centered moving averages for those quarters. The calculations of the two seasonal factors marked with an asterisk in Table 6–2 are as follows:

$$\text{For 1966Q1: SF} = 180.2/222.613 = 0.809$$

$$\text{For 1998Q2: SF} = 360.4/311.875 = 1.156$$

It makes sense that a first quarter would have a low SF (less than 1), since January, February, and March are often not good months in which to start building. The reverse is true in the second quarter (April, May, and June).

In Table 6–3 there are three seasonal factors for third quarters: 1.106, 1.039, and 1.100. These are all above 1 and all indicate that third quarters are generally high for private housing starts. See Table 6–2 for additional seasonal factors for private housing starts. Since the seasonal factors for each period are bound to have some variability, we calculate a seasonal index (SI) for each period, which is a standardized average of all of that period's seasonal factors.

The determination of the seasonal indexes are calculated as follows. The seasonal factors for each of the four quarters are summed and divided by the number of observations to arrive at the average, or mean, seasonal factors for each quarter.[3] The sum of the average seasonal factors should equal the number of periods (4 for quarters, 12 for months). If it does not, the average seasonal factors should be normalized by multiplying each by the ratio of the number of periods (4 for quarterly data) to the sum of the average seasonal factors.

Doing this we find that seasonal indexes for private housing starts are as follows (rounded to three decimal places):

First quarter: 0.797

Second quarter: 1.202

Third quarter: 1.113

Fourth quarter: 0.888

---

[3]A medial average is sometimes used to reduce the effect of outliers. The medial average is the average that is calculated after the highest and lowest values are removed from the data.

These add to 4.000 as expected. The warmer spring and summer months of quarters 2 and 3 are the strongest seasons for housing starts.

As shown above, the private housing starts' seasonal index for the first quarter is 0.797. This means that the typical first-quarter figure is only 79.7 percent of the average quarterly value for the year. Thus, if the housing starts for a year totaled 400, we would expect 79.7 to occur in the first quarter. The 79.7 is found by dividing the yearly total (400) by 4, and then multiplying the result by the seasonal index $[(400/4) \times 0.797 = 79.7]$. Following this process for the other three quarters gives us 120.2 for the second quarter, 111.3 for the third quarter, and 88.8 for the fourth quarter.

Another useful application of seasonal indexes is in projecting what one quarter's observation may portend for the entire year. For example, assume that you were working for a manufacturer of major household appliances in April 1998 and heard that housing starts for the first quarter were 258.4. Since your sales depend heavily on new construction, you want to project this forward for the year. Let's see how you would do this, taking seasonality into account. Once the seasonal indexes are known you can deseasonalize data by dividing by the appropriate index. That is:

$$\text{Deseasonalized data} = \text{Raw data/Seasonal index}$$

For 1998Q1 we have:

$$\text{Deseasonalized data} = 258.4/0.797 = 324.216$$

Multiplying this deseasonalized value by 4 would give a projection for the year of 1,296.864.

Finding the Long-Term Trend

The long-term trend is estimated from the deseasonalized data for the variable to be forecast. Remember that the centered moving average (CMA) is the series that remains after the seasonality and irregular components have been smoothed out by using moving averages. Thus, to find the long-term trend, we estimate a simple linear equation as:[4]

$$\text{CMA} = f(\text{TIME})$$

$$= a + b(\text{TIME})$$

where TIME = 1 for the first period in the data set and increases by 1 each quarter thereafter. The values of a and b are normally estimated by using a computer regression program, but they can also be found quickly on most hand-held business calculators.

Once the trend equation has been determined, it is used to generate an estimate of the trend value of the centered moving average for the historical and forecast periods. This new series is the centered moving-average trend (CMAT).

For our example involving private housing starts, the linear trend of the deseasonalized data (PHSCMA) has been found to be slightly positive. The centered moving-average

---

[4]A linear trend is most often used, but a nonlinear trend may also be used. Looking at a graph such as the one shown in Figure 6–2 is helpful in determining which form would be most appropriate for the trend line. We will apply an exponential trend in this context when we look at The Gap data later in this chapter.

FIGURE 6–3

*Private Housing
Starts (PHS)
with Centered
Moving Average
(PHSCMA) and
Centered Moving-
Average Trend
(PHSCMAT) in
Thousands of
Units*
(c6f3)

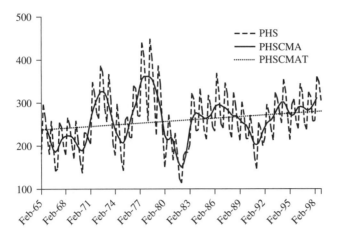

*The long-term trend in private housing starts is shown by the
straight dotted line (PHSCMAT). The dashed line is the raw
data (PHS), while the wavelike solid line is the deseasonalized
data (PHSCMA). The long-term trend is seen to be slightly
positive. The equation for the trend line is:* PHSCMAT
= 237.51 + 0.313(TIME).

trend for this example is denoted PHSCMAT, for "private housing starts centered moving-
average trend." The equation is:

$$PHSCMAT = 237.51 + 0.313(TIME)$$

where TIME = 1 for 1965Q1. This line is shown in Figure 6–3, along with the graph of
private housing starts (PHS) and the deseasonalized data (PHSCMA).

Measuring the Cyclical Component

The cyclical component of a time series is the extended wavelike movement about the
long-term trend. It is measured by a cycle factor (CF), which is the ratio of the centered
moving average (CMA) to the centered moving-average trend (CMAT). That is:

$$CF = CMA/CMAT$$

A cycle factor greater than 1 indicates that the deseasonalized value for that period is
above the long-term trend of the data. If CF is less than 1, the reverse is true.

The cycle factor is the most difficult component of a time series to analyze and to project into the forecast period. If analyzed carefully, however, it may also be the component
that has the most to offer in terms of understanding where the industry may be headed.

> Looking at the
> length and ampli-
> tude of previous
> cycles may enable
> us to anticipate the
> next turning point
> in the current cycle.

Looking at the length and amplitude of previous cycles may enable us to anticipate the
next turning point in the current cycle. This is a major advantage of the time-series
decomposition technique. An individual familiar with an industry can often explain cyclic
movements around the trend line in terms of variables or events that, in retrospect, can be
seen to have had some import. By looking at those variables or events in the present, one
can sometimes get some hint of the likely future direction of the cycle component.

FIGURE 6–4

*The General
Business Cycle*

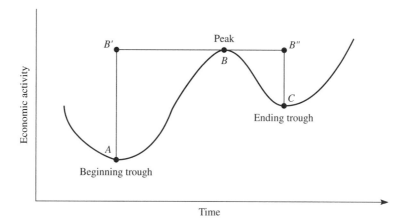

A business cycle goes through successive periods of expansion, contraction,
expansion, contraction, and so on.

Overview of Business Cycles

Business cycles are long-term wavelike fluctuations in the general level of economic
activity. They are often described by a diagram such as the one shown in Figure 6–4.
The period of time between the beginning trough (*A*) and the peak (*B*) is called the
expansion phase, while the period from peak (*B*) to the ending trough (*C*) is termed the
recession, or *contraction, phase.*

The vertical distance between *A* and *B'* provides a measure of the degree of the
expansion. The start of the expansion beginning at point *A* is determined by three consecutive months of increase in economic activity. Thus, the preceding recession is only
officially over three months after the economy has turned around. Similarly, the sever-
ity of a recession is measured by the vertical distance between *B"* and *C,* and the official
beginning of the recession is dated as the first of three consecutive months of decline.

If business cycles were true cycles, they would have a constant amplitude. That is,
the vertical distance from trough to peak and peak to trough would always be the same.
In addition, a true cycle would also have a constant periodicity. That would mean that
the length of time between successive peaks (or troughs) would always be the same.
However, with economic and business activity this degree of regularity is unlikely. As
you will see when we look at the cyclical component for private housing starts and for
domestic car sales, the vertical distances from trough to peak (or peak to trough) have
some variability, as does the distance between successive peaks and successive troughs.

Business Cycle Indicators

There are a number of possible business cycle indicators, but three are particularly note-
worthy:

1. The index of leading economic indicators
2. The index of coincident economic indicators
3. The index of lagging economic indicators

The individual series that make up each index are shown in Table 6–4.

It is possible that one of these indexes, or one of the series that make up an index, may be useful in predicting the cycle factor in a time-series decomposition. This could be done in a regression analysis with the cycle factor (CF) as the dependent variable. These indexes, or their components, may also be quite useful as independent variables in other regression models, such as those discussed in Chapters 4 and 5.

TABLE 6–4   U.S. Business Cycle Indicators

Components of the Composite Indexes*

Leading Index

Average weekly hours, manufacturing

Average weekly initial claims for unemployment insurance

Manufacturers' new orders, consumer goods and materials

Vendor performance, slower deliveries diffusion index

Manufacturers' new orders, nondefense capital goods

Building permits, new private housing units

Stock prices, 500 common stocks

Money supply, M2

Interest-rate spread, 10-year Treasury bonds less federal funds

Index of consumer expectations

Coincident Index

Employees on nonagricultural payrolls

Personal income less transfer payments

Industrial production

Manufacturing and trade sales

Lagging Index

Average duration of unemployment

Inventories to sales ratio, manufacturing and trade

Labor cost per unit of output, manufacturing

Average prime rate

Commercial and industrial loans

Consumer installment credit to personal income ratio

Consumer price index for services

*A short description of each of the indicators is found in the appendix to this chapter.

SOURCE: The Conference Board (www.globalindicators.org). Data in this table are from The Conference Board, which produces the U.S. Business Cycle Indicators.

Figure 6–5 shows what are considered the official business cycles for the U.S. economy in recent years. This graph focuses on real gross domestic product per capita as a broad measure of economic activity. The shaded vertical bars identify the officially designated periods of recession.

FIGURE 6–5

Official Business Cycles in the United States

U.S. Leading Index
(1996 = 100)

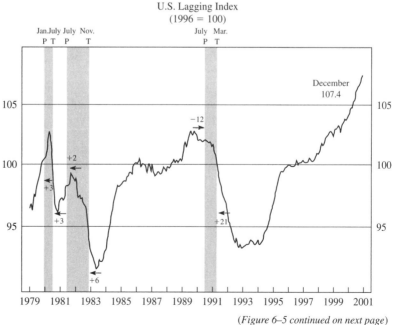

U.S. Lagging Index
(1996 = 100)

(*Figure 6–5 continued on next page*)

FIGURE 6–5
(*Continued*)

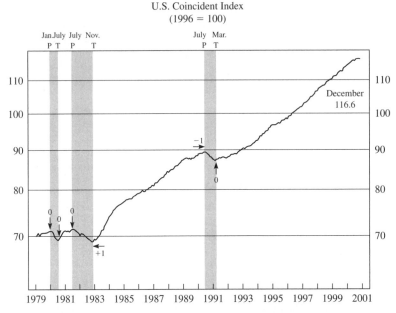

NOTE: P (peak) indicates the end of general business expansion and the beginning of recession; T (trough) indicates the end of general business recession and the beginning of expansion (as designated by the NBER). Thus, shaded areas represent recessions. Arrows indicate leads (−) and lags (+) in months from business cycle turning dates.

SOURCE: The Conference Board (www.globalindicators.org).

The Cycle Factor for Private Housing Starts

Let us return to our example involving private housing starts to examine how to calculate the cycle factor and how it might be projected into the forecast period. In Table 6–2 the cycle factors (CF) are shown in column seven. As indicated previously, each cycle factor is the ratio of the deseasonalized data (CMA) to the trend value (CMAT). For the private housing starts data, we have:

$$CF = PHSCMA/PHSCMAT$$

The actual calculations for 1966Q3 and 1998Q2 are:

$$1966Q3: CF = 190.513/239.700 = .795$$

$$1998Q2: CF = 311.875/279.512 = 1.116$$

You can see in Figure 6–3 that in 1966Q3 the centered moving average was below the trend line and that in 1998Q2 it was above the trend line.

The cycle factor is plotted in Figure 6–6. You can see that the cycle factor (CF) moves above and below the line at 1.00 in Figure 6–6 exactly as the centered moving average moves above and below the trend line in Figure 6–3. By isolating the cycle factor in Figure 6–6, we can better analyze its movements over time.

You see that the cyclical component for private housing starts does not have a constant amplitude or periodicity. The dates for peaks and troughs are shown in Figure 6–6,

FIGURE 6–6

Cycle Factor (CF) for Private Housing Starts (c6f6)

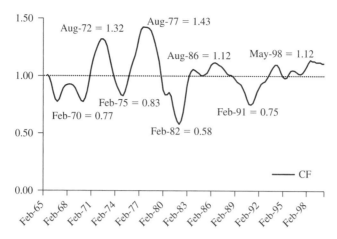

The cycle factor is the ratio of the centered moving average to the long-term trend in the data. As this plot shows, the cycle factor moves slowly around the base line (1.00) with little regularity. Dates and values of cycle factors at peaks and troughs are shown.

along with the values of the cycle factor at those points. Identification of these dates and values is often helpful in considering when the cycle factor may next turn around (i.e., when the next trough or peak may occur). For example, for the PHS cycle factor, the decline from 1972Q3 through 1975Q1 covered 10 quarters, the 1977Q3 to 1982Q1 decline was 18 quarters long, and the 1986Q3 through 1991Q1 decline was 18 quarters in duration. The average of these three contractions was 15.3 quarters, with a standard deviation of 4.6. The corresponding troughs had cycle factors of 0.83, 0.58, and 0.75, for an average of about 0.72 (with a standard deviation of about 0.13). The most recent peak of the CF in Figure 6–6 was 1998Q2, and so a trough was likely sometime near the beginning of 2000. Thus, the next trough was expected beyond our 1999 forecast horizon.[5]

The determination of where the cycle factor will be in the forecast horizon is a difficult task. One approach would be to examine the past pattern visually, focusing on prior peaks and troughs, with particular attention to their amplitude and periodicity, and then making a subjective projection into the forecast horizon. Another approach would be to use another forecasting method to forecast values for CF. Holt's exponential smoothing may sometimes be a good candidate for this task, but one must remember that such a model will not pick up a turning point until after it has occurred. Thus, the forecaster would never predict that the current rise or fall in the cycle would end. If we have recently observed a turning point and have several quarters of data since the turning point, and *if* we believe another turning point is unlikely during the forecast horizon, then Holt's exponential smoothing may be useful. In this example we used a Box-Jenkins forecast of the cycle factor for private housing starts with the following

---

[5]As of the date of this edition of the text, a new trough had not yet been identified.

results (the Box-Jenkins method is presented in Chapter 7):

Period	CF Forecast
1998Q3	1.14
1998Q4	1.13
1999Q1	1.13
1999Q2	1.12
1999Q3	1.12
1999Q4	1.12
2000Q1	1.11
2000Q2	1.11

It is important to recognize that there is no way to know exactly where the cycle factor will be in the forecast horizon, and there is no a priori way to determine the best technique for projecting the cycle factor. A thorough review of the past behavior of the cycle factor, along with alternative forecasts, should be evaluated for consistency and congruity before selecting values of the cycle factor for the forecast horizon.

We see that this forecast projects continued upward movement in the cycle factor for one quarter, then a gradual downturn. Note that we have to forecast the cycle factor for the last two quarters of 1998, even though we had original PHS data for all of 1998. This is because we lost the last two observations in developing the centered moving averages.

Perhaps most frequently the cycle factor forecast is made on a largely judgmental basis by looking carefully at the historical values, especially historical turning points and the rates of descent or rise in the historical series. You might look at the peak-to-peak, trough-to-trough, peak-to-trough, and trough-to-peak distances by dating each turning point, such as we show in Figure 6–6. Then, as we did above, you could calculate the average distance between troughs (or peaks) to get a feeling for when another such point is likely. You can also analyze the rates of increase and/or decrease in the cycle factor as a basis on which to judge the expected slope of the forecast of the cycle factor.

In our private housing starts example, the Box-Jenkins forecast seems reasonable and is the one we shall use for the purpose of this example. It is important to recognize that there is no way to know exactly where the cycle factor will be in the forecast horizon, and there is no a priori way to determine the best technique for projecting the cycle factor. A thorough review of the past behavior of the cycle factor, along with alternative forecasts, should be evaluated for consistency and congruity before selecting values of the cycle factor for the forecast horizon.

The Time-Series Decomposition Forecast

You have seen that a time series of data can be decomposed into the product of four components:

$$Y = T \cdot S \cdot C \cdot I$$

where Y is the series to be forecast. The four components are:

$T =$ The long-term trend based on the deseasonalized data. It is often called the *centered moving-average trend* (CMAT), since the deseasonalized data are centered moving averages (CMA) of the original Y values.

$S =$ Seasonal indexes (SI). These are normalized averages of seasonal factors that are determined as the ratio of each period's actual value (Y) to the deseasonalized value (CMA) for that period.

C = The cycle component. The cycle factor (CF) is the ratio of CMA to CMAT and represents the gradual wavelike movements in the series around the trend line.

I = The irregular component. This is assumed equal to 1 unless the forecaster has reason to believe a shock may take place, in which case I could be different from 1 for all or part of the forecast period.

Previous sections of this chapter have illustrated how these components can be isolated and measured.

To prepare a forecast based on the time-series decomposition model, we simply reassemble the components. In general terms, the forecast for Y (FY) is:

$$FY = (CMAT)(SI)(CF)(I)$$

For our private housing starts example we will denote the forecast value based on the model as PHSFTSD. Thus,

$$PHSFTSD = (PHSCMAT)(SI)(CF)(I)$$

where PHSCMAT is the private housing starts centered moving-average trend. The irregular factor (I) is assumed equal to 1, since we have no reason to expect it to be greater or less than 1 because of its random nature. These calculations are shown in Table 6–5 for 1965Q1–1966Q4 and 1997Q1–2000Q2. You will note that this method takes the trend (PHSCMAT) and makes two adjustments to it: the first adjusts it for seasonality (with SI), and the second adjusts it for cycle variations (with CF).

The actual and forecast values for private housing starts are shown for 1991Q1 through 2000Q2 in Figure 6–7. The actual values (PHS) are shown by the dashed line; forecast values based on the time-series decomposition model are shown by the solid line.

FIGURE 6–7

Private Housing Starts (PHS) and a Time-Series Decomposition Forecast (PHSFTSD) for 1991Q1 Through 2000Q4 (c6f7)

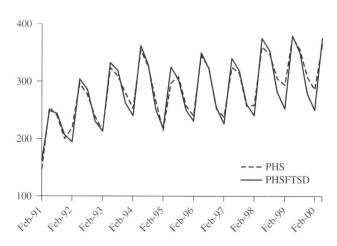

The actual values for private housing starts are shown by the dashed line, and the time-series decomposition forecast values are shown by the solid line.

(c6t5)   **TABLE 6–5   The Time-Series Decomposition Forecast**

Period	Time Index	PHS	PHSCMAT	CF	SI	PHSFTSD
Feb-1965	1	181.5	237.819		0.797	
May-1965	2	296.7	238.132		1.202	
Aug-1965	3	266.2	238.446	1.010	1.113	267.956
Nov-1965	4	219.4	238.759	0.988	0.888	209.351
Feb-1966	5	180.2	239.073	0.931	0.797	177.524
May-1966	6	258.8	239.386	0.854	1.202	245.686
Aug-1966	7	197.9	239.700	0.795	1.113	212.008
Nov-1966	8	141.7	240.013	0.774	0.888	164.953
⋮	⋮	⋮	⋮	⋮	⋮	⋮
Feb-1997	129	237.8	277.945	1.020	0.797	226.079
May-1997	130	324.5	278.259	1.017	1.202	340.075
Aug-1997	131	314.6	278.572	1.027	1.113	318.270
Nov-1997	132	256.8	278.886	1.051	0.888	260.093
Feb-1998	133	258.4	279.199	1.081	0.797	240.613
May-1998	134	360.4	279.512	1.116	1.202	374.939
Aug-1998	135	348.0	279.826	**1.140**	1.113	353.748
Nov-1998	136	304.6	280.139	**1.130**	0.888	281.369
Feb-1999	137	294.1	280.453	**1.130**	0.797	252.208
May-1999	138	377.1	280.766	**1.120**	1.202	379.376
Aug-1999	139	355.6	281.080	**1.120**	1.113	350.384
Nov-1999	140	308.1	281.393	**1.120**	0.888	278.772
Feb-2000	141	286.0	281.707	**1.110**	0.797	249.928
May-2000	142	365.3	282.020	**1.110**	1.202	375.990

Historical period RMSE = 65.70

Holdout period RMSE = 68.45

NOTES:

1. The cycle factors in bold are estimated values rather than actual ratios of PHSCMA to PHSCMAT.

2. Forecast values for private housing starts (PHSFTSD) are determined as follows:
   PHSFTSD = (PHSCMAT)(SI)(CF)

Because time-series decomposition models do not involve a lot of mathematics or statistics, they are relatively easy to explain to the end user. This is a major advantage, because if the end user has an appreciation of how the forecast was developed, he or she may have more confidence in its use for decision making.

Forecasting Domestic Car Sales by Using Time-Series Decomposition

We have applied the classic time-series decomposition method, as described in this chapter, to the problem of forecasting domestic car sales. Figure 6–8 shows the original series (DCS) as the dashed line that fluctuates widely. The deseasonalized series,

FIGURE 6–8

Domestic Car Sales Time-Series Decomposition (c6f8)

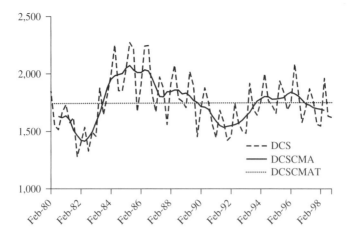

Actual domestic car sales (DCS) are shown by the dashed line, the centered moving averages (DCSCMA) are shown by the solid line, and the long-term trend values (DCSCMAT) are shown by the dotted line.

represented by the centered moving averages (DCSCMA) and the trend (DCSCMAT), are shown by solid and dotted lines, respectively. Note how the original series moves above and below the deseasonalized series in a fairly regular seasonal pattern. The seasonal indexes, based on the normalized mean of the seasonal factors for domestic car sales, are:

Quarter	Seasonal Index
1	0.961
2	1.105
3	1.009
4	0.925

The long-term trend (DCSCMAT), as shown in Figure 6–8, has a slope that is almost perfectly flat.

The cycle factor (CF) is shown in Figure 6–9. The values of CF from 1980Q3 through 1998Q2 were calculated as follows:

$$CF = DCSCMA/DCSCMAT$$

and are shown by the CF curve in Figure 6–9. For 1998Q3 through 1999Q4 they were determined through an analysis and projection of the behavior of the cycle pattern from 1980Q3 through 1998Q2. The dashed line labeled CFF represents a forecast of the cycle factor based on a Box-Jenkins model.

FIGURE 6–9

*The Domestic Car
Sales Cycle Factor
(c6f9)*

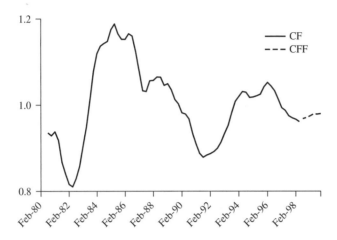

*The cycle factor (CF) for domestic car sales is shown along with a
forecast using a Box-Jenkins model (CFF).*

FIGURE 6–10

*The Time-Series
Decomposition
Forecast of
Domestic Car
Sales
(c6f10)*

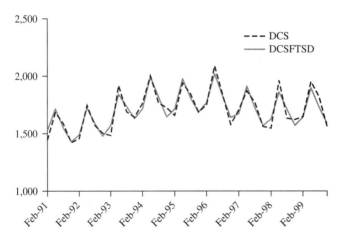

*The actual values for domestic car sales (DCS) are shown by
the dashed line, while the values forecast using the time-series
decomposition method (DCSFTSD) are shown by the solid line.*

The classic time-series decomposition forecast of domestic car sales (DCSFTSD)
is found by multiplying the trend (DCSCMAT) by the seasonal indexes (SI) and the
cycle factors (CF). That is:

$$DCSFTSD = DCSCMAT \times SI \times CF$$

The actual and forecast values for 1991Q1 through 1999Q4 are shown in Figure 6–10
by the dashed and solid lines, respectively.

We now have six different forecasts of domestic car sales for 1999Q1–1999Q4. The
fit and accuracy of these six models are summarized in Table 6–6.

TABLE 6–6   Summary Table of RMSEs for Domestic Car Sales

Chapter	Method	Period	RMSE
1	Naive—with 4-period lag	Historical	187.13
		Holdout	112.26
2	Not applicable		
3	Winters' exponential smoothing	Historical	144.45
		Holdout	61.79
	Holt's with seasonal adjustment	Historical	200.46
		Holdout	62.21
4	Simple regression model using seasonally adjusted DCS as a function of disposable personal income	Historical	96.98
		Holdout	87.93
5	Multiple regression	Historical	107.89
		Holdout	162.59
6	Time-series decomposition	Historical before 1995	195.50
		Holdout 1995Q1–1995Q4	181.20

Forecasting Winter Daily Natural Gas Demand at Vermont Gas Systems

Mike Flock
Distribution Engineer, Vermont Gas Systems, Inc.

Vermont Gas Systems is a natural gas utility with approximately 26,000 residential, business, and industrial customers in 13 towns and cities in northwestern Vermont. Vermont Gas Systems' Gas Control Department forecasts the gas demand, and arranges the gas supply and transportation from suppliers in western Canada and storage facilities along the Trans-Canada Pipeline that deliver the gas to our pipeline. The quantities of gas must be specified to the suppliers at least 24 hours in advance. The Gas Control Department must request enough natural gas to meet the needs of the customers but must not over-request gas that will needlessly and expensively tax Trans-Canada Pipelines' facilities. Because Vermont Gas Systems has the storage capacity for only one hour's use of gas as a buffer between supply and demand, an accurate forecast of daily natural gas demand is critical.

SOURCE: *Journal of Business Forecasting* 13, no. 1 (Spring 1994), p. 23.

INTEGRATIVE CASE
THE GAP

Part 6: Forecasting The Gap Sales Data with Time-Series Decomposition

The sales of The Gap stores for the 56 quarters covering 1985Q1 through 1998Q4 are once again shown below.

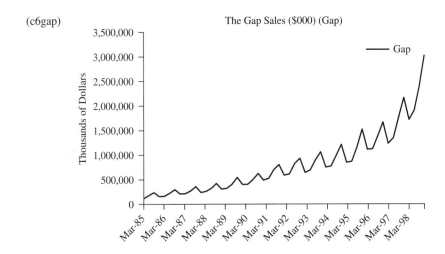

(c6gap)

Case Questions

1. Describe what you see in the 1985–1998 Gap sales in the terms used in time-series decomposition: *trend, seasonality,* and *cycle.*

2. Using The Gap sales data for 1985Q1 through 1998Q4, calculate the four-period centered moving average of The Gap sales (call it GAPCMA). Then, using a time index that goes from 1 for 1985Q1 through 60 for 1999Q4, estimate the trend of GAPCMA (call this trend GAPCMAT and extend it through the entire 1985Q1–1999Q4 period). Try three different trends: linear, quadratic, and exponential. Use the one you like the best. Plot The Gap sales, GAPCMA, and GAPCMAT on the same graph for the period from 1985Q1 through 1998Q4.

3. Calculate the seasonal factors and seasonal indices (SI) based on the 1985–1998 data. Are they consistent with your expectations? Explain.

4. Calculate the cycle factors (CF) for this situation and plot CF along with a horizontal line at one. Your calculated cycle factors end at 1998Q2. Why do they not extend farther? Make a forecast of CF for 1998Q3 through 1999Q4, explaining why you forecast as you do.

5. Prepare a forecast of The Gap sales for the four quarters of 1999 using the trend (GAPCMAT), cycle factors (CF), and the seasonal indices (SI) determined above. Plot the actual and forecast sales.

6. Use the historical period (1985Q1–1998Q4) and hold-out period (1999Q1–1999Q4) RMSEs to evaluate your results and to compare them with forecasts of The Gap sales prepared using other methods.

Solutions to Case Questions

1. The Gap sales exhibit an increasing positive trend over the time frame being evaluated and a very clear seasonal pattern that repeats itself year to year. It appears that the seasonality may be more pronounced in the more recent years than it was in the early years. From this graph it is not clear that there are the long-term swings that are normally associated with a seasonal pattern. However, because of the long-term nature of cycles, it may be that these 14 years of data are insufficient to make an identification of a cyclical pattern.

2. The actual Gap sales are shown by the dashed line in the graph below. The centered moving average is the darker solid line, and the centered moving-average exponential trend is the lighter solid line.

3. The seasonal factors (SF; SF = GAPSALES/GAPCMA) and the normalized seasonal indices (SI) are shown below.

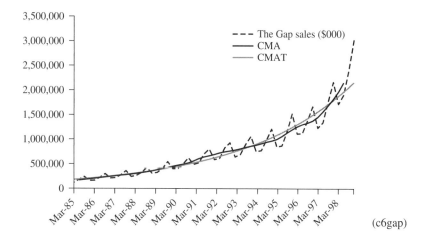

(c6gap)

Date	SF	SI	Date	SF	SI
Mar-1985		0.858	Mar-1997	0.846	0.858
Jun-1985		0.851	Jun-1997	0.860	0.851
Sep-1985	1.077	1.044	Sep-1997	1.046	1.044
Dec-1985	1.325	1.247	Dec-1997	1.190	1.247
Mar-1986	0.833	0.858	Mar-1998		0.858
Jun-1986	0.805	0.851	Jun-1998		0.851
Sep-1986	1.029	1.044			
Dec-1986	1.290	1.247			
⋮	⋮	⋮			
Mar-1996	0.886	0.858			
Jun-1996	0.860	0.851			
Sep-1996	1.035	1.044			
Dec-1996	1.210	1.247			

Notice that while the values for SF vary from year to year, the SI values repeat year after year. The seasonal factors for The Gap sales in quarters one through four indicate strong sales during the fall back-to-school buying season, followed by even stronger sales in the fourth quarter due to the Christmas season.

4. The cycle factors are calculated as: CF = GAPCMA/ GAPCMAT. The cycle factors are missing for 1985Q1, 1985Q2, 1998Q3, and 1998Q4 because the GAPCMA cannot be calculated for those quarters. The solid line in the graph of the cycle factors represents the actual values (CF), and the dashed line shows the forecast values (CFF). For this example, the "ProCast™" function of ForecastX™ was used to forecast CFF.

CFF Forecast by ProCast™ in ForecastX™

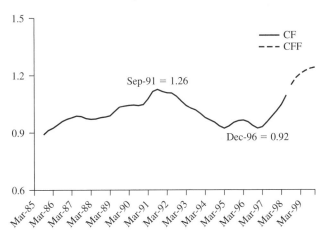

5. The forecast of The Gap sales based on the time-series decomposition method is calculated as: GAPFTSD = GAPCMAT ∗ SI ∗ CF. A time-series plot of these results follows.

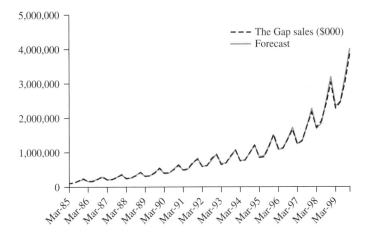

6. The actual (GAPSALES) and time-series decomposition forecast (GAPFTSD) of The Gap sales are shown below for the four quarters of 1999.

	GAPSALES	GAPFTSD
1999Q1	2,277,700	2,340,790
1999Q2	2,453,300	2,463,631
1999Q3	3,045,386	3,190,617
1999Q4	3,858,939	4,012,756

The root-mean-squared errors for the historical period (1985Q1–1998Q4) and for the holdout forecast period (1999Q1–1999Q4) are:

Using 1985Q1–1998Q4:

Root-mean-squared error = 44,013

Using 1999Q1–1999Q4:

Root-mean-squared error = 110,497

It is not uncommon for time-series decomposition models to yield historical RMSEs that are relatively small. This is because these models simply decompose the data and then reassemble the parts. As long as the seasonal factors are not dramatically different, the historical fit of the model will be excellent. However, due to the difficulty of projecting the cycle factor into the forecast horizon, forecast RMSEs are often considerably higher than those in the historical period. This is a good reason to test models in a holdout forecast horizon so that you get a realistic measure of forecast accuracy.

Table 6–7 provides a summary of root-mean-squared errors for various methods used thus far to forecast The Gap sales.

TABLE 6–7   Summary Table of RMSEs for The Gap Sales

Chapter	Method	Period	RMSE
1	Naive—with 4-period lag	Historical	233,092
		Holdout	654,976
2	Not applicable		
3	Winters' exponential smoothing	Historical	49,479
		Holdout	99,493
	Holt's exponential smoothing	Historical	42,388
	with seasonal readjustment	Holdout	74,034
4	Linear trend of deseasonalized	Historical	212,016
	data with forecast reseasonalized	Holdout	1,131,094
5	Multiple regression	Historical	114,995
		Holdout	510,068
6	Time-series decomposition	Historical	44,013
		Holdout	110,497

USING FORECASTX™ TO MAKE TIME-SERIES DECOMPOSITION FORECASTS

As usual, begin by opening your data file in Excel and start ForecastX™. In the **Data Capture** box identify the data you want to use, as shown below. Then click the **Forecast Method** tab.

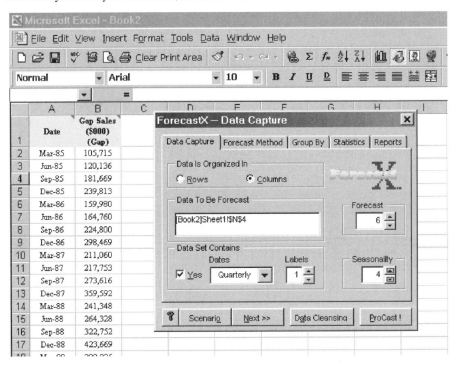

In the **Method Selection** box, click the down arrow in the **Forecasting Technique** box and select **Decomposition.** Click **Multiplicative** and select **Linear Regression** as the **Forecast Method for Decomposited Data.** Then click the **Statistics** tab.

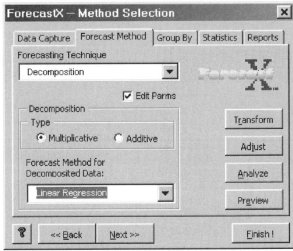

In this box select the statistics that you desire. Remember that there are more choices if you click the **More** button at the bottom.

After selecting the statistics you want to see, click the **Reports** tab.

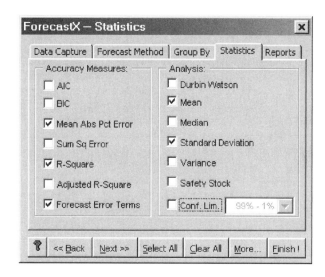

In the **Reports** box select those you want. Typical selections might be those shown here. When you click the **Standard** tab, be sure to select the **Show Charts** box. In the **Audit Trail** tab (the active tab shown here) click **Fitted Values Table.**

Then click the **Finish!** button.

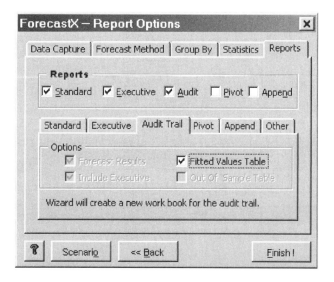

Suggested Readings

Austin, John S. "How to Use and Interpret Seasonal Factors." *Business Economics* 16, no. 4 (September 1981), pp. 40–42.

Campbell, Jeffrey R. "Entry, Exit, Embodied Technology, and Business Cycles." *Review of Economic Dynamics* 1 (1998), pp. 371–408.

Chatterjee, Satyajit. "From Cycles to Shocks: Progress in Business-Cycle Theory." *Business Review,* Federal Reserve Bank of Philadelphia (March/April 2000), pp. 27–37.

Chatterjee, Satyajit. "Productivity Growth and the American Business Cycle." *Business Review,* Federal Reserve Bank of Philadelphia (September/October 1995).

Espasa, Antoni; and Daniel Pena. "The Decomposition of Forecast in Seasonal ARIMA Models." *Journal of Forecasting* 14, no. 7 (December 1995), pp. 565–83.

Layton, Allan P. "Dating and Predicting Phase Changes in the U.S. Business Cycle." *International Journal of Forecasting* 12, no. 3 (September 1996), pp. 417–28.

Majani, Bernard E. "Decomposition Methods for Medium-Term Planning and Budgeting." In *The Handbook of Forecasting.* Eds. Spyros Makridakis and Steven C. Wheelwright. New York: John Wiley & Sons, 1982, pp. 153–72.

Makridakis, Spyros; Steven C. Wheelwright; and Victor E. McGee. *Forecasting Methods and Applications.* 2nd ed. New York: John Wiley & Sons, 1983, pp. 130–78.

Sommers, Albert T. *The U.S. Economy Demystified.* Rev. ed. Lexington, MA: Lexington Books, 1988.

Temin, Peter. "The Causes of American Business Cycles: An Essay in Economic Historiography." In *Beyond Shocks: What Causes Business Cycles?* Eds. Jeffrey Fuhrer and Scott Schuh. Federal Reserve Bank of Boston, 1998.

Veloce, William. "An Evaluation of the Leading Indicators for the Canadian Economy Using Time Series Analysis." *International Journal of Forecasting* 12, no. 3 (September 1996), pp. 403–16.

Zellner, Arnold, ed. *Seasonal Analysis of Economic Time Series.* U.S. Department of Commerce, Bureau of the Census, 1978.

Exercises

1. Using your own words, write a description of each of the four components of the classic time-series decomposition technique. Avoid using mathematical relationships and technical jargon as much as possible so that your explanations can be understood by almost anyone.

2. Define each of the components of the classic time-series decomposition method. Explain how the trend, seasonal, and cyclical components are determined.

3. Suppose that sales of a household appliance are reported to be 13,000 units during the first quarter of the year. The seasonal index for the first quarter is 1.24. Use this information to make a forecast of sales for the entire year. Actual sales for the year were 42,000 units. Calculate your percentage error for the year. What percentage error would result if you forecast sales for the year by simply multiplying the 13,000 units for the first quarter by 4?

4. In a time-series decomposition of sales (in millions of units), the following trend has been estimated:

$$CMAT = 4.7 + 0.37(T)$$

The seasonal indexes have been found to be:

Quarter	Seasonal Index
1	1.24
2	1.01
3	0.76
4	0.99

For the coming year the time index and cycle factors are:

Quarter	T	CF
1	21	1.01
2	22	1.04
3	23	1.06
4	24	1.04

a. From this information prepare a forecast for each quarter of the coming year.

b. Actual sales for the year you forecast in part (a) were 17.2, 13.2, 10.8, and 14.2 for quarters 1, 2, 3, and 4, respectively. Use these actual sales figures along with your forecasts to calculate the root-mean-squared error for the forecast period.

5. A tanning parlor located in a major shopping center near a large New England city has the following history of customers over the last four years (data are in hundreds of customers):

(c6p5)

Year	Q1	Q2	Q3	Q4
1	3.5	2.9	2.0	3.2
2	4.1	3.4	2.9	3.6
3	5.2	4.5	3.1	4.5
4	6.1	5.0	4.4	6.0
Yearly totals	18.9	15.8	12.4	17.3

a. Construct a table in which you show the actual data (given in the table), the centered moving average, the centered moving-average trend, the seasonal factors, and the cycle factors for every quarter for which they can be calculated in years 1 through 4.

b. Determine the seasonal index for each quarter.

c. Do the best you can to project the cycle factor through year 5.

d. Make a forecast for each quarter of year 5.

e. The actual numbers of customers served per quarter in year 5 were 6.8, 5.1, 4.7, and 6.5 for quarters 1 through 4, respectively (numbers are in hundreds). Calculate the RMSE for year 5.

f. Prepare a time-series plot of the actual data, the centered moving averages, the long-term trend, and the values predicted by your model for years 1 through 5 (where data are available).

6. Barbara Lynch, the product manager for a line of skiwear produced by HeathCo Industries, has been working on developing sales forecasts for the skiwear that is sold under the Northern Slopes and Jacque Monri brands. She has had various regression-based forecasting models developed (see Exercises 7 and 8 in Chapter 4 and Exercises 6 and 7 in Chapter 5). Quarterly sales for 1988Q1 through 1997Q4 are as follows:

(c6p6)

	Sales			
Year	Q1	Q2	Q3	Q4
1988	72,962	81,921	97,729	142,161
1989	145,592	117,129	114,159	151,402
1990	153,907	100,144	123,242	128,497
1991	176,076	180,440	162,665	220,818
1992	202,415	211,780	163,710	200,135
1993	174,200	182,556	198,990	243,700
1994	253,142	218,755	225,422	253,653
1995	257,156	202,568	224,482	229,879
1996	289,321	266,095	262,938	322,052
1997	313,769	315,011	264,939	301,479

a. Prepare a time-series plot of the data, and on the basis of what you see in the plot, write a brief paragraph in which you explain what patterns you think are present in the sales series.

b. Smooth out seasonal influences and irregular movements by calculating the centered moving averages. Add the centered moving averages to the original data you plotted in part (a). Has the process of calculating centered moving averages been effective in smoothing out the seasonal and irregular fluctuations in the data? Explain.

c. Determine the degree of seasonality by calculating seasonal indexes for each quarter of the year. Do this by finding the normalized average of the seasonal factors for each quarter, where the seasonal factors are actual sales divided by the centered moving average for each period. If you have done Exercise 7 in Chapter 5, explain how these seasonal indexes compare with the seasonality identified by the regression model.

d. Determine the long-term trend in the sales data by regressing the centered moving average on time, where $T = 1$ for 1988Q1. That is, estimate the values for b_0 and b_1 for the following model:

$$CMAT = b_0 + b_1(T)$$

Plot this equation, called the *centered moving-average trend* (CMAT), along with the raw data and the CMA on the same plot developed in part (*a*).

e. Find the cycle factor (CF) for each quarter by dividing the CMA by the CMAT. Plot the cycle factors on a new graph and project (CF) forward through 1998Q4.

f. Develop a forecast for Ms. Lynch for the four quarters of 1998 by calculating the product of the trend, the seasonal index, and the cycle factor. Given that actual sales were 334,271, 328,982, 317,921, and 350,118 for quarters 1 through 4, respectively, calculate the RMSE for this model based only on the 1998 forecast period.

g. If you have done Exercises 7 and 8 in Chapter 4 and Exercises 6 and 7 in Chapter 5, write a comparison of your findings.

7. Mr. Carl Lipke is the marketing VP for a propane gas distributor. He would like to have a forecast of sales on a quarterly basis, and he has asked you to prepare a time-series decomposition model. The data for 1985Q1 through 1996Q4 follow:

(c6p7) **Propane Gas Sales in Millions of Pounds**

Year	Q1	Q2	Q3	Q4
1985	6.44	4.85	4.67	5.77
1986	6.22	4.25	4.14	5.34
1987	6.07	4.36	4.07	5.84
1988	6.06	4.24	4.20	5.43
1989	6.56	4.25	3.92	5.26
1990	6.65	4.42	4.09	5.51
1991	6.61	4.25	3.98	5.55
1992	6.24	4.34	4.00	5.36
1993	6.40	3.84	3.53	4.74
1994	5.37	3.57	3.32	5.09
1995	6.03	3.98	3.57	4.92
1996	6.16	3.79	3.39	4.51

a. To help Mr. Lipke see how propane gas sales have varied over the 12-year period, prepare a time-series plot of the raw data and the deseasonalized data (i.e., the centered moving averages).

b. Prepare seasonal indexes for quarters 1 through 4 based on the normalized averages of the seasonal factors (the seasonal factors equal actual values divided by the corresponding centered moving averages). Write a short paragraph in which you explain to Carl Lipke exactly what these indexes mean.

c. Estimate the long-term trend for the sales series by using a bivariate linear regression of the centered moving average as a function of time, where TIME = 1 for 1985Q1.

d. Develop cycle factors for the sales data, and plot them on a graph that extends from 1985Q1 through 1996Q4. Analyze the plot of the cycle factor and project it through the four quarters of 1997. Write a brief explanation of why you forecast the cycle factor as you did.

e. Plot the values of sales that would be estimated by this model along with the original data. Does the model appear to work well for this data series?

f. Prepare a forecast for 1997Q1 through 1997Q4 from your time-series decomposition model. Write your forecast values in the accompanying table. Given the actual values shown in the table, calculate the root-mean-squared error (RMSE) for 1997.

	Sales		
Period	Forecast	Actual	Squared Error
1997Q1		5.39	
1997Q2		3.56	
1997Q3		3.03	
1997Q4		4.03	

Sum of squared errors =
Mean-squared error =
Root-mean-squared error =

8. Kim Brite and Larry Short have developed a series of exclusive mobile-home parks in which each unit occupies a site at least 100×150 feet. Each site is well landscaped to provide privacy and a pleasant living

environment. Kim and Larry are considering opening more such facilities, but to help manage their cash flow they need better forecasts of mobile-home shipments (MHS), since MHS appears to influence their vacancy rates and the rate at which they can fill newly opened parks. They have 16 years of data on mobile-home shipments, beginning with 1980Q1 and ending with 1995Q4, as shown:

(c6p8) **Mobile Home Shipments (MHS) (000s)**

Year	Q1	Q2	Q3	Q4
1980	56.6	49.1	58.5	57.5
1981	54.9	70.1	65.8	50.2
1982	53.3	67.9	63.1	55.3
1983	63.3	81.5	81.7	69.2
1984	67.8	82.7	79.0	66.2
1985	62.3	79.3	76.5	65.5
1986	58.1	66.8	63.4	56.1
1987	51.9	62.8	64.7	53.5
1988	47.0	60.5	59.2	51.6
1989	48.1	55.1	50.3	44.5
1990	43.3	51.7	50.5	42.6
1991	35.4	47.4	47.2	40.9
1992	43.0	52.8	57.0	57.6
1993	56.4	64.3	67.1	66.4
1994	69.1	78.7	78.7	77.5
1995	79.2	86.8	87.6	86.4

Assuming that Kim Brite and Larry Short have hired you as a forecasting consultant:

a. Provide a time-series plot of the actual MHS data along with the deseasonalized data. Write a brief memo in which you report the nature and extent of the seasonality in the data. Include seasonal indexes in your report.

b. Develop a long-term linear trend for the data, based on the centered moving averages. Let time equal 1 for 1980Q1 in your trend equation. On the basis of this trend, does the future look promising for Brite and Short?

c. One of the things Ms. Brite and Mr. Short are concerned about is the degree to which MHS is subject to cyclical fluctuations. Calculate cycle factors and plot them in a time-series graph, including projections of the cycle factor through 1996. In evaluating

the cycle factor, see whether interest rates appear to have any effect on the cyclical pattern. The prime rate for 1980Q1 through 1995Q4 is provided in the following table, should you wish to use this measure of interest rates.

(c6p8) **Prime Interest Rate**

Year	Q1	Q2	Q3	Q4
1980	16.4	16.3	11.6	16.7
1981	19.2	18.9	20.3	17.0
1982	16.3	16.5	14.7	12.0
1983	10.9	10.5	10.8	11.0
1984	11.1	12.3	13.0	11.8
1985	10.5	10.2	9.5	9.5
1986	9.4	8.6	7.9	7.5
1987	7.5	8.0	8.4	8.9
1988	8.6	8.8	9.7	10.2
1989	11.0	11.4	10.7	10.5
1990	10.0	10.0	10.0	10.0
1991	9.2	8.7	8.4	7.6
1992	6.5	6.5	6.0	6.0
1993	6.0	6.0	6.0	6.0
1994	6.0	6.9	7.5	8.1
1995	8.8	9.0	8.8	8.7

d. Demonstrate for Ms. Brite and Mr. Short how well your time-series decomposition model follows the historical pattern in the data by plotting the actual values of MHS and those estimated by the model in a single time-series plot.

e. Prepare a forecast for 1996 and calculate the root-mean-squared error (RMSE), given the actual values of MHS for 1996 shown:

	MHS		
Period	Forecast	Actual	Squared Error
1996Q1		35.4	
1996Q2		47.3	
1996Q3		47.2	
1996Q4		40.9	

Sum of squared errors =
Mean-squared error =
Root-mean-squared error =

9. The Bechtal Tire Company (BTC) is a supplier of automotive tires for U.S. car companies. BTC has hired you to analyze their sales. Data from 1976Q1 through 1997Q4 are given in the following table (in thousands of units):

(c6p9)   **BTC Sales of Tires**

Year	Q1	Q2	Q3	Q4
1976	2,029	2,347	1,926	2,162
1977	1,783	2,190	1,656	1,491
1978	1,974	2,276	1,987	2,425
1979	2,064	2,517	2,147	2,524
1980	2,451	2,718	2,229	2,190
1981	1,752	2,138	1,927	1,546
1982	1,506	1,709	1,734	2,002
1983	2,025	2,376	1,970	2,122
1984	2,128	2,538	2,081	2,223
1985	2,027	2,727	2,140	2,270
1986	2,155	2,231	1,971	1,875
1987	1,850	1,551	1,515	1,666
1988	1,733	1,576	1,618	1,282
1989	1,401	1,535	1,327	1,494
1990	1,456	1,876	1,646	1,813
1991	1,994	2,251	1,855	1,852
1992	2,042	2,273	2,218	1,672
1993	1,898	2,242	2,247	1,827
1994	1,669	1,973	1,878	1,561
1995	1,914	2,076	1,787	1,763
1996	1,707	2,019	1,898	1,454
1997	1,706	1,878	1,752	1,560

a. Write a report to Bechtal Tire Company in which you explain what a time-series decomposition analysis shows about their tire sales. Include in your discussion seasonal, cyclical, and trend components. Show the raw data, the deseasonalized data, and the long-term trend on one time-series plot. Also provide a plot of the cycle factor with a projection through 1998.

b. In the last section of your report, show a time-series graph with the actual data and the values that the time-series decomposition model would predict for each quarter from 1976Q3 through 1997Q4, along with a forecast for 1998. If actual sales for 1998 were Q1 = 1,445.1, Q2 = 1,683.8, Q3 = 1,586.6, and Q4 = 1,421.3, what RMSE would result from your 1998 forecast?

10. A national supplier of jet fuel is interested in forecasting its sales. These sales data are shown for the period from 1980Q1 to 1995Q4 (data in billions of gallons):

(c6p10)   **Jet Fuel Sales (Billions of Gallons)**

Year	Q1	Q2	Q3	Q4
1980	23.86	23.97	29.23	24.32
1981	23.89	26.84	29.36	26.30
1982	27.09	29.42	32.43	29.17
1983	28.86	32.10	34.82	30.48
1984	30.87	33.75	35.11	30.00
1985	29.95	32.63	36.78	32.34
1986	33.63	36.97	39.71	34.96
1987	35.78	38.59	42.96	39.27
1988	40.77	45.31	51.45	45.13
1989	48.13	50.35	56.73	48.83
1990	49.02	50.73	53.74	46.38
1991	46.32	51.65	52.73	47.45
1992	49.01	53.99	55.63	50.04
1993	54.77	56.89	57.82	53.30
1994	54.69	60.88	63.59	59.46
1995	61.59	68.75	71.33	64.88

a. Convert these data to a time-series plot. What, if any, seasonal pattern do you see in the plot? Explain.

b. Deseasonalize the data by calculating the centered moving average, and plot the deseasonalized data on the same graph used in part (a). Calculate the seasonal index for each quarter, and write a short explanation of why the results make sense.

c. Develop a trend for the data based on the centered moving averages, and plot that trend line on the graph developed in part (a). Compare the deseasonalized data (CMA) and the trend line. Does there appear to be a cyclical pattern to the data? Explain.

d. Calculate the cycle factors and plot them on a separate time-series graph. Project the cycle factor ahead one year.

e. For the historical period, plot the values estimated by the time-series decomposition model along with the original data.

f. Make a forecast of sales for the four quarters of 1996, and given the following actual data for that year, calculate the root-mean-squared error:

Jet Fuel Sales

Period	Forecast	Actual	Squared Error
1		64.81	
2		75.52	
3		81.93	
4		72.89	

Sum of squared errors =
Mean-squared error =
Root-mean-squared error =

g. Develop two other forecasts of jet fuel sales with:

1. An exponential smoothing method; and
2. A regression model using just time and quarterly dummy variables.

Compare the RMSE for the three models you have developed and comment on what you like or dislike about each of the three models for this application.

11. The following table contains quarterly data on foreign car sales (FCS) in the United States for 1975Q1 through 1995Q4:

Foreign Car Sales (FCS)

Year	Q1	Q2	Q3	Q4
1975	407.6	431.5	441.6	306.2
1976	328.7	381.3	422.6	369.4
1977	456.3	624.3	557.5	436.7
1978	485.0	564.3	538.3	412.5
1979	555.0	682.7	581.3	509.7
1980	662.7	591.1	616.9	529.7
1981	641.2	632.7	576.6	475.0
1982	542.8	558.9	581.7	537.8
1983	588.1	626.5	590.9	580.1
1984	589.2	643.2	593.9	612.2
1985	586.1	699.4	734.4	753.8
1986	691.6	793.4	864.9	840.8
1987	653.9	754.8	883.6	797.7
1988	722.2	788.6	769.9	725.5
1989	629.3	738.6	732.0	598.8
1990	603.9	653.6	606.1	539.7
1991	461.3	548.0	548.4	480.4
1992	476.6	528.2	480.4	452.6
1993	407.2	498.5	474.3	403.7
1994	418.6	470.2	470.7	375.7
1995	371.1	425.5	397.3	313.5

a. Prepare a time-series plot of foreign car sales from 1975Q1 through 1995Q4.

b. On the basis of these data, calculate the centered moving average (FCSCMA) and the centered moving-average trend (FCSCMAT). Plot FCS, FCSCMA, and FCSCMAT on a single time-series plot.

c. Calculate a seasonal factor (SF = FCS/FCSCMA) for each quarter from 1975Q3 through 1995Q2. Calculate the seasonal indexes (SI) for this series. (c6p11)

d. Determine the cycle factors CF = FCSCMA/FCSCMAT for the period from 1975Q3 through 1995Q2 and plot them along with a horizontal line at 1.

e. Evaluate the cycle factor (CF) and project it forward from 1995Q3 through 1996Q4.

f. Prepare a time-series decomposition forecast of FCS (FCSFTSD = FCSCMAT × SI × CF).

g. Calculate the historic RMSE as a measure of fit; then calculate the RMSE for the 1996Q1–1996Q4 forecast horizon as a measure of accuracy, given that the actual values of FCS for 1996 were:

1996Q1	301.1
1996Q2	336.7
1996Q3	341.8
1996Q4	293.5

h. Prepare a Winters' exponential smoothing forecast of FCS using data from 1975Q1 through 1995Q4 as the basis for a forecast of 1996Q1–1996Q4. Compare these results in terms of fit and accuracy with the results from the time-series decomposition forecast.

12. a. Use the following data on retail truck sales (TS) to prepare a time-series decomposition forecast of DTS for 1996Q1–1996Q4:

Truck Sales

Year	Q1	Q2	Q3	Q4
1975	478124	612719	613902	646312
1976	712170	821845	784493	725615
1977	848323	934438	817396	885389
1978	894359	1126400	946504	947141
1979	921967	838559	764035	711234

(continued)

Truck Sales   (*Continued*)

Year	Q1	Q2	Q3	Q4
1980	634427	568758	532143	496188
1981	499968	559593	495349	417391
1982	597296	605965	516173	528238
1983	582202	722965	663528	740694
1984	852774	979159	828721	877681
1985	993431	1047300	982917	959867
1986	901757	1095580	1098730	932177
1987	935125	1145360	1071020	1022050
1988	1139130	1252900	1116670	1099110
1989	1080950	1222890	1195190	983803
1990	1085270	1172960	1081380	921370
1991	845992	1044490	1028720	922831
1992	957733	1240610	1171230	1143440
1993	1145370	1493980	1328300	1350470
1994	1430080	1636760	1456740	1502440
1995	1438960	1661130	1490620	1500120

(c6p12)

b. Evaluate your model in terms of fit and accuracy using RMSE.

c. Plot your forecast values of TS along with the actual values.

d. Compare the results from your time-series decomposition model with those obtained using a Winters' exponential smoothing model in terms of both fit and accuracy.

APPENDIX
COMPONENTS OF THE COMPOSITE INDEXES

The composite indexes of leading, coincident, and lagging indicators produced by The Conference Board are summary statistics for the U.S. economy. They are constructed by averaging their individual components in order to smooth out a good part of the volatility of the individual series. Historically, the cyclical turning points in the leading index have occurred before those in aggregate economic activity, cyclical turning points in the coincident index have occurred at about the same time as those in aggregate economic activity, and cyclical turning points in the lagging index generally have occurred after those in aggregate economic activity.

Leading Index Components

Average weekly hours, manufacturing   The average hours worked per week by production workers in manufacturing industries tend to lead the business cycle because employers usually adjust work hours before increasing or decreasing their work force.

Average weekly initial claims for unemployment insurance   The number of new claims filed for unemployment insurance are typically more sensitive than either total employment or unemployment to overall business conditions, and this series tends to lead the business cycle. It is inverted when included in the leading index; the signs of the month-to-month changes are reversed, because initial claims increase when employment conditions worsen (i.e., layoffs rise and new hirings fall).

Manufacturers' new orders, consumer goods and materials (in 1996 dollars)   These goods are primarily used by consumers. The inflation-adjusted value of new orders leads actual production because new orders directly affect the level of both unfilled orders and inventories that firms monitor when making production decisions. The Conference Board deflates the current dollar orders data using price indexes constructed from various sources at the industry level and a chain-weighted aggregate price index formula.

Vendor performance, slower deliveries diffusion index   This index measures the relative speed at which industrial companies receive deliveries from their suppliers. Slowdowns in deliveries increase this series and are most often associated with increases in demand for manufacturing supplies (as opposed to a negative shock to supplies), and therefore, tend to lead the business cycle. Vendor performance is based on a monthly survey conducted by the National Association of Purchasing Management (NAPM) that asks purchasing managers whether their suppliers' deliveries have been faster, slower, or the same as the previous month. The slower-deliveries diffusion index counts the proportion of respondents reporting slower deliveries, plus one-half of the proportion reporting no change in delivery speed.

Manufacturers' new orders, nondefense capital goods (in 1996 dollars)   New orders received by manufacturers in nondefense capital goods industries (in inflation-adjusted dollars) are the producers' counterpart to "Manufacturers' new orders, consumer goods and materials," listed above.

Building permits, new private housing units   The number of residential building permits issued is an indicator of construction activity, which typically leads most other types of economic production.

Stock prices, 500 common stocks   The Standard & Poor's 500 stock index reflects the price movements of a broad selection of common stocks traded on the New York Stock Exchange. Increases (decreases) of the stock index can reflect both the general sentiments of investors and the movements of interest rates, which is usually another good indicator for future economic activity.

Money supply (in 1996 dollars)   In inflation-adjusted dollars, this is the M2 version of the money supply. When the money supply does not keep pace with inflation, bank lending may fall in real terms, making it more difficult for the economy to expand. M2 includes currency, demand deposits, other checkable deposits, travelers checks, savings deposits, small denomination time deposits, and balances in money market mutual funds. The inflation adjustment is based on the implicit deflator for personal consumption expenditures.

Interest rate spread, 10-year Treasury bonds less federal funds   The spread or difference between long and short rates is often called the *yield curve*. This series is constructed using the 10-year Treasury bond rate and the federal funds rate, an overnight interbank borrowing rate. It is felt to be an indicator of the stance of monetary policy and general financial conditions because it rises (falls) when short rates are relatively low (high). When it becomes negative (i.e., short rates are higher than long rates and the yield curve inverts) its record as an indicator of recessions is particularly strong.

Index of consumer expectations   This index reflects changes in consumer attitudes concerning future economic conditions, and therefore, is the only indicator in the leading index that is completely expectations-based. Data are collected in a monthly survey conducted by the University of Michigan's Survey Research Center. Responses to the questions concerning various economic conditions are classified as positive, negative, or unchanged. The expectations series is derived from the responses to three questions relating to: (1) economic prospects for the respondent's family over the next 12 months; (2) the economic prospects for the nation over the next 12 months; and (3) the economic prospects for the nation over the next five years.

Coincident Index Components

Employees on nonagricultural payrolls   This series from the U.S. Bureau of Labor Statistics is often referred to as *payroll employment*. It includes full-time and part-time workers and does not distinguish between permanent and temporary employees. Because the changes in this series reflect the actual net hiring and firing of all but agricultural establishments and the smallest businesses in the nation, it is one of the most closely watched series for gauging the health of the economy.

Personal income less transfer payments (in 1996 dollars)   The value of the income received from all sources is stated in inflation-adjusted dollars to measure the real salaries and other earnings of all persons. This series excludes government transfers such as Social Security payments and includes an adjustment for wage accruals less disbursements (WALD) that smoothes bonus payments (to more accurately reflect the level of income upon which wage-earners would use to base their consumption decisions). Income levels are important because they help determine both aggregate spending and the general health of the economy.

Index of industrial production   This index is based on value-added concepts and covers the physical output of all stages of production in the manufacturing, mining, and gas and electric utility industries. It is constructed from numerous sources that measure physical product counts, values of shipments, and employment levels. Although the value-added of the industrial sector is only a fraction of the total economy, this index has historically captured a majority of the fluctuations in total output.

Manufacturing and trade sales (in 1996 dollars)   Sales at the manufacturing, wholesale, and retail levels are invariably procyclical. This series is inflation-adjusted to represent real total spending. The data for this series are collected as part of the National Income and Product Account calculations, and the level of aggregate sales is always larger than GDP when annualized because some products and services are counted more than once (e.g., as intermediate goods or temporary additions to wholesale inventories and a retail sale).

Lagging Index Components

Average duration of unemployment   This series measures the average duration (in weeks) that individuals counted as unemployed have been out of work. Because this series tends to be higher during recessions and lower during expansions, it is inverted when it is included in the lagging index (i.e., the signs of the month-to-month changes are reversed). Decreases in the average duration of unemployment invariably occur after an expansion gains strength and the sharpest increases tend to occur after a recession has begun.

Ratio, manufacturing and trade inventories to sales (in 1996 dollars)   The ratio of inventories to sales is a popular gauge of business conditions for individual firms, entire industries, and the whole economy. This series is calculated by the Bureau of Economic Analysis using inventory and sales data for manufacturing, wholesale, and retail businesses (in inflation- and seasonally adjusted form) based on data collected by the U.S. Bureau of the Census. Because inventories tend to increase when the economy slows, and sales fail to meet projections, the ratio typically reaches its cyclical peaks in the middle of a recession. It also tends to decline at the beginning of an expansion as firms meet their sales demand from excess inventories.

Change in labor cost per unit of output, manufacturing   This series measures the rate of change in an index that rises when labor costs for manufacturing firms rise faster than their production (and vice versa). The index is constructed by The Conference Board from various components, including seasonally adjusted data on employee compensation in manufacturing (wages and salaries plus supplements) from the BEA, and seasonally adjusted data on industrial production in manufacturing from the Board of Governors of the Federal Reserve System. Because monthly percent changes in this series are extremely erratic, percent changes in labor costs are calculated over a six-month span. Cyclical peaks in the six-month annualized rate of change typically occur during recessions, as output declines faster than labor costs despite layoffs of production workers. Troughs in the series are much more difficult to determine and characterize.

Average prime rate charged by banks   Although the prime rate is considered the benchmark that banks use to establish their interest rates for different types of loans, changes tend to lag behind the movements of general economic activities. The monthly data are compiled by the Board of Governors of the Federal Reserve System.

Commercial and industrial loans outstanding (in 1996 dollars)   This series measures the volume of business loans held by banks and commercial paper issued by nonfinancial companies. The underlying data are compiled by the Board of Governors of the Federal Reserve System. The Conference Board makes price level adjustments using the same deflator (based on personal consumption expenditures data) used to deflate the money supply series in the leading index. The series tends to peak after an expansion peaks because declining profits usually increase the demand for loans. Troughs are typically seen more than a year after the recession ends. (Users should note that there is a major discontinuity in January 1988, due to a change in the source data; the composite index calculations are adjusted for this fact.)

Ratio, consumer installment credit outstanding to personal income   This series measures the relationship between consumer debt and income. Consumer installment credit outstanding is compiled by the Board of Governors of the Federal Reserve System and personal income data is from the Bureau of Economic Analysis. Because consumers tend to hold off personal borrowing until months after a recession ends, this ratio typically shows a trough after personal income has risen for a year or longer. Lags between peaks in the ratio and peaks in the general economy are much more variable.

Change in Consumer Price Index for services   This series is compiled by the Bureau of Labor Statistics, and it measures the rates of change in the services component of the Consumer Price Index. It is probable that because of recognition lags and other market rigidities, service sector inflation tends to increase in the initial months of a recession and to decrease in the initial months of an expansion.

SOURCE: The Conference Board (www.globalindicators.org).

7 ARIMA (Box-Jenkins)-Type Forecasting Models

Introduction

A time series of data is a sequence of numerical observations naturally ordered in time. Some examples would be:

- Hourly temperatures at the entrance to Grand Central Station
- Daily closing price of IBM stock
- Weekly automobile production by the Pontiac Division of General Motors
- Data from an individual firm: sales, profits, inventory, back orders
- An electrocardiogram

When a forecaster examines time-series data, two questions are of paramount importance:

1. Do the data exhibit a discernible pattern?
2. Can this pattern be exploited to make meaningful forecasts?

We have already examined some time-series data by using regression analysis to relate sequences of data to explanatory variables. Sales (as the dependent variable), for instance, might be forecast by using the explanatory (or independent) variables of product price, personal income of potential purchasers, and advertising expenditures by the firm. Such a model is a structural or causal forecasting model that requires the forecaster to know in advance at least some of the determinants of sales. But in many real-world situations, we do not know the determinants of the variable to be forecast, or data on these causal variables are not readily available. It is in just these situations that the ARIMA technique has a decided advantage over standard regression models. ARIMA is also used as a benchmark for other forecasting models; we could use an ARIMA model, for example, as a criterion for our best structural regression model. The acronym ARIMA stands for "Autoregressive Integrated Moving

Average." Exponential smoothing, which we examined in Chapter 3, is actually just a special case of an ARIMA model.

The Box-Jenkins
methodology of
using ARIMA
models is a
technically
sophisticated
way of forecasting
a variable by
looking *only* at the
past pattern of the
time series.

The Box-Jenkins methodology of using ARIMA models is a technically sophisticated way of forecasting a variable by looking *only* at the past pattern of the time series. Box-Jenkins thus ignores information that might be contained in a structural regression model; instead, it uses the most recent observation as a starting value and proceeds to analyze recent forecasting errors to select the most appropriate adjustment for future time periods. Since the adjustment usually compensates for only part of the forecast error, the Box-Jenkins process is best suited to longer-range rather than shorter-range forecasting (although it is used for short-, medium-, and long-range forecasts in actual practice).

The Box-Jenkins methodology of using ARIMA models has some advantages over other time-series methods such as exponential smoothing, time-series decomposition, and simple trend analysis. Box-Jenkins methodology determines a great deal of information from the time series (more so than any other time-series method), and it does so while using a minimum number of parameters. The Box-Jenkins method allows for greater flexibility in the choice of the "correct" model (this, we will see, is called "identification" in Box-Jenkins terminology). Instead of a priori choosing a simple time trend or a specific exponential smoothing method, for example, as the correct model, Box-Jenkins methodology includes a process that allows us to examine a large variety of models in our search for the correct one. This "open-ended" characteristic alone accounts for its appeal to many forecasters.

The Philosophy of Box-Jenkins

Pretend for a moment that a certain time series is generated by a "black box":

$$\text{Black box} \rightarrow \text{Observed time series}$$

In standard regression analysis we attempt to find the causal variables that explain the observed time series; what we take as a given is that the black box process is actually approximated by a linear regression technique:

$$\begin{array}{ccccc} \text{Explanatory} & & \text{Black box} & & \text{Observed} \\ \text{variables} & \rightarrow & \text{(approximated} & \rightarrow & \text{time series} \\ & & \text{by linear} & & \\ & & \text{regression)} & & \end{array}$$

In the Box-Jenkins methodology, on the other hand, we do not start with any explanatory variables, but rather with the observed time series itself; what we attempt to discern is the "correct" black box that could have produced such a series from some white noise:

$$\text{White noise} \rightarrow \text{Black box} \rightarrow \text{Observed time series}$$

The term *white noise* deserves some explanation. Since we are to use no explanatory variables in the ARIMA process, we assume instead that the series we are observing started as white noise and was transformed by the black box process into the series we are trying to forecast.

White noise is essentially a purely random series of numbers.

White noise is essentially a purely random series of numbers. Some examples of white noise may serve to make its meaning clearer:

1. The winning numbers in the Illinois lottery's "Pick Four" game (where the four winning digits are drawn daily from four separate urns, each with 10 marked balls inside). Would knowledge of the numbers drawn for the past year help you pick a winner? (No, but there are those who actually believe some numbers are "better" than others.)

2. The last digit in the daily closing Dow Jones Industrial Average (or the last digit in the day-to-day change in the average). Would knowing the digit for the last two weeks help you to pick today's final digit?

White noise, then, has two characteristics:

1. There is no relationship between consecutively observed values.

2. Previous values do not help in predicting future values.

White noise is important in explaining the difference between the standard regression process and the Box-Jenkins methodology. The steps required in each method are shown in Table 7–1. In standard regression analysis we move from the explanatory variables (which we choose as a result of some knowledge of the real world) to applying

---

TABLE 7–1   Comparison of Standard Regression Analysis and Box-Jenkins Methodology

For standard regression analysis:

1. Specify the causal variables.
2. Use a linear (or other) regression model.
3. Estimate the constant and slope coefficients.
4. Examine the summary statistics and try other model specifications.
5. Choose the most desirable model specification (perhaps on the basis of RMSE).

Start here:

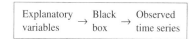

For Box-Jenkins methodology:

1. Start with the observed time series.
2. Pass the observed time series through a black box.
3. Examine the time series that results from passage through the black box.
4. If the black box is correctly specified, only white noise should remain.
5. If the remaining series is not white noise, try another black box.

Start here:

the linear regression technique in order to estimate the constant and slope coefficients of the model. We then use the regression equation to actually make up forecasts about future values of the time series. If our regression model does not have good summary statistics (e.g., *t*-statistics, *R*-squared), we may change some or all of the explanatory variables and try again until we are satisfied with the summary statistics (including the root-mean-squared error).

In Box-Jenkins methodology, however, we start instead with the observed time series itself (with no explanatory variables) and examine its characteristics in order to get an idea of what black box we might use to transform the series into white noise. We begin by trying the most likely of many black boxes, and if we get white noise, we assume that this is the "correct" model to use in generating forecasts of the series. If we try a particular black box and do not wind up with white noise, we try other likely black boxes until we finally wind up with white noise. The test to see whether we have succeeded in winding up with only white noise serves the same purpose as the set of summary statistics we generate with standard regression models.

When choosing the "correct" black box, there are really only three basic types of models for us to examine; there are, however, many variations within each of these three types. The three types of models are: (1) moving-average (MA) models, (2) autoregressive (AR) models, and (3) mixed autoregressive–moving-average models (called ARMA models). We will examine each of these three models in turn in the following sections.

Moving-Average Models

A moving-average (MA) model is simply one that predicts Y_t as a function of the past forecast errors in predicting Y_t. Consider e_t to be a white noise series; a moving-average model would then take the following form:

$$Y_t = e_t + W_1 e_{t-1} + W_2 e_{t-2} + \cdots + W_q e_{t-q}$$

where:

$$e_t = \text{The value at time } t \text{ of the white noise series}$$
$$Y_t = \text{The generated moving-average time series}$$
$$W_{1,2,\ldots,q} = \text{The coefficients (or "weights")}$$
$$e_{t-1,t-2,\ldots,t-q} = \text{Previous values of the white noise series}$$

The name *moving-average* is actually not very descriptive of this type of model; we would do better to call it a *weighted-average model,* since it is similar to exponential smoothing. An example of a moving-average model is constructed in Table 7–2. Table 7–2 is an abbreviated listing of the entire 200-observation data set. The complete data set is included on the CD accompanying this book.

In the first column of Table 7–2 we show a white noise series generated by randomly selecting numbers between 0 and 1. The moving-average series was constructed from the white noise series by using the following equation:

$$Y_t = e_t + W_1 e_{t-1}$$

(c7t2)   TABLE 7–2   **Box-Jenkins Example Data Series**

	White Noise	MA1	AR1	AR2	ARIMA111
1 .	0.256454	0.399867	0.240000	0.160000	0.160000
2 .	0.230240	0.409758	0.350240	0.040000	0.569758
3 .	0.675186	0.836354	0.850306	0.735186	1.40611
4 .	0.0475159	0.520146	0.472669	0.570146	1.92626
5 .	0.716827	0.750089	0.953162	1.26297	2.67635
6 .	0.854614	1.35639	1.33120	1.85272	4.03274
7 .	0.557983	1.15621	1.22358	2.10748	5.18895
8 .	0.0390320	0.429620	0.650822	1.88481	5.61857
9 .	0.184616	0.211938	0.510027	1.92548	5.83051
10 .	0.0167999	0.146031	0.271814	1.74160	5.97654
11 .	0.596069	0.607829	0.731976	2.20029	6.58437
12 .	0.235672	0.652921	0.601660	2.12419	7.23729
13 .	0.0724487	0.237419	0.373279	1.99944	7.47471
14 .	0.858917	0.909631	1.04556	2.68336	8.38434
15 .	0.830856	1.43210	1.35363	3.10910	9.81644
16 .	0.215927	0.797527	0.892744	2.92897	10.6140
17 .	0.223007	0.374156	0.669379	2.89511	10.9881
18 .	0.254166	0.410271	0.588855	2.86653	11.3984
19 .	0.764038	0.941954	1.05847	3.34963	12.3403
20 .	0.286438	0.821265	0.815671	3.20449	13.1616
191 .	0.323975	0.782538	0.820131	4.36400	150.720
192 .	0.162109	0.388892	0.572175	4.12794	151.109
193 .	0.702011	0.815488	0.988099	4.46437	151.924
194 .	0.854660	1.34607	1.34871	4.80531	153.270
195 .	0.480850	1.07911	1.15520	4.73744	154.349
196 .	0.843475	1.18007	1.42108	5.12074	155.530
197 .	0.408600	0.999033	1.11914	4.94061	156.529
198 .	0.581711	0.867731	1.14128	5.06429	157.396
199 .	0.975937	1.38313	1.54658	5.50906	158.779
200 .	0.683960	1.36712	1.45725	5.55316	160.147

where:

Y_t = The series generated, which appears in column 2

e_t = The white noise series appearing in column 1

W_1 = A constant (equal here to 0.7)

e_{t-1} = The white noise value lagged one period

This series [called an MA(1) series because it contains one lag of the white noise term] was constructed with known characteristics. Imagine how we might decide that a time series of unknown origin that we want to forecast could be similar to this known series. How could we go about examining this time series to determine whether it is an MA(1) series like that in column 2 of Table 7–2? We can get an insight into the answer by examining two characteristics of the time series we have purposely constructed to

First, we examine
the autocorrelation
(or "serial
correlation")
among successive
values of the
time series; this
will be the first of
two key tools in
determining
which model
(or black box) is
the appropriate
representation of
any given time
series.

be an MA(1) series in Table 7–2. These characteristics are the autocorrelations and the partial autocorrelations.

First, we examine the autocorrelation (or "serial correlation") among successive values of the time series; this will be the first of two key tools in determining which model (or black box) is the appropriate representation of any given time series. As described in Chapter 2, autocorrelation is the concept that the association between values of the same variable at different time periods is nonrandom—that is, that if autocorrelation does exist in a time series, there is correlation or mutual dependence between the values of the time series at different time periods.

As a simple example of autocorrelation, consider the data in Table 7–3. The first column could represent sales of an item during successive periods; the second column is the first column lagged one period; the third column is the first column lagged two periods. We can now calculate the simple correlation coefficient between the numbers in the first column and the numbers in the second column, treating each column as if it were a separate variable. Remember that the correlation coefficient will always vary between $+1$ and -1. If it is $+1$, it indicates that there is a perfect positive correlation between the two columns—that is, as one increases, so does the other. If the correlation coefficient is -1, it indicates a perfect negative correlation—that is, as one goes up, the other goes down. The closer the number is to $+1$, the more positively correlated the columns; the closer the number is to -1, the more negatively correlated the columns.

Here the correlation between the first and second columns is $+0.867$; the correlation between the first and third columns is $+0.898$. These values indicate the extent to which the original series values are correlated with themselves, lagged one and two periods (called *auto*correlation since the second and third columns of our table are not variables separate from column 1, but are actually the same variable at different periods).

Apparently, autocorrelation exists in this variable for both one and two lags, and the autocorrelation coefficients are approximately equal. These autocorrelations provide us

(c7t3)   **TABLE 7–3   A Simple Example of Autocorrelation**

Original Variable	One Time Lag	Two Time Lags
121	—	—
123	121	—
134	123	121
133	134	123
151	133	134
141	151	133
176	141	151
187	176	141
183	187	176
214	183	187

Correlation between original variable and one time lag = $+0.867$.
Correlation between original variable and two time lags = $+0.898$.

with the first important tool for identifying the correct model; if the original data in Table 7–3 had been completely random white noise (ours were not), the correlation among lagged values (one, two, or more lags) would have been approximately equal to zero, given a large enough data set. We will find that the pattern of the autocorrelations will help us identify a series that behaves as a moving-average model.

The partial autocorrelation coefficient is the second tool we will use to help identify the relationship between the current values and past values of the original time series. Partial autocorrelation coefficients measure the degree of association between Y_t and Y_{t-k} *when all the other time lags on Y are held constant.* The calculation of the partial autocorrelation terms is beyond the scope of this text, but they are calculated by ForecastX™ and most other statistical packages that deal with time-series analysis. It is possible, however, to indicate how these coefficients are calculated without presenting the rather lengthy derivation.

The partial autocorrelation coefficient is defined in terms of the last autoregressive (AR) term of an AR-type model with m lags. Partial autocorrelations are calculated when we are unsure of the correct order of the autoregressive process to fit the time series. Consider the AR(m) model (which will be explained in more detail in the section "Autoregressive Models") represented in the following equations:

$$Y_t = A_1 Y_{t-1} + e_t$$
$$Y_t = A_1 Y_{t-1} + A_2 Y_{t-2} + e_t$$
$$\vdots$$
$$Y_t = A_1 Y_{t-1} + A_2 Y_{t-2} + \cdots + A_m Y_{t-m} + e_t$$

By solving this system of equations for the $A_1, A_2, \ldots, A_{t-m}$ terms (which are the partial autocorrelation coefficients), we could determine their actual values.

It is most common to view both the autocorrelation coefficients and the partial autocorrelation coefficients in graphic form by constructing a correlogram of the autocorrelation coefficients and a partial correlogram for the partial autocorrelation coefficients; both graphics look very much like the residuals output in the ForecastX™ program.

Consider the typical MA(1) correlogram and partial correlogram in Figure 7–1. Two distinctive patterns in the autocorrelation and partial autocorrelation functions are characteristic of an MA(1) model. The *a* frame of Figure 7–1 displays the first of these patterns. Note the gradual falling to zero of the partial autocorrelation function and the single spike in the autocorrelation function. In general, if the autocorrelation function abruptly stops at some point, we know the model is of the MA type; the number of spikes (commonly referred to as q) before the abrupt stop tells us the "order" of the MA model. In frame *a* there is only one spike, and so we know the model is likely to be of the MA(1) variety.

Frame *b* represents a variation of this distinctive pattern; here the single spike (now negative) still appears in the autocorrelation function, but the partial autocorrelation function shows alternating positive and negative values, gradually falling to zero. This also would indicate to us an MA(1)-type model.

The partial autocorrelation coefficient is the second tool we will use to help identify the relationship between the current values and past values of the original time series.

FIGURE 7–1

*Examples of
Theoretical
Autocorrelation
and Partial
Autocorrelation
Plots for MA(1)
and MA(2) Models*

Autocorrelation Function

Partial Autocorrelation Function

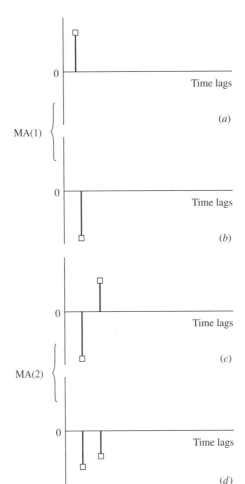

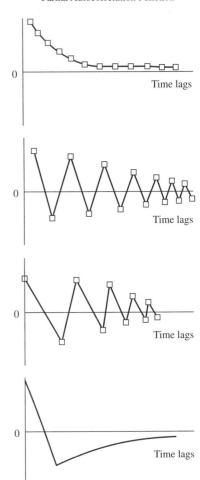

In any given data there may be more than one significant moving-average term; if there were two significant moving-average terms, for instance, we could find either of the patterns in frames *c* and *d*. Both of these situations are characteristic of an MA(2) model; both frames show two distinct spikes in the autocorrelation function while the partial autocorrelation function gradually slides to zero, either monotonically decreasing or alternating between positive and negative values.

We are now ready to examine the autocorrelation and partial autocorrelation functions for the MA(1) series in column 2 of Table 7–2. The correlograms for each are shown for the first 24 lags in Figure 7–2. If we had not previously known that this was an MA(1) series, we should have been able to deduce this from the characteristic patterns shown in Figure 7–2: note that the autocorrelation function has only one spike

FIGURE 7–2

*Autocorrelation
and Partial
Autocorrelation
Plots for the MA(1)
Series in Table 7–2
(c7t2)*

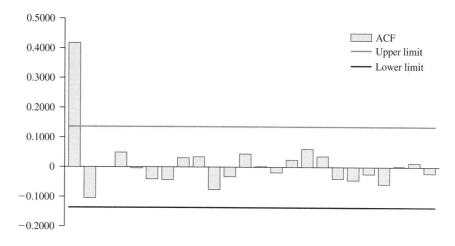

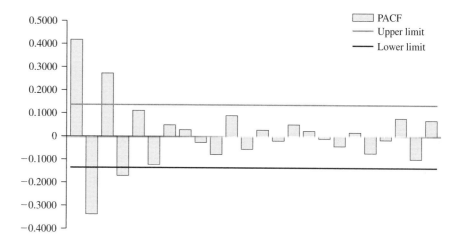

Obs	ACF	PACF	Obs	ACF	PACF
1	.4175	.4175	13	.0019	.0281
2	−.1046	−.3378	14	−.0185	−.0185
3	−.0003	.2724	15	.0246	.0517
4	.0490	−.1709	16	.0614	.0238
5	−.0040	.1112	17	.0363	−.0094
6	−.0405	−.1227	18	−.0392	−.0419
7	−.0429	.0490	19	−.0441	.0181
8	.0309	.0284	20	−.0233	−.0719
9	.0342	−.0262	21	−.0573	−.0146
10	−.0759	−.0779	22	.0020	.0790
11	−.0323	.0897	23	.0134	−.0973
12	.0444	−.0547	24	−.0210	.0703

that appears to be significantly different from zero. Also note that the partial autocorrelation function alternates from positive to negative *and* decreases in absolute value as it approaches zero. This pattern is similar to that shown in frame *b* of Figure 7–1 and identifies the time series for us as one of the MA(1) variety. This knowledge of what the autocorrelation and partial autocorrelation functions look like in an MA(1) model will allow us later to use Box-Jenkins methodology to model and forecast any similar time series accurately.

Autoregressive Models

The second of the three classes of models we need to examine is the autoregressive (AR) model. The equation for the autoregressive model is similar to the moving-average model, except that the dependent variable Y_t depends on its own previous values rather than the white noise series or residuals. The autoregressive model is produced from a white noise series by using an equation of the form:

$$Y_t = A_1 Y_{t-1} + A_2 Y_{t-2} + \cdots + A_p Y_{t-p} + e_t$$

where:

$$Y_t = \text{The moving-average time series generated}$$
$$A_1, A_2, \ldots, A_p = \text{Coefficients}$$
$$Y_{t-1}, Y_{t-2}, \ldots, Y_{t-p} = \text{Lagged values of the time series (hence the name}$$
$$\textit{autoregressive})$$
$$e_t = \text{White noise series}$$

If the model has only the Y_{t-1} term on the right-hand side, it is referred to as an AR(1) model; if it has Y_{t-1} and Y_{t-2} terms, it is an AR(2); and so on. Column 3 of Table 7–2 is an AR(1) series produced by the following equation:

$$Y_t = A_1 Y_{t-1} + e_t$$

where

$$Y_t = \text{The series generated, which appears in column 2}$$
$$e_t = \text{The white noise series appearing in column 1}$$
$$A_1 = \text{A constant (equal here to 0.5)}$$
$$Y_{t-1} = \text{The series lagged one period}$$

(Note: The first number in the column [i.e., 0.24] is chosen arbitrarily.)

Once again, as with the MA(1) model presented in the previous section, the AR(1) series in column 3 is constructed from the white noise series with known characteristics [that is, it is an AR(1) series because we constructed it to be one]. Again, ask the question: How might we decide that another time series, of unknown origin, that we were given to forecast could be similar to this AR(1) series? In other words, how would we go about examining a series to determine whether it is an AR(1)-type series?

We will answer the question by again examining the characteristics of the known series [the AR(1) series in column 3 of Table 7–2]. Once again we first examine the autocorrelation function of the series and then examine the partial autocorrelation function of the series. We are looking for distinctive patterns in each of these functions that will indicate that any time series under examination is an AR(1)-type series.

The typical correlograms and partial correlograms for an AR(1) series are shown in frames *a* and *b* of Figure 7–3. Either of two patterns is distinctive for an AR(1) model. In frame *a* the autocorrelation function falls monotonically to zero while the partial autocorrelation function shows a single spike; note that this is the exact opposite of the pattern exhibited by an MA(1) time series. In general, if the partial autocorrelation function abruptly stops at some point, the model is of the AR type; the number of spikes (p) before the abrupt stop is equal to the "order" of the AR model. In frame *a* there is just one spike in the partial autocorrelation function, and so the model is of the AR(1) type.

FIGURE 7–3

Examples of Theoretical Autocorrelation and Partial Autocorrelation Plots of AR(1) and AR(2) Models

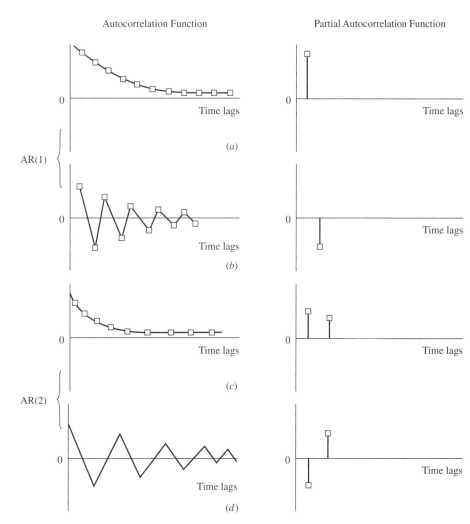

FIGURE 7–4

*Autocorrelation
and Partial
Autocorrelation
Plots for the AR(1)
Series in Table 7–2
(c7t2)*

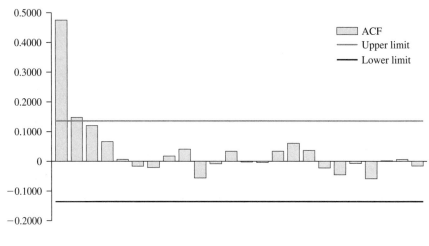

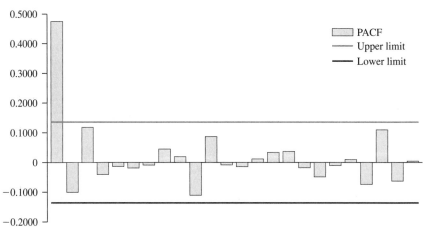

Obs	ACF	PACF	Obs	ACF	PACF
1	.4751	.4751	13	−.0026	−.0143
2	.1478	−.1006	14	−.0042	.0117
3	.1203	.1184	15	.0338	.0341
4	.0659	−.0406	16	.0604	.0376
5	.0064	−.0136	17	.0365	−.0179
6	−.0165	−.0187	18	−.0225	−.0485
7	−.0211	−.0088	19	−.0454	−.0105
8	.0175	.0456	20	−.0073	.0098
9	.0406	.0199	21	−.0587	−.0737
10	−.0562	−.1104	22	.0018	.1101
11	−.0085	.0874	23	.0062	−.0625
12	.0337	−.0084	24	−.0158	.0044

Frame *b* represents the second of two characteristic patterns for an AR(1) model; here the single spike (now negative) still appears in the partial autocorrelation function, but the autocorrelation function tends to zero by alternating between positive and negative values.

As in MA-type models, there may be more than one significant autoregressive term; if this is the case, patterns like those shown in frames *c* and *d* of Figure 7–3 could result. Patterns like those in either frame *c* or *d* would indicate an AR(2)-type model because of the two significant spikes in the partial autocorrelation function. Note again that the autocorrelation function in both cases falls to zero, either monotonically (as in frame *c*) or alternating between positive and negative values (as in frame *d*).

We should now be able to evaluate the autocorrelation and partial autocorrelation functions for the AR(1) series in column 3 of Table 7–2. Recall that we know that this particular time series was produced from a white noise series by using the equation

$$Y_t = A_1 Y_{t-1} + e_t$$

The correlograms for each are shown for the first 24 lags in Figure 7–4. If we had not known that this was an AR(1) series, we should have been able to deduce this from the characteristic patterns in Figure 7–4; note that the partial autocorrelation function has only one significant spike (i.e., it has only one spike that appears significantly different from zero, and so the order is $p = 1$). Also note that the autocorrelation function decreases in value, approaching zero. This pattern is similar to that shown in frame *a* of Figure 7–3, and this fact identifies the time series as one of the AR(1) variety.

Mixed Autoregressive and Moving-Average Models

The third and final of the three classes of models that we need examine is really a combination of an AR and an MA model. This third class of general models is called *ARMA*, which stands for *autoregressive–moving-average model*. This model could be produced from a white noise series by introducing the elements we have already seen in both moving-average and autoregressive models:

$$\begin{aligned} Y_t = A_1 Y_{t-1} + A_2 Y_{t-2} + \cdots \\ + A_p Y_{t-p} + e_t + W_1 e_{t-1} \\ + W_2 e_{t-2} + \cdots + W_q e_{t-q} \end{aligned}$$

This equation defines a mixed autoregressive–moving-average model of order *p, q,* and is usually written as ARMA(*p, q*). To identify an ARMA model, we again look for characteristic patterns in the autocorrelation and partial autocorrelation functions.

Figure 7–5 shows the characteristic patterns for an ARMA(1, 1) model; note that *any* of the four frames in Figure 7–5 could be patterns that would identify an ARMA(1, 1) model. In Figure 7–5, in each of the frames, both the autocorrelations and partial autocorrelations gradually fall to zero *rather than abruptly stop.* This observation (both functions falling off gradually) is characteristic of any ARMA(*p, q*) model.

FIGURE 7–5

Examples of Theoretical Autocorrelation and Partial Autocorrelation Plots of ARMA (1, 1) Models

Autocorrelation Function

Partial Autocorrelation Function

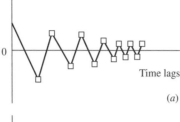

(a)

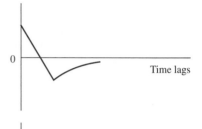

(b)

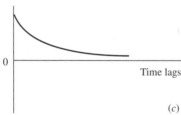

(c)

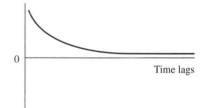

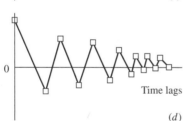

(d)

To identify the order of the AR and MA terms, we need to count the number of AR and MA terms significantly different from zero. In frame *b*, for instance, there is one spike in the AR process and one spike in the MA process; this would imply an ARMA(1, 1) model. The other patterns exhibited in Figure 7–5 are less easily identified as ARMA(1, 1) processes.

In fact, the particular identification process we have outlined requires some experience to apply in the real world. We have, however, outlined the basic steps to be followed in applying the identification process; skill in actual application requires the consideration of many examples and learning from past mistakes. We have already seen that according to Box-Jenkins methodology, if we are able to identify the type and order of model we are faced with when we are given a time series, then the repetitive pattern in that original time series offers us the method for forecasting it. When we are given a time series in the real world, however, we are not told the type of model that will fit it, and the first task is to figure out which of the infinite variations of the three models (autoregressive, moving-average, or mixed) is the "correct" model for our data.

Many real-world processes, once they have been adjusted for seasonality, can be adequately modeled with the low-order models.

Fortunately, for low-order processes like the ones we have examined so far, the correct specification of the p and q values is rather simple to make. Many real-world processes, once they have been adjusted for seasonality, can be adequately modeled with the low-order models [e.g., MA(1), MA(2), AR(1), AR(2), ARMA(1, 1)]. If low-order models are not adequate (how to determine whether a model is adequate will be explained in the section "The Box-Jenkins Identification Process"), the selection of the proper p and q becomes more difficult. As a rule of thumb, however, spikes in the autocorrelation function indicate moving-average terms, and spikes in the partial autocorrelation function indicate autoregressive terms.

When the correct model is not of a low order, you may be forced to determine an adequate p and q by trial and error; it will be possible, you will see, to check your guesses after the parameters of each model have been determined.

Stationarity

A *stationary* time series is one in which two consecutive values in the series depend *only* on the time interval between them and *not* on time itself.

In general we have been approaching our data as if they were stationary. A *stationary* time series is one in which two consecutive values in the series depend *only* on the time interval between them and *not* on time itself. For all practical purposes this would be consistent with a series whose mean value did *not* change over time. Real-world time series are most often nonstationary; that is, the mean value of the time series changes over time, usually because there is some trend in the series so that the mean value is either rising or falling over time. Nonstationarity can result in other ways (it could be that the variability of the time series changes over time; perhaps the variability becomes exaggerated through time), but the most common cause is simply some trend in the series.

If the series we examine are nonstationary, the autocorrelations are usually significantly different from zero at first and then gradually fall off to zero, or they show a spurious pattern as the lags are increased. Because autocorrelations dominate the pattern of a nonstationary series, it is necessary for us to modify a nonstationary series to make it stationary *before* we try to identify as the "correct" model one of the three models we have so far examined.

There is no single way to remove nonstationarity, but two methods help achieve stationarity most often in actual practice. First, if the nonstationarity is caused by a trend in the series, then differencing the time series may effectively remove the trend. Differencing refers to subtracting the previous observation from each observation in the data set:

$$Y_t' = Y_t - Y_{t-1}$$

where

Y_t' = The first difference of observation at time t

Y_t = Time-series observation at time t

Y_{t-1} = Time-series observation at time period $t - 1$

In some cases the first difference will not remove the trend and it may be necessary to try a higher order of differencing. For example, second-order differences can be found as follows:

$$Y''_t = Y'_t - Y'_{t-1}$$

where:

Y''_t = The second difference

Y'_t = The first difference of observation at time t

Y'_{t-1} = The first difference of observation at time $t - 1$

The second method for removing nonstationarity is used when there is a change in the variability of the series (i.e., when there is a trend in the variance). This method involves taking logs of the original time series, which usually transfers the trend in variance to a trend in the mean; this trend can then be handled by differencing. Other, more sophisticated methods of removing nonstationarity are sometimes used but will not be covered here.

Consider the series in column 5 of Table 7–2. Glancing at the numbers down the column, we can easily see that this series has some trend; the numbers are monotonically increasing throughout the time period. Figure 7–6 shows the autocorrelation function for this series. This autocorrelation function is entirely characteristic of series with a trend; that is, it shows dominant autocorrelations for the 24 lags shown, and these autocorrelations only gradually become smaller. Figure 7–7 shows the correlograms for the same series *after* first differences have been taken. Apparently, this series contains a trend and could probably easily be modeled with a simple time trend or a low-order ARMA model. Figure 7–7 (which shows the data after taking first differences) could perhaps be best modeled as an ARMA(3, 1), since there appear to be one dominant autocorrelation spike and three dominant partial autocorrelation spikes.

When differencing is used to make a time series stationary, it is common to refer to the resulting model as an ARIMA(p, d, q)-type model. The "I" that has been added to the name of the model refers to the integrated or differencing term in the model; the d inside the parentheses refers to the degree of differencing. An ARIMA(p, d, q) model is then properly referred to as an *autoregressive integrated moving-average model.* For example, a model with one autoregressive term, one degree of differencing, and no moving-average term would be written as an ARIMA(1, 1, 0) model. An ARIMA model is thus classified as an "ARIMA(p, d, q)" model, where:

- p is the number of autoregressive terms,
- d is the number of differences, and
- q is the number of moving-average terms.

FIGURE 7–6

*Autocorrelation
and Partial
Autocorrelation
Plots for the
ARIMA(1, 1, 1)
Series in
Table 7–2
(c7t2)*

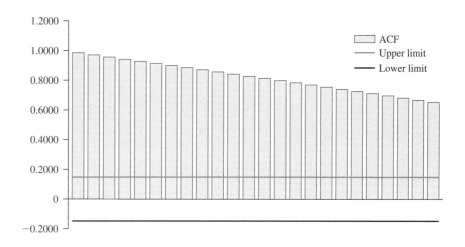

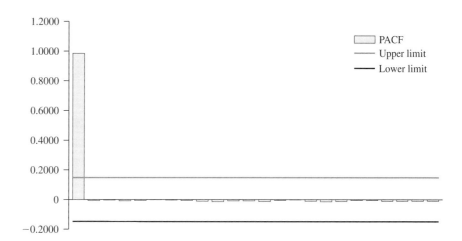

```
------------------------------------------------------------------------

Obs      ACF        PACF           Obs       ACF        PACF
------------------------------      ------------------------------
 1      .9854       .9854           13      .8124      -.0127
 2      .9707      -.0069           14      .7979      -.0045
 3      .9562      -.0031           15      .7836      -.0020
 4      .9417      -.0085           16      .7693      -.0103
 5      .9272      -.0064           17      .7547      -.0139
 6      .9129      -.0015           18      .7401      -.0123
 7      .8987      -.0031           19      .7255      -.0043
 8      .8845      -.0056           20      .7111      -.0052
 9      .8703      -.0105           21      .6966      -.0114
10      .8559      -.0138           22      .6820      -.0108
11      .8414      -.0084           23      .6674      -.0102
12      .8270      -.0085           24      .6527      -.0096

------------------------------------------------------------------------
```

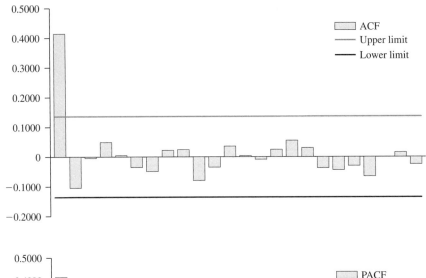

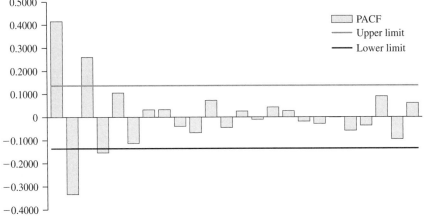

Obs	ACF	PACF	Obs	ACF	PACF
1	.4141	.4141	13	.0035	.0255
2	−.1046	−.3333	14	−.0087	−.0102
3	−.0047	.2594	15	.0246	.0424
4	.0486	−.1538	16	.0550	.0269
5	.0048	.1049	17	.0303	−.0188
6	−.0352	−.1130	18	−.0374	−.0286
7	−.0489	.0320	19	−.0442	−.0013
8	.0221	.0324	20	−.0301	−.0585
9	.0243	−.0396	21	−.0657	−.0367
10	−.0794	−.0677	22	.0003	.0894
11	−.0348	.0724	23	.0157	−.0963
12	.0357	−.0452	24	−.0248	.0603

The Box-Jenkins Identification Process

We are finally in a position to set down the Box-Jenkins methodology in a patterned format. The approach is an iterative one, in which we may loop through the process many times before reaching a model with which we are comfortable. The four steps of the Box-Jenkins process are outlined in Figure 7–8.

As a first step, the raw series is examined to *identify* one of the many available models that we will tentatively select as the best representation of this series. If the raw series is not stationary, it will initially be necessary to modify the original series (perhaps using first differences) to produce a stationary series to model.

The first step in the process is usually accomplished by using an *identify* function, which is a part of every standard Box-Jenkins software package; the identify function simply calculates and displays the autocorrelation and partial autocorrelation functions for the time series in question. Figure 7–2 shows these functions for the series in column 2 of Table 7–2 [which you will recall is the MA(1) data we produced from white noise]. By examining these correlograms we can observe the distinctive pattern (like that in frame *b* of Figure 7–1) that we earlier identified as representing an MA(1)-type model. It is this pattern produced by the identify function that leads us to the tentative choice of an MA(1) model. The general rules to be followed in this identification stage of the process can be summed up as follows:

1. If the autocorrelation function abruptly stops at some point—say, after *q* spikes—then the appropriate model is an MA(*q*) type.

As a first step, the raw series is examined to identify one of the many available models that we will tentatively select as the best representation of this series.

Figure 7–8

The Box-Jenkins Methodology

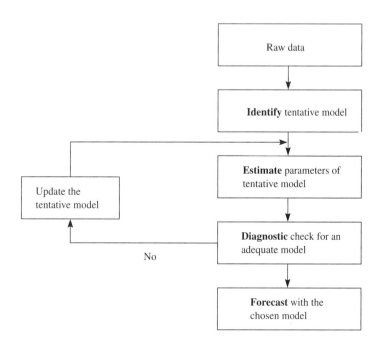

2. If the partial autocorrelation function abruptly stops at some point—say, after p spikes—then the appropriate model is an AR(p) type.

3. If neither function falls off abruptly, but both decline toward zero in some fashion, the appropriate model is an ARMA(p, q).

The second step in the process begins after the tentative model has been identified; the actual *estimation* of the parameters of the model is similar to fitting a standard regression to a set of data. If an MA(1) model had been tentatively identified as the "correct" model, we would fit the equation

$$Y_t = e_t + W_1 e_{t-1}$$

The ForecastX™ software package would estimate the value for W_1, using a mean-squared error minimization routine in order to select the optimal value.

Consider again the series in column 2 of Table 7–2; we "identified" these data as being distinctive of an MA(1)-type model when we examined the autocorrelation and partial autocorrelation functions in Figure 7–2. If we now specify an MA(1)-type model [this could also be written as an ARIMA(0, 0, 1) model] in the software package, the output will be as shown in Figure 7–9.

The third step in the Box-Jenkins process is to *diagnose* in order to determine whether the "correct" model has been chosen. In order to do this, again for the example in column 2 of Table 7–2, we will examine the autocorrelation function of the residuals produced by the estimation program; this is also presented in Figure 7–9. Recall that we originally produced the "raw data" series from white noise by specifying a function we knew would behave as an MA(1) model. That is, we passed an MA(1) box over the white noise and turned it into an MA(1) data set. If we now reverse the process and pass an MA(1) box over the contrived data set, we should wind up with white noise. A look at the autocorrelation function will tell us whether we have been left with just white noise, or whether we will have some unaccounted-for pattern in the series.

The second step in the process begins after the tentative model has been identified; the actual estimation *of the parameters of the model is similar to fitting a standard regression to a set of data.*

The third step in the Box-Jenkins process is to diagnose *in order to determine whether the "correct" model has been chosen.*

FIGURE 7–9

The MA(1) Model Estimate from ForecastX™ and Residual Autocorrelation Plot for the MA(1) Model Estimate (c7t2)

```
Audit Trail--Statistics

Accuracy Measure                              Value    Forecast Statistic          Value
---------------------------------------------------    ----------------------------------
AIC                                           75.20    Durbin-Watson                2.08
BIC                                           81.80    Mean                         0.80
Mean absolute percentage error (MAPE)         43.45%   Max                          1.64
Sum squared error (SSE)                       16.72    Min                          0.14
R-squared                                     35.63%   Sum squared deviation       25.97
Adjusted R-squared                            35.30%   Range                        1.50
Root-mean-squared error                        0.29    Ljung-Box                    7.33

Method Statistic                              Value
---------------------------------------------------
Method selected                       Box-Jenkins
Model selected           ARIMA(0,0,1) * (0,0,0)
T-test for constant                         39.07
T-test for nonseasonal MA                  -11.13
```

(continued)

FIGURE 7–9

(Continued)

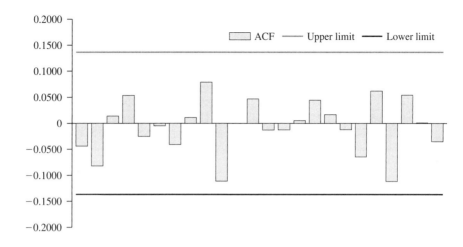

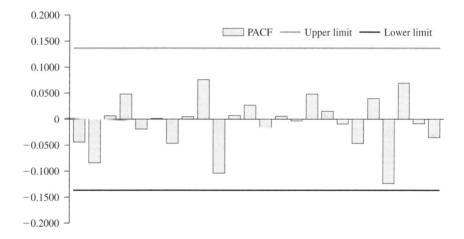

Obs	ACF	PACF	Obs	ACF	PACF
1	−.0440	−.0440	13	−.0128	−.0152
2	−.0820	−.0841	14	−.0125	.0055
3	.0140	.0064	15	.0053	−.0033
4	.0536	.0481	16	.0445	.0481
5	−.0254	−.0191	17	.0168	.0152
6	−.0048	.0013	18	−.0121	−.0093
7	−.0410	−.0463	19	−.0646	−.0466
8	.0113	.0049	20	.0620	.0396
9	.0789	.0761	21	−.1116	−.1239
10	−.1111	−.1040	22	.0542	.0694
11	.0000	.0072	23	.0010	−.0087
12	.0469	.0268	24	−.0350	−.0352

The autocorrelation function of the residual series in Figure 7–9 shows virtually no significant spikes. Apparently the MA(1)-type model we estimated was an accurate representation of the data. It is most importantly the autocorrelation function that tells the forecaster when the tentative model is actually the correct one. If you are left with only white noise in the residual series, the model chosen is likely the correct one.

A second test for the correctness of the model (but again, not a definitive test) is the Ljung-Box-Pierce Q statistic. This is referred to simply as the *Ljung-Box statistic* in the ForecastX™ printout. The statistic is used to perform a chi-square test on the autocorrelations of the residuals (or error terms). The test statistic is

$$Q_m = n(n + 2)\sum_{k=1}^{m} \frac{r_k^2}{n - k}$$

which is approximately distributed as a chi-square distribution with $m - p - q$ degrees of freedom, where

n = the number of observations in the time series

k = the particular time lag to be checked

m = the number of time lags to be tested

r_k = sample autocorrelation function of the kth residual term

Values of Q for different k may be computed in a residual analysis. For an ARMA (p,q) model, the statistic Q is approximately chi-square distributed with $m - p - q$ degrees of freedom if the ARMA orders are correctly specified.

Thus the Ljung-Box statistic tests whether the residual autocorrelations as a set are significantly different from zero. If the residual autocorrelations are significantly different from zero, the model specification should be reformulated. Note that the ForecastX™ software automatically checks for a lag length of 12 if a nonseasonal model has been selected; if a seasonal model has been selected, the lag is set equal to four times the seasonal length (e.g., the lag would be set to 16 if the data were quarterly).

The Ljung-Box statistic calculated for the Figure 7–9 model is 7.33 for the first 12 autocorrelations (which result in 11 degrees of freedom). A check with the chi-square table (see the appendix to this chapter) shows the critical value to be *about* 17 at the 0.10 significance level. Since the calculated value is less than the table value, the model is considered appropriate; that is, we believe the residuals to be uncorrelated. If this is the correct model, the residuals should be normally distributed and independent of one another (i.e., the residuals should resemble white noise).

If either the check of the residual series autocorrelations or the Ljung-Box statistic test had shown the model to be inappropriate, the tentative model would have been updated by trying another variation of the possible models. In Box-Jenkins methodology it is possible for two or more models to be very similar in their fit of the data; Occam's razor would suggest that the simpler of the similar models be chosen for actual forecasting. It is important to realize that the selection of an ARIMA model is an art and not a science.

The ForecastX™ software will automatically select a model using Box-Jenkins methodology. The reported model may be examined in the two ways we have shown for checking the adequacy of the model: examine the residual autocorrelations and use the Ljung-Box test. Any model, whether chosen by the forecaster manually or selected automatically by the ForecastX™ algorithm, is not necessarily the optimal model.

The final step in the Box-Jenkins process is to actually *forecast* using the chosen model. ForecastX™ performs this function by substituting into the chosen model in much the same manner as a standard regression forecast would be made. It should be remembered that as forecasts are made more than one period into the future, the size of the forecast error is likely to become larger.

When new observations of the time series become available, the model should be reestimated and checked again by the Box-Jenkins process; it is quite likely that the parameters of the model will have to be recalculated, or perhaps a different model altogether will be chosen as the best representation of the series. Consistent errors observed in estimation as more data become available are an indication that the entire model may require a change.

The final step in the Box-Jenkins process is to actually forecast *using the chosen model.*

ARIMA: A Set of Numerical Examples

Example 1

Return to the first column of Table 7–2; this is the column containing white noise from which we constructed the other time series in the table. When we run an *identify* test on the white noise (that is, observe the autocorrelation and partial autocorrelation functions), we should be able to see that this column actually contains white noise. Figure 7–10 contains these correlograms; in each case there is no distinctive pattern of spikes, or significant but descending values as we observed with earlier time series.

In this case the appropriate model would be an ARIMA(0, 0, 0); in other words, the best forecast would just be the mean value of the original time series (which is about 0.47).

Example 2

The series in column 3 of Table 7–2 was constructed to be an AR(1) or ARIMA(1, 0, 0) model. When we examined the autocorrelation and partial autocorrelation functions in Figure 7–4, one of the characteristic patterns for an ARIMA(1, 0, 0) model appeared; in addition, no trend is apparent in the series and so it is likely that no differencing is required. We should then be able to specify an ARIMA(1, 0, 0) model and correctly model the time series.

Figure 7–11 presents the results from estimating an AR(1) or ARIMA(1, 0, 0) model. Two tests will determine whether this model is an appropriate model: first, the examination of the autocorrelation coefficients of the residual series, and second, the Ljung-Box statistic.

The autocorrelation function for the residual series shows no distinctive pattern; it appears to be white noise. This would imply that we have chosen the correct model because when the original time series is modified by the model only white noise remains.

FIGURE 7–10

*Autocorrelation
and Partial
Autocorrelation
Plots for the
White Noise Series
in Table 7–2
(Example 1)*
(c7t2)

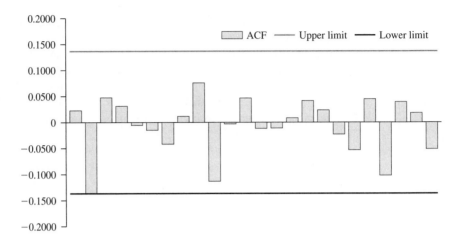

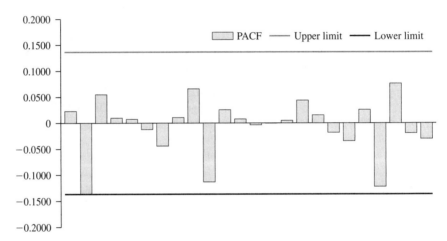

Obs	ACF	PACF	Obs	ACF	PACF
1	.0228	.0228	13	-.0117	-.0036
2	-.1366	-.1371	14	-.0112	-.0005
3	.0475	.0552	15	.0084	.0049
4	.0313	.0098	16	.0414	.0436
5	-.0055	.0074	17	.0235	.0153
6	-.0149	-.0122	18	-.0230	-.0183
7	-.0420	-.0440	19	-.0534	-.0344
8	.0117	.0107	20	.0447	.0257
9	.0757	.0661	21	-.1022	-.1223
10	-.1134	-.1132	22	.0392	.0763
11	-.0031	.0255	23	.0181	-.0193
12	.0465	.0078	24	-.0516	-.0302

FIGURE 7–11

*AR(1) Model
Estimate
(Example 2)
and Residual
Autocorrelation
Plot for the AR(1)
Model Estimate
(c7t2)*

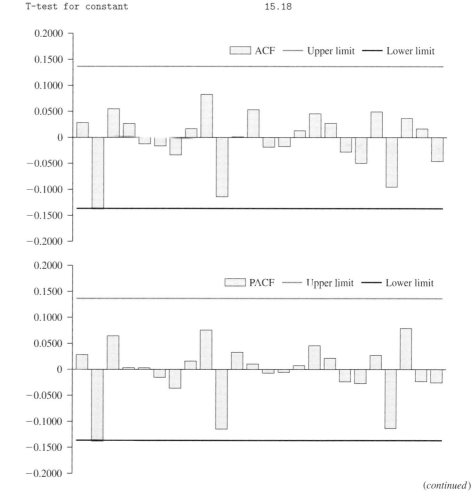

```
Audit Trail--Statistics
```

Accuracy Measure	Value
AIC	81.29
BIC	87.88
Mean absolute percentage error (MAPE)	33.12%
Sum squared error (SSE)	17.23
R-squared	23.75%
Adjusted R-squared	23.37%
Root-mean-squared error	0.29

Forecast Statistic	Value
Durbin-Watson	1.92
Mean	0.94
Max	1.71
Min	0.24
Sum squared deviation	22.60
Range	1.47
Ljung-Box	9.98

Method Statistic	Value
Method selected	Box-Jenkins
Model selected	ARIMA(1,0,0) * (0,0,0)
T-test for nonseasonal AR	8.00
T-test for constant	15.18

(continued)

FIGURE 7–11

(*Continued*)

```
------------------------------------------

Obs            ACF              PACF

------------------------------------------
 1            .0283            .0283
 2           -.1375           -.1384
 3            .0547            .0643
 4            .0266            .0033
 5           -.0124            .0030
 6           -.0163           -.0156
 7           -.0336           -.0365
 8            .0166            .0160
 9            .0827            .0755
10           -.1140           -.1148
11            .0011            .0330
12            .0531            .0104
13           -.0185           -.0071
14           -.0175           -.0055
15            .0129            .0074
16            .0454            .0456
17            .0272            .0217
18           -.0278           -.0240
19           -.0493           -.0274
20            .0492            .0272
21           -.0952           -.1135
22            .0366            .0787
23            .0167           -.0232
24           -.0457           -.0254

------------------------------------------
```

The Ljung-Box statistic offers further evidence that the correct model has been chosen. The calculated Ljung-Box Q is 9.98 for 12 autocorrelations (which give us 11 degrees of freedom). Checking the chi-square table shows the critical value to be *about* 17.275 at the 0.10 significance level. (See the appendix to this chapter for the chi-square table.) Since the calculated Ljung-Box is less than the table value, the model is termed appropriate.

Example 3

The AR(2) series in column 4 of Table 7–2 may be examined in like manner. Assume that we did not know the appropriate model for these data and examine the identification data presented in Figure 7–12. The autocorrelation function gradually falls over almost the entire 24 lags presented; the partial autocorrelation function shows two clear spikes (and possibly a third). The pattern looks like that in frame *c* of Figure 7–3; this identifies the tentative model as an AR(2) or ARIMA(2, 0, 0). No differencing *appears* to be needed, because there does not appear to be any trend.

When the AR(2) model is run, however, the coefficients fail to damp to zero, indicating a possible problem. In many cases like this, the use of a differencing term

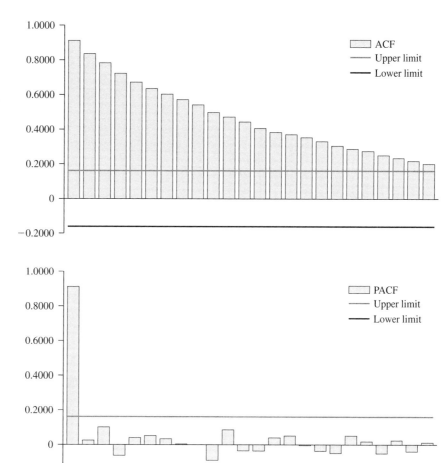

Obs	ACF	PACF		Obs	ACF	PACF
1	.9120	.9120		13	.4063	-.0358
2	.8360	.0252		14	.3834	.0399
3	.7833	.1012		15	.3710	.0511
4	.7222	-.0622		16	.3540	-.0045
5	.6715	.0406		17	.3313	-.0365
6	.6349	.0520		18	.3047	-.0493
7	.6030	.0335		19	.2871	.0514
8	.5716	.0042		20	.2746	.0182
9	.5416	-.0004		21	.2506	-.0508
10	.4979	-.0898		22	.2345	.0242
11	.4720	.0858		23	.2182	-.0394
12	.4435	-.0350		24	.2014	.0124

FIGURE 7–13

ARIMA(2, 1, 0)
Model Estimate
(Example 3)
and Residual
Autocorrelation
Plot for
ARIMA(2, 1, 0)
Model Estimate
(c7t2)

```
Audit Trail--Statistics
```

Accuracy Measure	Value
AIC	228.31
BIC	234.91
Mean absolute percentage error (MAPE)	9.42%
Sum squared error (SSE)	35.94
R-squared	83.61%
Adjusted R-squared	83.52%
Root-mean-squared error	0.42
Theil	0.83

Forecast Statistic	Value
Durbin-Watson	2.29
Mean	4.40
Max	6.36
Min	0.04
Sum squared deviation	219.27
Range	6.32
Ljung-Box	4.41

Method Statistic	Value
Method selected	Box-Jenkins
Model selected	ARIMA(2,1,0) * (0,0,0)
T-test for nonseasonal AR	-2.09
T-test for nonseasonal AR	7.04

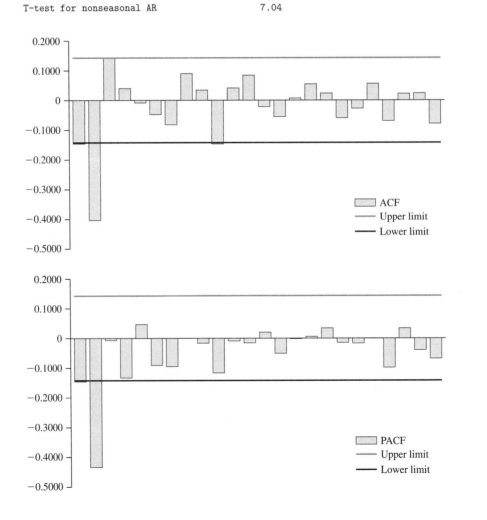

FIGURE 7–13

(*Continued*)

```
------------------------------------------
Obs           ACF              PACF
------------------------------------------
  1         -.1460            -.1460
  2         -.4033            -.4338
  3          .1423            -.0069
  4          .0405            -.1332
  5         -.0088             .0466
  6         -.0477            -.0909
  7         -.0819            -.0954
  8          .0904             .0004
  9          .0342            -.0163
 10         -.1466            -.1166
 11          .0411            -.0091
 12          .0845            -.0156
 13         -.0218             .0203
 14         -.0553            -.0506
 15          .0070            -.0017
 16          .0545             .0059
 17          .0234             .0342
 18         -.0596            -.0146
 19         -.0275            -.0168
 20          .0560            -.0006
 21         -.0694            -.0985
 22          .0221             .0339
 23          .0238            -.0396
 24         -.0787            -.0686
------------------------------------------
```

eliminates the problem. Figure 7–13 presents the results of applying an ARIMA(2, 1, 0) model to this series.

The autocorrelation function for the residuals shows largely white noise with some significant values in the 24 lags. The Ljung-Box statistic is 4.41 for the 12 autocorrelations (which give us 10 degrees of freedom). The table value from the chi-square table is about 15.987; this would indicate that the ARIMA(2, 1, 0) model chosen is an accurate representation of the series.

The reader may wish to allow ForecastX™ to select a model for this series. Because ForecastX™ uses an exhaustive iterative process, the results are often more satisfactory than manual selection. In this case, ForecastX™ selects an ARIMA(0, 1, 1) model that is significantly better than the model presented above.

Example 4

Consider finally the time-series data in Table 7–4 and assume we are given no clues to its origin. Applying the Box-Jenkins methodology, we would first use an identification function to examine the autocorrelation and partial autocorrelation functions; these are presented in Figure 7–14.

TABLE 7–4   Example 4 Data Series   (c7t4)

```
ARIMA
```
. . . .

1 . 0.160000	35 . 22.7092	69 . 45.2098	103 . 74.0750	137 . 99.5781	171 . 126.771
2 . 0.544113	36 . 23.8470	70 . 46.0228	104 . 74.7422	138 . 100.248	172 . 128.169
3 . 1.35744	37 . 24.4950	71 . 46.5587	105 . 75.1037	139 . 101.396	173 . 129.070
4 . 1.81007	38 . 24.7342	72 . 47.2307	106 . 76.1463	140 . 102.778	174 . 130.199
5 . 2.55541	39 . 25.0825	73 . 47.9890	107 . 76.9680	141 . 103.951	175 . 131.363
6 . 3.84012	40 . 25.6879	74 . 49.2088	108 . 77.2119	142 . 105.195	176 . 132.159
7 . 4.91087	41 . 26.9086	75 . 50.5534	109 . 78.1276	143 . 106.493	177 . 132.600
8 . 5.28469	42 . 27.6985	76 . 51.9717	110 . 78.8356	144 . 107.602	178 . 132.974
9 . 5.49273	43 . 27.9592	77 . 52.5793	111 . 79.2148	145 . 108.921	179 . 133.496
10 . 5.62030	44 . 29.0047	78 . 52.7499	112 . 79.4252	146 . 109.953	180 . 134.223
11 . 6.22645	45 . 30.5438	79 . 53.1405	113 . 80.0609	147 . 110.384	181 . 134.735
12 . 6.81976	46 . 31.8912	80 . 53.3826	114 . 81.1088	148 . 111.074	182 . 135.831
13 . 7.03361	47 . 32.7602	81 . 54.3375	115 . 81.5818	149 . 112.112	183 . 136.911
14 . 7.93600	48 . 33.0873	82 . 55.8604	116 . 82.5728	150 . 113.163	184 . 137.315
15 . 9.28220	49 . 33.2974	83 . 57.3969	117 . 83.4074	151 . 113.903	185 . 137.517
16 . 9.99665	50 . 33.7224	84 . 58.2719	118 . 84.0063	152 . 114.280	186 . 137.859
17 . 10.3492	51 . 34.4206	85 . 59.1758	119 . 84.8875	153 . 115.156	187 . 138.897
18 . 10.7372	52 . 35.0356	86 . 60.4877	120 . 86.0977	154 . 116.267	188 . 139.979
19 . 11.6537	53 . 35.6169	87 . 61.6198	121 . 87.1734	155 . 116.826	189 . 140.426
20 . 12.3986	54 . 35.9999	88 . 62.2831	122 . 88.2206	156 . 117.822	190 . 141.150
21 . 12.7508	55 . 36.4831	89 . 62.6991	123 . 88.9342	157 . 118.461	191 . 141.867
22 . 13.0273	56 . 36.8279	90 . 63.5748	124 . 89.6704	158 . 118.806	192 . 142.224
23 . 13.7149	57 . 37.0943	91 . 64.3452	125 . 90.6897	159 . 119.679	193 . 143.023
24 . 14.6099	58 . 37.6164	92 . 65.0968	126 . 91.4675	160 . 120.198	194 . 144.299
25 . 15.1324	59 . 38.7882	93 . 65.4967	127 . 91.7072	161 . 120.534	195 . 145.293
26 . 15.6525	60 . 39.9187	94 . 66.4900	128 . 92.1157	162 . 121.418	196 . 146.425
27 . 16.3994	61 . 40.9344	95 . 67.6714	129 . 92.9512	163 . 121.895	197 . 147.339
28 . 17.3193	62 . 41.5441	96 . 68.1611	130 . 93.4450	164 . 122.030	198 . 148.166
29 . 18.1561	63 . 42.5229	97 . 68.2980	131 . 94.4363	165 . 122.893	199 . 149.491
30 . 19.0496	64 . 43.1073	98 . 68.9562	132 . 95.6413	166 . 123.409	200 . 150.761
31 . 19.8106	65 . 43.4389	99 . 70.3170	133 . 96.2160	167 . 123.898	
32 . 20.7518	66 . 44.2401	100 . 71.5608	134 . 96.6762	168 . 124.924	
33 . 21.2347	67 . 44.6401	101 . 72.3279	135 . 97.2641	169 . 125.618	
34 . 21.5877	68 . 44.7896	102 . 73.2702	136 . 98.4736	170 . 125.903	

The autocorrelation function in Figure 7–14 is entirely characteristic of a series with a trend; that is, it shows dominant autocorrelations for the 24 lags shown. Look at the actual numbers in the original series in Table 7–4 and observe how they gradually creep upward in value. These data apparently have a trend and are therefore nonstationary. Before the Box-Jenkins process can be continued, the series must be transformed to a stationary series. The most common method of achieving stationarity is to take first differences of the original series; taking these first differences and again applying the identification program to the resulting series gives the autocorrelation and partial autocorrelation functions in Figure 7–15.

FIGURE 7–14

Autocorrelation and Partial Autocorrelation Plots for the Series in Table 7–4 (Example 4) (c7t4)

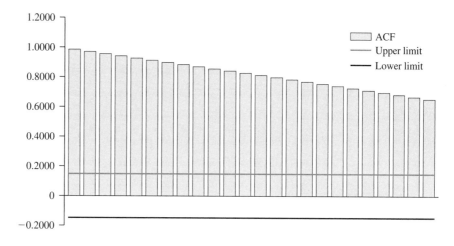

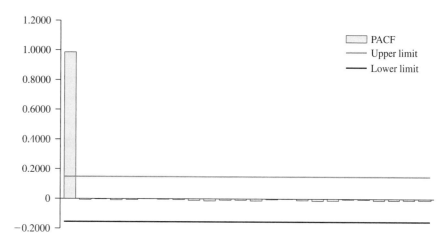

Obs	ACF	PACF	Obs	ACF	PACF
1	.9854	.9854	13	.8124	-.0129
2	.9707	-.0070	14	.7979	-.0043
3	.9562	-.0028	15	.7836	-.0017
4	.9417	-.0087	16	.7692	-.0104
5	.9272	-.0063	17	.7547	-.0138
6	.9129	-.0013	18	.7401	-.0124
7	.8987	-.0033	19	.7255	-.0043
8	.8845	-.0057	20	.7111	-.0051
9	.8703	-.0102	21	.6966	-.0116
10	.8559	-.0139	22	.6820	-.0107
11	.8414	-.0083	23	.6674	-.0100
12	.8270	-.0084	24	.6527	-.0096

FIGURE 7–15

*Autocorrelation
and Partial
Autocorrelation
Plots for the Series
in Table 7–4 after
First Differences
Have Been Taken
(Example 4)*
(c7t4)

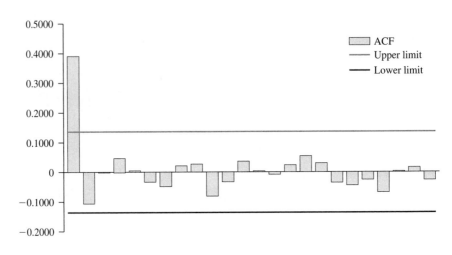

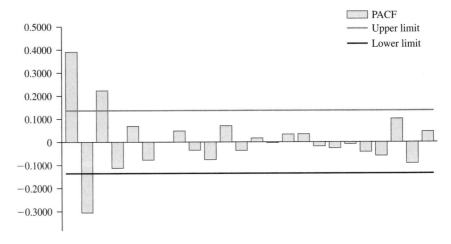

Obs	ACF	PACF	Obs	ACF	PACF
1	.3906	.3906	13	.0032	.0168
2	−.1063	−.3054	14	−.0085	−.0037
3	−.0021	.2231	15	.0233	.0333
4	.0481	−.1128	16	.0537	.0341
5	.0046	.0684	17	.0296	−.0186
6	−.0336	−.0772	18	−.0358	−.0266
7	−.0488	−.0006	19	−.0451	−.0084
8	.0209	.0480	20	−.0260	−.0424
9	.0266	−.0352	21	−.0684	−.0593
10	−.0812	−.0763	22	.0027	.1007
11	−.0333	.0702	23	.0158	−.0923
12	.0359	−.0366	24	−.0269	.0452

The pattern exhibited here (after differencing) is similar to frame *d* of Figure 7–5; perhaps the model is a mixed model, with both AR and MA terms in addition to the differencing required to make the series stationary. Figure 7–16 displays the results of estimating an ARIMA(3, 1, 2), that is, a model with three AR terms, one degree of differencing, and two MA terms.

FIGURE 7–16

ARIMA(3, 1, 2) Model Estimate (Example 4) and Residual Autocorrelation Plot for the ARIMA(3, 1, 2) Model Estimate (c7t4)

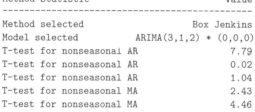

Audit Trail--Statistics

Accuracy Measure	Value		Forecast Statistic	Value
AIC	84.73		Durbin-Watson	1.84
BIC	101.22		Mean	72.55
Mean absolute percentage error (MAPE)	1.12%		Max	150.76
Sum squared error (SSE)	17.01		Min	0.16
R-squared	100.00%		Sum squared deviation	392,388.59
Adjusted R-squared	100.00%		Range	150.60
Root-mean-squared error	0.29		Ljung-Box	5.14

Method Statistic	Value
Method selected	Box Jenkins
Model selected	ARIMA(3,1,2) * (0,0,0)
T-test for nonseasonal AR	7.79
T-test for nonseasonal AR	0.02
T-test for nonseasonal AR	1.04
T-test for nonseasonal MA	2.43
T-test for nonseasonal MA	4.46

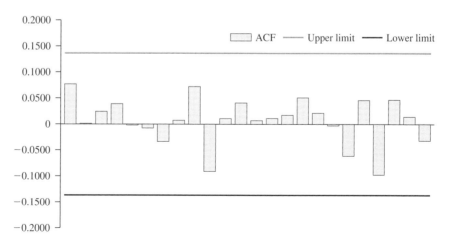

(continued)

FIGURE 7–16

(*Continued*)

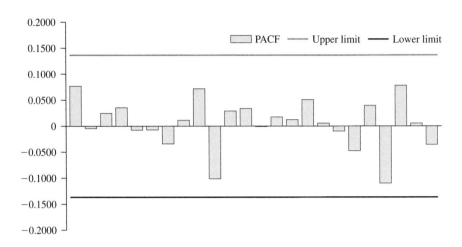

Obs	ACF	PACF
1	.0769	.0769
2	.0013	-.0046
3	.0244	.0248
4	.0390	.0355
5	-.0019	-.0076
6	-.0075	-.0072
7	-.0334	-.0343
8	.0074	.0114
9	.0721	.0718
10	-.0910	-.1013
11	.0108	.0291
12	.0410	.0340
13	.0071	-.0009
14	.0112	.0175
15	.0175	.0125
16	.0510	.0510
17	.0214	.0057
18	-.0027	-.0099
19	-.0614	-.0474
20	.0460	.0399
21	-.0976	-.1097
22	.0469	.0784
23	.0142	.0054
24	-.0317	-.0355

The results in the residual series autocorrelation function indicate that only white noise remains after applying the model. The Ljung-Box statistic is 5.14 for the 12 autocorrelations. The value from the chi-square table is about 12.017 for 7 degrees of freedom. We would then accept the ARIMA(3, 1, 1) model specification as a "correct" forecasting model for this series.

Forecasting Seasonal Time Series

In many actual business situations the time series to be forecast are quite seasonal. Recall that seasonality refers to a consistent shape in the series that recurs with some periodic regularity (sales of lawn mowers during summer months, for instance, are always higher than in winter months). This seasonality can cause some problems in the ARIMA process, since a model fitted to such a series would likely have a very high order. If monthly data were used and the seasonality occurred in every 12th month, the order of the model might be 12 or more. There is a process for estimating "seasonal MA" and "seasonal AR" terms for the ARIMA process along with seasonal differencing, but the details of estimating such terms are quite complicated. We will use the ability of ForecastX™ to estimate these parameters with the domestic car sales series.

Seasonality can cause some problems in the ARIMA process, since a model fitted to such a series would likely have a very high order.

Domestic Car Sales

Recall once again that the domestic car sales figures we have examined in past chapters show little trend and appear to exhibit a high degree of seasonality. The mean of the series also shifts significantly from period to period because of a strong seasonal variation. We will allow ForecastX™ to choose seasonal AR and MA terms as appropriate.

The domestic car sales data are seen again to be very seasonal. Quarters one and four appear to be "off" quarters for car sales, while quarter two is about 10 percent above average in sales.

Examining the autocorrelation and partial autocorrelation structure (Figure 7–17A), note the clear pattern of the autocorrelation plot. This pattern is very much like the one in Table 7–6 and this suggests that the series is nonstationary. Using a single degree of differencing on this series eliminates the pattern of nonstationarity. See Figure 7–17B and examine the plot; the nonstationarity characteristic is now absent and the data appear to be stationary. The high degree of seasonality is now clearly evident in the significant spikes in the autocorrelation function every four quarters.

Figure 7–18 is the estimation for an ARIMA(2, 0, 1) (0, 0, 2) model with a seasonal MA term *and second-degree seasonal differencing*. The residual plot for the first 24 lags of the residuals is also shown in Figure 7–18. Note that we now appear to have only white noise in the residuals, and so the choice of model is probably an accurate one. The Ljung-Box statistic for the first 16 lags is 13.48 and confirms the accuracy of the model.

Calculating the RMSE for the model gives 152.05. We can compare this with our previous results using other forecasting techniques.

FIGURE 7–17A

Autocorrelation and Partial Autocorrelation Plots for the Domestic Car Sales Series. Note That the Series Appears to Be Nonstationary. (c7f17)

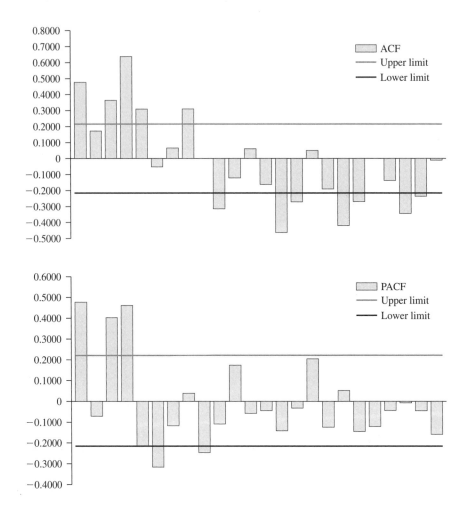

Obs	ACF	PACF	Obs	ACF	PACF
1	.4769	.4769	13	−.1621	−.0447
2	.1724	−.0713	14	−.4633	−.1421
3	.3636	.4027	15	−.2711	−.0323
4	.6376	.4614	16	.0498	.2041
5	.3090	−.2149	17	−.1903	−.1248
6	−.0525	−.3161	18	−.4199	.0523
7	.0662	−.1177	19	−.2695	−.1456
8	.3097	.0388	20	.0004	−.1217
9	−.0006	−.2470	21	−.1377	−.0437
10	−.3145	−.1094	22	−.3444	−.0073
11	−.1216	.1736	23	−.2359	−.0450
12	.0602	−.0575	24	−.0110	−.1591

FIGURE 7–17B

Autocorrelation and Partial Autocorrelation Plots for the Domestic Car Sales Series after First-Degree Differencing. Note That the Series Now Appears to Be Stationary. (c7f17)

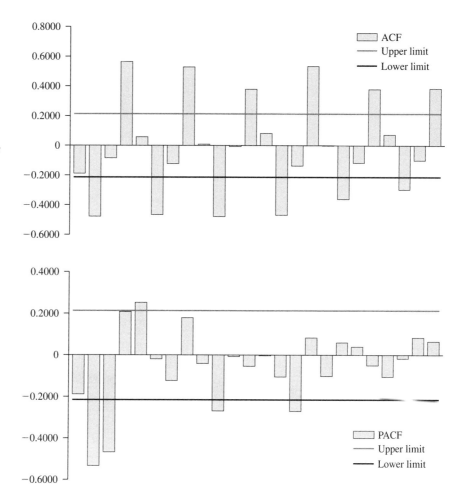

Obs	ACF	PACF	Obs	ACF	PACF
1	−.1884	−.1884	13	.0830	−.0033
2	−.4779	−.5323	14	−.4687	−.1048
3	−.0847	−.4671	15	−.1371	−.2703
4	.5650	.2085	16	.5339	.0835
5	.0571	.2525	17	−.0023	−.1022
6	−.4668	−.0196	18	−.3611	.0601
7	−.1230	−.1232	19	−.1178	.0399
8	.5279	.1792	20	.3782	−.0507
9	.0084	−.0411	21	.0729	−.1057
10	−.4791	−.2686	22	−.2975	−.0178
11	−.0068	−.0072	23	−.1011	.0833
12	.3792	−.0539	24	.3827	.0651

FIGURE 7–18

Domestic Car Sales Model Estimate of an ARIMA(2, 0, 1) (0, 0, 2) Model (c7f17)

Audit Trail--Statistics

Accuracy Measure	Value	Forecast Statistic	Value
AIC	1,017.13	Durbin-Watson	1.96
BIC	1,031.27	Mean	1,748.21
Mean absolute percentage error (MAPE)	7.04%	Standard deviation	223.30
R-squared	53.03%	Max	2,272.60
Adjusted R-squared	49.77%	Min	1,281.30
Root-mean-squared error	152.05	Mode	1,878.20
Theil	0.69	Range	991.30
		Ljung-Box	13.48

Method Statistic	Value
Method selected	Box Jenkins
Model selected	ARIMA(2,0,1) * (0,0,2)
T-test for nonseasonal AR	0.05
T-test for nonseasonal AR	0.02
T-test for constant	0.01
T-test for nonseasonal MA	0.00
T-test for seasonal MA	-1.34
T-test for seasonal MA	-1.02

Residual Autocorrelation and Partial Autocorrelation Plots for the ARIMA(1, 1, 0) (1, 2, 1) Model Estimate

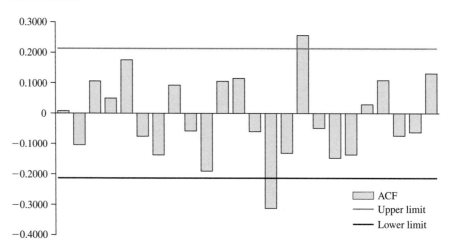

(continued)

FIGURE 7–18
(*Continued*)

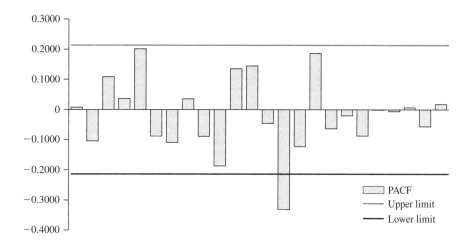

```
-------------------------------------------
Obs            ACF                 PACF
-------------------------------------------
  1           .0078                .0078
  2          -.1043               -.1044
  3           .1055                .1084
  4           .0496                .0365
  5           .1756                .2013
  6          -.0756               -.0882
  7          -.1372               -.1093
  8           .0924                .0354
  9          -.0579               -.0886
 10          -.1902               -.1868
 11           .1052                .1359
 12           .1148                .1451
 13          -.0605               -.0454
 14          -.3126               -.3310
 15          -.1312               -.1228
 16           .2564                .1865
 17          -.0492               -.0630
 18          -.1472               -.0200
 19          -.1362               -.0868
 20           .0293               -.0011
 21           .1086               -.0060
 22          -.0741                .0069
 23          -.0629               -.0559
 24           .1310                .0178
-------------------------------------------
```

Summary Table of RMSEs for DCS

Chapter	Method	Period	RMSE
1	Naive—with 4-period lag	Historical	187.13
		Holdout	112.26
2	Not applicable		
3	Winters' exponential smoothing	Historical	144.45
		Holdout	61.79
	Holt's with seasonal adjustment	Historical	200.46
		Holdout	62.21
4	Simple regression model using seasonally adjusted DCS as a function of the University of Michigan Index of Consumer Sentiment	Historical	217.15
		Holdout	132.30
5	Multiple regression	Historical	107.89
		Holdout	162.59
6	Time-series decomposition	Historical	195.5
		Holdout	181.2
7	ARIMA(2, 0, 1)(0, 0, 2)	Historical	152.05
		Holdout	102.28

Comments from the Field

An Overview of INTELSAT Forecasting[1]
INTELSAT

At the International Telecommunications Satellite Organization (INTELSAT), forecasting techniques have been employed to assist in developing estimates of future demand for international satellite telecommunications. This is accomplished by using as a base the demand projections provided by each of the approximately 200 worldwide telecommunications entities located within 130 countries and territories. Every year, a new 15-year projection, which is needed for long-range financial and new spacecraft planning, is developed.

The provision of international telephone satellite trunk circuits represents a fundamental portion of INTELSAT business. It is practically impossible for INTELSAT to attempt to assemble accurate, worldwide point-to-point forecasts, because of the number of technical and economic details required on each system user. In order to develop such forecasts,

[1]This overview of forecasting at INTELSAT was provided by Martin J. Kelinsky, forecasting manager, INTELSAT, Washington, DC.

Comments from the Field concluded

an annual global traffic meeting (GTM) is held, attended by each of the system users. During this week-long meeting, users can discuss and negotiate with each of their worldwide correspondents their estimates of future mutual traffic demand. These discussions are based on the network planning and preliminary traffic projections each system user develops prior to the GTM. The GTM delegates submit their mutually agreed forecasts as they are completed, and these are entered into a database (Oracle) for subsequent analysis and processing.

In developing their forecast of satellite circuits, established system users will typically make use of quantitative forecasting methods, because there exists a historical base of measured or known traffic. In the new and emerging countries, such as the members of the Commonwealth of Independent States (formerly USSR), where there are either few data or none available, the less-experienced system users tend to accept the suggestions of their larger, more established correspondent countries. In some instances, user forecast estimates will not be determined from an analysis of computed demand, but decided by the funds projected to be available to purchase the necessary telecommunications equipment.

An additional significant service category that INTELSAT offers to telecommunications entities is leases for satellite capacity. These users' inputs describe the technical operating qualities needed for each lease, along with information on anticipated start date, duration, and renewal potential. These requests from all users are aggregated and sorted by geographic region. The aggregated near-term user data can provide, on a systemwide basis, fairly accurate estimates of the potential growth trends to be expected. The 15-year, long-term demand for leases is developed using nonlinear regression analysis, historical trend analysis, and the three- to five-year near-term growth rate projections. Studies indicate that historically, these projected trends closely correlate to the realized system usages.

Recently, work was begun to look into methodologies to supplement the forecasts as provided by the system users. Two approaches that are currently being investigated are econometric demand models and stochastic time-series models. The development of an econometric model is recognized as a considerable endeavor, and one method that is being considered is to define the model in terms of geographic groups of countries so as to limit the complexity of the demand function.

As a specific example of INTELSAT's forecasting, consider the occasional-use television channel-hours provided to TV broadcasters needing satellites to relay news coverage around the world. Data on such occasional-use television satellite use date back to 1983. A Box-Jenkins second-order autoregressive integrated moving-average model [ARIMA (2, 1, 1)] was applied to the quarterly data of usage statistics from 1983 through 1992Q4. The parameters of the model were estimated by excluding the 1992 data (holdout period), and an "ex-post" forecast was developed and compared with the 1992 period. Having accepted the model performance, an "ex-ante" forecast, for a future time period, was generated.

For the future, work will continue on evaluation and development of forecasting models appropriate to each of INTELSAT's many telecommunications services.

INTEGRATIVE CASE
FORECASTING SALES OF THE GAP

Case Questions

1. From your previous experience plotting The Gap sales over time, what ARIMA techniques should you keep in mind when approaching this data?

2. Prepare a plot of the autocorrelation and partial autocorrelation coefficients of The Gap sales data. Does this correlogram suggest an ARIMA approach that could be used for forecasting The Gap sales?

3. Apply a model suggested by the correlogram plot and calculate the RMSE for your forecast of the four quarters of 1999. Recall that the actual 1999 sales (in thousands) were: Quarter 1—2,277,700; Quarter 2—2,453,300; Quarter 3—3,045,386; Quarter 4—3,858,939.

Solutions to Case Questions

1. The seasonal pattern and trend should now be familiar. These data will not be stationary and some adjustment will have to be made to obtain stationarity. The strong seasonal pattern could require some adjustment. It is also the case that the pattern of the data is quite regular and some ARIMA technique should do an excellent job of fitting a model.

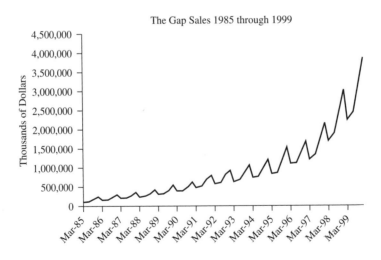

The Gap Sales 1985 through 1999

2. The correlogram for the unadjusted Gap sales shows the possibility of nonstationarity (see Figure 7–19). Since we already know that the data are seasonal, the nonstationarity and the seasonality might be accounted for by using seasonal differencing.

FIGURE 7–19

Autocorrelation and Partial Autocorrelation Plots for The Gap Sales (For the Historical Period of 1985Q1 through 1988Q4) (c7gap)

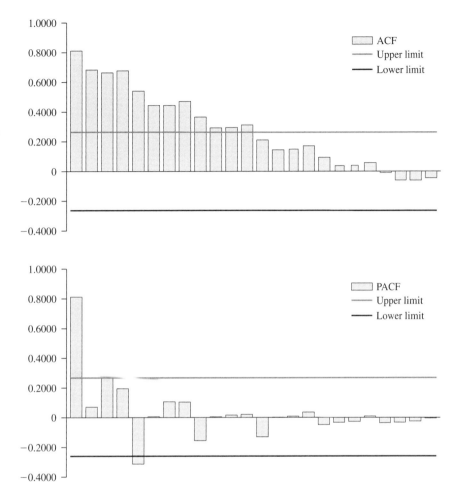

Obs	ACF	PACF	Obs	ACF	PACF
1	.8116	.8116	13	.2103	-.1297
2	.6827	.0705	14	.1442	.0018
3	.6631	.2676	15	.1488	.0086
4	.6768	.1953	16	.1707	.0368
5	.5407	-.3122	17	.0936	-.0487
6	.4445	.0060	18	.0377	-.0337
7	.4446	.1075	19	.0394	-.0275
8	.4709	.1049	20	.0577	.0098
9	.3660	-.1554	21	-.0087	-.0368
10	.2932	.0048	22	-.0602	-.0334
11	.2956	.0164	23	-.0608	-.0245
12	.3124	.0207	24	-.0449	-.0042

3. While a number of models may perform quite well, ARIMA(1, 0, 1) (0, 1, 0) seems to provide a good fit. The model estimation indicates that the Ljung-Box statistic is 1.01 for the 16 autocorrelations, which confirms the accuracy of the model.

The correlogram of the residuals to the model shows only white noise (see Figure 7–20).

The actual and predicted values for 1999Q3 through 2000Q2 are shown below. The RMSE for these four quarters is: RMSE = 178,559. This is about a 5.7 percent error based on the average quarterly sales for the year (12,335,536).

FIGURE 7–20

The Gap Sales Model Residual Autocorrelation and Partial Autocorrelation Plots for the ARIMA(1, 0, 1) (0, 1, 0) Model Estimate   (c7gap)

Audit Trail--Statistics

Accuracy Measure	Value
AIC	1,369.77
BIC	1,373.82
Mean absolute percentage error (MAPE)	3.88%
Sum squared error (SSE)	128,121,745,352
R-squared	99.41%
Adjusted R-squared	99.40%
Root-mean-squared error	47,831.88
Theil	0.21

Forecast Statistic	Value
Durbin-Watson	1.54
Mean	804,816.13
Max	3,029.900.00
Min	105,715.00
Sum squared deviation	21,706,814,750,732
Range	2,924,185.00
Ljung-Box	8.10

Method Statistic	Value
Method selected	Box-Jenkins
Model selected	ARIMA(1,0,1) * (0,1,0)
T-test for nonseasonal AR	18.98
T-test for nonseasonal MA	−1.13

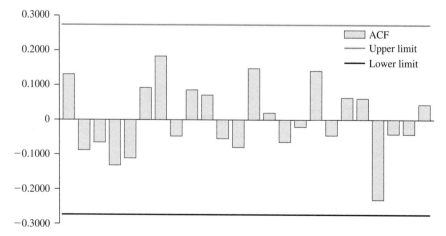

(continued)

FIGURE 7–20

(*Continued*)

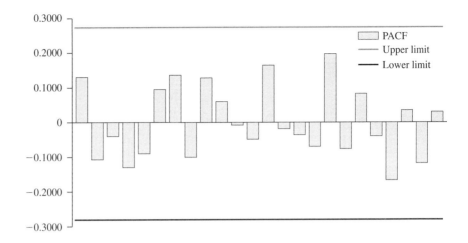

Obs	ACF	PACF	Obs	ACF	PACF
1	.1305	.1305	13	.1477	.1640
2	-.0882	-.1071	14	.0199	-.0186
3	-.0657	-.0402	15	-.0647	-.0365
4	-.1315	-.1298	16	.0211	-.0702
5	-.1111	-.0900	17	.1409	.1971
6	.0923	.0951	18	-.0452	-.0768
7	.1836	.1360	19	.0637	.0824
8	-.0474	-.1006	20	.0615	-.0399
9	.0861	.1277	21	-.2310	-.1668
10	.0713	.0599	22	-.0414	.0351
11	-.0546	-.0081	23	-.0421	-.1182
12	-.0798	-.0492	24	.0442	.0301

Date	The Gap Sales	Forecast	Date	The Gap Sales	Forecast
Mar-1989	105,715.00	105,715.00	Dec-1990	298,469.00	289,423.75
Jun-1989	120,136.00	120,136.00	Mar-1991	211,060.00	198,672.16
Sep-1989	181,669.00	181,669.00	Jun-1991	217,753.00	217,827.22
Dec-1989	239,813.00	239,813.00	Sep-1991	273,616.00	293,612.73
Mar-1990	159,980.00	157,571.01	Dec-1991	359,592.00	354,542.27
Jun-1990	164,760.00	179,278.16	Mar-1992	241,348.00	253,110.14
Sep-1990	224,800.00	241,169.89	Jun-1992	264,328.00	244,928.32

(*continued*)

FIGURE 7–20

(*Concluded*)

Date	The Gap Sales	Forecast	Date	The Gap Sales	Forecast
Sep-1992	322,752.00	335,213.42	Jun-1998	773,131.00	807,261.98
Dec-1992	423,669.00	417,606.16	Sep-1998	988,346.00	987,940.40
Mar-1993	309,925.00	283,327.20	Dec-1998	1,209,790.00	1,161,466.61
Jun-1993	325,939.00	342,818.86	Mar-1999	848,688.00	860,912.53
Sep-1993	405,601.00	389,970.78	Jun-1999	868,514.00	865,641.64
Dec-1993	545,131.00	532,069.50	Sep-1999	1,155,930.00	1,105,689.32
Mar-1994	402,368.00	396,754.25	Dec-1999	1,522,120.00	1,419,929.92
Jun-1994	404,996.00	419,875.08	Mar-2000	1,113,150.00	1,074,401.35
Sep-1994	501,690.00	495,302.13	Jun-2000	1,120,340.00	1,135,347.86
Dec-1994	624,726.00	670,220.24	Sep-2000	1,383,000.00	1,470,723.51
Mar-1995	490,300.00	451,191.83	Dec-2000	1,667,900.00	1,782,262.24
Jun-1995	523,056.00	498,773.32	Mar-2001	1,231,186.00	1,196,843.00
Sep-1995	702,052.00	647,978.11	Jun-2001	1,345,221.00	1,241,873.07
Dec-1995	803,485.00	877,833.97	Sep-2001	1,765,939.00	1,678,161.52
Mar-1996	588,864.00	611,487.05	Dec-2001	2,165,479.00	2,132,555.60
Jun-1996	614,114.00	618,044.09	Mar-2002	1,719,712.00	1,586,534.90
Sep-1996	827,222.00	817,529.61	Jun-2002	1,904,970.00	1,887,093.24
Dec-1996	930,209.00	942,750.61	Sep-2002	2,399,900.00	2,469,681.48
Mar-1997	643,580.00	675,481.87	Dec-2002	3,029,900.00	2,886,185.91
Jun-1997	693,192.00	661,336.33	Mar-2003	2,277,700.00	2,398,819.90
Sep-1997	898,677.00	939,006.20	Jun-2003	2,453,300.00	2,620,253.94	← Predicted values
Dec-1997	1,060,230.00	997,014.13	Sep-2003	3,045,386.00	3,257,001.95
Mar-1998	751,670.00	739,801.25	Dec-2003	3,858,939.00	4,059,460.48

The Gap Sales and Forecast

Summary Table of RMSEs for The Gap Sales

Chapter	Method	Period	RMSE
1	Naive—with 4-period lag	Historical	233,092
		Holdout	654,976
2	Not applicable		
3	Winters' exponential smoothing	Historical	49,479
		Holdout	99,493
	Holt's exponential smoothing with seasonal readjustment	Historical	42,388
		Holdout	74,034
4	Linear trend of deseasonalized data with forecast	Historical	
		Holdout	
5	Multiple regression	Historical	114,995
		Holdout	510,068
6	Time-series decomposition	Historical	44,013
		Holdout	110,497
7	ARIMA(1, 0, 1) (0, 1, 0)	Historical	47,831
		Holdout	178,559

USING FORECASTX™ TO MAKE ARIMA (BOX-JENKINS) FORECASTS

What follows is a brief discussion of how to use ForecastX™ for preparing an ARIMA (Box-Jenkins) forecast. As with other methods, start with your data in an Excel spreadsheet in column format, such as the sample of The Gap data shown in the table below. Once you have your data in this format, while in Excel highlight the data you want to use, then start ForecastX™. The dialog box to the right of the table appears.

A Sample of The Gap Data in Column Format

Date	The Gap Sales ($000)
Mar-1994	751,670
Jun-1994	773,131
Sep-1994	988,346
Dec-1994	1,209,790
Mar-1995	848,688
Jun-1995	868,514
Sep-1995	1,155,930
Dec-1995	1,522,120
Mar-1996	1,113,150
Jun-1996	1,120,340
Sep-1996	1,383,000
Dec-1996	1,667,900
Mar-1997	1,231,186
Jun-1997	1,345,221
Sep-1997	1,765,939
Dec-1997	2,165,479
Mar-1998	1,719,712
Jun-1998	1,904,970
Sep-1998	2,399,900
Dec-1998	3,029,900

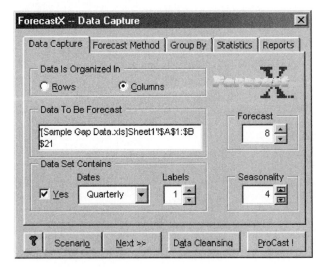

Set the **Dates** window to the periodicity of your data (**Quarterly** for this example), then click the **Forecast Method** tab at the top and the following appears.

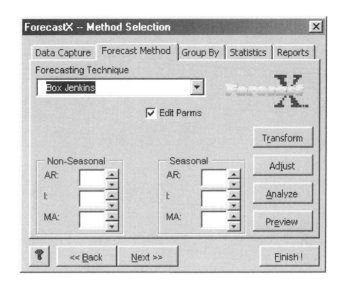

Click the down arrow in the **Forecasting Technique** window and select **Box Jenkins.** You can enter values for the **AR**, **I**, and **MA** terms, or you can leave those spaces blank and let ForecastX™ select the best set of values.

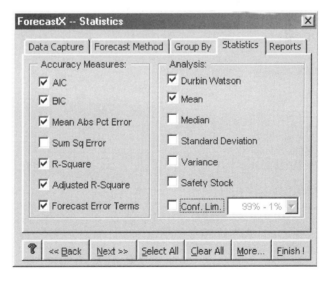

Next click the **Statistics** tab and the **Statistics** dialog box will appear.

Here you select the statistics you want to have reported. You will want to experiment with various selections. Use the **More** button to select the **Ljung-Box** statistic.

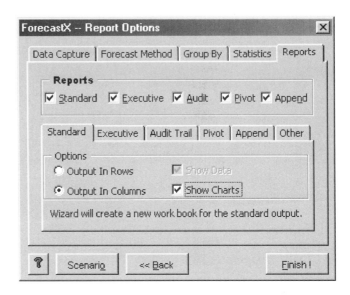

Next click the **Reports** tab and the **Report Options** dialog box will appear.

As you place a check next to each of the five boxes for various reports, the options available in that report will appear below. For example, in the **Standard** report box you will normally check **Output In Columns** and **Show Charts.**

Again you will want to experiment with the various reports to get a feel for the ones that will give you the output you want for your specific application.

After you click **Finish!** in the lower right corner, ForecastX™ will complete the forecast, and as part of the output, will identify the exact model used. Reports will be put in new Excel workbooks—Book 2, Book 3, and so forth. The numbers of the Books will vary depending on what you have done in Excel up to that point.

Suggested Readings

Armstrong, Scott J.; and Edward J. Lusk. "Research on the Accuracy of Alternative Extrapolation Models: Analysis of a Forecasting Competition Through Open Peer Review." *Journal of Forecasting* 2 (1983), pp. 259–62.

Box, G.; and G. Jenkins. *Time Series Analysis: Forecasting and Control.* Rev. cd. San Francisco: Holden-Day, 1976.

Brandon, Charles H.; Jeffrey E. Jarrett; and Saleha Khumawala. "Revising Forecasts of Accounting Earnings: A Comparison with the Box-Jenkins Method." *Management Science* 29 (1983), pp. 256–63.

Brown, Lawrence D.; and Michael S. Rozeff. "The Superiority of Analyst Forecasts as Measures of Expectations: Evidence from Earnings." *Journal of Finance* 33 (1978), pp. 1–16.

Chatfield, C.; and D. L. Prothero. "Box-Jenkins Seasonal Forecasting Problems in a Case Study." *Journal of the Royal Statistical Society* Series A 136 (1973), pp. 295–352.

Hill, Gareth; and Robert Fildes. "The Accuracy of Extrapolation Methods: An Automatic Box-Jenkins Package (SIFT)." *Journal of Forecasting* 3 (1984), pp. 319–23.

Libert, G. "The M-Competition with a Fully Automatic Box-Jenkins Procedure." *Journal of Forecasting* 3 (1984), pp. 325–28.

Ludlow, Jorge; and Walter Enders. "Estimating Non-Linear ARMA Models Using Fourier Coefficients." *International Journal of Forecasting* 16, no. 3 (July–September 2000), pp. 333–47.

Lusk, Edward J.; and Joao S. Neves. "A Comparative ARIMA Analysis of the 111 Series of the Makridakis Competition." *Journal of Forecasting* 3 (1984), pp. 329–32.

Nelson, Charles R. *Applied Time Series Analysis for Managerial Forecasting.* San Francisco: Holden-Day, 1973.

Pankratz, Alan. *Forecasting with Univariate Box-Jenkins Models.* New York: John Wiley & Sons, 1983.

Peña, Daniel. "George Box: An Interview with the International Journal of Forecasting." *International Journal of Forecasting* 17, no. 1 (January–March 2001), pp. 1–9.

Pindyck, Robert S.; and Daniel L. Rubinfeld. *Econometric Models and Economic Forecasts.* 3rd ed. New York: McGraw-Hill, 1991.

Exercises

1. A student collects data on the use of the university library on an hourly basis for eight consecutive Mondays. What type of seasonality would you expect to find in these data?

2. When would you use differencing and when would you employ seasonal differencing?

3. Evaluate the following statement: "If an ARIMA model is properly constructed, it has residual autocorrelations that are all equal to zero."

4. Of what use is the chi-square test as applied to residual autocorrelations?

5. *a.* Calculate and display the first 50 autocorrelations for the four data series in the accompanying table, labeled A, B, C, and D; consider each of the four data series to be a quarterly time series. How many of the autocorrelations fall outside the two-standard-deviation range (positive or negative)?

   b. Is there a pattern to those autocorrelation coefficients falling outside the two-standard-deviation range?

   c. Calculate and display the first 50 partial autocorrelations for the 100 time-series observations. How many of the partial autocorrelation coefficients fall outside the two-standard-deviation range?

   d. Is there a pattern to those partial autocorrelation coefficients falling outside the two-standard-deviation range?

   e. Estimate the appropriate model as determined from your inspections carried out in parts *a* through *d* and forecast for four quarters into the future. Calculate the RMSE for each model.

EXERCISE 5   Four Data Series

A	B	C	D	A	B	C	D
1.62	0.38	0.68	1.11	0.77	0.26	3.43	20.21
1.55	1.02	0.71	2.27	1.18	0.21	3.69	20.85
1.59	0.70	1.22	3.71	1.26	1.06	3.85	21.69
1.55	1.16	1.29	4.52	0.81	1.27	4.20	22.69
1.10	1.11	1.53	5.04	1.05	1.63	4.05	23.56
0.82	0.93	1.52	6.10	0.63	0.98	4.33	24.65
1.06	1.32	1.53	7.61	0.71	0.98	4.76	25.92
0.69	0.78	2.08	8.89	1.02	1.13	4.79	26.87
0.74	0.50	2.57	9.73	0.79	1.30	4.69	28.07
0.73	0.72	3.15	10.85	1.22	1.61	4.65	29.63
0.44	0.69	3.71	11.99	1.01	1.31	4.49	30.41
0.98	0.41	3.76	12.87	0.43	1.20	4.91	31.42
0.62	1.16	3.73	13.44	0.27	1.26	5.01	32.66
0.44	1.35	3.49	14.26	0.41	1.32	4.59	33.49
0.66	0.98	3.94	14.91	0.94	0.85	4.62	34.23
0.83	1.21	4.01	15.37	1.42	1.13	4.83	35.00
1.25	0.69	3.97	15.90	1.22	1.24	4.86	36.27
0.89	0.35	4.35	17.10	1.31	1.08	4.53	37.07
1.02	0.70	3.84	18.39	0.67	0.85	4.44	37.25
0.72	0.74	3.60	18.98	0.22	1.32	4.74	38.10
0.79	0.52	3.43	19.50	0.50	1.53	4.54	39.51

(continued)

EXERCISE 5   (*Continued*)

A	B	C	D	A	B	C	D
0.64	1.75	4.13	40.20	0.40	0.90	5.03	61.00
0.41	1.11	4.22	40.27	0.47	1.01	4.78	61.69
0.40	0.80	3.97	40.68	1.03	1.01	5.21	62.63
1.13	0.41	4.29	41.19	1.33	0.61	5.31	63.12
1.06	0.93	4.22	41.58	1.11	1.13	5.14	63.28
0.31	0.66	4.34	42.23	0.60	1.05	5.18	63.52
0.67	1.29	4.85	43.33	0.30	0.89	4.92	64.08
0.68	1.11	4.39	44.27	0.93	1.21	5.24	64.45
0.72	1.16	4.74	44.89	0.92	1.48	4.80	64.62
0.58	1.52	5.09	45.41	0.85	1.62	5.37	64.78
0.74	1.28	4.83	45.69	0.52	1.15	5.19	65.52
1.14	0.76	5.21	46.39	0.07	1.43	4.71	66.18
1.42	0.74	4.74	46.96	0.41	1.33	4.62	67.16
0.94	0.53	4.90	47.34	1.21	1.26	4.42	68.63
0.59	0.44	5.06	47.61	0.96	1.16	5.00	69.67
0.32	0.92	5.29	48.21	0.31	1.04	4.53	70.17
0.68	0.57	4.90	48.77	0.33	1.19	4.44	70.53
1.40	0.33	4.90	49.17	0.52	1.22	4.56	71.32
1.52	0.99	4.80	49.85	0.77	0.70	4.48	71.99
1.20	1.24	4.88	50.55	0.85	0.74	4.88	72.53
1.33	0.77	4.46	51.55	1.27	0.73	4.70	72.89
0.69	0.48	5.09	52.20	1.48	1.00	4.92	73.81
0.30	1.16	4.56	53.06	1.42	1.39	4.74	74.74
0.49	0.62	4.37	54.46	1.29	1.51	4.31	75.15
0.43	0.83	4.20	55.70	0.87	1.11	4.74	75.81
0.95	0.62	4.65	56.51	0.86	1.42	4.64	76.86
1.50	1.11	4.37	57.41	0.76	1.38	4.39	77.83
1.58	0.73	4.67	58.81	0.36	1.68	4.15	78.95
0.92	0.61	5.00	60.10	0.17	1.49	4.35	80.27

6. *a.* Calculate and display the first 50 autocorrelations for the four data series in the table for this exercise, labeled A, B, C, and D; consider each of the four data series to be a quarterly time series. How many of the autocorrelations fall outside the two-standard-deviation range (positive or negative)?

   b. Is there a pattern to those autocorrelation coefficients falling outside the two-standard-deviation range?

   c. Calculate and display the first 50 partial autocorrelations for the 100 time-series observations. How many of the partial autocorrelation coefficients fall outside the two-standard-deviation range?

   d. Is there a pattern to those partial autocorrelation coefficients falling outside the two-standard-deviation range?

e. Which frame in Figures 7–1, 7–3, and 7–5 does this pattern of autocorrelation and partial autocorrelation coefficients most closely resemble?

f. Estimate the appropriate model as determined from your inspections carried out in parts *a* through *e* and forecast for four quarters into the future. Calculate the RMSE for each model.

EXERCISE 6   Four Data Series

A	B	C	D	A	B	C	D
0.77	0.37	0.20	0.93	0.28	0.46	4.11	50.73
0.31	0.32	0.93	1.24	0.27	0.49	3.95	50.99
0.88	0.95	1.62	2.12	0.42	0.49	3.72	51.42
1.48	1.40	1.66	3.60	0.30	0.38	3.49	51.72
0.99	1.04	2.41	4.59	0.19	0.29	3.33	51.91
1.16	1.44	2.63	5.75	0.21	0.28	4.01	52.12
1.26	1.33	2.75	7.01	1.08	1.13	3.91	53.21
0.86	1.10	2.64	7.87	1.12	0.99	4.09	54.33
0.48	0.73	2.66	8.35	0.85	1.05	3.94	55.18
0.39	0.63	2.75	8.74	0.68	0.82	4.50	55.86
0.55	0.68	2.97	9.29	1.13	1.33	4.30	56.99
0.76	0.85	2.84	10.05	1.00	1.03	4.03	57.99
0.56	0.63	3.55	10.62	0.38	0.64	4.61	58.37
1.12	1.29	3.55	11.74	1.02	1.25	4.11	59.39
1.18	1.14	3.30	12.91	0.73	0.71	4.11	60.12
0.45	0.68	3.16	13.37	0.36	0.66	4.20	60.48
0.21	0.48	3.13	13.58	0.71	0.83	3.81	61.19
0.36	0.50	3.71	13.93	0.40	0.47	3.56	61.59
1.06	1.13	3.77	15.00	0.09	0.29	3.57	61.69
1.17	1.12	3.50	16.17	0.87	1.14	5.19	24.87
0.50	0.67	3.86	16.67	1.38	1.55	5.26	26.25
0.74	0.99	3.72	17.41	1.37	1.46	5.24	27.62
0.78	0.82	3.54	18.19	1.01	1.26	5.63	28.62
0.39	0.57	3.92	18.58	1.28	1.54	5.77	29.90
0.82	0.99	4.31	19.39	1.42	1.55	5.43	31.32
1.35	1.35	4.28	20.74	0.82	1.04	5.36	32.13
1.08	1.16	4.70	21.82	0.59	0.93	5.15	32.72
1.18	1.42	4.56	23.00	0.60	0.78	5.05	33.32
1.00	1.12	4.71	24.00	0.59	0.75	5.56	33.91
1.07	0.97	4.68	43.00	0.35	0.46	4.05	62.04
1.00	1.11	4.64	44.01	1.06	1.07	4.12	63.09
0.90	1.05	4.56	65.15	1.16	1.10	4.19	64.25
1.11	1.30	4.57	46.02	0.90	1.02	4.97	44.91
0.71	0.81	4.46	46.73	1.15	1.33	4.23	66.30
0.38	0.68	4.46	47.12	0.76	0.86	4.18	67.06
0.61	0.76	4.71	47.73	0.45	0.74	4.59	67.51
0.99	1.07	4.69	48.72	1.03	1.18	5.02	68.54
0.99	1.04	4.61	49.71	1.54	1.56	5.40	70.08
0.74	0.86	4.87	76.58	1.65	1.75	5.44	71.73

(*continued*)

EXERCISE 6 (*Continued*)

A	B	C	D	A	B	C	D
1.25	1.37	5.22	35.16	1.33	1.53	4.91	73.07
1.02	1.01	5.65	36.18	0.48	0.79	5.33	73.55
1.11	1.39	5.85	37.29	0.82	1.20	5.62	74.37
1.47	1.55	5.53	38.76	1.48	1.51	5.11	75.84
0.90	1.08	5.23	39.66	0.74	0.91	4.18	50.45
0.40	0.73	5.14	40.06	0.25	0.60	4.81	76.83
0.50	0.73	4.68	40.56	0.50	0.68	5.25	77.33
0.29	0.40	4.47	40.86	1.18	1.25	5.45	78.51
0.19	0.37	4.07	41.05	1.45	1.44	5.37	79.95
0.12	0.19	4.50	41.17	1.08	1.23	5.35	81.03
0.76	0.85	4.51	41.93	0.86	1.11	5.02	81.89

7. *a.* An autoregressive model is given by:

$$Y_t = 20.58 + 0.046Y_{t-1} + 0.019Y_{t-2}$$

where Y_t = sales of a product. Explain the meaning of the terms in this autoregressive model.

b. Write the expressions for the following models:

AR(3)	MA(4)
AR(4)	ARMA(1, 2)
MA(3)	ARIMA(2, 1, 2)

Appendix

Critical Values of Chi-Square

This table contains the values of χ^2 that correspond to a specific right-tail area and specific numbers of degrees of freedom (df).

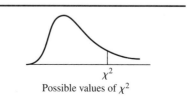

Possible values of χ^2

Degrees of Freedom (df)	Right-Tail Area			
	0.10	0.05	0.02	0.01
1	2.706	3.841	5.412	6.635
2	4.605	5.991	7.824	9.210
3	6.251	7.815	9.837	11.345
4	7.779	9.488	11.668	13.277
5	9.236	11.070	13.388	15.086
6	10.645	12.592	15.033	16.812
7	12.017	14.067	16.622	18.475
8	13.362	15.507	18.168	20.090
9	14.684	16.919	19.679	21.666
10	15.987	18.307	21.161	23.209
11	17.275	19.675	22.618	24.725
12	18.549	21.026	24.054	26.217
13	19.812	22.362	25.472	27.688
14	21.064	23.685	26.873	29.141
15	22.307	24.996	28.259	30.578
16	23.542	26.296	29.633	32.000
17	24.769	27.587	30.995	33.409
18	25.989	28.869	32.346	34.805
19	27.204	30.144	33.687	36.191
20	28.412	31.410	35.020	37.566
21	29.615	32.671	36.343	38.932
22	30.813	33.924	37.659	40.289
23	32.007	35.172	38.968	41.638
24	33.196	36.415	40.270	42.980
25	34.382	37.652	41.566	44.314
26	35.563	38.885	42.856	45.642
27	36.741	40.113	44.140	46.963
28	37.916	41.337	45.419	48.278
29	39.087	42.557	46.693	49.588
30	40.256	43.773	47.962	50.892

Source: From Owen P. Hall, Jr., and Harvey M. Adelman, *Computerized Business Statistics* (Homewood, IL: Richard D. Irwin, 1987), p. 95.

8   COMBINING FORECAST RESULTS

Introduction

The use of combinations of forecasts has been the subject of a great deal of research in forecasting. An indication of the importance of this concept is the fact that the prestigious *International Journal of Forecasting* had a special section, composed of seven articles, entitled "Combining Forecasts" in the year-end issue of the volume for 1989. These articles are listed in the "Suggested Readings" section at the end of this chapter. In December 1992 an article in the same journal provided strong evidence on the importance of combining forecasts to improve accuracy. It was found that 83 percent of expert forecasters believe that combining forecasts will produce more accurate forecasts than could be obtained from the individual methods![1]

The idea of combining business forecasting models was originally proposed by Bates and Granger.[2] Since the publication of their article, this strategy has received immense support in almost every empirical test of combined forecasts versus individual uncombined forecasts.

---

[1] Fred Collopy and J. Scott Armstrong, "Expert Opinions about Extrapolation and the Mystery of the Overlooked Discontinuities," *International Journal of Forecasting* 8, no. 4 (December 1992), pp. 575–82.

[2] Some of the material in this chapter is taken from the original Bates and Granger article; we recommend that readers consult the original article and other articles listed in the bibliography for more detail. J. M. Bates and C. W. J. Granger, "The Combination of Forecasts," *Operational Research Quarterly* 20, no. 4 (1969), pp. 451–68.

We have also drawn from and highly recommend J. Scott Armstrong's book, which is a virtual encyclopedia of forecasting methods. J. Scott Armstrong, *Long-Range Forecasting from Crystal Ball to Computer,* 2nd ed. (New York: John Wiley & Sons, 1985). For a nice overview of the state of the art in combining forecasts, see Robert T. Clemen, "Combining Forecasts: A Review and Annotated Bibliography," *International Journal of Forecasting* 5, no. 4 (1989), pp. 559–83.

Throughout this book we have emphasized the use of the root-mean-squared error (RMSE) as a measure of the effectiveness of a particular forecasting model (*forecast optimality*). The emphasis is very different in this chapter; instead of choosing the best model from among two or more alternatives, we are going to combine the forecasts from these different models to obtain *forecast improvement.* It may actually be unwise to simply determine which of a number of forecasting methods yields the most accurate predictions. A more reasoned approach, according to the empirical evidence, is to combine the forecasts already made in order to obtain a combined forecast that is more accurate than any of the separate predictions.

Any time a particular forecast is ignored because it is not the "best" forecast produced, it is likely that valuable independent information contained in the discarded forecast has been lost. The information lost may be of two types:

1. Some variables included in the discarded forecast may not be included in the "best" forecast.
2. The discarded forecast may make use of a type of relationship ignored by the "best" forecast.

In the first of these cases it is quite possible for several forecasts to be based on different information; thus, ignoring any one of these forecasts would necessarily exclude the explanatory power unique to the information included in the discarded model. In the second situation, it is often the case that different assumptions are made in different models about the form of the relationship between the variables. Each of the different forms of relationship tested, however, may have some explanatory value. Choosing only the "best" of the relationships could exclude functional information.

Bias

To be useful, forecasts we wish to combine must be unbiased. That is, each of the forecasts cannot consistently overestimate or underestimate the actual value. Note that if we combined an unbiased forecast with one that consistently overestimated the true value, we would always wind up with a biased estimate. Combining forecasts is not a method for eliminating bias in a forecast.

Bias can arise from a number of sources, but perhaps the most common source is the forecaster's preconceived notions. Predictions of forecasters not only reflect what they believe to be the truth, but also what they would *like* the truth to be. This statement is best demonstrated by the results obtained by Hayes in a survey of voters two weeks before the Roosevelt-Hoover election. Hayes found that of the people who intended to vote for Hoover, 84 percent thought that he would win the election. Of the people who intended to vote for Roosevelt, however, only 6 percent thought that Hoover would win. Apparently those who intended to vote for a particular candidate are biased in the sense that they also believe that their favorite will actually win the election.[3]

---

[3]S. P. Hayes, Jr., "The Predictive Ability of Voters," *Journal of Social Psychology* 7 (1936), pp. 183–91.

A forecaster should spend some time examining multiple forecasting models in the hope of combining some or all of these models into a combined forecast that is superior to any of the individual forecasts.

Professional forecasters may suffer from the same bias as voters—they may look for forecasting models that confirm their own preconceived ideas. To eliminate bias a forecaster will have to examine models that may contradict his or her current beliefs. What this means is that you must do something that runs counter to your intuition in order to examine models you may feel are incorrect; you must examine forecasting models that you may believe to be inferior to your "favorite" model. This prescription is more difficult to implement than it sounds. Much of a forecaster's time is spent in confirming existing beliefs of how the world works. However, we are suggesting that a forecaster should spend some time examining multiple forecasting models in the hope of combining some or all of these models into a combined forecast that is superior to any of the individual forecasts.

An Example

Consider a situation in which two separate forecasts are made of the same event. It is not atypical for a forecaster to attempt in this situation to choose the "best" of the two forecasting models on the basis of some error-minimization criterion such as RMSE. The model not chosen is discarded as being second-best, and therefore unusable.

If, however, the two forecasting models use different methods, or if the two models use different information, discarding one of the models may cause the loss of some valuable information. To prevent this loss of useful information requires some method for combining the two forecasts into a single "better" forecast.

To illustrate, we will use a classic example taken from an appendix to the original Bates and Granger article. In Table 8–1 we show output indexes for the gas, electricity, and water sectors of the economy, drawn from the 1966 edition of *National Income and Expenditure*. The actual index data in column 2 are in 1958 dollars. Our task is to estimate a forecasting model for these data that has a low RMSE.

We will use two separate forecasting techniques that have already been introduced in the text:

1. A linear time-series regression model (see Chapter 4)
2. An exponential or logarithmic model (see Chapter 5)

The regression model for forecasting with a simple linear trend in Chapter 4 was:

$$Y = b_0 + b_1(\text{TIME})$$

where Y is the series we wish to forecast. The linear-trend forecast in column 3 of Table 8–1 is calculated by using the year in column 1 as the independent variable and the actual data in column 2 as the dependent variable. The equation—estimated with simple linear regression—for making the first forecast (the one for 1950) used only the data for 1948 and 1949:

$$Y = -7{,}734 + 4(\text{YEAR})$$

Substituting the year 1950 gives the linear forecast for 1950, which appears in column 3:

$$Y = -7{,}734 + 4(1950) = 66$$

TABLE 8–1 Forecast of Output Indexes for Gas, Electricity, and Water (c8t1)

1	2	3	4	5	6	7	8	9	10
Year	Actual Index Data	Linear Forecast	Squared Deviations	Exponential Forecast	Squared Deviations	Combined Forecast (0.16 Weight)*	Squared Deviations	Combined Forecast (0.5 Weight)†	Squared Deviations
1948	58								
1949	62								
1950	67	66.000	1.0	66.276	0.5	66.23	0.59	66.14	0.74
1951	72	71.333	0.4	71.881	0.0	71.79	0.04	71.61	0.15
1952	74	76.500	6.3	77.385	11.5	77.24	10.52	76.94	8.66
1953	77	79.200	4.8	80.289	10.8	80.11	9.70	79.74	7.53
1954	84	81.933	4.3	83.215	0.6	83.01	0.98	82.57	2.03
1955	88	87.000	1.0	88.632	0.4	88.37	0.14	87.82	0.03
1956	92	91.607	0.2	93.656	2.7	93.33	1.76	92.63	0.40
1957	96	95.972	0.0	98.476	6.1	98.08	4.31	97.22	1.50
1958	100	100.200	0.0	103.187	10.2	102.71	7.34	101.69	2.87
1959	103	104.345	1.8	107.843	23.4	107.28	18.34	106.09	9.57
1960	110	108.106	3.6	112.108	4.4	111.47	2.15	110.11	0.01
1961	116	112.846	9.9	117.444	2.1	116.71	0.50	115.15	0.73
1962	125	117.967	49.5	123.241	3.1	122.40	6.77	120.60	19.32
1963	133	124.152	78.3	130.228	7.7	129.02	14.02	127.19	33.76
1964	137	130.850	37.8	137.864	0.7	136.74	0.07	134.36	6.99
1965	145	136.978	64.4	145.034	0.0	143.74	1.58	141.01	15.95
	Sum of squares =		263.3		84.4		78.82		110.25
	RMSE =		4.06		2.30		2.22		2.63

*The 0.16 weight refers to the weight on the linear model. The weight on the exponential model must then be 0.84, since the two weights must sum to 1.

†The 0.5 weight refers to the weight on the linear model. The weight on the exponential model must then be 0.5, since the weights must sum to 1. Note also that the RMSE for the column 9 combined model is not as low (and, therefore, not as good) as the RMSE for the column 7 combined model.

SOURCE: J. M. Bates and C. W. J. Granger, "The Combination of Forecasts," *Operational Research Quarterly* 20, no. 4 (1969), pp. 451–68.

The simple linear-trend estimating equation is then estimated again, this time using the data for the first three years (1948–50); this equation is used to forecast for the year 1951, and that value (which is 71.3) is placed in column 3 of Table 8–1. This procedure is repeated for each year, so that the forecast for year t is always made by extrapolating the regression line formed by the least-squares regression of the actual figures for 1948 through the year $t - 1$. The results obtained and displayed in the table would be similar to the results an actual forecaster might record as he or she makes annual forecasts by always using new data as they become available.

For each forecast in column 3, we also calculate the squared deviation from the actual figure as an intermediate step in calculating the RMSE (see Chapter 1 for an explanation of root-mean-squared error). The RMSE for the simple linear-trend approach to forecasting the index is given at the bottom of column 4.

The second model used to forecast the index is the exponential model (it is sometimes called the *logarithmic* or *constant-rate-of-growth* model). The assumption in this model is that the value we are forecasting does not produce a straight-line plot when graphed over time. Instead the data may plot as a curve on arithmetic paper but as a straight line on semilogarithmic paper (graph paper with one arithmetic axis and one logarithmic axis). The equation to estimate is:

$$Y = b_0 m^x$$

where:

Y = The actual value of the index

b_0 = Value of the trend when $x = 0$

m = The constant rate of growth (which could be negative)

x = The time value (in the present case, 1948 = 1, 1949 = 2, etc.)

The equation can be estimated with a standard regression package by using the equation:

$$\ln Y = \ln b_0 + x \ln m$$

To obtain the equation for the first exponential estimate in Table 8–1, the natural logs of the actual index data for the years 1948 and 1949 were taken and regressed on time (with 1948 = 1 and 1949 = 2). This produced the estimate:

$$\ln Y = \ln 3.994 + (\text{Year}) \ln 0.067$$

Taking the antilogs of the log values gives the following equation:

$$Y = (54.258)(1.069)^{\text{Year}}$$

Note that the antilog of 3.994 = 54.258 and the antilog of 0.067 = 1.069. The first forecast (the one for 1950) is calculated by making the substitution for year into this equation (recall that the year 1950 = 3):

$$Y = (54.258)(1.069)^3 = 66.276$$

This first exponential forecast is the first number (66.276) in column 5 of Table 8–1. The forecast for the following year (71.9) requires the fitting of another equation of the same form, utilizing the actual index data from all three previous years. Each subsequent forecast then requires the equation to be estimated once again.

For each forecast in column 5 we again calculate the squared deviation from the actual figure as an intermediate step in calculating the RMSE. The results in column 6 are again what could be expected if a forecaster were to use the exponential method over time and keep careful track of the errors made each year as the current year's actual data became available. The RMSE for the exponential model over the 16-year period from 1950 to 1965 is given at the bottom of column 6.

The RMSE for the exponential forecasting model is clearly smaller (and therefore better) than the corresponding figure for the simple linear-trend forecasting model. If we were to choose the "best" model, the exponential model would be the clear choice.

However, since the two forecasts assume different forms of the relationship between the variables, there may be a combination of the two forecasts that will yield considerable improvements from either single model. A combined forecast is a weighted average of the different forecasts, with the weights reflecting in some sense the confidence the researcher has in each of the models. Some forecasters have suggested that the weights should be selected before the forecasts are generated in order to reduce the possibility of bias introduced by the researcher. The use of a mechanical rule to make the selection of weights would also satisfy this objection and will be discussed in what follows.

In our particular situation it appears that we should have more confidence in the exponential model because it has the lower RMSE. This would suggest that in combining the two forecasts we should weight the exponential model more heavily than the simple linear-trend model. In column 7 of Table 8–1 we have arbitrarily weighted the simple linear-trend model by 0.16 and the exponential model by 0.84 (the two weights must sum to 1). The first forecast in column 7 is then calculated as follows:

$$(0.16)(\text{Linear forecast}) + (0.84)(\text{Exponential forecast}) = \text{Combined forecast}$$
$$(0.16)(66.000) + (0.84)(66.276) = 66.23$$

This procedure is repeated for each of the years from 1950 to 1965. Column 8 contains the squared deviations of the combined forecast from the actual index data, and the RMSE for the combined forecast (2.22) is at the bottom of the column.

Note that the RMSE for the combined forecast is better (i.e., lower) than for either individual forecasting model. The combining of forecasts is a practical tool for increasing forecast accuracy and has the attraction of being both automatic and conceptually quite simple; apparently even the less accurate simple linear-trend model contained important information that made it possible to obtain a better forecast. Following this approach, it should be clear that most forecast methods contain some information that is independent of the information contained in other forecast methods. If this is the case, combination forecasts will, quite likely, outperform individual forecasts.

Two important observations need to be made about the results in Table 8–1:

1. Considerable improvements in forecast accuracy can be achieved by combining forecast models with an optimal weight. In this case the optimal

weight turned out to be 0.16 for the simple linear-trend model (and therefore, 0.84 for the exponential model).

2. While the forecaster cannot assume that combining forecasts will always yield better results, it can be shown that the combined forecasts will have an error variance not greater than the smallest error variance of the individual forecasts.[4]

What Kinds of Forecasts Can Be Combined?

The example of combining forecasts we used in the previous section is one of the simpler combinations a researcher could try. In actual practice it would be more common to find a forecaster using very different types of models in order to construct a combination forecast.

Recall that the premise in constructing combined forecasts is:

1. That the different forecasting models *extract different predictive factors* from essentially the same data, or

2. That the different models offer different predictions because they *use different variables.*

We should expect that combinations of forecasts that use very different models are likely to be effective in reducing forecast error.

We should expect that combinations of forecasts that use very different models are likely to be effective in reducing forecast error.

Consider Figure 8–1, which conceptually presents a 10-year forecast of air travel in the United States. The judgmental method represents a mail survey of experts outside the airline industry. The extrapolation method could be a form of exponential smoothing. The segmentation method surveys airline travelers in different segments of the market and then combines the results to obtain a total picture of the industry. The econometric method refers to a causal regression model. All four methods could be employed and predictions weighted by the values w_1 to w_4 in order to calculate the combined forecast. Such a diverse combined forecast would benefit from both the use of the different techniques *and* from the use of different sources of data. If each of the methods

FIGURE 8–1

Combining Forecasts from Different Methods

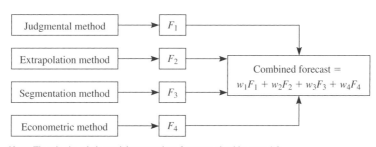

NOTE: The w's, the relative weights on various forecasts, should sum to 1.0.

[4]David A. Bessler and Jon A. Brandt, "Composite Forecasting: An Application with U.S. Hog Prices," *American Journal of Agricultural Economics* 63 (1981), pp. 135–40.

employed was also constructed and estimated by a different forecaster, another source of possible bias may also have been minimized; this provides a safeguard by making it difficult to cheat.

Considerations in Choosing the Weights for Combined Forecasts

Combined forecasts are used in place of individual forecasts in order to reduce forecast error, and the results of the combined method are quite often impressive. Armstrong has reported results from reanalyzing eight separate studies that provided sufficient information to test the combined forecasting method against individual forecast models.[5] In each case Armstrong used equal weights for the individual forecasts, following his belief that weight should be chosen *ex ante*. The combinations of two forecasts reduced error (measured as mean absolute percentage error) by a significant 6.6 percent. In no single case did the accuracy ever suffer; when more than two forecasts were combined, further improvements were noted (in one case observed by Armstrong, the forecast error was reduced by 17.9 percent).

Even though the use of equal weights for each of the individual forecasts offers the advantage of simplicity and also precludes the forecaster's own bias in the selection of weighting factors, there may be a good reason for weighting one individual forecast more than another, as we have done in the previous example. Equal weights do not take into account the relative accuracy of the individual forecasting models that are combined. Bates and Granger were the first to indicate that by weighting the more accurate of the methods more heavily, the overall forecast could be improved.[6] You have seen in Table 8–1 that the combination using equal weights is not as effective, on the basis of RMSE, as a combination that assigns a smaller weight to the individual forecast having the larger RMSE.

In general, a combined forecast will have a smaller error, as measured by RMSE, *unless individual forecasting models are almost equally good and their forecast errors are highly correlated.*

Consider Table 8–2, which presents data on the gross national product (GNP) of the communications industry for the years 1968 to 1985 (i.e., the total value of all goods and services produced by the communications industry, valued at market prices). The actual GNP figures appear in column 2; in columns 3 and 5, respectively, are the linear and exponential forecasts calculated in the manner of the previous example. The squared deviations of these forecasts from the actual data are given in columns 4 and 6. By calculating the RMSE for each of the forecasting models, it is clear that the linear model is a superior forecasting tool (RMSE of 2.66 for the linear model versus 3.63 for the exponential model).

Of interest here is the correlation of the forecast errors (squared) between the two models. To do this we calculate the correlation coefficient between columns 4 and 6 of Table 8–2, which yields −0.62; from this low correlation coefficient it is apparent that

---

[5]See Armstrong, *Long-Range Forecasting,* p. 292.
[6]See Bates and Granger, p. 452.

TABLE 8–2 GNP: Communications, 1982 Dollars (Billions) (c8t2)

1 Year	2 Actual Data	3 Linear Forecast	4 Squared Deviations	5 Exponential Forecast	6 Squared Deviations	7 Combined Forecast (0.9 Weight)	8 Squared Deviations	9 Combined Forecast (0.8 Weight)	10 Squared Deviations	11 Combined Forecast (0.7 Weight)	12 Squared Deviations	13 Combined Forecast (0.5 Weight)	14 Squared Deviations	15 Combined Forecast (0.3 Weight)	16 Squared Deviations
1968	33.9														
1969	37.4														
1970	40.9	40.9	0.0	41.3	0.1	40.94	0.00	40.97	0.01	41.01	0.01	41.08	0.03	41.15	0.06
1971	43	44.4	2.0	45.0	4.0	44.46	2.13	44.52	2.30	44.58	2.49	44.70	2.87	44.81	3.29
1972	47	46.5	0.3	47.2	0.1	46.57	0.18	46.65	0.13	46.72	0.08	46.87	0.02	47.01	0.00
1973	50.5	50.0	0.3	51.0	0.2	50.08	0.18	50.18	0.10	50.28	0.05	50.48	0.00	50.68	0.03
1974	53	53.5	0.3	54.8	3.4	53.64	0.41	53.77	0.60	53.91	0.82	54.17	1.38	54.44	2.07
1975	55.2	56.5	1.6	58.1	8.6	56.64	2.07	56.81	2.58	56.97	3.14	57.31	4.44	57.64	5.95
1976	58.1	59.0	0.9	61.0	8.5	59.23	1.29	59.43	1.78	59.63	2.34	60.03	3.72	60.43	5.41
1977	61.9	61.7	0.0	64.0	4.5	61.95	0.00	62.18	0.08	62.41	0.26	62.87	0.95	63.34	2.06
1978	67.7	64.8	8.3	67.5	0.0	65.09	6.81	65.36	5.47	65.63	4.28	66.17	2.33	66.72	0.97
1979	72.5	68.9	12.9	72.1	0.1	69.23	10.69	69.55	8.70	69.87	6.91	70.51	3.94	71.16	1.81
1980	78.4	73.3	26.2	77.1	1.7	73.66	22.46	74.04	18.99	74.42	15.81	75.19	10.32	75.95	6.00
1981	82.8	78.2	21.5	82.7	0.0	78.62	17.47	79.07	13.88	79.53	10.70	80.44	5.57	81.35	2.11
1982	85.6	83.0	6.9	88.4	7.6	83.51	4.38	84.05	2.41	84.59	1.03	85.66	0.00	86.74	1.30
1983	92.1	87.3	23.2	93.6	2.2	87.91	17.54	88.54	12.67	89.17	8.59	90.43	2.80	91.68	0.17
1984	92.7	92.2	0.3	99.5	45.6	92.89	0.04	93.62	0.85	94.35	2.73	95.81	9.67	97.27	20.87
1985	93.2	96.1	8.3	104.4	124.4	96.90	13.71	97.73	20.52	98.56	28.71	100.21	49.19	101.87	75.15
Sum of squares =			112.8		211.1		99.4		91.1		87.94		97.24		127.25
RMSE =			2.66		3.63		2.49		2.39		2.34		2.47		2.82

Note that the weights listed in parentheses are those assigned to the linear forecasting model. The exponential model must then have a weight of 1 minus the weight listed in parentheses.
SOURCE: CITIBASE, Citicorp Database Services.

these two forecasting models are not highly correlated. This result indicates that possible improvements would result from some combination of the two models.

The simplest combination of the two models is obtained by weighting each equally; this is done in column 13 of Table 8–2. The RMSE for this combined model is 2.47, which is lower (and therefore better) than for either the linear or the exponential model.

If, however, the forecast model with the lower RMSE is more heavily weighted, the combined forecast should improve even further. In column 9 of Table 8–2, a weight of 0.8 is applied to the linear model and a weight of 0.2 to the exponential model. This results in an RMSE of 2.39, which is the best yet. Further experimentation shows that a weighting of 0.7 for the linear model (and 0.3 for the exponential model) yields even better results (an RMSE of 2.34).

If, however, you ignore the rule of thumb that the more accurate forecast should receive the larger weight, the accuracy of the combined forecast may deteriorate. Notice that in the final two columns of the table we use a weighting of 0.3 for the linear model (and 0.7 for the exponential model), which results in an RMSE that is larger than that for the linear model alone.

In Table 8–3 the data for GNP in the retail trade industry for the same years are presented. Again we calculate a linear forecast and an exponential forecast by using the same methods we have employed, so that the data represent what a forecaster would have collected during 16 years of forecasting these numbers one year at a time and using only the data available in the given year.

In this case both forecasts have very similar errors, as shown by their RMSEs (11.23 for the linear model and 11.53 for the exponential model). In addition, the correlation between the squared deviations of the linear model and the squared deviations of the exponential model (located in columns 4 and 6) is high—the coefficient is 0.81. We should expect little, if any, improvement by using a combined forecast in this situation.

Using an equal-weighting scheme for the two models yields a combined forecast with an RMSE of 11.28, which is better than the exponential model but worse than the linear model. By using heavier weights for the "better" forecasting model (in this case the linear model), we are able to improve the forecast only slightly. Weights of 0.9 or 0.8 for the linear model (and correspondingly 0.1 or 0.2, respectively, for the exponential model) result in an RMSE of 11.22 for the combined model. This result emphasizes that it is the diversity of information included in the individual models that allows the combined forecast model to assemble the pieces to form a more powerful forecasting model than any one of the parts.

It is the diversity of information included in the individual models that allows the combined forecast model to assemble the pieces to form a more powerful forecasting model than any one of the parts.

Three Techniques for Selecting Weights When Combining Forecasts

Is there any way to choose the weights to use in combining the individual forecasts other than by trying all possible combinations? Yes; several researchers have suggested techniques for choosing weights that take advantage of the facts we have just demonstrated. We will present three of these techniques here.

TABLE 8–3   GNP: Retail Trade, 1982 Dollars (Billions)   (c8t3)

1	2	3	4	5	6	7	8	9	10	11	12	13	14	15	16
Year	Actual Data	Linear Forecast	Squared Deviations	Exponential Forecast	Squared Deviations	Combined Forecast (0.9 Weight)	Squared Deviations	Combined Forecast (0.8 Weight)	Squared Deviations	Combined Forecast (0.7 Weight)	Squared Deviations	Combined Forecast (0.5 Weight)	Squared Deviations	Combined Forecast (0.3 Weight)	Squared Deviations
1968	211.6														
1969	212.7														
1970	215.6	213.8	3.2	213.8	3.2	213.80	3.24	213.80	3.24	213.80	3.23	213.80	3.23	213.80	3.23
1971	224.5	217.3	51.8	217.3	51.5	217.30	51.80	217.31	51.77	217.31	51.73	217.31	51.66	217.32	51.58
1972	239.8	226.5	176.9	226.6	173.9	226.51	176.59	226.52	176.29	226.53	176.00	226.56	175.40	226.58	174.81
1973	255.6	241.3	204.5	241.7	193.9	241.34	203.41	241.38	202.34	241.41	201.27	241.49	199.14	241.56	197.02
1974	245.2	257.7	155.1	258.6	180.1	257.75	157.50	257.85	159.94	257.94	162.40	258.14	167.37	258.33	172.41
1975	247.5	259.4	141.6	260.7	274.0	259.53	144.70	259.66	147.82	259.79	150.98	260.05	157.39	160.30	163.93
1976	262.8	261.0	3.3	262.5	0.1	261.13	2.80	261.27	2.33	261.42	1.90	261.72	1.17	262.01	0.62
1977	275.1	268.3	45.9	270.2	24.3	268.51	43.43	268.69	41.04	268.88	38.71	269.25	34.25	269.62	30.06
1978	288.1	277.7	108.3	280.0	65.7	277.92	103.57	278.15	98.94	278.38	94.42	278.84	85.70	279.30	77.40
1979	294.4	288.5	34.7	291.4	9.2	288.79	31.45	289.08	28.32	289.37	25.35	289.94	19.90	290.51	15.12
1980	286.9	298.0	122.6	301.5	213.5	298.33	130.53	298.68	138.75	299.03	147.21	299.74	164.88	300.45	183.56
1981	288.9	302.3	179.4	306.3	303.9	302.70	190.34	303.10	201.66	303.50	213.30	304.31	237.56	305.12	263.13
1982	287.5	305.8	335.9	310.3	518.6	306.27	352.43	306.72	369.31	307.16	386.59	308.05	422.33	308.94	459.65
1983	307	307.9	0.8	312.6	31.5	308.39	1.93	308.86	3.46	309.33	5.42	310.27	10.67	311.21	17.69
1984	328.6	314.2	207.0	319.4	85.0	314.73	192.40	315.25	178.34	315.76	164.81	316.80	139.35	317.83	116.03
1985	339.8	324.1	246.5	329.8	99.2	324.67	228.81	325.25	211.77	325.82	195.39	326.97	164.60	328.12	136.46
	Sum of squares =		2,017.6		2,127.7		2,015.0		2,015.3		2,018.70		2,034.63		2,062.72
	RMSE =		11.23		11.53		11.22		11.22		11.23		11.28		11.35

Note that the weights listed in parentheses refer to the weighting on the linear forecasting model. The exponential model must then have a weight of 1 minus the weight listed in parentheses.
SOURCE: CITIBASE, Citicorp Database Services.

First, Bates and Granger have suggested a method that assumes the individual fore-casts are consistent over time and that minimizes the variance of the forecast errors over the time period covered. The weight assigned to the first forecast model, k, is calculated in the following manner (note that the second forecast model would receive a weight of $1 - k$):

$$k = \frac{(\sigma_2)^2 - \rho\sigma_1\sigma_2}{(\sigma_1)^2 - (\sigma_2)^2 - 2\rho\sigma_1\sigma_2}$$

where:

k = The weight assigned to the first forecast model

$(\sigma_1)^2$ = The variance of errors for the first model

$(\sigma_2)^2$ = The variance of errors for the second model

ρ = The coefficient of correlation between the errors in the first set of forecasts and those in the second set

A second, and quite different, approach to selecting the best weighting scheme in-volves allowing the weights to adapt or change from period to period. The power of this method rests on the assumption that forecasting models may not have a constant perfor-mance over time. An adaptive set of weights may be calculated in the following manner:

$$\alpha_{1,T+1} = \sum_{t=T-\nu}^{T} \frac{e_{2t}^2}{e_{1t}^2 + e_{2t}^2}$$

where:

$\alpha_{1,T+1}$ = The weight assigned to forecast model 1 in period $T + 1$

e_{it} = The error made by forecast model i in period t

ν = The choice variable, which represents the number of periods included in the adaptive weighting procedure

T = The total number of periods for which there is a history of forecast errors

What is not clear is the superiority of these two methods for choosing weights in a combined model. Bessler and Brandt[7] examined the two weighting methods and con-cluded:

1. Forecasts from individual models are not likely to be the most accurate forecasts.
2. Even with no record of prior forecast performance, it may make some sense to combine forecasts using a simple averaging method (i.e., equal weights).
3. If prior forecasting records are available, the user should weight forecasts on the basis of past performance (with the most accurate forecast receiving the highest weight).

---

[7]See Bessler and Brandt, p. 139.

At least one other technique is used to combine forecasts in order to improve accuracy. This technique involves the use of a regression analysis in determining the weights. Charles Nelson[8] suggests that if we are trying to weight a portfolio of forecasts in order to minimize the forecast error, an optimal linear composite forecast would be:

$$F^* = b_1 F(1) + b_2 F(2)$$

where:

$$F^* = \text{Optimal combined forecast}$$
$$F(1) = \text{First individual forecast}$$
$$F(2) = \text{Second individual forecast}$$
$$b_1 = \text{Weight allocated to the first forecast}$$
$$b_2 = \text{Weight allocated to the second forecast}$$

The actual values of b_1 and b_2 would be calculated by running a regression with the past actual values as the dependent variable and the forecasted values for each individual model as the independent variables. Note that this is not exactly the type of regression we have run before in the text; this regression has no intercept term, and so the equation must be calculated in a manner different from that we have used earlier.

Using this method, if the two (or more) individual forecasts are free of systematic bias, the values of b_1 and b_2 will sum to roughly 1. The t-ratios for the regression essentially answer the question: Does individual forecast 1 add any explanatory power to what is already present in forecast 2? and similarly for forecast 2. If the b_1 value passed the t-test at some reasonable confidence level, we would be assured that the first individual model, $F(1)$, did add explanatory power when combined with the second model, $F(2)$, using the weights calculated by the regression.

To apply this method and to determine the best values for b_1 and b_2, a two-step regression process is used. First, you perform a standard multiple regression of the actual values (dependent variable) on the values predicted from the individual forecasting methods (independent variables in this regression). We can express this as:

$$A = a + b_1 F(1) + b_2 F(2)$$

The value of the intercept (a) should be zero if there is no bias in the combined forecast. A standard t-test can be used to test whether the intercept is significantly different from zero.[9] Note that a two-tailed test would be appropriate here.

Assuming that you conclude that $a = 0$, you then redo the regression, forcing the regression through the origin. Most regression programs provide an option that allows this to be done quite easily. The result of regressing the actual values on the two forecast series, without an intercept, yields the desired result to determine the best weights to be used in combining the forecasts. We have:

$$F^* = b_1 F(1) + b_2 F(2)$$

[8]Charles R. Nelson, "A Benchmark for the Accuracy of Econometric Forecasts of GNP," *Business Economics* 19, no. 3 (April 1984), pp. 52–58.

[9]This is one of the few cases for which we are interested in testing to see whether the intercept is different from zero. Normally, we do this test only for the slope terms.

Using these values of b_1 and b_2, along with the $F(1)$ and $F(2)$ forecast series, the optimal combined forecast, F^*, is easily determined.

As was indicated, the values of b_1 and b_2 should sum roughly to 1. On occasion one of these weights may be negative, in which case interpretation is tenuous. Some forecasters use such a model even if b_1 or b_2 is negative, as long as the RMSE for F^* is lower than for $F(1)$ or $F(2)$ alone. However, we advise using this method only when both weights are positive. It should be noted that this method can be extended to include more than two forecast series in the combination process. Remember, however, that each method should have unique information content.

An Application of the Regression Method for Combining Forecasts

To illustrate the widely used regression method of combining forecasts, we will apply it to the problem of forecasting private housing starts (PHS) using data from 1990Q2 through 1998Q4. Regressing PHS as a function of the mortgage rate (MR) yields:

$$\text{PHS} = 471.08 - 24.47(\text{MR})$$
$$(\text{RMSE} = 45.33)$$

Forecasts based on this model will be referred to as RFCST. A Winters' exponential smoothing model for PHS results in an RMSE of 15.12. We will refer to the Winters' forecast as WFCST.

Regressing PHS on RFCST and WFCST, and using the standard method including an intercept term, yields the following results (using 1990Q2 to 1998Q4):

$$\text{PHS} = -44.30 + 0.29(\text{RFCST}) + 0.88(\text{WFCST})$$
$$(-1.64) \quad (2.71) \quad\quad (18.71)$$

The values in parentheses are t-ratios. On the basis of these t-ratios, the intercept (-44.30) is not significantly different from zero, but the slope terms are significantly positive. Since the intercept is essentially zero, we conclude that there is no bias in combining these two methods.

Repeating the regression without an intercept yields the following (again using 1990Q2 to 1998Q4):

$$\text{PHS} = 0.13(\text{RFCST}) + 0.88(\text{WFCST})$$
$$(2.7) \quad\quad (18.18)$$
$$(\text{RMSE} = 13.66)$$

We see that the combined RMSE of 13.66 is less than the root-mean-squared error of either the regression model (RMSE = 45.33) or the Winters' model (RMSE = 15.12). Notice also that the coefficients sum nearly to 1 ($0.13 + 0.88 = 1.01$).

Note that the two methods combined in this example contain quite different information. The regression model includes only the effect of mortgage rates on private housing starts, while the Winters' model takes into account trend and seasonal components of the time series (but not the effect of the mortgage rate). Incidentally, the correlation coefficient between the squared errors for the two individual models is -0.14 in this case (quite small, as we would expect).

The values for PHS, CFCST (the combined forecast), RFCST, and WFCST are shown in Table 8–4. Figure 8–2 shows the combined forecast and the actual PHS data

(c8t4) **TABLE 8–4   Private Housing Starts (PHS) and Three Forecasts of PHS**

Period	PHS	CFCST	RFCST	WFCST
Jun-1990	271.3	267.22	218.08	272.62
Sep-1990	233.0	249.87	223.80	251.93
Dec-1990	173.6	187.63	227.44	180.28
Mar-1991	146.7	162.93	238.55	150.40
Jun-1991	254.1	249.91	237.92	249.86
Sep-1991	239.8	234.41	244.07	231.24
Dec-1991	199.8	195.91	258.44	185.09
Mar-1992	218.5	186.60	257.91	174.54
Jun-1992	296.4	311.87	258.69	317.54
Sep-1992	276.4	279.62	275.08	278.24
Dec-1992	238.8	231.93	270.26	224.48
Mar-1993	213.2	227.83	281.81	218.06
Jun-1993	323.7	309.08	288.71	309.85
Sep-1993	309.3	304.98	297.85	303.81
Dec-1993	279.4	265.86	298.44	259.02
Mar-1994	252.6	262.32	292.52	255.87
Jun-1994	354.2	342.91	264.59	352.12
Sep-1994	325.7	327.58	260.89	335.16
Dec-1994	265.9	277.27	248.42	279.55
Mar-1995	214.2	246.50	255.40	243.35
Jun-1995	296.7	313.80	276.58	317.06
Sep-1995	308.2	280.33	282.60	277.93
Dec-1995	257.2	261.98	291.17	255.67
Mar-1996	240.0	240.10	293.81	230.28
Jun-1996	344.5	332.67	272.71	339.20
Sep-1996	324.0	324.28	271.39	329.82
Dec-1996	252.4	275.66	282.38	272.62
Mar-1997	237.8	237.47	280.41	229.29
Jun-1997	324.5	330.77	277.11	336.38
Sep-1997	314.6	309.27	288.28	310.14
Dec-1997	256.8	265.93	294.91	259.63
Mar-1998	258.4	244.98	298.42	235.17
Jun-1998	360.4	347.57	297.46	352.52
Sep-1998	348.0	342.70	303.05	346.12
Dec-1998	304.6	296.44	305.55	292.89

PHS = Private housing starts
CFCST = A combination forecast of PHS where: CFCST = 0.13(RFCST) + 0.88(WFCST)
RFCST = Regression forecast of PHS
WFCST = Winters' exponential smoothing forecast of PHS

FIGURE 8–2

*Private Housing
Starts (PHS) and
the Combined
Forecast (CFCST)
(c8t4)*

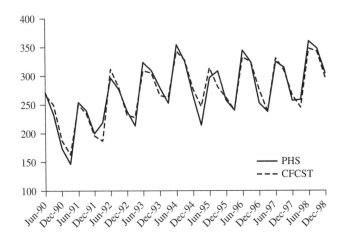

for the historical period. The period is missing early observations for CFCST because of
the loss of initial data in developing the Winters' forecast. The forecast values for
Jun-1990–Dec-1998 certainly appear reasonable.

Forecasting Domestic Car Sales with a Combined Forecast

We will now apply the forecasting concepts of this chapter to the problem of forecasting
domestic car sales. We will combine two of the forecasting models we have presented
in previous chapters (using a holdout period). The models chosen for combination are a
multiple-regression model (Chapter 5) and a Winters' exponential smoothing model
(Chapter 3). These two models were chosen because they differ in both the variables
included and in the type of relationship hypothesized.

The multiple-regression model contains information from disposable personal
income and the prime interest rate. The regression model appeared in the upper section
of Table 5–9.

$$DCS = 2,175.97 - 18.67(PR) - 0.01(DPI)$$

The root-mean-squared error for this forecasting model is 217.15 in the historical period
and 132.34 in the 1999Q3–2000Q2 forecast horizon.

The Winters' exponential smoothing model takes both trend and seasonality into
account. The root-mean-squared error for the Winters' forecasting model for DCS is
144.45 in the historical period and 61.79 in the 1999Q3–2000Q2 forecast horizon.

If we were to simply choose the optimum forecasting model from only these two,
we would choose the smoothing model. The RMSE for the smoothing model of about

73 is less than the RMSE of the regression model. Recall, however, that the objective in combining forecasts is not to choose the optimum forecasting model (forecast optimality) but to improve the forecast (forecast improvement).

Let us see what happens when we combine these forecasts using the regression method of selecting the best set of weights. For notational simplicity we will let DCSFR (domestic car sales forecast regression) refer to the multiple-regression forecast, and DCSFW (domestic car sales forecast Winters) refer to the Winters' forecast. DCSCF (domestic car sales combined forecast) will be used to represent the combined forecast.

We begin by regressing the actual values of domestic car sales (DCS) on DCSFR and DCSFW, using standard regression techniques to determine whether the intercept is essentially equal to zero. The results are:

$$DCS = -713.66 + 0.51(DCSFR) + 0.90(DCSFW)$$
$$(-1.13) \quad (1.41) \quad (10.06)$$

where the *t*-ratios are in parentheses. Given a *t*-ratio of -1.13 for the intercept, we would conclude that it is not statistically different from zero at any meaningful significance level.

Next we do the same regression, except that this time we force it through the origin by eliminating the constant term (i.e., the intercept). The new regression results are:

$$DCS = 0.12(DCSFR) + 0.89(DCSFW)$$
$$(1.29) \quad (9.98)$$

where the *t*-ratios are in parentheses. These results are interesting. First, they show that the coefficients do sum approximately to 1 ($0.12 + 0.89 = 1.01$). Second, we see that by far the greatest weight is assigned to the smoothing model, which has an RMSE about three-quarters the size of the RMSE for the regression model. Third, we see that after accounting for the contribution of the regression model, the amount of explanatory power added by the Winters' model is substantial (note the large *t*-ratio for DCSFW). This is not surprising, since the correlation coefficient between the squared error terms resulting from DCSFR and DCSFW is quite low. These results suggest that the amount of improvement from combining these models may be significant.

Using this set of weights to determine the combined forecast (DCSCF), we have:

$$DCSCF = 0.12(DCSFR) + 0.89(DCSFW)$$

The resulting root-mean-squared error of 141.69 does show modest improvement over the 144.45 RMSE based on the Winters' model alone. The forecast values based on DCSCF are plotted for the historical period as well as for the forecast horizon, along with actual DCS, in Figure 8–3. The data are shown in tabular form in Table 8–5.

Table 8–6 contains a summary of RMSEs for various models we have used to forecast domestic car sales throughout the text. We see that, on the basis of known information, the combined forecast has one of the lowest RMSEs during the historical period.

FIGURE 8–3

*Domestic Car
Sales (DCS) and
Combined Forecast
(DCSCF)*
(c8t5)

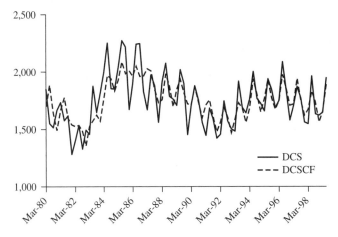

This graphic shows actual DCS and a combined forecast (DCSCF)
that is based on a combination of a multiple-regression forecast
(DCSFR) and a Winters' exponential smoothing forecast (DCSFW)
The combined forecast is:

$$DCS = 0.12(DCSFR) + 0.89(DCSFW)$$

**TABLE 8–5   Regression with a Constant Term (Note That the Constant Term Is
Not Statistically Significant)** (c8t5)

Audit Trail--ANOVA Table (Multiple Regression Selected)

Source of Variation	SS	df	MS	SEE
Regression	2,273,415.26	2	1,136,707.63	
Error	1,565,899.68	75	20,878.66	144.49
Total	3,839,314.93	77		

Audit Trail--Coefficient Table (Multiple Regression Selected)

Series Description	Included in Model	Coefficient	Standard Error	T-test	F-test	Elasticity	Overall F-test
DCS	Dependent	-713.66	633.31	-1.13	1.27		54.44
DCSFR	Yes	0.51	0.36	1.41	1.99	0.51	
DCSFW	Yes	0.90	0.09	10.06	101.16	0.90	

(continued)

TABLE 8-5 (*Continued*)

```
Audit Trail--Statistics
```

Accuracy Measure	Value
AIC	996.12
BIC	998.48
Mean absolute percentage error (MAPE)	6.41%
Sum squared error (SSE)	1,565,899.68
R-squared	59.21%
Adjusted R-squared	58.13%
Mean absolute error	110.60
Mean error	0.00
Mean squared error	20,075.64
Root-mean-squared error	141.69
Theil	0.62

Forecast Statistic	Value
Durbin-Watson	2.00
Mean	1,748.21
Standard deviation	223.30
Max	2,272.60
Min	1,281.30
Range	991.30
Ljung-Box	0.01

Regression without a Constant Term—This Regression Is Used for the Combined Forecast

```
Audit Trail--ANOVA Table (Multiple Regression Selected)
```

Source of Variation	SS	df	MS	SEE
Regression	2,117,010.84	2	1,058,505.42	
Error	1,592,412.12	75	21,232.16	145.71
Total	3,839,314.93	77		

```
Audit Trail--Coefficient Table (Multiple Regression Selected)
```

Series Description	Included in Model	Coefficient	Standard Error	T-test	F-test	Elasticity	Overall F-test
DCS	Dependent	0.00	0.00	0.00	0.00		53.62
DCSFR	Yes	0.12	0.09	1.29	1.68	0.00	
DCSFW	Yes	0.89	0.09	9.98	99.54	0.89	

```
Audit Trail--Statistics
```

Accuracy Measure	Value
AIC	997.43
BIC	999.79
Mean absolute percentage error (MAPE)	6.39%
Sum squared error (SSE)	1,592,412.12
R-squared	58.52%
Adjusted R-squared	57.42%
Mean absolute error	110.28
Mean error	-0.48
Mean squared error	20,415.54
Root-mean-squared error	142.88
Theil	0.62

Forecast Statistic	Value
Durbin-Watson	1.95
Mean	1,748.21
Standard deviation	223.30
Max	2,272.60
Min	1,281.30
Range	991.30
Ljung-Box	0.02

**TABLE 8–6   Domestic Car Sales (DCS) and
Three Forecasts of DCS** (c8t5)

Date	DCS	DCSFR	DCSFW	DCSCF
Mar-1980	1849.9	1,668.21	1,684.22	1,684.34
Jun-1980	1550.8	1,673.88	1,909.65	1,884.67
Sep-1980	1515.3	1,761.16	1,623.20	1,641.02
Dec-1980	1665.4	1,662.13	1,466.35	1,490.66
Mar-1981	1733.0	1,616.07	1,671.16	1,666.76
Jun-1981	1576.0	1,622.43	1,794.03	1,776.33
Sep-1981	1618.5	1,592.63	1,595.42	1,596.96
Dec-1981	1281.3	1,654.86	1,523.06	1,540.04
Mar-1982	1401.4	1,669.56	1,504.22	1,525.06
Jun-1982	1535.3	1,664.28	1,515.52	1,534.46
Sep-1982	1327.9	1,697.42	1,454.11	1,483.88
Dec-1982	1493.6	1,749.36	1,302.16	1,355.28
Mar-1983	1456.9	1,768.85	1,492.69	1,526.30
Jun-1983	1875.8	1,774.99	1,547.06	1,575.17
Sep-1983	1646.2	1,766.33	1,602.95	1,623.67
Dec-1983	1814.1	1,758.69	1,544.67	1,571.17
Mar-1984	1994.6	1,752.78	1,765.13	1,765.76
Jun-1984	2251.8	1,725.93	1,998.18	1,969.10
Sep-1984	1854.3	1,709.68	1,966.85	1,939.47
Dec-1984	1851.0	1,730.89	1,846.10	1,834.97
Mar-1985	2042.2	1,754.85	1,949.99	1,929.75
Jun-1985	2272.6	1,757.40	2,128.49	2,088.16
Sep-1985	2217.7	1,772.18	2,008.70	1,983.75
Dec-1985	1672.2	1,770.56	2,038.86	2,010.28
Mar-1986	1898.7	1,770.67	1,982.92	1,960.74
Jun-1986	2242.2	1,782.89	2,081.59	2,049.56
Sep-1986	2246.9	1,796.49	1,978.67	1,959.96
Dec-1986	1827.2	1,803.82	1,981.33	1,963.16
Mar-1987	1669.3	1,801.45	2,053.19	2,026.54
Jun-1987	1972.8	1,793.87	2,032.68	2,007.49
Sep-1987	1878.2	1,783.37	1,850.55	1,844.96
Dec-1987	1560.6	1,772.09	1,724.12	1,731.67
Mar-1988	1914.0	1,774.48	1,752.05	1,756.69
Jun-1988	2076.0	1,769.60	2,007.69	1,982.56
Sep-1988	1787.1	1,750.77	1,889.02	1,875.28
Dec-1988	1762.3	1,739.97	1,687.40	1,695.44
Mar-1989	1707.4	1,723.06	1,859.98	1,846.36
Jun-1989	2018.6	1,717.21	1,959.16	1,933.53
Sep-1989	1898.5	1,730.35	1,825.39	1,816.56
Dec-1989	1453.6	1,732.79	1,717.53	1,721.30
Mar-1990	1706.2	1,738.43	1,705.73	1,711.49
Jun-1990	1878.2	1,738.52	1,886.40	1,871.54

(*continued*)

TABLE 8–6 (*Continued*)

Date	DCS	DCSFR	DCSFW	DCSCF
Sep-1990	1752.1	1,738.82	1,731.73	1,734.57
Dec-1990	1560.4	1,741.21	1,578.78	1,599.37
Mar-1991	1445.1	1,756.42	1,702.66	1,710.85
Jun-1991	1683.9	1,765.03	1,752.46	1,755.96
Sep-1991	1586.6	1,769.81	1,585.60	1,608.71
Dec-1991	1421.3	1,784.86	1,435.20	1,477.22
Mar-1992	1455.4	1,801.33	1,527.78	1,561.13
Jun-1992	1746.1	1,800.21	1,671.12	1,687.96
Sep-1992	1571.7	1,810.12	1,576.67	1,605.45
Dec-1992	1503.4	1,806.34	1,423.30	1,469.17
Mar-1993	1483.5	1,811.87	1,555.25	1,586.68
Jun-1993	1917.9	1,808.96	1,716.61	1,729.27
Sep-1993	1690.3	1,809.47	1,664.67	1,683.32
Dec-1993	1642.3	1,806.74	1,523.50	1,557.96
Mar-1994	1762.3	1,808.98	1,665.14	1,683.68
Jun-1994	2001.5	1,788.92	1,955.22	1,938.31
Sep-1994	1766.6	1,776.41	1,803.58	1,802.55
Dec-1994	1724.8	1,761.72	1,632.77	1,649.56
Mar-1995	1658.2	1,748.23	1,764.65	1,764.82
Jun-1995	1938.4	1,745.86	1,957.12	1,935.03
Sep-1995	1845.3	1,749.07	1,771.16	1,770.68
Dec-1995	1686.9	1,748.77	1,660.79	1,672.88
Mar-1996	1749.4	1,754.65	1,743.79	1,747.08
Jun-1996	2087.7	1,755.41	2,001.08	1,975.07
Sep-1996	1837.1	1,753.14	1,863.29	1,852.75
Dec-1996	1579.5	1,752.66	1,699.61	1,707.72
Mar-1997	1704.1	1,751.23	1,712.97	1,719.38
Jun-1997	1870.6	1,745.19	1,965.25	1,942.15
Sep-1997	1769.7	1,743.32	1,746.21	1,747.91
Dec-1997	1561.8	1,740.72	1,604.17	1,621.80
Mar-1998	1547.3	1,736.83	1,660.73	1,671.45
Jun-1998	1961.6	1,734.29	1,843.00	1,832.61
Sep-1998	1633.1	1,732.60	1,733.21	1,735.16
Dec-1998	1621.9	1,741.53	1,535.30	1,560.89
Mar-1999	1646.3	1,743.20	1,643.42	1,656.85
Jun-1999	1951.0	1,741.82	1,906.88	1,890.06

DCSFR = Multiple regression forecast of DCS

DCSFW = Winters' exponential smoothing forecast of DCS

DCSCF = A combination forecast of DCS where:
    DCSCF = 0.115391*(DCSFR) + 0.885778*(DCSFW)

TABLE 8–7   Summary Table of RMSEs for DCS

Chapter	Method	Period	RMSE
1	Naive—with 4-period lag	Historical	187.13
		Holdout	112.26
2	Not applicable		
3	Winters' exponential smoothing	Historical	144.45
		Holdout	61.79
	Holt's with seasonal adjustment	Historical	200.46
		Holdout	62.21
4	Simple regression model using seasonally adjusted DCS as a function of disposable personal income	Historical	96.98
		Holdout	87.93
5	Multiple regression	Historical	107.89
		Holdout	162.59
6	Time-series decomposition	Historical	195.5
		Holdout	182.2
7	ARMA(1, 1, 0) (1, 2, 1)	Historical	172.56
		Holdout	120.09
8	Combined Winters' and multiple-regression forecast (note: regression model includes only DPI and MR as explanatory variables)		141.69
			53.79

Comments from the Field

Combining Forecasts Can Improve Results

Delfield

This statement was made by Deborah Allison-Koerber, a product-line manager at the Delfield Company, a leading manufacturer of food-service equipment. Delfield uses a production-planning system consisting of a master production schedule and a corresponding material requirements planning (MRP) system. The MRP system is driven in large part by sales forecasts. For some time, management had been relying on a heavily judgmental sales forecast that started with a three-month moving average, incorporated judgmental factors from an informal "jury of executive opinion," and was finally adjusted by "add factors" provided by the person who was responsible for the MRP system.

According to Ms. Allison-Koerber, the results from this approach to forecasting were unsatisfactory from an operational perspective, and so she started to test some more quantitative forecasting methods. She focused her initial attention on a particular three-door reach-in freezer that represented a large cost when held in inventory, and so accurate forecasts of sales were important. A review of the sales history for this product showed some trend and some seasonality. Thus, Ms. Allison-Koerber believed that a multiple-regression model and a Winters' exponential smoothing model would be good candidates.

For a multiple-regression model she "reviewed a large set of potential causal variables, but settled on GNP and the prime interest rate as the most important." In addition, "dummy variables were used to account for seasonality and a temporary demand surge" that reflected the rollout of new menu items by a large fast-food chain that purchases Delfield food-service equipment. Ms. Allison-Koerber commented,

> A regression model based on this information is comprehensive enough to forecast sales of these freezers and yet simple enough to be easily communicated to others in the organization. In addition, the model is desirable because it necessitates having to develop forecasts for only two independent variables.

For the first six months of actual use, this model resulted in an RMSE of 20.185, which compared with an RMSE of 42.821 based on the traditional subjective method.

Ms. Allison-Koerber found a Winters' exponential smoothing forecast to also outperform the subjective forecast by producing an RMSE of 29.081 for the first six months of use. Because the regression model and the Winters' model contain different information, they were combined. The resulting RMSE was 17.198, lower than the regression model (20.185) or the Winters' model (29.081), and much better than the subjective approach (42.821).

However, as Ms. Allison-Koerber commented, it was felt that "the personnel who make the subjective forecasts have good insights about the industry and these insights should be utilized when possible." Thus, she used a regression technique to combine the quantitative and subjective forecasts. Even though the RMSE for the subjective forecast was much higher, the results demonstrated that the subjective method contained information not found in the other models. The results are summarized in the following table:

Model	RMSE
A. Regression	20.185
B. Winters'	29.081
C. Subjective	42.821
D. A and B combined	17.198
E. C and A combined	17.944
F. C and B combined	16.724
G. C and D combined	16.168

These results confirmed for Delfield that the use of quantitative forecasting methods and the combination of subjective and quantitative forecasts can improve results.

INTEGRATIVE CASE
THE GAP

Forecasting The Gap Sales Data with a Combination Model

The sales of The Gap stores for the 56 quarters covering 1985Q1 through 1998Q4 are again shown in the graph below. Recall that The Gap sales data are quite seasonal and are increasing over time.

(c8gap)

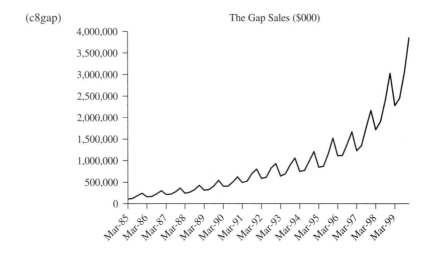

The Gap Sales ($000)

Case Questions

1. Assume you would like to use a Winters' model and combine the forecast results with the multiple-regression model presented previously (see Chapter 5). Use the regression technique to decide on the weighting to attach to each forecast.

2. Combine the two methods (i.e., the Winters' and the multiple-regression models) with the calculated weighting scheme and make a combined forecast.

3. Calculate the root-mean-squared errors for both the historical period and for the 1999Q1 through 1999Q4 forecast horizon.

Solutions to Case Questions

1. To see if both models may reasonably be used in a combined forecast, run the regression that uses The Gap sales as the dependent variable and the two forecasts (one from the Winters' model and the other from the multiple-regression model) as the explanatory variables. The regression (shown in Table 8–8) indicates that there is little significance attached to the constant term (because of its *t*-statistic of −0.63), and so we may reasonably attempt to combine the models.

TABLE 8–8 **Regression with a Constant Term (Note That the Constant Term Is Not Statistically Significant)** (c8gap)

```
Audit Trail--Coefficient Table (Multiple Regression Selected)
```

Series Description	Included in Model	Coefficient	Standard Error	T-test	F-test	Elasticity	Overall F-test
Gap Sales ($000)	Dependent	-6,467.84	10,332.93	-0.63	0.39		5,005.67
Gapsales_RFC	Yes	0.11	0.04	2.60	6.75	0.11	
Gapsales_WFC	Yes	0.91	0.04	22.58	510.08	0.90	

```
Audit Trail--Statistics
```

Accuracy Measure	Value	Forecast Statistic	Value
AIC	1,361.38	Durbin-Watson	1.75
BIC	1,363.41	Mean	804,816.13
Mean absolute percentage error (MAPE)	5.21%	Standard deviation	628,227.16
Sum squared error (SSE)	114,310,689,710.20	Max	3,029,900.00
R-squared	99.47%	Min	105,715.00
Adjusted R-squared	99.45%	Range	2,924,185.00
Mean absolute error	34,833.08	Ljung-Box	0.76
Mean error	0.00		
Mean squared error	2,041,262,316.25		
Root-mean-squared error	45,180.33		
Theil	0.27		

Regression Without a Constant Term—This Regression Is Used for the Combined Forecast

```
Audit Trail--ANOVA Table (Multiple Regression Selected)
```

Source of Variation	SS	df	MS	SEE
Regression	21,381,353,823,704.90	2	10,690,676,911,852.50	
Error	115,155,739,746.46	53	2,172,749,806.54	46,612.76
Total	21,706,814,750,732.10	55		

```
Audit Trail--Coefficient Table (Multiple Regression Selected)
```

Series Description	Included in Model	Coefficient	Standard Error	T-test	F-test	Elasticity	Overall F-test
Gap Sales ($000)	Dependent	0.00	0.00	0.00	0.00		5,062.49
Gapsales_RFC	Yes	0.10	0.04	2.54	6.47	0.00	
Gapsales_WFC	Yes	0.91	0.04	22.70	515.50	0.91	

(continued)

TABLE 8–8   *(Continued)*

Audit Trail--Statistics

Accuracy Measure	Value	Forecast Statistic	Value
AIC	1,361.80	Durbin-Watson	1.72
BIC	1,363.82	Mean	804,816.13
Mean absolute percentage error (MAPE)	5.08%	Standard deviation	628,227.16
Sum squared error (SSE)	115,155,739,746.46	Max	3,029,900.00
R-squared	99.47%	Min	105,715.00
Adjusted R-squared	99.45%	Range	2,924,185.00
Mean absolute error	34,538.72	Ljung-Box	0.94
Mean error	-2,333.11		
Mean squared error	2,056,352,495.47		
Root-mean-squared error	45,347.02		
Theil	0.27		

---

2. The two models are combined by running the same regression through the origin (shown below). Here the dependent variable is again The Gap sales. Note that the weight on the Winters' forecast is larger than the weight on the multiple-regression forecast; this seems appropriate because the Winters' forecast alone has a lower RMSE than does the multiple-regression forecast when considered separately.

Note the very close association of the forecast with the original data:

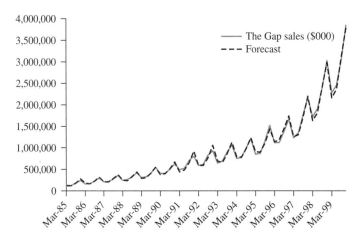

3. The combined forecast gives the following results in the forecast horizon:

	Combined Forecast	Actual
Mar-1999	2,160,500.79	2,277,700
Jun-1999	2,359,986.28	2,453,300
Sep-1999	3,111,234.20	3,045,386
Dec-1999	3,788,377.03	3,858,939

The RMSEs for the historical period and the 1999 forecast horizon are:

Historical root-mean-squared error = 45,347
(shortened period due to missing data)

Forecast period root-mean-squared error = 89,103

If we compare these results with the results presented at the end of Chapters 3 and 5 (see Table 8–9), we find that

TABLE 8–9   **Summary Table of RMSEs for The Gap Sales**

Chapter	Method	Period	RMSE
1	Naive—with 4-period lag	Historical	233,092
		Holdout	654,976
2	Not applicable		
3	Winters' exponential smoothing	Historical	49,479
		Holdout	99,493
	Holt's exponential smoothing with seasonal readjustment	Historical	42,388
		Holdout	74,034
4	Linear trend of deseasonalized data with forecast	Historical	212,016
		Holdout	1,131,894
5	Multiple regression	Historical	114,995
		Holdout	510,068
6	Time-series decomposition	Historical	44,013
		Holdout	110,497
7	ARMA(1, 0, 1) (0, 1, 0)	Historical	47,831
		Holdout	178,559
8	Combined Winters' and the multiple regression from Chapter 5	Historical	45,347
		Holdout	89,103

both the historical period RMSE and the forecast horizon RMSE are lower with the combination forecast than with either individual method. Each forecasting method must be adding some unique explanatory power to the combined regression.

Date	The Gap Sales ($000)	Forecast
Mar-1985	105,715	128,432.67
Jun-1985	120,136	117,673.17
Sep-1985	181,669	175,930.97
Dec-1985	239,813	278,478.31
Mar-1986	159,980	179,624.91
Jun-1986	164,760	163,652.09
Sep-1986	224,800	223,174.53
Dec-1986	298,469	319,385.89
Mar-1987	211,060	209,980.59
Jun-1987	217,753	207,241.22
Sep-1987	273,616	284,054.66
Dec-1987	359,592	376,779.77
Mar-1988	241,348	248,114.87
Jun-1988	264,328	235,781.00
Sep-1988	322,752	334,471.80
Dec-1988	423,669	437,785.95
Mar-1989	309,925	290,960.33
Jun-1989	325,939	304,930.33
Sep-1989	405,601	410,286.34
Dec-1989	545,131	544,983.28
Mar-1990	402,368	378,695.71

(*continued*)

Date	The Gap Sales ($000)	Forecast
Jun-1990	404,996	400,233.20
Sep-1990	501,690	510,648.05
Dec-1990	624,726	670,601.36
Mar-1991	490,300	441,299.94
Jun-1991	523,056	483,931.16
Sep-1991	702,052	652,912.49
Dec-1991	803,485	922,498.88
Mar-1992	588,864	589,943.42
Jun-1992	614,114	590,031.61
Sep-1992	827,222	764,993.83
Dec-1992	930,209	1,055,775.05
Mar-1993	643,580	692,292.21
Jun-1993	693,192	655,522.80
Sep-1993	898,677	861,478.40
Dec-1993	1,060,230	1,127,062.10
Mar-1994	751,670	790,980.72
Jun-1994	773,131	780,986.97
Sep-1994	988,346	973,744.30
Dec-1994	1,209,790	1,232,904.78
Mar-1995	848,688	906,218.16
Jun-1995	868,514	896,763.13
Sep-1995	1,155,930	1,105,609.54
Dec-1995	1,522,120	1,435,325.94
Mar-1996	1,113,150	1,135,359.60
Jun-1996	1,120,340	1,184,936.18
Sep-1996	1,383,000	1,449,400.76
Dec-1996	1,667,900	1,738,949.42
Mar-1997	1,231,186	1,252,211.19
Jun-1997	1,345,221	1,299,983.06
Sep-1997	1,765,939	1,711,828.15
Dec-1997	2,165,479	2,197,866.06
Mar-1998	1,719,712	1,633,074.69
Jun-1998	1,904,970	1,808,804.42
Sep-1998	2,399,900	2,415,684.97
Dec-1998	3,029,900	2,980,082.27
Mar-1999	2,277,700	2,160,500.79
Jun-1999	2,453,300	2,359,986.28
Sep-1999	3,045,386	3,111,234.20
Dec-1999	3,858,939	3,788,377.03

Holdout Period Forecast RMSE

Actual	Forecast	$(A_t - F_t)$	$(A_t - F_t)^2$
2,277,700	2,160,500.79	117,199.21	13,735,654,881.86
2,453,300	2,359,986.28	93,313.72	8,707,451,216.03
3,045,386	3,111,234.20	−65,848.20	4,335,985,454.27
3,858,939	3,788,377.03	70,561.97	4,978,991,983.65

RMSE = 89,103.99

USING FORECASTX™ TO COMBINE FORECASTS

As usual, begin by opening your data file in Excel and start ForecastX™. In the **Data Capture** box identify the data you want to use, as shown here. Note that in this case you want a sheet that has the date, the actual values for the series you are forecasting, and then two or more of the forecasts you have developed. Then click the **Forecast Method** tab.

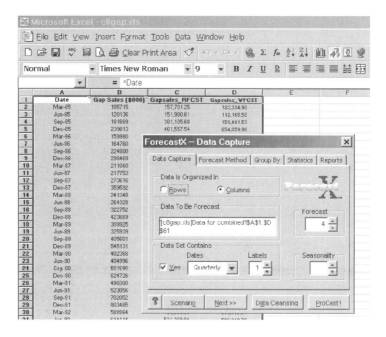

In the **Method Selection** box click the down arrow in the **Forecasting Technique** box and select **Multiple Regression.** Make sure the desired variable is selected as the **Dependent Series,** which is the actual value of **Gap Sales** in this example. Then click the **Statistics** tab.

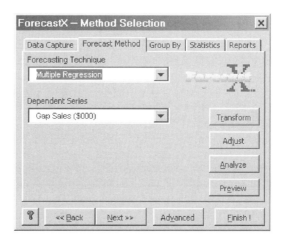

In this box select the statistics that you desire. Remember that there are more choices if you click the **More** button at the bottom.

After selecting the statistics you want to see, click the **Reports** tab.

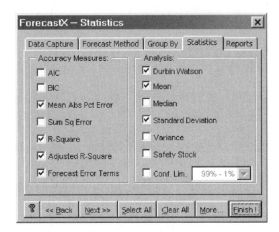

In the **Reports** box select those you want. Typical selections might be those shown here. When you click the **Standard** tab make sure to select the **Show Charts** box. In the **Audit Trail** tab (the active tab shown here) click **Fitted Values Table.**

Then click the **Finish!** button.

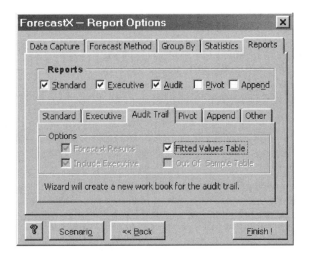

ForecastX™ will automatically apply a time-series method to forecast the independent variables. The methods used are identified in the **Standard Report.** Check the results to see that the constant term is *not* significantly different than zero. This provides a way to check for systematic bias.

If the constant term *is* essentially zero (the significance level is greater than 0.05), you want to redo the regression, forcing the line through the origin. To do this, estimate the regression model again, but this time in the **Method Selection** screen click the **Advanced** button at the bottom. In the dialog box that appears, check the box **Constant is Zero.** The regression coefficients in the resulting model are the optimum weights for the combined forecast, and the results provided by ForecastX™ are the combined forecast values.

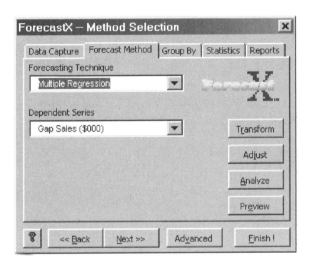
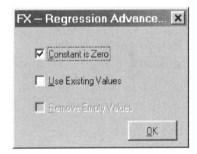

Suggested Readings

Armstrong, J. Scott. "Combining Forecasts: The End of the Beginning or the Beginning of the End?" *International Journal of Forecasting* 5, no. 4 (1989), pp. 585–88.

_____. *Long-Range Forecasting from Crystal Ball to Computer.* 2nd ed. New York: John Wiley & Sons, 1985.

Bates, J. M.; and C. W. J. Granger. "The Combination of Forecasts." *Operational Research Quarterly* 20, no. 4 (1969), pp. 451–68.

Bessler, David A.; and Jon A. Brandt. "Composite Forecasting: An Application with U.S. Hog Prices." *American Journal of Agricultural Economics* 63 (1981), pp. 135–40.

Chase, Charles W., Jr. "Composite Forecasting: Combining Forecasts for Improved Accuracy." *Journal of Business Forecasting* 19, no. 2 (Summer 2000), pp. 2, 20–22.

Clemen, Robert T. "Combining Forecasts: A Review and Annotated Bibliography." *International Journal of Forecasting* 5, no. 4 (1989), pp. 559–83.

_____. "Linear Constraints and the Efficiency of Combined Forecasts." *Journal of Forecasting* 5 (1986), pp. 31–38.

Collopy, Fred; and J. Scott Armstrong. "Expert Opinions about Extrapolation and the Mystery of the Overlooked Discontinuities." *International Journal of Forecasting* 8, no. 4 (December 1992), pp. 575–82.

Diebold, Francis X. "Forecast Combination and Encompassing: Reconciling Two Divergent Literatures." *International Journal of Forecasting* 5, no. 4 (1989), pp. 589–92.

Flores, Benito E.; David L. Olson; and Christopher Wolfe. "Judgmental Adjustment of Forecasts: A Comparison of Methods." *International Journal of Forecasting* 7, no. 4 (1992), pp. 421–33.

Fullerton, Thomas M., Jr. "A Composite Approach to Forecasting State Government Revenues: Case Study of the Idaho Sales Tax." *International Journal of Forecasting* 5, no. 3 (1989), pp. 373–80.

Goodwin, Paul. "Connect or Combine? Mechanically Integrating Judgemental Forecasts with Statistical Methods." *International Journal of Forecasting* 16, no. 2 (April–June 2000), pp. 261–275.

Hayes, Samuel P., Jr. "The Predictive Ability of Voters." *Journal of Social Psychology* 7 (1936), pp. 183–91.

Hogarth, Robin M. "On Combining Diagnostic 'Forecasts': Thoughts and Some Evidence." *International Journal of Forecasting* 5, no. 4 (1989), pp. 593–97.

Lobo, Gerald I. "Analysis and Comparison of Financial Analysts' Time Series, and Combined Forecasts of Annual Earnings." *Journal of Business Research* 24 (1992), pp. 269–80.

Mahmoud, Essam. "Combining Forecasts: Some Managerial Issues." *International Journal of Forecasting* 5, no. 4 (1989), pp. 599–600.

Makridakis, Spyros. "Why Combining Works." *International Journal of Forecasting* 5 (1989), pp. 601–603.

Moriarity, Mark M.; and Arthur I. Adams. "Management Judgment Forecasts, Composite Forecasting Models, and Conditional Efficiency." *Journal of Marketing Research* 21 (1984), pp. 239–50.

Nelson, Charles R. "A Benchmark for the Accuracy of Econometric Forecasts of GNP." *Business Economics* 19, no. 3 (April 1984), pp. 52–58.

Wilson, J. Holton; and Deborah Allison-Koerber. "Combining Subjective and Objective Forecasts Improve Results." *Journal of Business Forecasting* 11, no. 3 (1992), pp. 3–8.

Winkler, Robert L. "Combining Forecasts: A Philosophical Basis and Some Current Issues." *International Journal of Forecasting* 5, no. 4 (1989), pp. 605–609.

Exercises

1. Explain why a combined model might be better than any of the original contributing models. Could there be cases in which a combined model would show no gain in forecast accuracy over the original models? Give an example where this situation might be likely to occur.

2. Outline the different methods for combining forecast models explained in the chapter. Can more than two forecasting models be combined into a single model? Does each of the original forecasts have to be the result of the application of a quantitative technique?

3. *Air Carrier Traffic Statistics Monthly* is a handbook of airline data published by the U.S. Department of Transportation. In this book you will find revenue passenger-miles (RPM) traveled on major airlines on international flights. Airlines regularly try to predict accurately the RPM for future periods; this gives the airline a picture of what equipment needs might be and is helpful in keeping costs at a minimum.

   The revenue passenger-miles for international flights on major international airlines is shown in the accompanying table for the period Jan-1979 to Feb-1984. Also shown is personal income during the same period, in billions of dollars.

Date	RPM	Personal Income
Jan-1979	4,114,904	1,834.3
Feb-1979	3,283,488	1,851.4
Mar-1979	4,038,611	1,872.1
Apr-1979	4,312,697	1,880.7
May-1979	4,638,300	1,891.6
Jun-1979	6,661,979	1,905.1
Jul-1979	6,221,612	1,933.2
Aug-1979	6,489,078	1,946.5
Sep-1979	5,258,750	1,960.1
Oct-1979	4,720,077	1,979.2
Nov-1979	4,037,529	2,000.0
Dec-1979	4,240,862	2,022.5
Jan-1980	4,222,446	2,077.2

(continued)

Date	RPM	Personal Income
Feb-1980	3,540,027	2,086.4
Mar-1980	4,148,262	2,101.0
Apr-1980	4,106,723	2,102.1
May-1980	4,602,599	2,114.1
Jun-1980	5,169,789	2,127.1
Jul-1980	5,911,035	2,161.2
Aug-1980	6,236,392	2,179.4
Sep-1980	4,700,133	2,205.7
Oct-1980	4,274,816	2,235.3
Nov-1980	3,611,307	2,260.4
Dec-1980	3,794,631	2,281.5
Jan-1981	3,513,072	2,300.7
Feb-1981	2,856,083	2,318.2
Mar-1981	3,281,964	2,340.4
Apr-1981	3,694,417	2,353.8
May-1981	4,240,501	2,367.4
Jun-1981	4,524,445	2,384.3
Jul-1981	5,156,871	2,419.2
Aug-1981	5,465,791	2,443.4
Sep-1981	4,320,529	2,462.6
Oct-1981	4,036,149	2,473.5
Nov-1981	3,272,074	2,487.6
Dec-1981	3,514,227	2,492.1
Jan-1982	3,558,273	2,499.1
Feb-1982	2,834,658	2,513.8
Mar-1982	3,318,250	2,518.6
Apr-1982	3,660,038	2,535.5
May-1982	4,014,541	2,556.2
Jun-1982	4,487,598	2,566.3
Jul-1982	5,088,561	2,588.3
Aug-1982	5,292,201	2,592.0
Sep-1982	4,320,181	2,597.2
Oct-1982	4,069,619	2,611.5
Nov-1982	3,125,650	2,621.3
Dec-1982	3,381,049	2,636.8
Jan-1983	3,513,758	2,652.6
Feb-1983	2,876,672	2,650.5
Mar-1983	3,536,871	2,670.1
Apr-1983	3,744,696	2,689.0
May-1983	4,404,939	2,719.3
Jun-1983	5,201,363	2,732.6
Jul-1983	5,915,462	2,747.6
Aug-1983	6,022,431	2,756.4
Sep-1983	5,000,685	2,781.6
Oct-1983	4,659,152	2,812.8
Nov-1983	3,592,160	2,833.1
Dec-1983	3,818,737	2,857.2
Jan-1984	3,828,367	2,897.4
Feb-1984	3,221,633	2,923.5

a. Build a multiple-regression model for the data to predict RPM for the next month. Check the data for any trend, and be careful to account for any seasonality. You should easily be able to obtain a forecast model with an R-squared of about 0.70 that exhibits little serial correlation.

b. Use the same data to compute a time-series decomposition model, and again forecast for one month in the future.

c. Judging from the root-mean-squared error, which of the models in parts (a) and (b) proved to be the best forecasting model? Now combine the two models, using a weighting scheme like that shown in Table 8–1; choose various weights until you believe you have come close to the optimum weighting scheme. Does this combined model perform better (according to RMSE) than either of the two original models? Why do you believe the combined model behaves in this way?

d. Try one other forecasting method of your choice on these data and combine the results with the multiple-regression model. Do you obtain a better forecast (according to RMSE) than either of your two original models?

4. Estimating the volume of loans that will be made at a credit union is crucial to effective cash management in those institutions. In the table that follows are quarterly data for a real credit union located in a midwestern city. Credit unions are financial institutions similar to banks, but credit unions are not-for-profit firms whose members are the actual owners (remember their slogan, "It's where you belong"). The members may be both depositors in and borrowers from the credit union.

Quarter	Loan Volume	Assets	Members	Prime Rate
Mar-1977	$2,583,780	$4,036,810	3,522	6.25%
Jun-1977	2,801,100	4,164,720	3,589	6.75%
Sep-1977	2,998,240	4,362,680	3,632	7.13%
Dec-1977	3,032,720	4,482,990	3,676	7.75%
Mar-1978	3,094,580	4,611,300	3,668	8.00%
Jun-1978	3,372,680	4,696,720	3,689	8.63%
Sep-1978	3,499,350	4,844,960	3,705	9.41%
Dec-1978	3,553,710	4,893,450	3,722	11.55%
Mar-1979	3,651,870	5,089,840	3,732	11.75%
Jun-1979	3,832,440	5,185,360	3,770	11.65%

(*continued*)

Quarter	Loan Volume	Assets	Members	Prime Rate
Sep-1979	4,013,310	5,381,140	3,845	12.90%
Dec-1979	3,950,100	5,413,720	3,881	15.30%
Mar-1980	3,925,100	5,574,160	3,923	18.31%
Jun-1980	3,717,480	5,838,990	3,941	12.63%
Sep-1980	3,712,300	6,150,350	3,955	12.23%
Dec-1980	3,677,940	6,133,030	3,943	20.35%
Mar-1981	3,724,770	6,119,030	3,960	18.05%
Jun-1981	3,787,760	6,221,090	3,971	20.03%
Sep-1981	3,981,620	6,229,000	3,993	20.08%
Dec-1981	3,848,660	6,412,230	4,011	15.75%
Mar-1982	3,619,830	6,795,830	4,040	16.50%
Jun-1982	3,623,590	7,538,210	4,103	16.50%
Sep-1982	3,632,120	8,496,080	4,133	13.50%
Dec-1982	3,482,000	9,979,390	4,173	11.50%
Mar-1983	3,378,500	11,475,300	4,218	10.50%
Jun-1983	3,433,470	12,116,900	4,266	10.50%
Sep-1983	3,615,430	12,686,500	4,305	11.00%
Dec-1983	3,865,780	13,457,600	4,657	11.00%
Mar-1984	3,955,270	14,118,300	4,741	11.21%
Jun-1984	4,394,140	14,448,600	4,826	12.60%
Sep-1984	4,803,630	14,687,200	4,943	12.97%
Dec-1984	4,952,740	14,885,800	4,945	11.06%
Mar-1985	5,249,760	16,106,300	5,007	10.50%
Jun-1985	5,943,390	17,079,400	5,112	9.78%
Sep-1985	6,387,000	17,846,800	5,164	9.50%
Dec-1985	6,435,750	19,435,600	5,210	9.50%
Mar-1986	6,482,780	19,714,100	5,255	9.10%
Jun-1986	6,683,800	21,185,800	5,289	8.50%
Sep-1986	7,094,210	22,716,700	5,391	7.50%
Dec-1986	7,329,770	23,790,500	5,461	7.50%

Obs	TIME	SALES	INC	NRUR
1988Q1	1	72,962	218	8.4
1988Q2	2	81,821	237	8.2
1988Q3	3	97,729	263	8.4
1988Q4	4	142,161	296	8.4
1989Q1	5	145,592	318	8.1
1989Q2	6	117,129	359	7.7
1989Q3	7	114,159	404	7.5
1989Q4	8	151,402	436	7.2
1990Q1	9	153,907	475	6.9
1990Q2	10	100,144	435	6.5
1990Q3	11	123,242	574	6.5
1990Q4	12	128,497	622	6.4
1991Q1	13	176,076	667	6.3
1991Q2	14	180,440	702	6.2
1991Q3	15	162,665	753	6.3
1991Q4	16	220,818	796	6.5
1992Q1	17	202,415	858	6.8
1992Q2	18	211,780	870	7.9
1992Q3	19	163,710	934	8.3
1992Q4	20	200,135	1,010	8.0
1993Q1	21	174,200	1,066	8.0
1993Q2	22	182,556	1,096	8.0
1993Q3	23	198,990	1,162	8.0
1993Q4	24	243,700	1,187	8.9
1994Q1	25	253,142	1,207	9.6
1994Q2	26	218,755	1,242	10.2
1994Q3	27	225,422	1,279	10.7
1994Q4	28	253,653	1,318	11.5
1995Q1	29	257,156	1,346	11.2
1995Q2	30	202,568	1,395	11.0
1995Q3	31	224,482	1,443	10.1
1995Q4	32	229,879	1,528	9.2
1996Q1	33	289,321	1,613	8.5
1996Q2	34	266,095	1,646	8.0
1996Q3	35	262,938	1,694	8.0
1996Q4	36	322,052	1,730	7.9
1997Q1	37	313,769	1,755	7.9
1997Q2	38	315,011	1,842	7.9
1997Q3	39	264,939	1,832	7.8
1997Q4	40	301,479	1,882	7.6

a. Estimate a multiple-regression model to estimate loan demand and calculate its root-mean-squared error.

b. Estimate a time-series decomposition model to estimate loan demand with the same data and calculate its root-mean-squared error.

c. Combine the models in parts (a) and (b) and determine whether the combined model performs better than either or both of the original models. Try to explain why you obtained the results you did.

5. HeathCo Industries, a producer of a line of skiwear, has been the subject of exercises in several earlier chapters of the text. The data for its sales and two potential causal variables, income (INC) and the northern-region unemployment rate (NRUR), are repeated in the following table:

a. Develop a multiple-regression model of SALES as a function of both INC and NRUR:

$$SALES = a + b_1(INC) + b_2(NRUR)$$

Use this model to forecast sales for 1998Q1–1998Q4 (call your regression forecast series SFR), given that INC and NRUR for 1998 have been forecast to be:

Quarter	INC	NRUR
1998Q1	1,928	7.6
1998Q2	1,972	7.7
1998Q3	2,017	7.5
1998Q4	2,062	7.4

b. Calculate the RMSE for your regression model for both the historical period (1988Q1–1997Q4) and the forecast horizon (1998Q1–1998Q4).

Period	RMSE
Historical	———
Forecast	———

c. Now prepare a forecast through the historical period and the forecast horizon (1998Q1–1998Q4) using Winters' exponential smoothing. Call this forecast series SFW, and fill in the RMSEs for SFW:

Period	RMSE
Historical	———
Forecast	———

d. Solely on the basis of the historical data, which model appears to be the best? Why?

e. Now prepare a combined forecast (SCF) using the regression technique described in this chapter. In the standard regression:

$$SALES = a + b_1(SFR) + b_2(SFW)$$

Is the intercept essentially zero? Why? If it is, do the following regression as a basis for developing SCF:

$$SALES = b_1(SFR) + b_2(SFW)$$

Given the historical RMSEs found in parts (b) and (c), do the values for b_1 and b_2 seem plausible? Explain.

f. Calculate the RMSEs for SCF:

Period	RMSE
Historical	———
Forecast	———

Did combining models reduce the RMSE in the historical period? What about the actual forecast?

6. Annual U.S. billings for the Leo Burnett advertising agency (LBB) for the period from 1950 through 1990 are shown in the following table (data are from various issues of *Advertising Age*):

Year	LBB*	Year	LBB*	Year	LBB*
1950	22.0	1964	160.1	1978	604.0
1951	28.0	1965	184.7	1979	639.8
1952	37.6	1966	212.2	1980	734.6
1953	46.4	1967	250.0	1981	838.4
1954	55.0	1968	255.6	1982	919.8
1955	69.2	1969	288.2	1983	914.1
1956	79.0	1970	283.6	1984	1,132.9
1957	78.7	1971	296.8	1985	1,269.9
1958	98.7	1972	313.6	1986	1,361.6
1959	110.5	1973	330.9	1987	1,550.0
1960	116.7	1974	366.1	1988	1,765.0
1961	136.1	1975	400.0	1989	1,945.3
1962	151.9	1976	508.0	1990	2,035.2
1963	139.3	1977	575.0	1991	MISSING

*Data are in billions of dollars.

a. Prepare an exponential trend forecast of LBB through 1995, calling this forecast LBBFET. The development of such a trend was discussed in this chapter in the section "An Example." Start by entering the LBB data; then establish a time index (T) equal to 1 for 1950 through 46 for 1995. The model you want is:

$$LBB = b_0 m^T$$

Thus, start by regressing the natural log of LBB on T, to obtain

$$\ln LBB = \ln b_0 + T(\ln m)$$

Forecast $\ln LBB$ throughout the 1950–1995 period; then convert back to LBBFET as follows:

$$LBBFET = e^{\ln LBB}$$

or

$$LBBFET = \exp(\ln LBB)$$

(Note: The regression must be done using the 1950–1990 time frame; then forecast [fit] the model for 1950–1995.)

b. Calculate the root-mean-squared error for this forecast model during the historical period.

c. Plot actual LBB for 1950–1990 along with the predicted or forecast values (LBBFET) for 1950–1995. On the basis of this plot, does the forecast seem reasonable? Why or why not?

d. Now use Holt's exponential smoothing to make a forecast of this series through 1995. Call this forecast LBBFH. What is the historical RMSE for your Holt's forecast?

e. Plot LBB and LBBFH using the 1950–1995 period. On the basis of this plot, does the forecast seem reasonable? Why or why not?

f. Now use the regression method described in this chapter to prepare a combined forecast (called LBBCF). For the regression model

$$LBB = a + b_1(LBBFET) + b_2(LBBFH)$$

is the intercept essentially zero? How can you tell?

For the regression model

$$LBB = b_1(LBBFET) + b_2(LBBFH)$$

do the values of b_1 and b_2 seem logical? Explain.

g. Complete the following table:

Model	RMSE
LBBFET	_____
LBBFH	_____
LBBCF	_____

On the basis of this information, which of these models would you expect to provide the best forecast for the 1991–1995 forecast horizon? Explain.

h. Calculate the correlation coefficient between the squared forecast errors from LBBFET and LBBFH. Is the value consistent with your other findings? Explain.

9　FORECAST IMPLEMENTATION

In this chapter we discuss the forecasting process and provide a framework that will help you get the most out of any forecasting effort. While every forecasting problem has unique features, there is enough commonality in forecasting that guidelines can be helpful in several ways. First, the guidelines we provide will help you come to grips with some of the nuts-and-bolts issues related to data problems. Second, these guidelines will help you in making certain that the effort that goes into forecasting has the desired result in terms of the decision process. Finally, the guidelines discussed in this chapter will help you make logical choices regarding the technique(s) you should use for any particular situation.

Keys to Obtaining Better Forecasts

As part of an ongoing research study that has focused on very practical forecasting issues, a group of researchers led by John Mentzer has identified key elements to improving forecasts.[1] These elements are summarized in Table 9–1. One of the findings of Mentzer's group is that blind reliance on computer-generated quantitative forecasts is not a good management practice. As indicated in Chapter 1 of this text, judgments are important in forecasting even when quantitative methods are used. You have spent considerable time and effort developing a working knowledge of many quantitative techniques and how they can be implemented using a software package. Our own personal experiences, as well as the experiences of others, provide convincing evidence that quantitative forecasting methods tend to outperform solely qualitative forecasts. However, the best software cannot automatically take into account the specific industry,

---

[1] Mark A. Moon, John T. Mentzer, Carlo D. Smith, and Michael S. Garver, "Seven Keys to Better Forecasting," *Business Horizons,* September–October 1998, pp. 44–52; and Mark A. Moon and John T. Mentzer, "Improving Salesforce Forecasting," *Journal of Business Forecasting,* Summer 1999, pp. 7–12.

TABLE 9–1   Seven Keys to Better Forecasting

Keys	*Issues and Symptoms*	*Actions*	*Results*
Understand what forecasting is and is not	Computer system as focus, rather than management processes and controls Blurring of the distinction between forecasts, plans, and goals	Establish forecasting group Implement management control systems before selecting forecasting software Derive plans from forecasts Distinguish between forecasts and goals	An environment in which forecasting is acknowledged as a critical business function Accuracy emphasized and game-playing minimized
Forecast demand, plan supply	Use of shipment history as the basis for forecasting demand rather than actual demand	Identify sources of demand information Build systems to capture key demand data	Improved customer service and capital planning
Communicate, cooperate, and collaborate	Duplication of forecasting effort Mistrust of the "official" forecast Little understanding of the impact throughout the firm	Establish a cross-functional approach to forecasting Establish an independent forecast group that sponsors cross-functional collaboration	All relevant information used to generate forecasts Forecasts trusted by users More accurate and relevant forecasts
Eliminate islands of analysis	Mistrust and inadequate information leading different users to create their own forecasts	Build a single "forecasting infrastructure" Provide training for both users and developers of forecasts	More accurate, relevant, and credible forecasts Islands of analysis eliminated Optimized investments in information and communication systems
Use tools wisely	Relying solely on either qualitative or quantitative methods	Integrate quantitative and qualitative methods Identify sources of improved accuracy and increased error Provide instruction	Process improvement in efficiency and effectiveness
Make it important	No accountability for poor forecasts Developers not understanding how forecasts are used	Training developers to understand implications of poor forecasts Include forecast performance in individual performance plans and reward systems	Developers take forecasting more seriously A striving for accuracy More accuracy and credibility
Measure, measure, measure	Not knowing if the firm is getting better Accuracy not measured at relevant levels of aggregation Inability to isolate sources of forecast error	Establish multidimensional metrics Incorporate multilevel measures Measure accuracy whenever and wherever forecasts are adjusted	Forecast performance can be included in individual performance plans Sources of errors can be isolated and targeted for improvement Greater confidence in forecast process

SOURCE: Adapted from Mark A. Moon, John T. Mentzer, Carlo D. Smith, and Michael S. Garver, "Seven Keys to Better Forecasting," *Business Horizons,* September–October 1998, p. 45. Reprinted with permission from *Business Horizons* by The Board of Trustees at Indiana University, Kelley School of Business.

marketing, and economic knowledge that a business professional may have. To obtain the best forecast outcomes, both quantitative and qualitative information should be valued, and when possible, combined in preparing a forecast.

The work of Mentzer and others has also helped to clarify the distinction between forecasts, plans, and goals. In a recent discussion, a veteran forecaster in the automobile industry commented: "I prepared what I thought was a logical and well-thought-out forecast, but when it was presented to management the response was that the forecast was wrong and that I should go back and redo it." In this individual's case, what management wanted was a plan (what the company intends to do) or a goal (the company target) rather than an objective projection of what is likely given the current business environment. This scenario is not uncommon. What it points out is a serious confusion on the part of many between a forecast, a plan, and a goal. The forecast should be one piece of objective information that plays a part in the development of plans and/or goals, but it should not be confused with the planning or goal-setting functions.

The emergence of widely available and sophisticated forecasting software has made it possible for people to implement complex forecasting methods quickly and easily. However, there is danger in implementing a technique about which one does not have a reasonable level of understanding. For example, suppose that you are a brand manager who has some forecasting responsibility for certain brands, but that this function is only about 10 percent of your overall work load. In this situation you might be inclined to make relatively simple judgmental forecasts, or if you have come to realize that quantitative methods can improve forecast accuracy, you might be tempted to use an automated forecast "black box" to develop your forecasts. In either case you are likely to have difficulty explaining and/or justifying the forecast to those to whom you report. However, if you have a basic understanding of forecast methods (which you have now developed), you can articulate the reasoning behind your forecast and how the quantitative methods employed are well suited to the type of data that represent sales of your products. You will be able to make qualitative judgments and adjustments to the forecasts and be able to explain why such adjustments may be necessary. You may not be able to derive the formulas for the Winters' exponential smoothing model or for developing an ARIMA forecast, but you know enough about how these methods work to know when they are appropriate.

As we will discuss in more detail later in this chapter, communication, cooperation, and collaboration are important if the forecasting effort is to be as successful as it can be. Many times the people who develop a forecast do so in a vacuum of sorts. They look at the data and prepare a forecast, which is then sent to users who have had little or no input into the forecast process. The forecast may not be in a form that is useful to the end user, or the units forecast may be inappropriate for their use, or they may simply not have enough understanding of the forecast to use it properly.

Often there are two particular groups that need to communicate well: the analysts or number crunchers, and the sales, marketing, and customer service people. Each of these groups may have quite different perspectives on the forecasting process. Sean Reese, demand planner at Ocean Spray Cranberries, Inc., has observed that for collaborative forecasting to be successful, all parties need to work together by treating the perspectives and biases of others as valuable inputs rather than as obstacles to overcome.[2] These days the need for communication, cooperation, and collaboration goes beyond company boundaries. To maximize the benefits to be derived from the forecast process, communication, cooperation, and collaboration should involve the entire supply chain.

Everyone is well aware that inventory is expensive and there may be substantial savings if inventory levels can be reduced. Such reduction was the premise upon which "Just in Time" processes were developed. As Moon reports,

> When demand can be predicted accurately, it can be met in a timely and efficient manner, keeping both channel partners and final customers satisfied. Accurate forecasts help a company avoid lost sales or stock-out situations, and prevent customers from going to competitors . . . . Perhaps most important, accurate forecasting can have a profound impact on a company's inventory levels. In a sense, inventory exists to provide a buffer for inaccurate forecasts. Thus, the more accurate the forecasts, the less inventory that needs to be carried, with all the well-understood cost savings that brings.[3]

"The more accurate the forecasts, the less inventory that needs to be carried, with all the well-understood cost savings that brings."

In Chapter 1 you read an example based on the brake parts company in which *savings of $6 million per month* resulted from an improved forecasting system.[4]

The Forecast Process

The forecast process begins with a need to make one or more decisions that depend, at least in part, on the future value(s) of some variable(s) or on the future occurrence of some event. Subjective forecasting methods, such as the Delphi method, are usually the most useful in forecasting future events such as the nature of the home computer market 20 years from now. The quantitative techniques you have studied in this text are widely used in providing forecasts of variables such as sales, occupancy rates, income, inventory needs, and personnel requirements. Regardless of the specific scenario, the forecast is needed to help in making the best possible decision.

We have divided the entire forecasting process into the nine steps first introduced in Chapter 2 and shown again in Figure 9–1. These begin and end with communication, cooperation, and collaboration between the managers who use the forecasts and the technicians who prepare them. This communication and cooperation are critical if forecasting is to have the desired positive effect on decisions. Most of the students who study this text will probably be managers and will be better able to communicate with their professional forecasters because they have developed an understanding of the methods that can be used.

Communication, cooperation, and collaboration are critical if forecasting is to have the desired positive effect on decisions.

---

[2]Sean Reese, "The Human Aspects of Collaborative Forecasting," *Journal of Business Forecasting,* Winter 2000–2001, pp. 3–9.

[3]Mark A. Moon, John T. Mentzer, Carlo D. Smith, and Michael S. Garver, "Seven Keys to Better Forecasting," *Business Horizons,* September–October 1998, p. 44.

[4]John T. Mentzer and Jon Schroeter, "Multiple Forecasting System at Brake Parts, Inc.," *Journal of Business Forecasting,* Fall 1993, pp. 5–9.

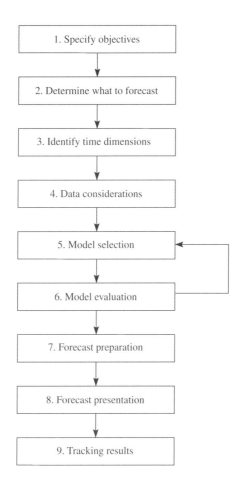

FIGURE 9–1

A Nine-Step Forecasting Process

1. Specify objectives

2. Determine what to forecast

3. Identify time dimensions

4. Data considerations

5. Model selection

6. Model evaluation

7. Forecast preparation

8. Forecast presentation

9. Tracking results

Step 1. Specify Objectives

The objectives related to the decisions for which a forecast is important should be stated clearly. Management should articulate the role that the forecast will have in the decision process. If the decision will be the same regardless of the forecast, then any effort devoted to preparing the forecast is wasted. This may sound too obvious to deserve mention. However, it is not uncommon for a manager to request a forecast only to ignore it in the end. One reason that this happens is that the manager does not understand or have faith in the forecast. This issue will be addressed more fully in steps 7, 8, and 9, but a grounding of faith and understanding should begin here in step 1. If the manager who needs the information from a forecast and the technician who prepares the forecast take the opportunity to discuss the objectives and how the forecast will be used, there is increased likelihood that the ultimate forecast will be one that the manager understands and has faith in using.

Step 2. Determine What to Forecast

Once your overall objectives are clear, you must decide exactly what to forecast. For example, it is not sufficient to say that you want a sales forecast. Do you want a forecast of sales revenue or unit sales? Do you want an annual forecast or a quarterly, monthly, or weekly forecast? It is generally better to base sales forecasts on units rather than dollars so that price changes do not cloud actual variations in unit sales. The unit sales forecast can then be converted to a dollar figure easily enough. If the effect of price on sales is important, you may want to use a regression-based technique that incorporates causality. Good communication between forecast user and forecast preparer is important in making certain that the appropriate variables are being forecast.

Step 3. Identify Time Dimensions

There are two types of time dimensions to consider. First, one must establish the length of the forecast horizon. For annual forecasts this might be from one to five years or more, although forecasts beyond a few years are likely to be influenced by unforeseen events that are not incorporated into the model used. Quarterly forecasts are probably best used for one or two years (four to eight quarters), as are monthly forecasts (perhaps as long as 12 to 18 months). The objectives dictate the time interval (year, quarter, and so forth) that is appropriate in preparing the forecast. For inventory control, short time periods are often necessary, whereas an annual forecast may be sufficient for the preparation of an estimated profit-and-loss statement for the coming year.

Second, the manager and the forecaster must agree on the urgency of the forecast. Is it needed tomorrow? Is there ample time to explore alternative methods? Proper planning is appropriate here. If their forecasting process is integrated into ongoing operations, then the forecasting personnel can plan an appropriate schedule, which will contribute to better forecasts.

Step 4. Data Considerations

The data necessary in preparing a forecast may come from within or may be external. Let us first consider internal data. Some people may believe that internal data are readily available and easy to incorporate into the forecasting process. It is surprising how often this turns out to be far from correct. Data may be available in a technical sense yet not readily available to the person who needs them to prepare the forecast. Or the data may be available but not expressed in the right unit of measurement (e.g., in sales dollars rather than units sold).

Data are often aggregated across both variables and time, but it is best to have disaggregated data. For example, data may be kept for refrigerator sales in total but not by type of refrigerator, type of customer, or region. In addition, what data are maintained may be kept in quarterly or monthly form for only a few years and annually thereafter. Such aggregation of data limits what can be forecast and may limit the appropriate pool of forecasting techniques. Communication and cooperation among the personnel involved in database maintenance, forecast preparation, and forecast use can help alleviate many unnecessary problems in this regard.

External data are available from a wide variety of sources, many of which have been discussed in Chapter 1. Data from national, state, and local government agencies are generally available at low cost. The more local the level of government unit, the more likely it is that the data will not be available as quickly as one might like or in the desired detail. Other sources of secondary data include industry or trade associations and private companies, such as some of the major banks. Often, secondary data are available on computer disk, a CD, or on the Internet.[5]

How to Evaluate and Improve a Forecasting Process

Mark Walden
Sales Forecasting Manager, Partylite Gifts, Inc.

One of the fundamentals of making good forecasts is to understand exactly what comprises the historical data to be used in preparing forecasts. Do not accept the data at face value. In fact, this is one of the reasons why forecasts, and the resulting financial decisions based on those forecasts, can go awry. This may also be part of the reason a forecast department can lack credibility. The best statistical model in the world is only as good as the input data. To provide effective forecasts and market analyses, one has to fully understand the business. The best way to begin is to inquire into the systems that feed your source data. There is no single answer as to what constitutes the best data.

SOURCE: *Journal of Business Forecasting* 15, no. 2 (Summer 1996), p. 23.

Step 5. Model Selection

There are many methods to select from when you set out to make any forecast. There are subjective or judgmental methods, some of which were reviewed in Chapter 1, and a growing set of quantitative methods is available. The most widely used of these quantitative methods have been discussed in the previous chapters. Now, how can you decide which methods are most appropriate for a particular situation? Some of the things that should be included in making the selection are:

1. The type and quantity of data available
2. The pattern that the data have exhibited in the past
3. The urgency of the forecast
4. The length of the forecast horizon
5. The technical background of the people preparing and using the forecast

---

[5]At this time, one of the best starting points for finding data on the Internet is http://www.economagic.com.

This issue of selecting the appropriate methods to use is of sufficient importance that we will come back to it in the next section. There we provide specific guidelines for each of the methods discussed in the text.

Step 6. Model Evaluation

Once the methods that we want to use have been selected we need to do some initial evaluation of how well they work. For the subjective or judgmental methods, this step is less appropriate than for the quantitative methods that have been stressed in this text. For those subjective methods, the comparable sixth step would be to organize the process to be used (e.g., setting up procedures for gathering information from a sales force or Delphi panel).

For quantitative methods, we should apply the techniques to historical series and evaluate how well they work in a retrospective sense. We have referred to this as an evaluation of the "fit" of the model. If they do not work well in the historical context there is little reason to believe that they will perform any better in the unknown domain of the future.

If we have sufficient historical data, a good approach to model testing is to use a "holdout" period for evaluation. For example, suppose we have quarterly data on sales for 10 years. We might use only the earliest nine years (36 data points) and make a forecast for the 10th year. If the model performs well when the forecast values are compared with the known values for the four quarters of year 10, we have reason to believe that the technique may also work well when the forecast period is indeed unknown. Out-of-sample evaluations such as this provide a measure of forecast "accuracy."

Once you are satisfied with a model based on historical and holdout period evaluations, you should respecify the model using all the available data (historical and holdout) and then use it for your actual forecast.

Once you are satisfied with a model based on historical and holdout period evaluations, you should respecify the model using all the available data (historical and holdout) and then use it for your actual forecast.

Suppose a technique turns out not to perform well when tested. The purpose of testing is, at least in part, to help us avoid applying a method that does not work well in our unique situation. Therefore, we should go back to step 5 and select another method that is appropriate to the problem at hand. It is not always possible to tell ahead of time how well a particular method will actually perform in a specific forecasting environment. We can apply reasoned judgment to our initial selection, but ultimately "the proof is in the pudding." We must apply the method to see whether it performs adequately for the purpose at hand.

Step 7. Forecast Preparation

At this point, some method or set of methods has been selected for use in developing the forecast, and from testing you have reasonable expectations that the methods will perform well. We recommend using more than one forecasting method when possible, and it is desirable for these to be of different types (e.g., a regression model and Holt's exponential smoothing rather than two different regression models). The methods chosen should be used to prepare a range of forecasts. You might, for example, prepare a worst-case forecast, a best-case forecast, and a most-likely forecast. The latter may be based on a combination of forecasts developed by following the procedures suggested in Chapter 8.

Step 8. Forecast Presentation

For a forecast to be used as intended, it must be presented to management clearly, in a way that provides an understanding of how the numbers were obtained and that elicits confidence in the forecast. It does not matter how much work is put into developing the forecast. It does not matter how confident the preparer is in the results. It does not matter how sophisticated the methodology may be. What matters is whether or not the manager understands and has confidence in the forecast. All too often, quantitative analyses are put on a shelf and do not play the role in decision making that they should, because the results are not effectively presented to management. Mark J. Lawless, who has been involved with forecasting within a number of corporations, including Chrysler, NCR, Ponderosa, and Hanson Industries Housewares Group, has commented that:

"The forecaster must be capable of communicating the findings in language which the functional managers can understand. . . ."

> In communicating the forecast results to management, the forecaster must be capable of communicating the findings in language which the functional managers can understand and which is compatible with the corporate culture.[6]

The forecast should be communicated to management both in written form and in an oral presentation. The written document should be at a level that is appropriate to the reader. In most cases the managers who read the forecast document will have little interest in technical matters. They need just enough information to give them a general understanding of the method used. They do not need the amount of background and detail to be able to prepare the forecast themselves.

Tables should be kept relatively short. Rarely would it be desirable to include an entire history of the data used and historical forecasts. The most recent observations and forecasts are usually sufficient. The long series should, however, be shown graphically and should include both actual and forecast values. In such graphic displays, colors and/or patterns can be used effectively to distinguish actual and forecast values.

The oral presentation should follow the same form and be made at about the same level as the written document. Generous use should be made of flip charts, slides, overheads, or projections of computer displays to heighten interest and involvement in the presentation. This oral presentation provides an excellent opportunity for discussion and clarification, which help the manager gain a more complete understanding of the forecast and confidence in its usefulness.

Step 9. Tracking Results

Neither the preparer nor the user is done with the forecast after the presentation and incorporation of results into the relevant decisions. The *process* continues. Deviations from the forecast and the actual events should be discussed in an open, objective, and positive manner. The objectives of such discussions should be to understand why errors occurred, to determine whether the magnitude of the errors was sufficient to have made a difference in the decisions that were based on the forecast, and to reevaluate the entire

---

[6]Mark J. Lawless, "Effective Sales Forecasting: A Management Tool," *Journal of Business Forecasting* 9, no. 1 (Spring 1990), p. 10.

process with the intent of improving performance in the next round of forecasts. Input from both managers and technicians is important for the continual refinement of the forecasting process.

It is important to stress once more the critical role that communication and cooperation between managers and technicians play in building and maintaining a successful forecasting process. This is true whether forecasts are prepared "in house" or by outside suppliers. Without a commitment to communication and cooperation, it is not likely that any organization can get a maximum return from the forecasting effort.

Choosing the Right Forecasting Techniques

In the Spring 1991 issue of the *Journal of Business Forecasting,* Charles W. Chase, Jr. (former director of forecasting at Johnson & Johnson Consumer Products, Inc.), commented that:

"The key task of a practicing forecaster is to determine at the outset the best match possible between the situation and the methods. . . ."

> The key task of a practicing forecaster is to determine at the outset the best match possible between the situation and the methods before doing anything else.[7]

Now that you have an understanding of a variety of forecasting techniques, you need a general framework that will help you determine when to use each method. There are few hard-and-fast rules in this regard, but there are guidelines to assist in making the determination. If you understand how to use the methods discussed in this text, you have a good start toward determining when each method is likely to be useful. For example, if you are preparing a quarterly forecast of sales for a product that exhibits considerable seasonality, you would want to use one of the methods that is designed to handle such seasonal fluctuations.

In this section we evaluate the forecasting methods presented earlier in the text relative to the underlying conditions for which they are most likely to be useful. There are many characteristics of a forecasting situation that might be considered in selecting an appropriate method. We will focus attention on three major areas: data, time, and personnel. For data, we consider the type and quantity of data that are available as well as any pattern that may exist in the data (e.g., trend, cycle, and/or seasonality). The time dimension focuses on the forecast horizon. For personnel we consider the necessary technical background of both the preparer and the user of the forecast. We begin with the methods discussed in Chapter 1 and progress sequentially through the text, ending with the ARIMA technique. Table 9–2 provides a quick reference summary of the data and time issues.

Sales Force Composite (SFC)

In using the sales force composite method, little or no historical data are necessary. The data required are the current estimates of salespeople regarding expected sales for the forecast horizon. Historical data may be considered by the sales force, but not

---

[7]Charles W. Chase, Jr., "Forecasting Consumer Products," *Journal of Business Forecasting* 10, no. 1 (Spring 1991), p. 3.

TABLE 9–2   A Guide to Selecting an Appropriate Forecasting Method

Forecasting Method	*Data Pattern*	*Quantity of Historical Data (Number of Observations)*	*Forecast Horizon*
Subjective Methods			
Sales force composite	Any	Little	Short to medium
Customer surveys	Not applicable	None	Medium to long
Jury of executive opinion	Any	Little	Any
Delphi	Any	Little	Long
Naive			
	Stationary[a]	1 or 2	Very short
Moving Averages			
	Stationary[a]	Number equal to the periods in the moving average	Very short
Exponential Smoothing			
Simple	Stationary[a,b]	5 to 10	Short
Adaptive response	Stationary[a,b]	10 to 15	Short
Holt's	Linear trend[b]	10 to 15	Short to medium
Winters'	Trend and seasonality	At least 4 or 5 per season	Short to medium
Regression-Based			
Trend	Linear and nonlinear trend with or without seasonality	Minimum of 10 with 4 or 5 per season if seasonality is included	Short to medium
Causal	Can handle nearly all data patterns	Minimum of 10 per independent variable	Short, medium, and long
Time-Series Decomposition			
	Can handle trend, seasonal, and cyclical patterns	Enough to see 2 peaks and troughs in the cycle	Short, medium, and long
ARIMA			
	Stationary[a]	Minimum of 50	Short, medium, and long

[a]Or data that have been transformed to a stationary series.
[b]May be used for seasonal data if the data are first deseasonalized.

necessarily. Thus, this method may not reflect patterns in the data unless they are obvious to the sales force (e.g., Christmas season sales of jewelry). The method may, however, provide early warning signals of pending change (positive or negative) because of the closeness of the sales force to the customer. SFC is probably best used for short- to medium-term forecasts.[8] The preparation time is relatively short once a system for gathering data from the sales force is in place. This method requires little quantitative sophistication on the part of the preparer or the user, which contributes to its ease of use and to ready acceptance of results.

Customer Surveys (CS)

Forecasts that are based on surveys of buyers' intentions require no historical data, and thus the past plays no explicit role in forecasting the future. Customer surveys are most appropriate for medium- to long-term forecasting. For example, a natural gas utility has used this method to help in long-term planning by gathering survey data on customers' plans for future energy use, including long-term capital expansion plans. The time necessary to develop, conduct, and analyze a survey research project can be relatively extensive. Rarely can such a project be completed in less than two to three months. If the same survey is used year after year, however, this time can be shortened considerably. CS is not a method to consider if there is a sense of urgency in getting the forecast. Those involved in preparing such a forecast need considerable technical expertise in the area of survey research. Users, on the other hand, need not have a sophisticated technical background, as long as they know enough about survey research to interpret the results appropriately.

Jury of Executive Opinion (JEO)

The executives included do not need a formal data set. They need only the body of experience that they have developed to make judgments concerning the most likely value of the forecast variable during the period of interest. Historical data patterns may or may not be reflected in the opinions expressed, although regular patterns such as seasonality are very likely to receive attention, albeit implicit attention. JEO may be used for any forecast horizon and is generally a relatively quick procedure. This method does not require much quantitative sophistication on the part of either preparers or users, but it does require a substantial base of expertise on the part of the participants.

Delphi Method

The Delphi method does not require a historical data series, other than what is in the knowledge base of the panel members, and therefore does not necessarily reflect patterns that may have existed in the past. It is most often applicable for long-range forecasting but

---

[8]Short-term, medium-term, and long-term forecasts will be mentioned throughout this section. Short-term forecasts include up to three months, medium-term forecasts cover four months to about two years, and long-term forecasts are for periods longer than two years.

can be applied to medium-term projects as well. In these respects it is much like JEO. However, the time to develop the Delphi forecast can be considerable unless the responses of panel members stabilize quickly. Computers can be effectively used to speed the flow of information and thus shorten the time considerably. The Delphi method requires only modest technical sophistication on the part of the preparer, and no particular technical sophistication is necessary for the end user, other than to understand the process through which the forecast was developed. The Delphi approach, as well as jury of executive opinion and customer surveys, are sometimes useful in forecasting the sales of new products. We will discuss new product forecasting in more detail later in this chapter.

Naive

The basic naive model requires only one historical value as a basis for the forecast. An extended naive model that takes the most recent trend into account requires just two past values. This method is best suited to situations in which the data are stationary or in which any trend is relatively stable. Seasonality can sometimes be accounted for in a reasonably stationary series using a seasonal time lag, such as was demonstrated for domestic car sales and The Gap sales in Chapter 1. The naive approach is suited only for very short-term forecasts. Preparation time is minimal, and no technical sophistication is necessary on the part of either the preparer or the user.

Moving Averages

Moving averages are most appropriate when the data are stationary and do not exhibit seasonality. Relatively few historical data are necessary. The number of past observations must be at least equal to the number of periods in the moving average. For example, if a four-period moving average is used, one needs at least four historical data points. Moving averages are normally used to forecast just one period ahead and require very little quantitative sophistication.

Simple Exponential Smoothing (SES)

Historical data are necessary to establish the best weighting factor in simple exponential smoothing, but thereafter only the most recent observed and forecasted values are required. Five to ten past values are sufficient to determine the weighting factor. The data series should be stationary (i.e., have no trend and no seasonality) when SES is used. This method is appropriate for short-term forecasting and requires little technical sophistication. While the arithmetic work can be done by hand, a computer can be helpful in determining the best weighting factor. Once the weighting factor is known, forecasts can be developed very quickly.

Adaptive-Response Exponential Smoothing (ADRES)

The adaptive-response exponential smoothing model may be used when the data are stationary and exhibit no seasonality. Ten to fifteen historical observations should be available when ADRES is used, and forecasts should be for only a short forecast horizon, typically one or two periods ahead. This method requires a bit more quantitative sophistication by the preparer than does SES, but users need little quantitative background.

Holt's Exponential Smoothing (HES)

As in SES, Holt's exponential smoothing model requires historical data to determine weighting values, but only the very recent past is required to apply the model. It is desirable to have at least 10 to 15 historical observations in determining the two weights. HES can be used effectively with data series that exhibit a positive or negative trend, and thus this method has a much wider scope of application than SES. However, it should not be used when the data contain a seasonal pattern unless the data have been deseasonalized. HES is appropriate for short- and medium-term forecasts, and like SES, can be implemented rapidly once the weights have been selected. Some technical expertise is required of the preparer, but users with little sophistication can understand HES well enough to use it properly. A computer is desirable, but not necessary, for model development.

Winters' Exponential Smoothing (WES)

Sufficient historical data to determine the weights are necessary in using Winters' exponential smoothing model. A minimum of four or five observations per season should be used (i.e., for quarterly data, 16 or 20 observations should be used). Because this method incorporates both trend and seasonal components, it is applicable to a wide spectrum of data patterns. Like HES, this method is most appropriate for short- to medium-term forecasts. Once the weights have been determined, the process of making a forecast moves quickly. The preparer needs some technical expertise, but the nature of the method can be understood by users with little technical sophistication. Use of a computer is recommended for the process of selecting the best values for the weights in the WES model. Even if weights are restricted to one decimal place, the number of combinations that might be evaluated becomes too cumbersome to do by hand.

Regression-Based Trend Models

The data requirement for using a regression-based trend depends to a considerable extent on the consistency in the trend and whether or not the trend is linear. We look for enough data that the t-statistic for the slope term (i.e., the trend) is significant (a t-value of 2 or more in absolute value is a handy rule of thumb). For a simple linear trend, 10 observations may be quite sufficient. A simple trend model can be effective when the series being forecast has no pattern other than the trend. Such a model is appropriate for short- to medium-term forecasts and can be developed and implemented relatively quickly. The preparer needs to have a basic understanding of regression analysis but does not need a sophisticated background for simple linear trends. More complex nonlinear trends require deeper understanding. Using a computer simplifies preparation of the forecast. The method is sufficiently straightforward that the user needs little technical sophistication.

Regression-Based Trend Models with Seasonality

To include seasonality in a regression-based trend model, it is desirable to have at least four or five observations per season. Thus, for quarterly data a minimum of 16 observations would be appropriate. For monthly data, 48 or more observations should be used. Regular seasonal patterns in the series are often modeled quite well by using dummy variables. As with simple trend models, linear or nonlinear forms can be used; the models are best for short- to medium-term forecasts, and the time necessary for preparation is short. Except when nonlinear models are used, little mathematical sophistication is necessary on the part of either the preparer or the user of the forecast. A computer regression program is a virtual necessity, however.

Comments from the Field

James G. Steen
Forecasting Analyst,
Sensormatic Electronics Corporation

Team Work: Key to Successful Forecasting

Sensormatic Electronics is a manufacturer of electronic surveillance equipment. The most challenging part of our forecasting effort is getting the market management and product development groups together to come up with a consensus forecast. This is important because they are in frequent contact with salespeople, customers, and account managers, and thus have access to information vital for forecasting. But, due to their hectic schedule, the information is often not communicated in a timely manner to be used effectively in preparing forecasts. Because of the lead time of certain products, ample time is needed to plan and manufacture products. We often don't hear of a large order or potential order until the end of our fiscal quarter. At that point, there is little or no time left to react.

Once every quarter we have a meeting in which we discuss, review, and update our forecasts. Such meetings are very helpful but not quite adequate to do the job. Many things change during the period between one meeting and the next. But the information about the changes is not passed on to those responsible for preparing the forecasts. We are currently working on improving the flow of information from our sales force to those involved in forecasting at our head office.

The "team" approach is the only way we can be successful since no one person has all the necessary information to prepare forecasts. By working together, we can all benefit and keep our customers satisfied.

Adapted from: *Journal of Business Forecasting* 11, no. 2 (Summer 1992), p. 22. Reprinted by permission.

Regression Models with Causality

The quantity of data required for the development of a causal regression model depends on the number of independent variables in the model and on how much contribution each of those variables makes in explaining variation in the dependent variable. One rule of thumb is that you should expect to have a minimum of 10 observations per independent variable. Thus, for a model with three independent variables you should have at least 30 observations. You can see that developing and maintaining a database for multiple-regression models can be a significant undertaking. The effort may be worthwhile, however, since multiple-regression models are often effective in dealing with complex data patterns and may even help identify turning points. Seasonality can be handled by using dummy variables. Causal regression models can be useful for

---

Comments from the Field

Debra M. Schramm
Manager, Sales Forecasting,
Parke-Davis

How to Sell Forecasts to Management

One of the universal problems forecasters have is "selling" their forecast to others, especially marketing management. Management is reluctant, at best, to use numbers from a group or individual who is viewed as only able to analyze numbers. They question why our crystal ball should be any better than theirs. Our company was no exception. Five years ago the forecast area was viewed as a department that did something with the sales numbers. No one seemed to know what our role was in the organization or how we meshed with the big picture. Although our forecasts were used to feed manufacturing and distribution, they were not considered in the management review process, which took place each month, to determine the division's sales numbers. It became our goal to change our image or the lack of it.

Today the forecasting department and its forecasts are an integral part of the management process. Our system forecasts are used as the basis for the monthly review, the annual, and longer-term plans. We continue to support marketing with reliable information, anticipating their future needs and experimenting with external data in order to improve the forecasts. There is no point lower than to work at something, then find you are the only one who believes in what you do. If we as forecasters are to raise our image in business, we must be able to prove ourselves and prove the integrity of the data we supply. The process can be long and frustrating, but it is attainable with determination, patience, and perseverance. Once achieved it is immensely rewarding.

Adapted from: *Journal of Business Forecasting* 10, no. 4 (Winter 1991–92), p. 22. Reprinted by permission.

short-, medium-, or long-term forecasts. Because the causal variables must usually be forecast as well, regression models may take more effort to develop. It can take a long time to develop a good causal regression model. Once the model is developed, preparation of a forecast can be done reasonably quickly. In using causal regression models, you should reestimate equations at least once a year so that structural changes are identified in a timely manner. The technician who prepares regression forecasts needs to have a solid background in regression analysis. Managers, on the other hand, can use such forecasts effectively as long as they have a basic understanding of regression methods.

Time-Series Decomposition (TSD)

The quantity of data needed for time-series decomposition should be enough for you to see at least two peaks and two troughs in the cycle factor, if the cycle factor is important. If the cycle factor does not appear important (i.e., has not been far above or below 1.0 during the historical period), then the quantity of data needed should be determined by what is necessary to adequately identify the seasonal pattern. A rule of thumb would be at least four or five observations per season (e.g., for quarterly data you should have at least 16 to 20 observations). TSD is quite good at picking up patterns in the data. The challenge is for the analyst to successfully project the patterns through the forecast horizon. This is generally fairly easy for the trend and seasonal pattern, but is more difficult for the cyclical pattern. TSD is especially appropriate for short-term and medium-term forecasting. If the cycle pattern is not important or if it can be projected with confidence, the method can also be used effectively for long-term forecasts. This method may be one of the best in terms of being able to identify and incorporate turning points. Doing so is dependent on the analyst's ability to correctly interpret when the cycle factor may turn up or down. The preparation time for a TSD forecast is relatively short, and this method does not require much sophistication on the part of the preparer or the user. In fact, most managers find the concepts inherent in the TSD model quite consistent with how they see the world.

ARIMA

A long data series (at least 50 data points—more if data are seasonal) is necessary to make use of the ARIMA models. These models can handle variability in the data as long as the series is stationary or can be transformed to a stationary series. This method can be applied to short-, medium-, or long-term forecast horizons. Because of the complexity of model identification, forecast preparation can take an extended period of time. This complexity also means that the preparer needs a highly sophisticated technical background. Users of ARIMA forecasts must also be quite sophisticated, because even achieving a basic understanding of the method is not easy. It is rare to find a manager who has a good feel for how an ARIMA forecast is developed, and rarer still to find a manager capable of explaining the forecast derivation to others who must use the results. This may be part of the reason that ARIMA models have had relatively low ratings in terms of importance, accuracy, and use by business managers.

New Product Forecasting

The vast majority of products for which we are likely to have to prepare a sales forecast are products with a substantial amount of sales history for which the methods you have learned in earlier chapters will work quite well. However, often we are faced with new, or substantially altered, products with little sales history. These new products pose particularly vexing issues for a forecaster. Before we consider the problem of forecasting new products, it will be helpful to review the concept of a product life cycle (PLC). An example of a PLC curve is shown in Figure 9–2. There is actually an additional and important preliminary stage called *product development* that precedes the actual introduction of the product to the market. Businesses are working diligently to reduce this initial stage of new product development so that new products can be brought to market in a more timely manner.

During the introductory stage of the product life cycle, only consumers who are classified as "innovators" are likely to buy the product. Sales start low and increase slowly at first; then, near the end of this stage, sales start to increase at an increasing rate. Typically products in this introductory stage are associated with negative profit margins as high front-end costs and substantial promotional expenses are incurred.

As the product enters the growth stage of the life cycle, sales are still increasing at an increasing rate as "early adopters" enter the market. Eventually in this stage the rate of growth in sales starts to decline and profits typically become positive. Near the end of the growth stage, sales growth starts to level off substantially as the product enters the maturity stage. Here profits normally reach the maximum level. Businesses often employ marketing strategies to extend this stage as long as possible. However, all products eventually reach the stage of decline in sales and are, at some point, removed from the market (such as Oldsmobile cars, which had been in the automobile market for a century).

This notion of a product life cycle can be applied to a product class (such as personal passenger vehicles), to a product form (such as sport utility vehicles), or to a brand (such as Jeep Cherokee—whose life cycle ended after many years and has now been replaced with the Jeep Liberty). Product life cycles are not uniform in shape or duration

FIGURE 9–2

A Product Life Cycle Curve

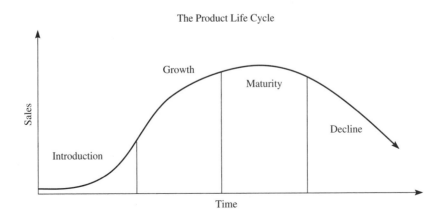

The Product Life Cycle

and vary from industry to industry. The Jeep example illustrates a relatively long life cycle. For high-tech electronic products, life cycles may be as short as six to nine months. An example would be a telephone that has a design based on a movie character.

The forecasting approach that is best will vary depending on where a product or product class is in the life cycle. Once the mid-to-late growth stage is reached, there is probably sufficient historical data to consider a wide array of quantitative methods. The real forecasting problems occur in the introductory stage (or in the pre-introductory product development stage). Here the forecaster finds traditional quantitative methods of limited usefulness and must often turn to marketing research techniques and/or qualitative forecasting techniques. We will discuss several potential approaches to new product forecasting in this section: analog forecasts, test marketing, and product clinics.

Analog Forecasts

The basic idea behind the analog method is that the forecast of the new product is related to information that you have about the introduction of other similar products in the past.[9] Suppose that you work for a toy company that sells toys to children in the 4-to-14 age group. Two years ago for the Christmas season you introduced a toy that was based on a popular Christmas animation movie. The percentage of total market households who purchased that product was 1.3 percent, 60 percent of potential toy stores stocked the product, and your company spent $750,000 on promotions. Now you have a new toy to bring to market this next Christmas season and you need some estimate of sales. Suppose that this new product appeals to a narrower age range such that the likely percentage of households who would purchase the product is 1.1 percent, and that you can expect comparable promotional support as well as comparable acceptance by retailers in stocking the product. Assuming that the only change is the percentage of households likely to purchase the product, the relation of sales of the new product to the old one would be 1.1 ÷ 1.3 (which equals 0.84615). If the previous product sold 100,000 units in the first quarter of introduction and 120,000 in the second quarter of introduction, you might forecast sales for your new product as 84,615 in the first quarter and 101,538 in the second quarter. If the size of the relevant population, the percentage of stores stocking the product, or the promotional effort change, you would adjust the forecast accordingly.

Test Marketing

Test marketing involves introducing a product to a small part of the total market before doing a full product rollout. The test market should have characteristics that are similar to those of the total market along relevant dimensions. For example, usually we would look for a test market that has a distribution similar to the national market in terms of

---

[9]See for example: Scott E. Pammer, Duncan K. H. Fong, and Steven F. Arnold, "Forecasting the Penetration of a New Product—A Bayesian Approach," *Journal of Business & Economic Statistics* 18, no. 4 (October 2000), pp. 428–35; and David A. Aaker, V. Kumar, and George S. Day, *Marketing Research* (New York: John Wiley & Sons, 2001), pp. 628–39.

age, ethnicity, and income, as well as any other characteristics that would be relevant for the product in question. The test market should be relatively isolated in terms of the product being tested to prevent product and/or information flow to or from other areas. For example, Kansas City, Missouri, would not usually be a good test market because there would be a good deal of crossover between Kansas City, Missouri, and Kansas City, Kansas. Indianapolis, Indiana, on the other hand, might be a better choice of a test market for many types of products because it has a demographic mix that is similar to the entire country and is relatively isolated in the context discussed here.[10] Suppose we do a test market in one or more test cities and sell an average of 1.7 units per 10,000 households. If, in the total market, there are 100 million households, we might project sales to be 17,000 units ([1.7 ÷ 10,000] × 100,000,000 = 17,000). The cost of doing a local roll-out is far less than a national roll-out and can provide significant new information.

Product Clinics

The use of product clinics is a marketing research technique in which potential customers are invited to a specific location and are shown a product mockup or prototype, which in some situations is essentially the final product. These people are asked to "experience the product," which may mean tasting a breakfast cereal, using a software product, or driving a test vehicle. Afterwards they are asked to evaluate the product during an in-depth personal interview and/or by filling out a product evaluation survey. Part of this evaluation would normally include some measure of likelihood to purchase the product. From these results a statistical probability of purchase for the population can be estimated and used to predict product sales. The use of in-home product evaluations is a similar process. A panel of consumers is asked to try the product at home for an appropriate period of time and then is asked to evaluate the product, including an estimate of likelihood to purchase.

Type of Product Affects New Product Forecasting

All products have life cycles and the cycles have similar patterns, but there may be substantial differences from one product to another. Think, for example, about products that are fashion items or fads in comparison with products that have real staying power in the marketplace. Fashion items and products that would be considered fads typically have a steep introductory stage followed by short growth and maturity stages and a decline that is also very steep.

High-tech products often have life cycles that are relatively short in comparison with low-technology products. It has been found that "high-technology businesses show a significant preference for data-less, qualitative, internal judgment forecasting

---

[10]A small sample of stores can also be selected for this purpose as reported in Marshall Fisher and Kumar Rajaram, "Accurate Retail Testing of Fashion Merchandise: Methodology and Application," *Marketing Science* 19, no. 3 (Summer 2000), pp. 266–78.

methods" in comparison with low-technology businesses, which are more likely to use external sources such as surveys of consumer-buying intentions.[11]

Artificial Intelligence and Forecasting

As you discovered earlier in this chapter, a manager must make a number of potentially difficult decisions during the forecast process. For example, to select an appropriate forecasting method, a manager must first consider the many characteristics of the forecasting situation and then choose a specific forecasting technique from a large number of available judgmental and quantitative techniques. Fortunately, recent improvements in microcomputer hardware and software technology have aided managers in making more effective and efficient forecasting decisions. One computer technology application that shows significant promise for improving forecasting decision making involves the use of artificial intelligence.

Artificial intelligence (AI) is concerned with making machines perform in ways that we would normally associate with human intelligence. AI includes (1) natural language processing, the focus of which is on computer programs that are able to speak, read, and understand spoken language; (2) robotics, which is concerned with providing machines with human abilities such as vision, a sense of touch, and intelligent movement; and (3) reasoning abilities that can solve problems, such as expert systems and neural networks. Expert systems and neural networks have the potential to make significant contributions to business forecasting.

Expert systems are intelligent computer programs that use expert knowledge and reasoning to solve problems. In developing an expert system, one begins by interviewing recognized experts to capture their knowledge about a problem area and the problem-solving logic they apply when making related decisions. Then a computer program is developed that replicates the experts' problem-solving process. There are commercially available expert system "shells," which provide a structure in which the knowledge base can be operationalized.

An example of the use of an expert system would be in the selection of an appropriate forecast method. The software would lead a manager through some simple questions concerning such things as data availability, data patterns, and other issues like those shown in Table 9–2. The program could combine the manager's responses to these questions with the knowledge base that has been supplied from forecast experts to determine an appropriate forecast method to be used in the manager's current situation.

Neural networks are computer programs that take inputs similar to those used in the forecasting methods discussed in this text and process them to provide an output that is the forecast. In a limited way, neural networks are similar to the methods you have already learned. Exponential smoothing models have inputs (past data and weights) that combine to yield an output (the forecast). Regression analysis takes inputs (past data and a statistical model) that are combined to produce an output in the form of a

---

[11]Gary S. Lynn, Steven P. Schnaars, and Richard B. Skov, "Survey of New Product Forecasting Practices in Industrial High Technology and Low Technology Businesses," *Industrial Marketing Management* 28 (November 1999), pp. 565–71.

forecast. What is different about neural networks is that they incorporate artificial intelligence in the process that connects inputs to outputs.[12]

In a neural network there are input and output pairs that are used to "train" the network. There can be multiple inputs (causal factors) and multiple outputs (forecasts of different variables) in a neural network. Between the inputs and outputs there is a layer (or multiple layers) of processing that mimics the working of the human mind attempting to reason out the logical connections between inputs and outputs. Then, given a new set of inputs, the neural network can produce a new output (forecast) based on what it has learned from the pairs of actual inputs and outputs that were provided. The analyst can control some aspects of the process, such as the learning rate and the desired precision of the output (forecast). As with expert systems, there are commercially available neural network "shells" that simplify the development of a neural network forecast system.

Comments from the Field

Mark J. Lawless
Senior Vice President of the Business Group,
National Fire Protection Association

Forecasts Must Be Relevant and Effective

The environment of business is continuing to change at an increasing rate, and the demands on management to create value are increasing with it. The role of forecasters is changing as well, and the value created by the forecaster is very much a consideration in the role which forecasting plays in the management-decision process.

If management must create value for the shareholder, the forecaster must create value for the shareholder as well. Hence, rather than pining for earlier times when things were better for forecasters, we need to adapt to the changing environment as well. We need to be continuously asking: "How can we create value? How can we enhance value? How can we assist others in creating value?" If forecasters will ask themselves these simple questions, and act upon their answers, the ability of forecast functions to be effective and credible will take care of itself. Looking to the needs of the management decisions, using whatever information that is available (imperfect though it may be), and developing the forecasts and recommendations in the context of these management needs are important parts of the forecast function.

To be successful in the future, there are two important ground rules for all forecasters—be relevant and be effective.

Adapted from: "Ten Prescriptions for Forecasting Success," *Journal of Business Forecasting* 16, no. 1 (Spring 1997), pp. 3–5.

---

[12]For a more complete description of neural networks and an example of their potential application in a forecasting environment, see Chin Kuo and Arthur Reitsch, "Neural Networks vs. Conventional Methods of Forecasting," *Journal of Business Forecasting* 14, no. 4 (Winter 1995–96), pp. 17–22.

Summary

The forecasting process begins with the need to make decisions that are dependent on the future values of one or more variables. Once the need to forecast is recognized, the steps to follow can be summarized as follows:

1. Specify objectives
2. Determine what to forecast
3. Identify time dimensions
4. Data considerations
5. Model selection
6. Model evaluation
7. Forecast preparation
8. Forecast presentation
9. Tracking results

Throughout the process, open communication between managers who use the forecasts and the technicians who prepare them is essential.

You have been introduced to the most widely used forecasting methods and need to know when each is appropriate. The section entitled "Choosing the Right Forecasting Techniques" provides a guide to help you in determining when to use each technique and when each should not be used. Table 9–2 also provides a handy summary of that discussion.

As you have seen, there is potential for the application of artificial intelligence technology to the forecast process. For example, expert-system decision-support tools would allow managers to make better forecasting decisions in forecasting method selection. Artificial intelligence concepts are also applied to forecasting through the use of neural networks. These are computer programs that take inputs and process them to provide an output that is the forecast. In a limited way neural networks are similar to other forecast methods, but they differ in that they incorporate artificial intelligence in the process that connects inputs to outputs. As with expert systems, there are commercially available neural network "shells" that simplify the development of a neural network forecast system.

Developing a forecast for new products is an especially difficult task. Because no historical data are available we are forced to use methods based on judgments and/or various marketing research methods. Often, looking at the sales history of relatively similar products can provide a basis upon which a forecast for the new product can be built. Information gathered using a survey technique about intention to purchase on the part of potential customers may also provide helpful insight.

USING "PROCAST™" IN FORECASTX™
TO MAKE FORECASTS

As usual, begin by opening your data file in Excel and start ForecastX™. In the **Data Capture** box identify the data you want to use, as shown below. Then click the **Forecast Method** tab.

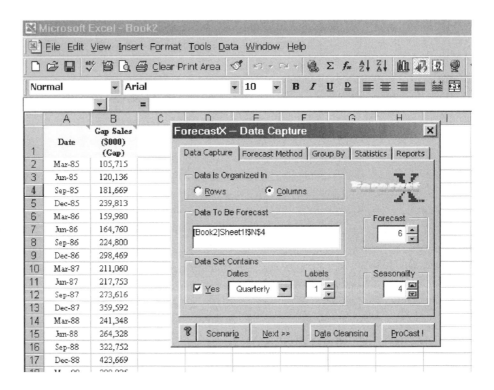

In the **Method Selection** box click the down arrow in the **Forecasting Technique** box and select **ProCast™.** Click the down arrow in the **Error Term** box and select **Root Mean Squared Error** (or another error term you want to use). Then click the **Statistics** tab.

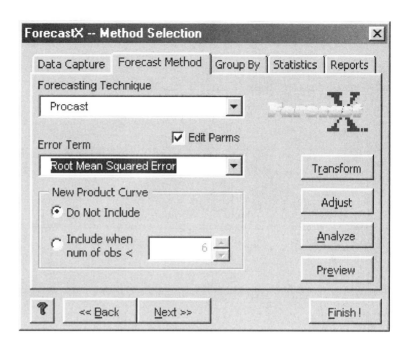

In this box select the statistics that you desire. Remember that there are more choices if you click the **More** button at the bottom.

After selecting the statistics you want to see, click the **Reports** tab.

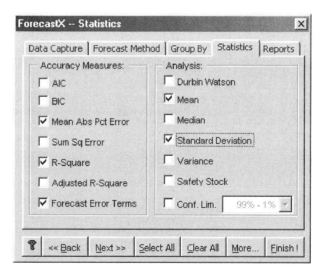

In the **Reports** box select those you want. Typical selections might be those shown here. When you click the **Standard** tab be sure to select the **Show Charts** box. In the **Audit Trail** tab (the active tab shown here) click the **Fitted Values Table.**

Then click the **Finish!** button. In the Audit Trail output you will find the method that ProCast™ used to make the requested forecast.

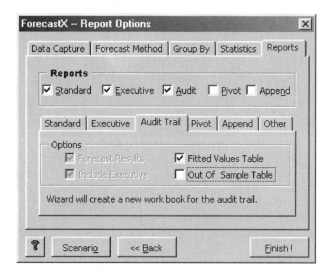

Using an automated forecasting method such as ProCast™ is all right if you understand the selected method well enough to evaluate whether it is truly a logical choice. It is wise to exercise some caution when allowing any software to select a method automatically. By using a software package over a period of time, such as ForecastX™, you may develop confidence in the selections it makes. Then using an automated process may provide considerable time savings—such as in situations where there are hundreds or thousands of items that must be forecast frequently.

Suggested Readings

Armstrong, J. Scott. "Research Needs in Forecasting." *International Journal of Forecasting* 4, no. 3 (1988), pp. 449–65.

Chase, Charles W., Jr. "Business Forecasting: A Process Not an Application." *Journal of Business Forecasting* 11, no. 3 (Fall 1992), pp. 12–13.

Fisher, Marshall; and Kumar Rajaram. "Accurate Retail Testing of Fashion Merchandise: Methodology and Application." *Marketing Science* 19, no. 3 (Summer 2000), pp. 266–78.

Keating, Barry; and J. Holton Wilson. "Forecasting Practices and Teachings." *Journal of Business Forecasting* 7, no. 4 (Winter 1987–88), pp. 10–13, 16.

Larréché, Jean-Claude; and Reza Moinpour. "Managerial Judgement in Marketing: The Concept of Expertise." *Journal of Marketing Research* 20, no. 2 (May 1983), pp. 110–21.

Lawless, Mark J. "Effective Sales Forecasting: A Management Tool." *Journal of Business Forecasting* 9, no. 1 (Spring 1990), pp. 2–11.

———. "Ten Prescriptions for Forecasting Success." *Journal of Business Forecasting* 11, no. 4 (Spring 1997), pp. 3–5.

LeLee, Gary S. "The Key to Understanding the Forecasting Process." *Journal of Business Forecasting* 11, no. 4 (Winter 1992–93), pp. 12–16.

Lynn, Gary S.; Steven P. Schnaars; and Richard B. Skov. "Survey of New Product Forecasting Practices in Industrial High Technology and Low Technology Businesses." *Industrial Marketing Management* 28 (November 1999), pp. 565–71.

Mentzer, John T.; and Kenneth B. Kahn. "State of Sales Forecasting Systems in Corporate America." *Journal of Business Forecasting* 11, no. 4 (Spring 1997), pp. 6–13.

Moon, Mark A.; and John T. Mentzer. "Improving Salesforce Forecasting." *Journal of Business Forecasting* 18, no. 2 (Summer 1999), pp. 7–12.

Moon, Mark A.; John T. Mentzer; Carlo D. Smith; and Michael S. Garver. "Seven Keys to Better Forecasting." *Business Horizons* (September–October 1998), pp. 44–52.

Pammer, Scott E.; Duncan K. H. Fong; and Steven F. Arnold. "Forecasting the Penetration of a New Product—A Bayesian Approach." *Journal of Business & Economic Statistics* 18, no. 4 (October 2000), pp. 428–35.

Reese, Sean. "The Human Aspects of Collaborative Forecasting." *Journal of Business Forecasting* 19, no. 4 (Winter 2000–2001), pp. 3–9.

Reyes, Luis. "The Forecasting Function: Critical Yet Misunderstood." *Journal of Business Forecasting* 14, no. 4 (Winter 1995–96), pp. 8–9.

Szmania, Joe; and John Surgent. "An Application of an Expert System Approach to Business Forecasting." *Journal of Business Forecasting* 8, no. 1 (Spring 1989), pp. 10–12.

Tkacz, Greg. "Neural Network Forecasting of Canadian GDP Growth." *International Journal of Forecasting* 17, no. 1 (January–March 2001), pp. 57–69.

Weitz, Rob R. "NOSTRADAMUS—A Knowledge-Based Forecast Advisor." *International Journal of Forecasting* 2, no. 1 (1986), pp. 273–83.

Wilson, J. Holton; and Hugh G. Daubek. "Marketing Managers Evaluate Forecasting Models." *Journal of Business Forecasting* 8, no. 1 (Spring 1989), pp. 19–22.

Exercises

1. You have read the statement that the forecast process begins with a need to make one or more decisions that depend on the future value of some variable. Think about this as it relates to the daily weather forecast you hear, and write a list of five decisions that might depend on such a forecast.

2. Why do you think communication between the person preparing a forecast and the forecast user is important? Give several specific places in the nine-step forecast process where you think such communication is especially important and explain why.

3. The availability and form of data to be used in preparing a forecast are often seen as especially critical areas. Summarize, in your own words, the database considerations in the forecasting process (step 4).

4. Suppose that you have been asked to recommend a forecasting technique that would be appropriate to prepare a forecast, given the following situational characteristics:

   a. You have 10 years of quarterly data.

   b. There is an upward trend to the data.

   c. There is a significant increase in sales prior to Christmas each year.

   d. A one-year forecast is needed.

   e. You, as the preparer of the forecast, have good technical skills, but the manager who needs the forecast is very nontechnical.

   f. You need to have the forecast done and the presentation ready in just a few days.

   What method(s) would you consider using and why?

5. Write an outline of what you would like to see in a forecast presentation from the perspective of a manager who needs to use the forecast.

6. Explain in your own words how artificial intelligence can be used in a forecasting environment.

7. If you had been assigned the task of forecasting the demand for CD players when they were a new product, how might you have approached the problem?